# SCANDAL ON
# PLUM
# ISLAND

Benjamin Koehler as a West Point cadet.
*Courtesy Mary Elke.*

# SCANDAL ON
# PLUM
# ISLAND

## A COMMANDER BECOMES THE ACCUSED

### [ A TRUE STORY ]

## MARIAN E. LINDBERG

**EAST END PRESS**
**BRIDGEHAMPTON • NEW YORK**

SCANDAL ON PLUM ISLAND:
A Commander Becomes the Accused

Copyright © 2020 by Marian E. Lindberg

Published by
EAST END PRESS
Bridgehampton, NY

ISBN: 978-1-7324912-7-4
Ebook ISBN: 978-1-7324912-8-1

Library of Congress Control Number: 2020904007

First Edition

Book Design by Neuwirth & Associates
Cover Design by Mark Karis

Manufactured in the United States of America

10 9 8 7 6 5 4 3 2 1

An island is one great eye

    gazing out, a beckoning lighthouse,

searchlight, a wishbone compass,

    or counterweight to the stars.

        —Yusef Komunyakaa, *Islands*

# CONTENTS

## PART THREE

## PART FOUR

# SCANDAL ON
# PLUM
# ISLAND

# PART ONE

CHAPTER ONE

# Cross-Dressing for Halloween

THE CAPTAIN WORE a see-through dress. No dispute about that.
Even the captain admitted that in a certain light, guests at the
party could see the outline of his body through the muslin shift.

Months later, a lawyer would press for details: Was the dress tied at
the waist? What color and length were the captain's socks? Did others
treat him "as if you were a woman?"[1]

But on this night, the night of November 1, 1913, a carefree party
was in progress on an island with spectacular sea views, whose sole
inhabitants, except for the lighthouse keeper, were employees of the
U.S. Army and their families. Peace prevailed on Plum Island, as in
the rest of the nation, allowing late Halloween revelry to be the order
of the evening for some.

Cold winds off the Atlantic announced the approach of winter, but
conditions were more enticing inside Captain Philip Worcester's spa-
cious two-story house. Dance tunes from a player piano set a high-spir-
ited tone, and a basement furnace supervised by an Army private kept
the rooms warm—warm enough for the host to wear a light dress with
little underneath.[2]

Worcester would later say he had borrowed "an old, loose dress of
my wife's."[3] The highest-ranking officer at the party, Major Benjamin
M. Koehler, found that hard to believe. Mabel Worcester was petite,
nothing like her husband—the six-foot, athletic new leader of the

100th Company at Fort Terry, a sprawling coast defense post off eastern Long Island.

Worcester, 34 years old, also bore little resemblance to Major Koehler, Fort Terry's commanding officer, who stood at best five foot three. Koehler, 41 and single, had gained weight since his West Point days and service in the Philippines, where food was both scarce and vile. A live-in cook prepared his meals now, and there was a slight bulge between the fourth and fifth buttons of his uniform, in contrast to Worcester's toned physique.

Worcester's leadership of the 100th Company had taken effect the day of the party. Come midnight, guests could also toast the Worcesters' first wedding anniversary. Though he claimed the party was his wife's idea, Worcester certainly acted like a celebrant. He led the dancing, gestured gaily with his arms, and greeted guests in mock flirtation with a fling of his skirt.

Yet the host's cavorting belied a deep resentment over his new place of residence. Geologically, 840-acre Plum Island was a marvel, the outer lands of a glacially created moraine with seventeen soil types and a freshwater wetland supporting many species of plants and birds.[4] To the Worcesters, though, the island was a backwater, an earthen slab with more gulls than people—and a five-hour trip by boat and train if Mabel wanted to see her family in New York City.

Major Koehler, the watchful leader of the island's seven hundred soldiers, did not make Worcester any happier about his new assignment. In a mere three months, the two had differed several times, from a dispute over a private labeled the major's "pet" by one of Worcester's friends to Worcester's "dancing and kissing parties," which Koehler considered "not respectable."[5]

It had been a long day for Koehler, cantering around the island to monitor the monthly exchange of soldiers. A book, a cocktail, and his favorite chair would have made for a perfect evening, but fatigue was no match for the persuasive powers of his younger sister, Sophia, who lived with him on Officers Row in a shingled house just like the Worcesters'. When Koehler had arrived home, Sophia was "dressed up to go to the party and she wanted me to go," Koehler later said.[6] Sophia assured her brother that he could leave early and he agreed to accompany her, surprising no one by showing up in his dress uniform rather than a costume.

Not so for Captain Richard Ellis, who tied a ribbon around his neck and came as the cartoon character Buster Brown—a wealthy boy with long blond hair, pantaloons, Mary Jane shoes, and other feminine features. Lieutenant John Smith also cross-dressed for the occasion, but Worcester went the furthest. In addition to the diaphanous dress, he wore a bonnet pinned with a fake braid of hair, and he periodically raised his hands to his face, curtsied, and affected shyness, supposedly imitating the behavior of a "country girl," in his words.[7]

Worcester's manner of feigning a "country girl" disgusted several women present, including Sophia, especially when she saw the sheerness of the dress in the bright light of the basement, where a dinner of ham, peas, and beans was served. Pillars created a nook in which the Worcesters placed a tablecloth on the floor, surrounded by seats of sandbags and straw, cornstalks, pumpkin lanterns, and witches cut from black cloth. The decorations may have been appropriate, but the host's costume was not. Sophia called it "indecent."[8]

Guests descended to the basement by means of a cobweb game. As Koehler described it, "each person was given a piece of ribbon or string and we were told to follow that out and see what was the end of it and these strings went into different rooms and up the stairs and circulated around and finally lead [sic] to the basement, where we had supper."[9]

Both Koehler and his sister remembered guests dancing before the game, passing time until everyone arrived. Sophia recalled that Mabel "insisted upon my going into the parlor where they were dancing, because I had on a zerape, and she wanted them to see it."[10] Worcester, in contrast, said no one danced until after dinner.[11]

Whenever it occurred, the dancing was another strike against Worcester, who had "a very peculiar way of holding one, in the first place, and then he sort of wiggled," according to Sophia, who found it "not at all pleasant to dance with him. It was vulgar."[12]

At one point, Worcester danced the Highland fling, a Scottish reel that originated to mark battle victories and later came to serve as a test of men's stamina. While the performance of a dance signifying masculine strength by a man dressed as a woman may have seemed like a parody, the scene was more like a warning, for Worcester would soon be claiming that one of the men at the party deserved to be thrown out of the Army and imprisoned as a traitor to his gender.

Ben Koehler did not dance at the party, neither the fling nor the turkey trot, and certainly not the hoochie-coochie, a Middle Eastern import that Worcester demonstrated by gyrating his hips in imitation of the belly dance made famous by Farida Mazhar, a star of the Chicago World's Fair known as Little Egypt.[13]

Koehler said he left the party to walk home around ten o'clock. He'd had enough of Worcester's brand of merriment. According to Koehler, as he walked toward the smoking room after dinner, Worcester "was jumping along towards me with his hands up to his face, sticking his stomach out."[14] "I said 'Worcester, suck up your stomach. It looks as if you were in a family way,'" Koehler recalled. Koehler claimed he told Worcester, "You have not enough clothes," and said he "struck him in the stomach" with his thumb to make his point.[15]

In a few weeks, Worcester would paint a very different picture of what had happened in the basement between the two men. He would make the long trip to New York City not to visit his in-laws but to meet with leaders of the Army's Eastern Department on Governors Island. Sitting in a neo-Gothic brick building designed to exalt order and discipline, Worcester would tell of scandalous behavior at his party— but having nothing to do with his dress, his dancing, or any kissing.

Rather, Worcester would say, it was when his commanding officer grabbed him "by the testicles"—not once, but twice.[16]

# CHAPTER TWO

# *Perversion*

WORCESTER'S ACCUSATIONS CAME "like a thunderbolt from a clear sky" in the words of Charles Sloan, a Nebraska congressman who knew Koehler's pioneer German family and backed Koehler's denials, declaring it impossible that he had groped another man.[1]

The charges also shocked the leaders of the Army's Eastern Department, who had only a month earlier selected Koehler to be acting district commander, a move understandably seen by him as proof of his bosses' approval and worth to the Army. "I considered him an unusually good officer," wrote one colonel, saying he would hold that opinion "[i]n the absence of any official or definite knowledge on the subject [of the charges]."[2]

By 1913, gay subcultures existed in America's large cities, though "[s]exual attraction to a person of the same sex was considered a disorder of gender, closer to what we today think of as 'being transgender' than 'being gay.'"[3] Homosexual men were defined by outsiders "almost entirely in terms of their masculinity, or rather, in terms of its absence."[4] Plucked eyebrows, powdered faces, and falsetto voices were some of the styles associated with so-called fairies, who "constituted the dominant public image of the male homosexual," visible on the streets of some neighborhoods, seen in clubs and shows, and referenced in newspapers.[5]

Ben Koehler, who wore his uniform to a party where other men dressed in drag, could hardly be taken for a fairy or effeminate male prostitute—men who, according to a New York investigator testifying in 1899, "get up and sing as women, and dance; ape the female character; call each other sisters and take people out for immoral purposes."[6] Koehler had not swished his skirt or danced the hoochie-coochie at Worcester's party.

Nor did Koehler fit the profile of an "invert," "pervert," or "degenerate," as those terms were used by federal bureaucrats newly concerned with keeping "pederasts or sodomites" out of the United States based on a 1909 report about same-sex promiscuity in Europe.[7] Koehler was not foreign, poor, uneducated, or lazy, the characteristics immigration officials initially linked with men "who exhibited gender inversion, had anatomical defects, or engaged in sodomy."[8]

It may have been acceptable for sponsors of the 1893 World's Fair to import sexually provocative Little Egypt for patrons' amusement, but the population, government, and concerns of the United States had grown since then, and the head of the Bureau of Immigration now worried about "a new species of undesirable immigrant not heretofore met with in the enforcement of the immigration law"—people inclined toward nonconforming sex acts.[9] Their bodily practices might corrupt Americans, not merely entertain them.

The 1909 report is "one of the earliest pieces of evidence to document federal-level concern with homosexuality," according to historian Margot Canaday.[10] Lacking laws that expressly matched that concern, officials used what they had: authority to exclude or deport foreigners "likely to become a public charge" or guilty of "crimes of moral turpitude."[11] The latter regulation was fairly simple to apply. The "public charge" clause, in contrast, was "a status charge—it required no evidence that a crime had been committed, but only that a person *seem to be something* (likely to be poor)."[12]

Accordingly, while Ben Koehler drilled soldiers on Plum Island to repel foreign threats that might arrive by ship, immigration inspectors worked at Ellis Island to exclude individuals on moral and economic grounds—the specious but largely unchallenged legal justification being that a sexual deviant would or could not hold a job and would become a "public charge." Fusing "moral deficiency and economic dependency," and applying the idea that sexual deviance in men was caused by or associated with effeminate traits, immigration inspectors looked for such "signs" as deformed genitals, lack of muscle tone, high-pitched voices, or atypical gait and clothing.[13]

The Bureau of Immigration was the first federal agency to target suspected homosexuals as a class.[14] In 1917–18, the Army would follow suit, instructing draft boards "to watch for male recruits who 'present the general body conformation of the opposite sex, with sloping narrow shoulders, broad hips, excessive pectoral and pubic adipose deposits, with lack of masculine [hair] and muscular markings.'"[15]

In 1913, however, the worlds of Plum Island and Ellis Island seemed quite separate—until Worcester leveled charges against his boss, a respected officer with sixteen years of service.

Back in 1908, the Army had considered Koehler such a good judge of men's fitness for military service that it assigned him to manage recruitment in Brooklyn, then Manhattan. Between fifteen and thirty applicants stripped naked for his inspection every day "to see that there were no defects," according to a sergeant who worked with him.[16] Based on praise for his performance in that job, the Army promoted Koehler to major and commander of Fort Terry in 1911.

Koehler's education, family prosperity, whiteness, and years of employment contradicted the Immigration Bureau's early homosexual paradigm, but the Army did not need to find someone a "public charge" to declare him unfit. A mere six weeks after Worcester's tell-all trip to Governors Island, the Army proposed to court-martial Koehler as a "man whose sexual desires are reversed, [having] the same desires toward men that normal men have towards women," in the words of the Army prosecutor assigned to the case. He called Koehler a "homo-sexualist," underscoring the newness of the term "homosexual."[17]

Court-martialing a senior officer for homoerotic acts was also new. No laws passed by Congress and no administrative regulations explicitly prohibited homosexual conduct in the military, and New York's sodomy law did not apply to groping.[18] What the Army did have was an archaic code called the Articles of War, imported from Great Britain in 1775-76 and virtually unchanged since 1806. One section prohibited conduct "unbecoming an officer and a gentleman." Another proscribed actions to "the prejudice of good order and military discipline."[19] Those broadly worded clauses had been interpreted to allow prosecution of an officer for "almost any improper or irregular act" or behavior "disapproved by superiors."[20] Army leaders planned to use those clauses to court-martial Koehler—but there was pushback.

Worcester said he complained about Koehler "in order that the Army should remain clean,"[21] but Koehler's supporters claimed Worcester was throwing dirt for the sole purpose of ridding himself of a strict boss. Koehler was the true victim, his defenders maintained, not Worcester and the other men who told an Army inspector that Koehler had groped them, too.

No one was more upset than Sophia, who had left a pleasant midwestern life of tennis matches and dinner parties to live at Fort Terry and was now in her third winter of providing the Army with free labor as a hostess and operator of the post's Sunday school. She was fiercely loyal to her brother, signified by something they had in common from the earliest moments of their lives: Both had been born on New Year's Day, five years apart.

"Some scoundrels have been making trouble for Ben," she wrote to a longtime friend, Roy Dimmick. "A couple of officers whom Ben has had occasion to correct have gotten a dozen or more soldiers to swear to a lot of lies."[22]

The other officer Sophia referred to was Second Lieutenant Austin G. Frick, a friend of Worcester's. Young, tall, and single, Frick had befriended Sophia upon her arrival, playing cards and tennis with her, but just as quickly, he began to collect reprimands from Ben.[23] Now, all the tennis balls Sophia had hit with Frick and their hands of bridge seemed like a long warm-up to betrayal, for Frick told the Army inspector that Ben tried to kiss him one evening in 1912 when the Koehlers invited him to stay for dinner, as well as grabbing his testicles at a dance in the spring of 1913.[24]

"He is entirely innocent of their charges," Sophia lamented to her friend, "but they are of the character that is most difficult to fight— They couldn't bring a decent charge but had to resort to things no man with any manhood would even think of—"

Sophia may have graduated college and resisted social pressure to marry, but her iconoclasm only went so far. Her words intoned the era's cultural preoccupation with male strength that underlay much of the ramped-up hostility toward men suspected of homosexuality. Yes, manhood was important. Yes, her brother had it.

Sociologist Michael Kimmel has written that "the story of America [is] a story of proving and testing manhood."[25] In the 1800s, it could be "unmanly" to support abolition and women's rights, and "unmanly" not to, for, in the words of historian Stacey Robertson, "various notions of manhood became representations of larger competing ideologies."[26]

The manhood fixation changed as America changed, economically and socially, with old hierarchies declining, former slaves obtaining the right to vote, and women advocating for rights as never before. The result as America entered the twentieth century was one of those "moments of crisis when masculinity was seen as threatened and people worked hard to try and salvage, revitalize, and resurrect it."[27] New standards of masculinity were emerging, including a hyper-masculinity focused on the body—how it looked, and how one used it.

During the Civil War, Walt Whitman openly kissed and hugged injured soldiers.[28] His actions were considered tender, not perverted.[29] Through most of the 1800s, young men expressed intimacy with their close male friends in physical ways, such as holding hands.[30] Men shared beds, including Abraham Lincoln with a close friend when he was in his late twenties.[31] As historian E. Anthony Rotundo has written, "In the absence of a deep cultural anxiety about homosexuality, men did not have to worry about the meaning of those moments of contact."[32]

By 1913, at least in middle-class culture, those days were gone.[33] "Toughness was now admired, while tenderness was cause for scorn," according to Rotundo, who coined the term "passionate manhood" to denote that aggressive male traits, previously considered socially undesirable and warranting restraint, were now seen as virtues, particularly in the view of younger men—such as Worcester and Frick.[34]

On their surface, the charges against Koehler revolved around specific acts and whether or not they occurred. As Sophia alluded to, answering that question took one into spongy "he said–they said" terrain. That was an unstable place from an evidentiary standpoint, potentially allowing "could he have done it?" to eclipse "did he do it?"—especially given the vagueness of the articles under which Ben would be prosecuted.[35] Sophia went straight to Ben's "manhood" to rebut the charges, but that was not a stable defense either. Was it the manhood of a brave soldier—a late nineteenth-century standard Ben could easily satisfy—or the newer "passionate manhood" that focused on personal traits such as toughness, muscular appearance, and obvious sexual interest in women?[36] The latter test posed a problem for a middle-aged, short, and stocky bachelor who lived with his sister on a remote island.

When Sophia wrote to Roy Dimmick in January 1914, both she and Ben were on edge, awaiting a report that could exonerate Ben and end the threat of a court-martial. A second investigation had taken place, ordered at the urging of Representative Sloan and an influential senator based on Ben's claim of a plot involving Worcester, Frick, and men in their "clique."

"Every one in the post outside the clique is for Ben," Sophia informed Roy.[37]

That was the status she was accustomed to—people being *for* her beloved brother, not against him.

# CHAPTER THREE

# Embryo Generals

Sophia had lived through the Floyd River flood of May 1892, those terrible days when Iowans died and stockyard cattle swam for their lives, but three years later, when she was 18 and about to graduate LeMars High School, she expected nature to provide more favorable conditions for the outdoor celebration she had arranged.

Rowing on the Floyd was the plan, followed by a picnic in her favorite grove, "but it rained so hard the evening before that we couldn't," Sophia lamented in her first letter to Roy, then 19, which he received in Blue Hill, Nebraska, where he lived with his family near two of Sophia and Ben's older brothers.[1] Rain had also spoiled Sophia's post-graduation stay with her cousins in nearby Marcus, Iowa, where her uncle was mayor. She had "such a dull time," she confided to Roy.

In June, when Sophia wrote her letter, the Floyd was still running high and Sophia doubted her mother would let her handle oars anytime soon, but Sophia let Roy know of other upcoming amusements—a dance and horse races. She flirtatiously suggested that if Roy's sister visited over the summer, "don't you think you had better be her escort, she might get lost?" Still, Sophia reserved her strongest enthusiasm for Ben, who "is to be home one week from today" from West Point.

"I am so glad," she wrote, for Ben had been her anchor after their father died, and she missed him, even though it was unquestionably an honor to have a brother at the United States Military Academy.

This admiration was underscored by *The New York Times* when it published a photograph of Ben and his sixty-six classmates two years later. The graduates were "embryo Generals" in the unctuous words of the *Times*, pictured solemnly in dark uniforms of the sort many, including Ben, expected to wear for the rest of their lives.[2] Someone with neat penmanship had labored over the photograph, writing a small number in white ink on each man's chest that corresponded to an index printed below the photo, so that readers could know the names of the men whose years of drills and "practical experience . . . will stand them in good stead should the country ever need their services."[3]

Today, the graduating class at West Point numbers more than one thousand, and no newspaper of general circulation devotes enough space to print all those names.

It was different in the late 1800s, not only because of class size. The military formed a large portion of the daily news diet in part because of its role in the recently completed westward drive through Native American land, and also because a major cultural glorification of the Civil War was in progress. Many young adults had grown up hearing their fathers and grandfathers speak of the glory days of the Civil War, mythologized as a time of hardy men of high character willing to die for what they believed. Such "intergenerational storytelling" by veterans, plus a "massive Civil War literary genre [and] widespread production of popular and official historical memory of the conflict" led Americans of the late 19th century to understand the Civil War "as a national treasure," in the words of historian John Pettegrew.[4] The racial cause of the war was downplayed as "popular historical memory of the Civil War fixed on the scale and excitement of battle."

A number of U.S. senators and representatives were veterans. Joined by younger hawks, and supported by Civil War memoirs that stressed the "man-making power of war," they propounded the idea of military life and service in war—"the soldierly virtues," in Theodore Roosevelt's words—as incubators of strong men and exemplary citizens, in contrast, it was said, to weak men molded by industrial progress, material comforts, women's influence, and peace.[5]

Books and articles offered much advice on how teenage boys could attain vigorous manhood as the milestone year of 1900 neared, but for Ben, West Point was the fulfillment of a dream formed earlier—in a boyhood that exposed him to the most illustrious Civil War hero of them all, Ulysses S. Grant.[6]

Ben spent the first years of his life in Galena, Illinois, which claimed Grant as a favorite son due to his having worked in his father's store located there. The Grant & Perkins leather goods shop stood down the street from the establishment where Christian Koehler made wagons, and where an employee, Louis Gund, created something else—a lifelong relationship—when he introduced his sister to his boss. Christian Koehler and Margaret Gund soon married after finding that they had much in common, including former lives in Rhineland, Germany. Fate, or an innate desire to replicate the past, had brought them both to the watershed of the Mississippi, a U.S. river that rivaled the Rhine; for Galena's stately red brick buildings sloped down to a Mississippi tributary, the Galena River.

Ben, the couple's ninth child, was born on January 1, 1872, during Grant's first term as president.[7]

Grant and his wife made annual visits to Galena, feted by marching bands, fluttering flags, and red, white, and blue bunting.[8] Ben was the right age to soak up the pageantry, too young to know about either the death and discrimination that lay underneath such heraldic nods to the Civil War, or the allegations of corruption and ineffectiveness that bedeviled Grant's administration.

Nor did Ben know that Grant had not always been a hero, that he had experienced years of failure after developing a drinking problem while living apart from his wife in an isolated California fort. Grant had resigned rather than face a court-martial, and after several financial missteps, he had reluctantly gone to work in his father's store in 1860, turning it into "a small hotbed of political debate" until the shelling of Fort Sumter made war a reality.[9] After that, Grant's ties to a U.S. representative, Elihu Washburne, and almost unbelievable fortuity brought his innate military abilities to President Lincoln's attention and made possible Grant's transformation from antislavery saddle-seller to head of the Union Army and two-term president.

Later, when Ben faced the loss of all he had lived for, those come-back aspects of Grant's story likely mattered more than the boyhood idolatry he had felt.

Ben was four when his parents left Galena with their youngest children to be closer to the older ones, whose aspirations had taken them west. The year was 1876, the nation's centennial, and Margaret was pregnant. In the spring, the Koehlers crossed the Mississippi into Iowa at Dubuque, passing farms, wide-open vistas, and many a steeple catching the light. They kept on moving past Waterloo, Webster City, and Fort Dodge toward the Midwest's other Rhine-like river, the Missouri. With about twenty-five miles to go until the Missouri border, they veered northwest to the Floyd River Valley and stopped in Le-Mars. Other Germans had settled there, and local business leaders were congratulating themselves on their "success and prosperity," the "exceptionally fine location of the town," and "the splendid farming country that surrounds it."[10]

In LeMars, Christian set up a new wagon business and Margaret gave birth to Sophia. Very soon, different sorts of immigrants began arriving: second and third sons of British aristocrats, born in the wrong order to inherit their family homesteads, sent to Iowa to buy tracts of its fertile farmland, learn farm management, and live like lords for a pittance. Soon after the Koehlers' arrival, LeMars laid claim to one of the first golf courses west of the Mississippi.[11]

In the 1880s, LeMars became famous among upper-class Brits, though its name predated the English. In 1869, a railroad builder had arrived with big intentions in what was then called Saint Paul Junction, where two train lines intersected. He invited the women in his party to rename the place. They played around with the first letters of their names—Lucy, Elizabeth, Mary, Anna, Rebecca, Sarah—until the result was articulable, but to say "LeMars" made sense would be a stretch: Ben and Sophia grew up in an Iowa prairie town dominated by Brits bearing the name of the fourth planet from the sun—or the Roman god of war—juxtaposed with a French article.

That was where Ben spent the next twelve years, in "an American town which wasn't American," in the words of a prominent anthropologist who grew up in LeMars and credited its "crossing of cultures" for his subconscious sense that "something in my background was different."[12]

In 1913, a few men on a small East Coast island would allege that Ben was different in an unmanly way, and some would see as confirmation of that difference Ben's behaviors that seemed out of step with American practices. Take sports, for example.

"No boy can grow to a perfectly normal manhood today without the benefits of at least a small amount of baseball experience and practice," according to the wisdom imparted by the American author of *Training the Boy*.[13] In LeMars, however, boys played cricket, not baseball. Apparently, the Brits of LeMars did not believe that baseball was essential to "normal manhood," nor did Ben and his family.[14] Years later, Ben would be the top arbiter of, but not a player in, Fort Terry's version of America's pastime—inter-company baseball games—and this would put him in direct conflict with one of his accusers, Austin Frick, who was the fort's baseball athletic director.

British tastes in sports also left their mark on Sophia. A rower and polo player from Cambridge, England, William Close, first saw the "rolling prairie" of western Iowa in 1876 when a land speculator took him there after he competed in a centennial rowing regatta on Philadelphia's Schuylkill River.[15] Within a year, Close and one of his brothers had bought their first 2,500 acres of Iowa land undervalued due to past grasshopper plagues. The next year, with a third brother and family money, they formed a land company, purchased sixteen thousand acres outside of LeMars, negotiated for another fifty thousand acres, and began promoting the area to "English people of the better class," leading to "the largest class-based British colony in the West."[16] Bartenders poured Bass ale and Guinness at the House of Lords tavern, and polo matches took place weekly, with women as well as men watching. Sophia and other girls, whether English, German, or Swedish, learned to row and play tennis and golf, while in the rest of the country females were largely excluded from sports. "There was nowhere else like it in the United States," writes British producer and author Peter Pagnamenta.[17]

Cricket aside, Ben's upbringing included activities widely accepted as masculine, such as the excellent horsemanship he learned and the manual labor that went along with prairie life. With few boys his age in LeMars—there was only one other, Ned Sibley, in his high school class—Ben spent much of his adolescence working and studying.[18] He tended the family garden, chopped wood, and helped his mother raise his younger brother, Rudolph, and Sophia after their father died and three older brothers, Henry, Barthold, and Edgar, left home. But with its fancy opera house, highbrow forms of entertainment, and commitment to education, LeMars nurtured in Ben an appreciation for classical music, theater, and reading—traits that would be associated with effeminacy as men's policing of other men's sexuality increased.[19] Ben's own lawyer would call him "a little bit too refined."[20]

While British upper-class norms molded Ben in LeMars, his dream of American military service was kept alive by his brother Louis, nine years older, who had received an appointment to West Point after graduating in the first LeMars High School class. Ben wanted to follow suit, but there was little chance of another Koehler being nominated for a coveted place at West Point by Iowa officials, even though Ben was an excellent student of history, geography, and Latin who gave a scholarly graduation speech on "Historical Turning Points," prescient in ways Ben never could have imagined.[21]

To enhance his chances, Ben moved to Nebraska after high school. He went to work for one of his older brothers, Henry, as a bank cashier in Blue Hill, the same town where the Dimmicks lived—a little north of the immigrant farms where, in the words of Willa Cather, "there was nothing but land: not a country at all, but the material out of which countries are made."[22]

Ben's bet paid off. His brothers made the right introductions, and Ben did well on the West Point entrance exam. There followed an appointment to West Point from the 5th Congressional District of

Nebraska.[23] Like his lack of baseball experience, Ben's shortness was not held against him. One did not need to be tall to be brave and smart or to pull a trigger. Grant proved that, having started at West Point when he stood the same height as Ben—five foot two—though Grant grew to five foot eight."[24]

Ben's short stature was evident to others, but it did not prevent him from having confidence in his abilities.[25] He had grown up with two visions of male success on display within his large family: military service and business-building. There was never any question which future Ben wanted. While he would always note his banking background on Army forms, along with fluent German, Ben and the United States struck their first deal when he was 21. He would be a military man and leave civilian life behind.

Back in Iowa, Sophia had her own dreams for the future. "One of my girl friends left his morning for [the University of] Nebraska," she informed Roy. "How I wish that it was me, but then I think that it won't be long before I can go."[26] Sophia signed her letter, "I am as ever, 'The Bum,'" an ironic word choice given the emerging association between hoboes—or "bums"—and male-male sexual promiscuity.[27] Presumably, Sophia was using the word to mean a loafer or transient, but even that description bore little relation to her circumstances. She would never again sign her letters to Roy so flippantly.


IN THE *TIMES* PHOTOGRAPH of the West Point class of 1897, Ben is seated in the first row, his lean body angled so that only one side of his face is visible, drawing attention to his aquiline nose—or "large nose," as a newspaper would put it in 1914.[28] The blond hair of his youth is gone; it is brown now. Like some other cadets, Ben is gazing downward, solemnly. In his youth, Ben posed cockily for family photos with his hand on his hip, but in the West Point photo his posture is perfect: erect shoulders, straight back. To his right stands Andrew Moses, one of Ben's good friends, blond even in his twenties and boyish compared to the sterner-looking Ben.

Appearances notwithstanding, the two had much in common, Moses being from a pioneer family and an accomplished rider like Ben. Neither man anticipated on this occasion of pride that in seventeen years they would assume markedly different roles on a small island, Ben as the accused and Moses as a key witness, asserting that Ben could not possibly have groped a sergeant as alleged, for Moses had sat in the same small room, a few feet away, the whole time.

Now, the graduates focused on securing favorable assignments. According to the *Times*, "never was the survival of the fittest better exemplified than in the class of '97," described as "superior" in athletics, academics, and discipline.[29] More than fifty entrants had "dropped by the wayside," but Ben was one of the survivors, having persevered despite intestinal upset, boils, and eye infections. Graduating with a class rank of forty-six, "sound and normal" muscle systems, and 20/20 vision, Ben, at 25, was older than many of his classmates.[30] He was single, but so were they all, marriage being prohibited for cadets.[31] Indeed, there were some who proclaimed that an Army man had only one true life partner, and it wasn't a human being.

Henry Koehler, the banker, advocated for his younger brother, writing to the Army that Ben "is a Nebraska boy and of course we all feel very proud of him and feel that in the distribution of the good assignments that [sic] Nebraska boys should not be neglected."[32] Two weeks later, another letter arrived in Washington from the bank's vice president, a former Civil War colonel.[33] He sought the help of Nebraska Senator John Thurston, who forwarded the letter to the assistant secretary of war with his own brief and pointed note: "This young man is from our State, and he ought to be looked after."[34]

The senator's request was soon granted. In July, the newly minted Additional Second Lieutenant of Infantry Benjamin Martin Koehler signed his first oath of office, in elegant script, and moved to Fort Logan in Colorado—but not for long.[35] In the late 1890s, it was not only wind and salt air that seas brought to land, nor immigrants to its increasingly crowded coastal cities. Fear lapped at the shores of the United States, fear of an attack by Spanish ships. The Indian Wars had been fought in deserts and canyons west of the Mississippi, but now newspaper reports of misery and violence in Cuba under Spanish rule—fanned by those who favored war—turned attention to the country's coastline, which suddenly seemed too easy a target.

Ben would be swept up in the current of fear, while from across the Atlantic came hints of a different factor that would influence his life. A famous man had been released from prison a few weeks before Ben's graduation. The man had served two years, the maximum sentence under British law for sodomy, though the judge would gladly have made the term longer, calling it "totally inadequate for such a case as this"—"the worst case I have ever tried."[36]

The convict's name was Oscar Wilde, the Irish playwright and wit who was greatly damaged physically and emotionally by his imprisonment and died three years after his release. As Ben would later do, Wilde had ignored signs of his vulnerability to legal process instigated by someone willing to use a charge of homosexuality to get what he wanted.[37]

"[W]hat is said of a man is nothing. The point is, who says it." That was one of many aphorisms Wilde left behind.[38] Eventually, Ben would learn how much the wrong words from the right people could hurt a man, but first, as a young officer, he faced the threats of war and earned the praise of generals. In the years immediately following Ben's West Point graduation, the words of others seemed to be his allies, not the vectors of mutiny they would become.

# CHAPTER FOUR

# *Islands*

M ASS FEARS COME and go. In the late 1800s, Spanish ships were poised to enter Long Island Sound, destroy munitions factories in Connecticut, and bombard New York City, according to yellow journalists William Randolph Hearst and Joseph Pulitzer. Even *The New York Times*, the usually less alarmist "gray lady," joined in.[1] An early casualty of the fear-mongering was New Jersey's summer rental market, as prospective tenants allowed the known pleasures of sun and surf to be outweighed by the speculative risk of enemy fire.[2]

Responding to calls for greater preparedness, Congress voted to militarize the wide mouth of Long Island Sound by building forts on islands at its eastern end—Plum, Great Gull, Gardiners, and Fishers. Those sandy islands had been connected for thousands of years by an underwater ridge, and now they were connected above the sea by a political effort to calm anxious citizens.[3] The first purchase of land on Plum Island took place in 1897, the year of Ben's West Point graduation.[4]

The flip side of Americans' fear of the Spanish was compassion for Cubans being repressed, tortured, and killed for seeking independence. American men and women contributed to food drives and wrote letters urging Congress to intervene, having read articles such as those by Richard Harding Davis, a friend of Roosevelt's, about the execution of a young Cuban man and the strip search of a Cuban woman.[5] At home, Geronimo and other Apaches had been relocated against their will to northern Florida, Alabama, and Oklahoma. Seminole Indians, considered a deterrent to Florida's development, were killed or driven into the Everglades over a period of thirty years. But now, one hundred miles south of Florida, Americans were outraged because the Spanish were mistreating Cubans.

The crusading newspapers of Pulitzer and Hearst, engaged in their own war over readership, helped incite the public outcry, but as historian Kristin Hoganson convincingly argues, correspondents for Hearst, Pulitzer, and other publishers wrote about events in Cuba in highly gendered terms, producing "accounts [that] portrayed the entire island as a pure woman who was being assaulted by Spain."[6]

At a time when American men were anxious about their roles at home, and influenced by Civil War nostalgia linking manhood with martial spirit, the Cuban issue became "nothing less than a test of American manhood."[7]

Cubans had been seeking independence for years, but the rebellion intensified in the mid-1890s when Spain imposed martial law and forced citizens to live in shanty towns—virtual concentration camps— without proper food or sanitation.[8] American officials joined the press in depicting the Spanish as decadent and "effeminate aristocrats" and "bestial and unchivalrous" degenerates engaged in abusing docile Cuban women, who were said to want nothing more than to be good wives and mothers—unlike the rabble-rousing New Women in the United States who sought the right to vote.[9] Cuban men were portrayed as brave heroes fighting for the noble ideal of self-government, in contrast to "sapped" American men who had turned into "money-making machines," in the words of one member of Congress.[10]

As Hoganson puts it, the "tendency to depict Cuban revolutionaries as if they were the heroes and heroines of a chivalric drama" said less about what hawkish American men wanted for Cuba than what they wished for at home: defeat of women's suffrage and perpetuation of a patriarchal political and social system in which men dominated and women assumed dependent, homebound roles in exchange for "protection."[11] The argument went like this: Women no longer trusted men to lead and protect because men had become weak, but if men were stronger, as they supposedly had been in the Civil War, women would retreat from public life, to the betterment of the nation. War would make men strong again, so war was desirable.[12]

The link between strong men and a strong country was a rallying cry of Theodore Roosevelt, but there were plenty of others who complained that men—especially white middle- and upper-class men—were growing too soft for their own and the nation's good.[13]

An influential rabbi warned in 1892 that female teachers were feminizing boys, a refrain that would grow louder as the number of women teaching in elementary schools increased.[14] Other factors blamed for the erosion of manly strength included masturbation, insufficient consumption of red meat, the growth of a consumer culture, joyless factory work, nonwhites and women in the workplace, and cities (an "enormity devouring manhood," said Frank Lloyd Wright). Also blamed were homes "built to meet the needs of women, whose tendency is still to emphasize emotion—to minimize reason," in the words of Gustav Stickley, the mission-style furniture maker whose "designs, with their disciplined geometry, generous proportions, and sturdiness offered men the possibility of return to their castles."[15]

"The emergence of a visible gay male subculture in many large American cities at the turn of the century gave an even greater moral urgency to men's flight from being perceived as sissies," writes Michael Kimmel.[16] Beginning in the 1890s, "fairies" congregated openly in clubs in downtown Manhattan, where they "were the most famous symbols of gay life, and the impression of that life they conveyed was reinforced by the countless other effeminate men who [came to be] visible in the streets of the city's working-class and amusement districts," according to historian George Chauncey.[17]

In politics, men who opposed intervention in Cuba drew the label of "sissy," a word that had morphed from meaning "sister" to an effeminate or cowardly male. President William McKinley, who initially resisted the calls for war, found himself characterized in some newspapers as an old woman; for it was clear to the same people who depicted Cuban women as feminine and worthy of rescue that the last person who should be making U.S. foreign policy was a woman.[18] While serving as assistant secretary of the Navy, Roosevelt accused McKinley of having "no more backbone than a chocolate éclair," and McKinley's Civil War service was trotted out by his supporters to shore up his image.[19]

On hikes outside Washington, Roosevelt frequently discussed his wish to "drive the Spaniard from the Western World" with a man responsible for care of McKinley's actual backbone. That man was Leonard Wood, the president's medical adviser, who had won over Roosevelt with his tales of serving in the "inconceivably harassing" campaign to capture Apache leader Geronimo.[20] The two spoke of their shared belief, in Roosevelt's words, that a war against Spain "would be as righteous as it would be advantageous to the honor and the interests of the nation."[21] "Honor" in that context was bound up with manly strength, and Roosevelt wrote admiringly that Wood had "qualities of entire manliness."[22]

Yet "entire manliness" as a governing paradigm was threatened by women's growing participation in public life, especially in cities. Women worked in the labor force in increasing numbers, rallied for local reforms, testified at congressional hearings, participated in the trade-union movement, and advocated for international arbitration with Spain rather than war.[23] Through their involvement in the temperance movement, women were telling men to stop drinking, and women had secured voting rights in four states by 1896: Wyoming, Colorado, Idaho, and Utah. They nearly won in California, but for heavy opposition by liquor interests.[24] In the 1896 presidential campaign, women "attained new heights of political visibility," attending conventions, holding candidate forums, and distributing campaign literature.[25]

Ben Koehler did not have to look far for evidence of strong women. His sister Lizzie taught school and approved of western states' progressive attitude toward women's suffrage.[26] While Sophia was less political, she expressed her opinions, aspired to attend college, and enjoyed the company of male friends, including her partners in the mixed doubles tournaments she often entered and sometimes won.[27]

Ben's sisters gave him reason enough to respect women as independent beings, but he gained a ringside seat to the struggle for women's rights when his older brother Louis married Susan B. Anthony's niece, Maude Anthony, during Ben's final year at West Point. The couple met when Louis was stationed in Leavenworth, Kansas, where Maude's father, Daniel Read Anthony, played an outsized role. The owner of a local newspaper, he had come to Kansas from the Anthony farm near Rochester, New York, to oppose slavery. His maverick life in Kansas included duels, whippings, burning buildings owned by Confederate sympathizers, and being shot by a rival newspaper owner in the Leavenworth Opera House.[28]

"She has a lot of Anthony in her and is a bright girl," Susan B. Anthony wrote proudly of her niece.[29] By the time Louis married Maude, he was a well-regarded captain in the cavalry with a strong personality himself. Perhaps Louis was drawn to a woman raised to stand up for principles—as Louis would later do against Leonard Wood, in a controversy that landed on Roosevelt's desk with no good outcomes for anyone, least of all Ben Koehler.

When Louis and Maude married, he was 33, she 31—"what the world calls late," Susan wrote to Maude, "yet I think plenty early."[30]

"Well it makes me happy to feel that you & he are happy," Susan wrote on the occasion of the couple's first anniversary. Susan referenced Charlotte Brontë's *Shirley* for the idea "that a marriage would be happy provided that after the delusions & illusions of love had passed—there were real character left in each on which could be founded a true & lasting friendship."[31]

"A true [and] lasting friendship" between husband and wife was a radical idea at a time when some men warned against too much contact with women lest it cause a man to become homosexual, and men who supported women's rights were likely to find their manhood questioned.[32] Women, too, were beginning to emphasize their differences from men in positive, political ways.[33]

Circumstance had provided Ben with unusual influences. First there were the Brits, who gave Ben an English pedigree in education and habits, and now his brother's spouse meant that Ben's family-by-marriage included a top leader of the National Woman Suffrage Association and a strident opponent of racial inequality. First and foremost, however, Ben Koehler was a skilled artillery officer, a disciplined young man whose high school motto had been "duty before position."[34] In the late 1890s, "duty" was rapidly leading him and many other American men toward war.

President McKinley, trying to appease both hawks and proponents of arbitration, sent the U.S.S. *Maine* to Cuba at the end of 1897 for the vague purposes of protecting American interests and showing strength.[35] Less than three weeks after the *Maine*'s arrival in Havana Harbor, the ship exploded, killing 267 American soldiers.

"MAINE EXPLOSION CAUSED BY BOMB OR TORPEDO?" screamed the banner headline of *The World*, Pulitzer's paper, even though the cause of the explosion was far from clear.[36] The *New York Journal* did not bother with a question mark, proclaiming on its front page "DESTRUCTION OF THE WAR SHIP MAINE WAS THE WORK OF AN ENEMY."[37] Spain denied responsibility, asserting that an accident must have taken place on the ship, but few listened. A writer in *Harper's* opined that "a nation needs a war from time to time to prevent it from becoming effeminate."[38]

As Pettegrew puts it, "personal concern over proving one's manhood" was being effectively joined "with the foreign-war-making interests of the United States."[39]

After the *Maine*'s explosion, McKinley still urged restraint, but Congress voted to expand the military, including the creation of two new Coast Artillery divisions. Army headquarters telegraphed instructions that "desirable men" should be selected to fill the new divisions.[40] One man deemed "desirable" was Ben Koehler, and so Ben left the inland location his brothers had helped secure and traveled to Fort McHenry in Baltimore to join the new 6th Artillery Division as a second lieutenant.[41] He remained short in stature and romantically unattached, but apparently no one in the Army thought him a sissy.

On April 13, a brawl occurred in the House of Representatives between the war and peace factions.[42] McKinley told Spain to leave Cuba, to which Spain responded with a declaration of war against the United States. The next day, April 25, Congress declared war on Spain.

The hawks had won, and the Spanish colonies of Cuba, Puerto Rico, and the Philippines would all be transformed in ways still playing out today.[43] The war sent American ships across multiple seas, and in 1898, less than a year after his graduation from West Point, the Army dispatched Ben Koehler, eager to prove his worth to his country, to some of the most valuable real estate on earth—and then to some of the poorest.

# CHAPTER FIVE

# Mock Battle, Real Death

I F BEN HAD BENEFITED as a "Nebraska boy," he was about to witness a whole new world of privilege courtesy of John Jacob Astor IV, a New York City socialite and heir to a fortune amassed by his great-grandfather from fur trading, shipping, and real estate. In leisure times, Astor had sailed his yacht near Plum Island. In 1898, he directed his opulence toward war.

Heeding the call from McKinley for volunteers to fight the Spanish, Astor offered not one man but ninety-nine men—an entire battery. Astor would provide their uniforms (blue with red-lined overcapes, brown leggings, and gray caps), equip them with guns direct from the factory (rapid-firing Hotchkiss 12-pounders), house them in one of his Manhattan buildings, and pay for their salaries, transportation, mules, and other expenses.[1] The press ate it up. "It would be hard to imagine a finer looking lot of men than these members of the Astor Battery," oozed *The New York Times* at the end of May 1898. The battery included "college graduates, with records on field and track, and there are doctors, lawyers, policemen, bookkeepers."[2]

The uniforms and guns may have been of the highest quality, but the soldiers also needed leaders. Up from Baltimore came Ben, "ordered to report to First Lieut. Peyton C. Marsh [sic], at New York, for duty in connection with this battery," reported *The New York Times*.[3] Eleven months after his graduation, Ben was back in the pages of the

East Coast's dominant paper, drawing the sort of attention the *Times* gave those whom its editors and reporters deemed worthy, such as Roosevelt, who for months had "preached, with all the fervor and zeal I possessed, our duty to intervene in Cuba" and had eagerly left his desk job with the Navy to volunteer.[4]

Roosevelt's service with the Rough Riders in Cuba may be the most enduring narrative from the Spanish-American War, but the war's first battle took place in the Philippines, an archipelago of nearly seven thousand islands where Spanish rule was also being challenged. On May 1, 1898, just days after the declarations of war, the Navy, under Commodore George Dewey, destroyed the Spanish fleet anchored in Manila Bay. One of the most decisive naval battles in history had already occurred by the time Roosevelt left for mobilization in San Antonio, Texas, and Ben bedded down at 552 Broadway in New York City in a new Astor building.

Despite the quick sea victory, Dewey asked for ground forces to garrison Manila in the event of a Spanish attack. The Astor Battery boarded a train in mid-July to San Francisco. From there, they sailed to Manila.

A month later, on August 13, 1898, Ben and his battery began fighting Spanish troops, joining two other units under the command of General Arthur MacArthur Jr., father of the future five-star general Douglas MacArthur. After seven hours, the Spaniards retreated into "a thick jungle of bamboo trees, where the enemy made the last stand." MacArthur called for an officer to lead a charge, to which "Capt. March instantly cried, 'Come on, men,' and dashed into the wilderness, followed by every one of his artillerymen."[5] Ben, head of the artillery section, was in the fore. The artillerymen "drew their pistols, their only weapons, and, after a desperate encounter, won a signal victory," wrote the *Times*. Three men in the battery—two sergeants and a private—were shot and killed. Eight others were wounded.[6]

For his conduct, Ben earned recognition for "gallantry and meritorious services in campaign ending with capture of Manila" by MacArthur and Major General Wesley Merritt.[7] He rose to first lieutenant in the regular Army and captain in the volunteers within a year.[8]

Such a rapid advance suggested a bright future, but later, as if presaging the reversal of his fortunes, the ground-fighting that Ben helped lead would become known as the "Mock Battle of Manila." The word "mock" was added once it came to light that representatives of Spain and the United States had secretly met in Hong Kong to settle their differences, such that the pistol fight and chase involving the Astor Battery were essentially for show—to allow Spain to save face rather than surrender—not that Ben, nor the three men who died, knew that.

Eventually, it also came to appear that an engine room fire, not a mine, caused the *Maine*'s explosion.[9] Yet the war was celebrated as "a glorious display of American manhood."[10] In early 1899, the "heroes of the famous pistol charge before Manila" were "cheered and feasted" at "nearly every way station as they journeyed eastward."[11] Arriving home, they looked as good to the *Times* as when they had left, bearing "a closer resemblance to returning tourists than to veterans of one of the most arduous and brilliant campaigns of the war." The Battery's members paraded down Park Avenue for a viewing by the mayor, "a blue and brawn column of giants with the bronzed cheeks and springy step of athletes."

Even the Battery's dog, Bonjum, made news. Though the fox terrier's master died in the Philippines, comrades had rescued Bonjum and brought him to New York, where he "made friends with a host of admirers," the *Times* wrote.

The Army could keep track of a dog, but as events showed, it could also lose sight of one of its desirable men.

"Had I better revoke this order?" wrote an officer in January. "Yes," underscored twice, was the reply.[12] The order directed Ben to fulfill administrative functions in New York City in connection with the "muster out of service"—or discharge—of Astor Battery members.[13] However, Ben was nowhere near New York. He remained in the Philippines.[14] The Spaniards had surrendered, but the United States found reasons to linger in both the Philippines and Cuba. Cuban men, pictured before the war as heroic, were now deemed incapable of governing themselves, prompting establishment of a provisional government by the United States. While Congress had specified that the United States could not assert sovereignty over Cuba, no such restraint applied to the Philippines, which was purchased from Spain, along with Guam and Puerto Rico, for $20 million.

The American West had been won, and Spain had been trounced. Hawks felt vindicated, having won a war that was "a defining moment in America's emergence as a global power."[15] Now, the rest of the world shimmered with opportunity, including proximity to the China market. Members of Congress debated how far to follow the rainbow, but for Filipino nationalists, control of their country by a different foreign power was not the desired outcome. Fighting broke out between Filipino troops and American soldiers in February, and a new war began over control of the Philippines. Pro-interventionists became imperialists, who in turn recast the Filipinos, no longer allies, as "insurgents," savages," and "children"—"not *men.*"[16]

According to Kristin Hoganson, the fast, decisive victory in Cuba "did everything its backers hoped it would do to shore up American manhood," exalting physical strength and aggressiveness over traits such as "intelligence and morality," which elder statesmen such as 72-year-old George Frisbie Hoar, a senator from Massachusetts, considered the hallmarks of a man.[17] "In the heady celebration of the victory, triumphant Americans crowed that the prowess demonstrated by U.S. soldiers in the war had placed American men beyond reproach."[18]

But there was always the danger of relapse, and so many, including Roosevelt and Senators Albert Beveridge and Henry Cabot Lodge, argued that American men ought to continue their masculine educations by fighting in the Philippines. Echoing the gender-based arguments that preceded intervention in Cuba, imperialists portrayed their domestic opponents as sissies and old women, while the antis portrayed the imperialists as hot-headed and immature.[19]

In the end, the arguments that Asian expansion would be good for America and its men, if not its women, prevailed. As Hoganson notes, the imperialists "might have seemed boyish but always seemed male."[20] Some believed that holding colonies could counter "modern civilization's seemingly dangerous tendency to make young, middle-class, and wealthy men soft, self-seeking, and materialistic [and] create the kind of martial character so valued in the nation's male citizens . . . and that, in so doing, it would prevent national and racial degeneracy."[21]

Ben might have wondered whether his youthful ideals deserved re-assessment. He had given his all and lost men in a "mock" battle, and he would now be fighting forces in the Philippines led by Emilio Aguinaldo, whom months earlier the United States had brought back from exile and proclaimed its ally. And as Ben put his life on the line again, the men calling the plays from Washington were so removed that they ordered him to perform tasks in New York, not realizing he had stayed in the Philippines while the "bronze-cheeked athletes" returned home to a heroes' welcome. But Ben held too much faith in the Army to find fault, nor could he foresee how disparagements applied to the Spanish and Filipinos to justify war—effeminate, lustful, animalistic, lacking in self-control—would later be repurposed to apply to him.

In 1899, in what was now the Philippine-American War, Ben served in all the expeditions led by General Henry Ware Lawton, a preeminent figure in the nineteenth-century Army, who wrote that Ben "distinguished himself for gallantry, ability and courage in the presence of the enemy."[22] Praise also came from Lieutenant Harry Hawthorne, who commended Ben for "cool courage and perfect judgment," and recommended his promotion "because of . . . his splendid service."[23]

As he dutifully acted the role that leaders such as Roosevelt had scripted for him as an American man—a role, it was said, that would bring personal gratification and prevent softness—Ben could not have imagined that in fifteen years he would be held up as the epitome of male degeneracy. He could not have imagined that he would turn to Hawthorne, his wartime comrade, to protect him as his counsel, and that Hawthorne would be questioned on the witness stand not about Ben's bravery and military skills but about his sleeping practices and whether Ben made sexual advances when the two men slept side by side in the sticky heat of the tropics.[24]

Back in 1899, it seemed that Ben was precisely the kind of man the Army wanted, though the effort took its toll. In August, he was diagnosed with an acute gastric problem—a typical ailment among American soldiers in the Philippines. After a month of sick leave spent in Japan, Ben returned to Manila, but all of his "cool courage" and willingness to do his duty abroad could not keep tragedy from striking close to home.[25]

# CHAPTER SIX

# Three Sons at Risk

W HILE THE REASONS FOR Ben's bachelorhood can only be guessed at, his self-image as a person devoted to duty is traceable to his parents. "No more honorable or high-minded people ever lived," wrote a Chicago lawyer who grew up in LeMars.[1]

Ben's father, Christian, was "an upright man" of "sterling character" who volunteered for several government posts—from town trustee to "poor master"—and "always placed the public interests to the front."[2] Ben's mother, Margaret, raised a small army of siblings and children over a period that spanned forty-five years, being 14 when her parents, George and Sophia Gund, moved the family from Germany to the United States, and only 16 when her parents died of cholera on a farm in Illinois.

Taking on responsibility for her younger siblings proved to be good training for raising the eleven children she bore with Christian, and yet, after all that labor on Margaret's part, her husband left the world before her, dying in 1885 of heart disease with Henry, 24, Barthold, 20, Edgar, 16, Ben, 13, Rudolph, 9, and Sophia, 8, still at home.[3] Barthold and Henry soon eased the burden by joining their older brothers in Nebraska, and Edgar left for law school in Michigan.

"To know her [is] to love her," wrote the local paper, but her children knew a more austere version of their mother.[4] "Little of this world's pleasure [is] her fashion" was how Sophia's older sister characterized Margaret's life of hard work.[5] Judging from her youthful appearance well into middle age, Margaret's strength had physical as well as emotional components.

While Margaret's brother Louis Gund was a prominent businessman in Marcus, Iowa, that did not compare to the success of their brother John, who ran a major brewery in La Crosse, Wisconsin, having started making beer in a log cabin. By the time Ben finished West Point, his uncle's brewery supplied beer to six states. The success of this branch of the family would continue, with two of John Gund's great-grandsons owning the Cleveland Cavaliers, and his great-granddaughter, Agnes Gund, serving as president and board chair of New York's Museum of Modern Art, among many other distinguished philanthropic positions.[6]

Margaret's life was a long way from such prestige, but she took great satisfaction in her children, all of whom had lived into adulthood and excelled in some way. Yet, as the end of the nineteenth century neared, she faced a new challenge. Three sons were abroad facing danger, for Edgar had left his law practice to join the Army—and what a soldier he made, according to the local paper, "a manly, gallant young man," with "courteous bearing, polished manner."[7]

Letters were slow to arrive, and Margaret never knew if her sons were all safe at the same time, but she could take some solace in reports of their courage.

On July 1, 1898, a month before the Astor Battery's Manila fight, Edgar astonished comrades in Cuba with his horseback skills. Quartermaster of the 3rd Brigade, he rode to the front in the Battle of Fort San Juan Hill, "bearing dispatches and orders, and though constantly exposed to the fire of the enemy, he remained mounted," wrote an eyewitness. After his brigade commander was mortally wounded, Edgar assisted in getting "all troops in to proper position for the assault that followed, and materially assisted in the assault by rapidly transmitting orders for the forward movement, and by his splendid example." Then, as "the first line moved across the field and up the hill, Lieut. Koehler rode rapidly forward, and reached the crest." He was "the only officer who reached the summit of the hill mounted, within the limits of his Brigade, or within sight of the position held by his Brigade."[8] All the while he was being fired at, ignoring calls from fellow soldiers to dismount and take cover.

Quickly inspecting the Spanish positions, Edgar "at once rode back to the crest of the hill from which our still advancing troops could be seen, and by words and signals encouraged and hurried the advance."[9] Soon after General Hamilton Hawkins reached the summit, Edgar rode to the rear "on some mission for General Hawkins, thus immediately passing under fire again."

Numerous officers, including the brigade commander, recommended Edgar for a medal of honor for "specially heroic" acts "that distinguished him above others" during what turned out to be a key battle, despite heavy American casualties, leading to the surrender of the Spanish.[10]

Some of the recommendations were written from Camp Wikoff in Montauk, at the eastern end of Long Island, not far from where Edgar's younger brother would later be accused of homoerotic acts.[11] The Army sent Edgar to Camp Wikoff to be quarantined, along with many others, including Roosevelt. A nearby park was named after Roosevelt until 1998, when questions about his actual ties to eastern Long Island led to the park's renaming.

But back in 1898, the Roosevelt name carried weight. He was a favorite of the press, and he publicized his participation in the Battle of San Juan Hill in a firsthand account. Roosevelt and the Rough Riders had charged up a different hill from the 3rd Brigade, later named Kettle Hill, from which Roosevelt observed Hawkins's ascent up San Juan Hill, though there is no evidence he saw Edgar Koehler ride alone to the summit, then ride back to the crest.[12] Roosevelt commended numerous members of his contingent, but according to one historian, "the regulars received little recognition because their charge seemed only expertly routine while 'a bespectacled volunteer officer, charging the Spanish earthworks at a gallop, with a blue polka-dotted handkerchief floating like a guidon from his sombrero' was the stuff from which heroes were made. Thus Roosevelt, not the regulars, received the publicity."[13]

One cannot help but wonder whether the rush to cast Roosevelt as the battle's hero is why an unknown lawyer-turned-soldier from Iowa never received a medal.[14] But whether or not Edgar was snubbed for political reasons, he drew the attention of someone who came to matter to him far more than a medal. Eight months after the battle, Edgar married Nellie Powell, the daughter of his infantry's commander. The newlyweds soon parted in San Francisco, where they had traveled so that Edgar could deploy to the Philippines to join his unit. Before she headed back to Governors Island to live with her father during Edgar's absence, Nellie wrote a secret letter to President McKinley apologizing for her "anxiety to see justice done her husband," and asking that Edgar be given a command post in new regiments she had read were being formed.[15]

Louis also received orders to head to the Philippines and so, by late 1899, all three of Margaret's Army sons were stationed in the same set of unpredictable islands. General Lawton, who had fought in Cuba, served with Louis in the Indian Wars, and praised Ben for his courage, now commanded the three Koehlers as head of field forces in the Philippines—but not for long.

In December 1899, a Filipino killed Lawton while he stood on the ridge of a rice paddy, having shrugged off warnings that he was an easy target.[16] The killing of the popular six-foot-three "fighting giant" showed all readers of newspapers back home that the situation in the Philippines was dangerous—more dangerous than most realized. Consequently, it came as a shock that the first Koehler brother to die was one of the businessmen, not one of the soldiers. In February 1900, Anthony Koehler, who ran grain, coal and lumber enterprises in Geneva, Nebraska, died in a Chicago hospital a few weeks after a stomach operation. He was only 40.

Margaret fell so ill she could not attend Anthony's funeral. She had little time to recover before learning the devastating news that military service had indeed claimed the life of another son. On March 4, two weeks after Anthony's death, Edgar, 30, died in an ambush.

Edgar was in a unit in Luzon that detained nearly thirty Filipinos, some dressed as women, one carrying a baby. A Filipino offered to show where rifles were stored. Edgar and another officer followed him into the jungle. Edgar had just asked, "How much longer?" and suggested turning around when he fell, shot in the abdomen by a gunman hiding behind brush on a ridge.[17] Soldiers carried him to the barrio, gave him first aid and whiskey, and watched him die—silently, as the wound made him unable to speak.[18] At the time, Nellie was preparing to join him in the Philippines.

"Have you knowledge of death of my son, Edgar Lieutenant Ninth Infantry, answer," cabled Margaret to the secretary of war two days after Edgar's death.[19] The family had received word of the death unofficially before the government's notification.[20]

Ben was granted leave to bring his brother's remains back to LeMars. It was the last type of visit Margaret wanted from a child, coming home in a box. She had cause to worry about Ben and Louis until they both left the Philippines, alive, in 1901. By then, the members of a growing anti-imperialistic movement in the United States, including Mark Twain, were expressing alarm over the "quagmire" in the Philippines.

"I wanted the American eagle to go screaming into the Pacific," Twain wrote toward the end of 1900. "I said to myself, here are a people who have suffered for three centuries. We can make them as free as ourselves . . . But I have thought some more, since then, . . . and I have seen that we do not intend to free, but to subjugate the people of the Philippines. We have gone there to conquer, not to redeem."

"And so," Twain continued, "I am an anti-imperialist. I am opposed to having the eagle put its talons on any other land."[21]

In time, Twain's voice became louder, his satire stronger.[22] Some labeled him a traitor. Louis Koehler would also speak out after the Army sent him back to the Philippines to fight new battles against Islamic Filipinos in the south. Still incensed by his younger brother's death, Louis would complain that the commander of troops in the southern Philippines, Major Hugh Scott, was needlessly jeopardizing soldiers' lives.

Margaret Koehler may have raised her sons to speak their minds, but had she advised them of the consequences? Exemplifying Oscar Wilde's quip about the importance of a speaker's identity, Mark Twain could excoriate public officials and withstand it, but Louis Koehler was a military man subject to the rules of command. His criticism outraged Leonard Wood, Scott's superior and mentor. One Army officer named Koehler was dead. There would be hell to pay for the other two.

In the meantime, Ben's Nebraska brothers, pleased that Ben's service in the Philippines earned him a promotion to captain in August 1901, lamented that along with the title came a posting in San Francisco. The Army had sent a Nebraska boy to Baltimore, then to the island of Manhattan and an archipelago in the Pacific, and now to the shores of California. It seemed that Ben's destiny was tied to the coast.

And what a coast it was in San Francisco in 1901, whether Ben's family liked it or not.

# CHAPTER SEVEN

# Single in San Francisco

THE DEBUTANTE WORE WHITE orchids in her hair, looking "artis-tic, simple and elegant . . . in a decolette gown of white tulle over liberty satin."[1]

Lavish dinners introducing young women to "society" had been in short supply in Manila and Luzon, but now, in 1902, "San Francisco's exclusive set," "costly gowns," and American Beauty roses surrounded Ben at the coming-out party of Edith Huntington, grandniece of a railroad magnate. A year later, her marriage to the son of a sugar baron and newspaper publisher would be declared "the most brilliant wedding San Francisco has witnessed for years."[2]

The aristocratic ritual of the debutante ball began in England, and Ben blended right in with his British-honed manners. The invitation to attend the party as leader of the 92nd Company of Coast Artillery represented one of many ways in which Ben's new assignment meant an enormous step up from the Philippines in comfort and prestige.

"It was San Francisco before the fire," wrote Alice Roosevelt Long-worth, the popular first child of Theodore Roosevelt, now president, about her visit to the city around the same time. "I shall never forget those days. There was an exhilarating quality in the air, the place, the people, that kept me on my toes every moment of the time there."[3]

Ben was back on prime real estate in San Francisco, living and working on the Army post at the Presidio—named by the Spanish, deriving from the Latin word "to preside" or "defend." Every day, he could look out on beautiful, productive, and strategically located San Francisco Bay, a prize America had been eager to win by annexing California from Mexico. In an 1840s report, a Navy captain called it "one of the finest, if not the very best, harbour in the world."[4]

The bay lay across the Pacific from Asia, which is why the Presidio was packed with soldiers. Most of the seventy-five thousand troops who served in the Philippines passed through San Francisco, and Ben's first assignment was to help coordinate the mustering out of those coming home.

The soldiers disembarked into a place with a unique history, especially regarding gender roles. Whereas some Filipino men dressed as women to fool American soldiers, men in San Francisco had a history of dressing as women to fool no one, simply to have a good time.

At the height of the 1850s gold rush, 95 percent of the migrants streaming in were male. When dances took place, men played the role of women, signaling "female" status by placing patches over their genitals, tying handkerchiefs to their arms, or wearing dresses.[5] Sociologist Clare Sears notes that this practice, while appearing deviant on the surface, actually reinforced Anglo-Saxon gender norms—men dance with women, not other men—such that the *San Francisco Examiner* thought it fine to mark the 1895 inaugural ball of the governor by running a "full-page cartoon of the state's white male elite dancing, half of them in women's clothing."[6] Writes Sears, "As this cartoon demonstrates, cross-dressing practices and same-sex dancing retained a central place in high-society entertainment long after the gold rush passed, as cultural symbols of the state's economic and political development."[7]

The same rules did not apply to all. Decades before the cartoon ran, San Francisco supervisors voted to criminalize a person's appearing in public "in a dress not belonging to his or her sex," a law that authorities used selectively to clear the streets of sex workers and other "undesirables," but rarely against the elite.[8] The law was aimed primarily at female prostitutes who dressed as men, "indicating a transgressive sexuality that distinguished them from 'respectable' ladies."[9] Perhaps cross-dressers thought their self-presentation would increase business, playing upon men's ease with other men, or perhaps they just preferred to dress like men.

When the gold rush frenzy abated and corporate mining took over, former prospectors stayed and started businesses. Wives and children moved west, and San Francisco morphed from a singles compound into a family town. Civic and religious leaders began expressing concern for the place's "purity" lest middle-class white women and children be exposed to impropriety, and outsiders were deterred from investing. Such consternation led to the "decency" law that included the cross-dressing prohibition. Ten eastern cities had adopted similar laws, beginning with Columbus, Ohio, in 1848, and Chicago in 1851, but San Francisco was the first western city to do so.[10]

This paradigm shift began to make single men suspect for, as Sears writes, the purification forces "positioned the family man as the bedrock of good government and explicitly considered marital status when investigating men for political and moral transgressions."[11] A similar refrain could be heard at the national level, with senators publicly encouraging men to marry for, "[i]n addition to giving men a constructive outlet for their sexual energies, marriage, like fatherhood, promised to teach men to exercise authority."[12]

And yet, not everyone in San Francisco was willing to give up the gold rush forms of entertainment. Single men remained—living in housing built for transients—and "a permissive quality of life evolved around bachelor entertainments."[13] By 1890, San Francisco had more bars per person than New York or Chicago.[14] Many were located in the Barbary Coast district centered on Pacific Street (now Pacific Avenue) east of Stockton, a racy part of town analogous to New York's Bowery. There, "the rough-and-tumble [gold rush] saloons developed into dance halls, honky-tonks, and bawdy houses that provided a space for men to gamble, dance, and satisfy their sexual desires."[15]

Tension crackled between the purifiers and the partiers in the east end of San Francisco, but the Presidio was its own world to the west where even married men were likely to be living apart from their wives as they deployed to or returned from the Philippines. A uniform with

the insignia of a captain offered protection from marital status discrimination, especially if the wearer conducted himself in ways that
could be appreciated by the sorts of people who held debutante parties. On Memorial Day in 1902, Ben helped lead a parade from the
Palace Hotel to Golden Gate Avenue.[16] In 1903, his artillery prowess
made news: "Smashes Target into Splinters" was the headline after the
92nd Company struck a target pulled by a tugboat—"which from the
fort seemed but a speck on the waves."[17]

The first shot missed. "Captain Koehler then prepared for the second shot, which proved the surprise and pride of the day," reported
the *San Francisco Call.* "It was a great aim, and a steady and sure aim,
for the moving, bobbing, 15-foot triangular target, three miles out,
received the terrific shot and splinters flew in all directions." Witnesses to "the great shot . . . gave their congratulations . . . to young
Captain Koehler."[18]

Ben was a rising Army star in San Francisco, unlike the soldiers
who landed in jail one night after an alcohol-fueled brawl in the Barbary Coast. The next evening some two hundred fifty soldiers temporarily housed at the Presidio returned to seek revenge. A policeman
tipped off by a bar owner alerted the Presidio commander, who sent
Army police to round up the soldiers.[19]

That a bar owner turned to the police for support against unruly
soldiers—and obtained it—is only one example of the "tension between vice and regulation," the ongoing attention to which served to
"advertise San Francisco's nighttime entertainments" at the same time
that authorities "worked to curb and control them."[20] Despite the decency law, San Francisco capitalized on its licentiousness, sponsoring
"slumming tours" of places in the Barbary Coast and Chinatown
where tourists could see "sights and practices that existed against the
law" and experience the "voyeuristic pleasures of gazing at bodily difference."[21] Off-duty police and licensed guides led the tours.[22]

In New York City, curious residents tended to gawk on their own,
including well-to-do residents living uptown in Manhattan who went
downtown to see men wearing make-up vamping on the streets or
inside a "resort." Slumming was free entertainment.[23] George

Chauncey describes New York's "fairies" as congregating openly and mixing with "'normal' men publicly—and sexually—[with] remarkable ease."[24] But in San Francisco, sexual "attractions" were hidden and required an insider for access, for a man wearing female clothing or otherwise acting in sexually nonconforming ways was likely to be arrested.[25]

The law invited a surveillance mentality, not only among the police. Citizens turned in neighbors. Newspapers expressed both disapproval and fascination, as when they published sketches of men appearing in court in women's clothes and reported on their attire: a "pair of new black gloves," a "brand new russet leather satchel," a gray hat that was "[a] splendid sample of the milliner's art," or a "natty set of blue clothes."[26]

Violating the law was technically a misdemeanor, but the consequences could be extreme: incarceration, lifetime institutionalization for people whose cross-dressing was attributed to mental illness, and deportation for those caught entering the country disguised as a member of the opposite sex. Yet at least one bar on Pacific Street employed men who dressed as women to flirt with male customers and encourage them to drink. After a patron was robbed by a female impersonator, following a session of fondling in a private booth, newspaper stories mocked the victim for being duped, such was the expectation that citizens should be good gender detectives promoting binary sexuality and heterosexual coupling.[27]

Ben was diagnosed with bronchitis and malaria during his first year in San Francisco. In his second year, he underwent surgery for an anal fistula, a painful condition usually caused by an abscess.[28] Those illnesses, his general fastidiousness, and a six-month visit by Sophia and their mother make it highly doubtful that Ben frequented the same places as boisterous soldiers or tourists on slumming tours.[29] His focus was on the post, where he served as a court-martial juror in 1902 and led preparations in 1903 for a "delightful hop"—described in the *San Francisco Chronicle*'s "Society" column.[30]

But that wasn't the way Ben's time in San Francisco would be presented years later on Plum Island. Rather, a sergeant under Philip

Worcester's command, Jacob Campbell, would claim that Ben spoke to him about "women and about sporting houses on the Pacific Coast . . . and the different ways and manners that a man could get satisfaction in a sportinghouse" [*sic*]—including "that you could get screwed or you could get sucked or you could get a fat boy."[31]

Ben begged to differ. He said he recalled only discussing with Campbell the sport of fishing and a treatment for venereal disease, in answer to a question from the sergeant.[32]

But like the men on San Francisco's slumming tours who removed the clothes of Chinese women to check their anatomy, Worcester and the handpicked men under his authority offered themselves as diligent gender detectives capable of helping the Army see the real Ben Koehler beneath his uniform, excellent reputation, and protestations of innocence. The charges against Ben promised senior Army men their own slumming tour—a chance to indulge their fascination with sex on an officially sanctioned, voyeuristic odyssey.

It wasn't supposed to be that way. Having achieved the rank of major, eight years after the Army promoted him from San Francisco to an adjutant position in New York, Ben was supposed to be happy at Fort Terry. At least that was Sophia's expectation in the summer of 1911 when she cast her fate with his. That year, the heavy rains came to Iowa in July, but Sophia hardly noticed. She was mourning a loss far deeper than canceled rowing plans. Margaret Koehler had died in June.

Sophia took the death hard. After graduating from the University of Nebraska, she had returned to the large family home on Court Street in LeMars. For years it had been just her and her mother under the same roof, Rudolph having married and moved out. "Our house seems dreadfully lonely and no longer home," Sophia confided in a letter to Roy Dimmick's sister, Lucile, shortly after her mother's death. "I feel so restless and blue that I can't settle down to do anything."[33]

Sophia usually had no trouble staying busy, whether it was reading in a rocker on the covered porch, playing tennis or golf, working in Rudolph's real estate office, or caring for her mother with Lizzie, who lived nearby with her husband, a LeMars lawyer.

Margaret's passing ruptured those routines and obliged Sophia to make a choice about her future. She was 34 and single at a time when unmarried women were living on their own in coastal cities but not in midwestern towns like LeMars without raising eyebrows. Sophia had many friends but no beau or prospect of marriage. She could move in with Lizzie or Rudolph, but being spinster aunt to her siblings' children did not enthuse her in the least. No, it was clear to Sophia that her best option involved Ben, then in Manhattan awaiting a new assignment. As Sophia explained to Lucile:

> I am planning to make my home with Ben but don't know where "our" home will be. He has been made a Major and he thought he would know before this, where he is to be sent but as yet the War Department hasn't informed him of their intentions so I am up in the air and can't make any plans. For we may be in New York and we may land in the Phillippines [sic]. I don't care where they send him—if they would only let him know and relieve his uncertainty.

"I know we will be happy together no matter where Ben is sent," Sophia added.

The Army soon ended the suspense. Ben would not be sent back to the Philippines but would nonetheless lead an island life—at Fort Terry, where Ben's superiors thought he could improve morale and discipline. Sophia was welcome, too, to help manage the new commander's household and social duties. In the absence of a wife, a sister would do.

Destination Plum Island meant far more change for Sophia than Ben, who merely had to ride a train from Manhattan to New London, Connecticut, walk to the pier, and take a two-hour boat trip southeast across Long Island Sound—a routine he knew well, having pitched a tent on Plum Island during summer artillery drills. He was leaving the crowded city and heading to a rural place with fields and trails where he could ride every day and return to some of his adolescent pastimes, such as gardening.

For Sophia, the trip was longer—nearly 1,500 miles—and the adjustment in lifestyle immeasurable. She was leaving her hometown and active social life—including dinners in her honor before her departure—for an Army base far removed from a civilian population.

On October 15, 1911, amidst the bright oranges, yellows, and reds of autumn on the East Coast, Ben and Sophia arrived on Plum Island. Ben brought his dog, Sophia her cat, and both held great hopes for the future. From the front door of her new home, across the flat expanse of the grass parade ground, Sophia could see the ocean, a view she never had in Iowa.

For a time, she would even be happy.

# CHAPTER EIGHT

# Plum Island

P LUM ISLAND COULD BE brutal in winter, pounded by nor'easters, blizzards, and hail. Some days, the gusts were so strong that nothing alive could stand straight—not the native junipers, the imported soldiers, or the maple trees planted in rows along the main road—and the boats that provided the sole escape off the island barely stayed lashed to the docks. The lighthouse keeper had enough stories about shipwrecks in the treacherous waters of Plum Gut to keep soldiers up all night—if the Fort Terry curfew would have allowed it.

Yet also in winter, there could be days of intense beauty, the sky nearly the color of the indigo buntings that stopped to forage during spring and fall migrations, needing no boats, only stars, to leave when instinct dictated. On those calm days, the idyllic vistas could have come from a painter's hand: the sky, the steel-blue water, the sandy beaches across flat land tufted here and there with tall grasses, shrubs, and trees sculpted by the wind into dancer-like forms.

In summer the island was a paradise. The Algonquin people called it Manittuwond—"the island to which we go to plant corn"—well before Europeans named it for a less domesticated member of the plant kingdom: beach plums.[1] Unlike corn, beach plum shrubs required no sowing. They grew wild on the Atlantic coast from Maine to Maryland. In bloom, the plants could be seen from the deck of a ship, and that is how Plum Island got its name. It was as though a museumgoer, noticing a plum in a still-life painting on the wall, called the painting the "plum painting" for ever more, no matter the artist's title.

As explained by Long Island historians in *A World Unto Itself: The Remarkable History of Plum Island*, Dutchman Adriaen Block, a trader and navigator, bestowed the name.[2] Hailing from a country known for flowers, he apparently appreciated the plants, which looked like hedges of tiny pom-poms. The bushes grew in front of taller green shrubs, providing a beautiful contrast, the white and the green against the buff-colored sand and blue water.

Block was inspired by Henry Hudson, but Block saw a whole stretch of the "new world" that Hudson missed searching for a western passage to China. Hudson sailed north up the river that bears his name, whereas Block made a right turn out of New Amsterdam. As Block and his crew continued east in 1614, the land on their leeward side—the future Connecticut—was marked by numerous mouths of rivers. On the starboard side, Block passed smaller bays and harbors, and further east the land rose into high bluffs of compressed sand.

Those attractive features belonged to a very long island, and after about one hundred miles Block reached its northern tip. Compared to Long Island, Plum Island was a tiny accessory, shaped like a stout tobacco pipe with its handle pointing east, located a mile and a half northeast of Orient Point on what is now called Long Island's North Fork. From there, Block continued southeast to the tip of Long Island's southern extension, known as Montauk Point after the Montaukett tribe. Block then sailed northeast, passing another island that still bears his name, Block Island. Back home, Block reported his discoveries, and by the 1650s, European maps of the New World showed *Pruym Eylant*.

By then, activities on and around Plum Island were undergoing radical change. British settlers from Connecticut had begun to migrate across the Sound, bringing English styles and place names like Southampton and Maidstone to eastern Long Island. Yet not all the changes arose from newly arrived whites who were hunting game and cutting timber on lands the Native Americans had occupied for hundreds of years. War had broken out between the fearsome Pequots of southern Connecticut and opposing tribes. With British assistance from settler Lion Gardiner and others, the Pequots were defeated in 1637. No longer would tribes on Long Island have to send canoe-loads of wampum across the Sound to the Pequots.[3] Instead, sachems on Long Island, including Wyandanch of the Montauketts, asked the British what it would take to live in peace. The complete answer—everything you have and know—would not reveal itself for decades.

During Wyandanch's lifetime, due largely to his alliance with Gardiner, there was cooperation between the English and the eastern Long Island tribes.[4] In 1639, King Charles I issued a patent to Gardiner for a 3,400-acre island visible from Plum Island that Wyandanch had already gifted to Gardiner according to his traditions.[5] The British and Native Americans fought together to repel Dutch advances from the west. However, different understandings of gift-giving and conceptions of property—use versus ownership—plus the assertion of jurisdiction over eastern Long Island by Dutch-phobic British governors in Connecticut and New Haven Colony, began to dispossess the Native Americans of their land.[6] The Corchaugs and Montauketts deeded tracts they had long used in exchange for goods that seemed useful in the short run but could never be traded or invested to recoup what they had lost.

Several deeds involved Plum Island, including one signed by Wyandanch in 1659, selling the island for a coat, food, fish hooks, and one hundred muxes, which were used to cut holes in wampum beads. (Wampum started to lose monetary value in the 1700s, though it retained symbolic and spiritual importance.)[7]

Before being settled by humans, Long Island had been the southern terminus of an ice sheet more than half a mile thick that lay on the land for thousands of years. As the ice sheet melted and retreated northward, seas rose by hundreds of feet, creating a large estuary between the north and south forks, with numerous craggy coves. The land seemed to have been scraped with an immense rake wielded by an angry giant, leaving chunks of ice, boulders, and rubble.

Over time, the ice chunks melted and the holes filled with rain, becoming lakes and ponds. Erosion ground the rubble into fine sand,

spread by currents to create spectacular beaches and dunes and turning inlets into coastal ponds. Plants and trees evolved that could tol-
erate wind, sand, and salt. Salt-hardy grasses grew into tidal marshes,
offering shelter to numerous shellfish, finfish, and birds, and when
the marsh grasses decayed in winter, they left behind rich organic
matter that accumulated, supporting new and abundant animal and
insect life.

By the 1600s, the descendants of the first humans to migrate to the
area lived in a place rich with food and other resources. Hundreds of
species of plants and animals thrived. All the churned-up pebbles
made the soil porous and loamy, ideal for planting crops, and the Gulf
Stream lengthened the growing season. Trees provided ample wood
for fires. Such was the biologically diverse, life-sustaining world that
the English entered.

All the postglacial change had taken a long time, but events of the
seventeenth century showed that change could also happen quickly.
Sixty years after Adriaen Block had spied wild plums from a boat called
*Restless*, Samuel Willis—a prominent magistrate on the Connecticut
General Court—became the first British owner of "Plumme" Island
and the lord of the manor.[8]

Underneath the sea, Plum Island remained connected by a submerged ridge to the Long Island mainland, and northward to the
Rhode Island and Massachusetts shores. But up above, on the visible
surface of the land, Plum Island had gone in a matter of decades from
a place where many came to grow corn to a place controlled by one
man. That was the English way, but it would not last—not for Willis,
and not for royal governor to whom he paid his tithe.

The changes to Plum Island after it became "property" in the European sense resulted from human causes more than ecological ones.
Willis found that he preferred his comfortable life in Connecticut to
raising cattle and sheep on a desolate island. After thirteen years, he
sold the island, and in 1700 the "manor" became two holdings, farmed
by two families until the Revolutionary War changed everything
again. The settlers of eastern Long Island, having displaced Native
Americans, now faced some of the same treatment they had meted

out. British forces arrived and stole livestock. They cleared trees to build boats. Families who were living on Plum Island fled to the mainland.[9]

After the war, most who had left returned to Plum Island, but its location as a gateway to Long Island Sound led British and American ships to drop anchor in the surrounding waters during the War of 1812. Once more, the British raided livestock and used the island as a place to retreat after attacks. A treaty ended the war in late 1814, but the British fleet remained near Plum Island for several more months.[10]

By this point, two hundred years had passed since Block's naming of Plum Island. A period of peace ensued, even a return to communal sharing of the island—though not by the Algonquins.

A lighthouse started beaming on the island's southwestern shore, helping boaters navigate Plum Gut. The lighthouse keeper and his wife welcomed summer visitors, who slept on the floors, and a land-owner let clubs set up camps. These visitors were of modest means, but soon the wealthy discovered the island. Yachts navigated where Block had sailed, and famous people came for the fishing, which Grover Cleveland pronounced some of the finest in the world.[11]

Economic progress begat real estate speculation. Quietly, over the course of several years, a man bought the farms of Plum Island, not disclosing that he was acting as an agent for a former New York City mayor and a group of investors who had their sights on turning Plum Island into a resort with hotels and cottages.

Through a tricky move involving the agent's bankruptcy, the former mayor, Abram Hewitt, shed his investors and acquired virtually all of Plum Island—until events beyond his control abruptly ended his plans. When coastal residents worried about invasion once again, this time by Spain, Hewitt sold the eastern part of the island to a new buyer to whom he found it impossible to say no: the United States. The War Department began building Fort Terry, and in 1901, citing an overriding national interest, bought the rest of the island from Hewitt.[12]

That was how Ben Koehler came to command an island in whose waters John Jacob Astor IV—benefactor of Ben's first fighting unit—had sailed his yacht. Astor's stature had fallen significantly since that time. During the same season that Ben took command of Fort Terry, the 47-year-old Astor shocked New York society by marrying an 18-year-old after divorcing his first wife.[13]

In the fall of 1911, compared to Astor's disgrace, Ben was moving up in his world, running a fort of seven hundred soldiers, their families, and civilians who cooked, cleaned, and held other supporting jobs. While Astor was being excoriated for flouting social norms, Ben enjoyed a fine reputation in New York State thanks to his early service with the Astor Battery and later postings in Brooklyn, Manhattan, the Bronx, and Fort Niagara. Not a word had been put in Ben's file expressing concern about his personal life. To the contrary, he was being dispatched to Plum Island because higher-ups believed in his ability to bring order to a cadre of men who had grown a bit lazy in their peacetime post by the sea.

That is what he set out to do.

# CHAPTER NINE

# Grudges Take Hold

B EN KOEHLER WAS NO Samuel Willis, paying others to mind the sheep. His "sheep" were men in uniforms, and Ben inspected them and their surroundings nearly every day. He tried to learn each soldier's name.

Ben "was always trying to improve the post in every way possible," according to Lieutenant John Smith. "When we were out over the post his conversation was generally about something that he wanted improved somewhere, that he wanted done, and he would generally look after this personally himself."[1]

There was plenty for Ben to look after. Fort Terry resembled a college campus more than a traditional fort built to keep foes out. The 840 acres of Plum Island were their own fortress, encircled by a vast moat. With nature offering so much protection, the residents of Fort Terry did not need to live and work in bunkers or behind cement walls—except for the concrete gun batteries, built on the land's edge, using bluffs and dunes as camouflage.

More than sixty buildings served the population, some made of wood, some of brick, with stone foundations and interior framing of heavy timbers and steel columns. A few months before Ben's arrival, structures were retrofitted with electric lighting, and he presided over completion of the electric power plant. In January 1912, a new guardhouse opened with thirty-four metal cells. There were houses for officers, barracks where dozens of soldiers shared rooms, and separate quarters for noncommissioned officers, engineers, and hospital stewards. There were mess halls, the boxy two-story administration building where Ben had an office, a plumber's and blacksmith shop, a hospital, a pump house, bathhouses, an officers' club, a carpenter's shop, an oil house, a sawmill, a commissary, a bakery, a laundry, stables, a gymnasium and library building, a firemen's building, and the recently completed Post Exchange, with bowling lanes in the basement.[2]

Some structures were plain, some ornate, with arched windows and patterned iron railings. The two-story brick barracks could have passed as dormitories at an Ivy League university. Barracks #55 had balconies affording magnificent views of Gardiners Bay.

The most militaristic aspects of Fort Terry were its eleven gun batteries and the massive rectangular building on the southeast. Officially, it was the Torpedo Storage and Cable Tanks building, but everyone called it Building 257. Completed the year Ben arrived, it would develop a controversial reputation later in the century as Lab 257, officially part of a federal laboratory studying animal diseases but allegedly a place where ex-Nazis had researched biological warfare.[3]

Several batteries were perched at the end of a long spit of land on the northeastern part of the island—the pipe's handle—ending at East Point. Returning from East Point, any tired soldier would be soothed by the paradisiacal view: beaches, boulders, and water on both sides of the narrow road, where the entire width of the land was only a few hundred feet. Connecticut could be seen to the north, Gardiners Island to the south.

Most of the buildings were situated on a central plain that divided the southeast from a northwestern ridge where hills rose to one hundred feet above sea level. It was a short walk to the eastern beach from nearly all buildings, though the more than two hundred residents of Barracks #55 and the stable workers lived closest to the sound of breaking waves. Furthest from the hub was Plum Light, overlooking Plum Gut on the southwest.

"Don't anchor here" was the message from the Gut's sea floor, covered with rocks—and perhaps Ben should have heeded that warning.[4] "Don't be overconfident," was another of the Gut's tidings. Local boaters might recognize a pattern to the currents, but especially in fog or rain, the Gut's swift, crisscrossing waters, shifting winds, and hidden sand bars could flummox a newcomer, even a strong captain with a good vessel, and lead to a smashed and ruined end.

While Ben inspected the man-made parts of the island, Sophia explored its quiet areas, such as the large freshwater wetland to the south that attracted great blue herons, egrets, and falcons. The mild weather that greeted the Koehlers upon their arrival allowed Sophia to spend time outdoors—when she was not supervising the housekeeper, becoming acquainted with the officers and their wives, or helping Ben host visitors, including their sister Lizzie, who arrived November 1, planning to spend one month but staying for three.

"I like it here very much the only draw back is that we have had so much company that we are getting tired and long to be alone," Sophia wrote to Roy in January, signing her name "Sophia Koehler," a far cry from her teenage "the Bum."[5] As Sophia reported, "I am the only unmarried woman on the post but the married men are younger than I, at least 3 of them are, so I have plenty of company—There are six married officers and about six bachelors on the post so we have enough to get a bridge crowd and to bowl and have a good time."

Sophia and Lizzie played golf on Christmas, but a week later, a storm put an end to drives and putts—just when Roy sought to visit his old friends, especially Sophia, with whom he had been corresponding for more than fifteen years with little success in seeing her. There was the time in 1908 when he offered to visit LeMars, but the Koehler clan was convening to celebrate Margaret's seventy-fifth birthday. Roy sent the novel *Freckles* instead, about an itinerant orphan who found love while guarding timber in an Indiana swamp.[6] Roy, a traveling salesman, may have identified with the protagonist.

To usher in 1912, Roy traveled to New York City for New Year's and hoped to see Sophia and Ben in Manhattan or on Plum Island, but no boats were operating. It could not have eased Roy's disappointment to read in Sophia's letter that the storm was a fluke—"the worst weather we have had so far this winter [which] as a whole . . . has been delight-ful." Indeed, she informed him, "It's lovely today and I think I shall go skating after lunch."[7]

Sophia mailed her letter to a hotel in Omaha, Roy's last known address, but it had to travel much further to reach him, all the way to Portland, Oregon, where the growing lumber industry provided a strong market for the smokeless tobacco products he sold. Avoiding matches was a good thing in a place where so many jobs depended on trees.

DURING HIS FIRST EIGHT months as commander, Ben often made rounds with Lieutenant Charles Steese, the quartermaster. Since 1775, quartermasters had been responsible for Army supplies and transpor-tation, including trains, steamships, and even camels during a brief experiment in Texas. There were no camels on Plum Island. Horses and a wagon called a buckboard, led by horses or mules, were the primary means of transportation.

Steese was almost as new in his position as Ben. The two shared a zeal for their jobs and saw each other socially in Ben's home several nights a week.[8]

In November 1911, after working together for a month, Steese and Ben made a decision involving John Barrett, who would become one of Ben's accusers. Steese did not like how Barrett was performing as provost sergeant, involving supervision over the fort police. At Steese's request, Ben removed Barrett from the job for "being inefficient and unreliable."[9] Barrett complained to Steese that he had gotten "a rot-ten deal."[10]

Ben soon found himself confronting Barrett for another reason. One evening when a film was being shown in the gym, Barrett, a ser-geant named Palmer, and their wives occupied seats that a lieutenant had told the usher to reserve for him and his guests. Asked to move, the sergeants refused, and one muttered that he was as good as any-one else. The next day, Ben heard of the matter and summoned the men to his office.

A previous commander had given Barrett and Palmer permission to build small cottages by the stable rather than live in the general quarters for married noncommissioned officers. Ben told Palmer and Barrett that the cottages conferred "special privileges," which obliged them to "be men of high character."[11] That meant respecting rank.

In response, Palmer "was defiant," by Ben's account, and said "he was just as good as any other damn man on the post."[12] Ben revoked Palmer's right to live in the cottage.

Barrett took the opposite approach. He "came in and cried about it," according to Ben. "He had a family and some children and he said he was in the wrong and I allowed him to keep his house."[13]

Palmer bought his discharge rather than move into group housing—at no great loss to Fort Terry, in Ben's view. Barrett stayed on in his cottage, but any feelings of gratitude on his part were short-lived, for Ben objected when Barrett applied for a supervisory job in the stables. Ben had someone else in mind.

By that time, Steese had been transferred and his replacement as quartermaster, Captain Gordon Robinson, never developed a rapport with Ben, as later events would make all too clear. Robinson lived at Fort Wright on Fishers Island, on the same ferry run to and from New London as Fort Terry. Over Ben's objection, Robinson arranged for Barrett to get the stable job.[14]

And so, Barrett remained at Fort Terry, a stable hand with more loyalty to a captain on a different island than to his post commander. Barrett's charges against Ben, all set in the stable, would be elaborate. Barrett would claim that Ben "grasped me by the buttocks, talking about fat boys and comparing the relative size of one of the mules [*sic*] penises to his own and to mine." According to Barrett, Ben also "grasped me by the testicles outside my trousers," urinated "in front of me, always made it a point to come to the end of the stables where I was," regularly asked Barrett, "Did you wake up with a hard-on this morning?" and told Barrett not "to bother around women, you want to get a fat boy."[15]

Lieutenant Smith, who rode with Ben most days, would contradict Barrett, saying he and Ben avoided Barrett because he was incompetent with horses.[16]

The Army expected soldiers to follow orders and defer to superiors, but no rule prevented a sergeant from ruminating to himself against authority and waiting for a chance to get even. Ben Koehler may have been certain about his vision for a well-functioning Fort Terry, but John Barrett was not.[17]

PART TWO

# CHAPTER TEN

# A Chill in the Air

IN OREGON, THROUGHOUT THE summer of 1912, Roy pictured Sophia playing golf and cards and enjoying island life courtesy of the U.S. Army while he made a living in a rough lumber and fishing town selling products that discolored men's teeth.

Who could blame him for imagining Sophia in a state of contentment? When Roy last heard from her, she wrote of ice skating, golfing on Christmas, and having "a good time" with young officers. Sophia's life sounded pretty swell, as Roy suggested in a letter.

Sophia set him straight at summer's end, writing that there had been none of the "fishing, bathing, boating, etc" that she had expected. Rather, she felt as though she had run "a boarding house all summer and its [sic] hard work."

Who were the boarders? Not her sister or friends, but officers from other coastal forts—strangers to Sophia—who came to Fort Terry for summer drills. Boatloads of men arrived from as far away as Staten Island, lining the parade ground with neat rows of khaki tents.

"They sent all the companies from Fort Totten, Adams, Greble and Hamilton up here to be in camp for two weeks to do their firing and of course it makes extra work for our men and incidentally for me for as each set came Ben would feel that he must invite some of the officers to a meal," she told Roy.[1]

Sophia knew how to be a good hostess in LeMars, but not during multi-week conventions of Army companies on an island. She had help, a housekeeper and cook named Anna, but still she felt more like a servant herself than a hostess. The night firing exercises were the worst, "for I never knew how many to expect to a meal or when they would get in for it." There was no "run[ning] to the store when something is forgotten," she informed Roy, "for we have to send to town by boat for everything."

All the hard work might have been borne more easily if Sophia felt connected to others at the post, but she did not. As she told Roy: "You imagine I have little to do but play bridge and have a good time and you may doubt my word when I tell you I haven't been to a bridge party or afternoon party of any kind all summer—and I might almost say since I have been here, for with the exception of a card club that met for a few months during the Winter, there has been nothing doing."[2]

This account so deviated from Sophia's initial enthusiasm that she realized Roy might not believe her—"you may doubt my word"—but more than that, she seemed to be reevaluating her own first impressions. Maybe, in hindsight, there were not as many fun times as she had thought.

In January 1912, Sophia had written of having "plenty of company" among the young officers, but by the end of the summer she felt rejected, telling Roy, "If I were only about ten years younger I might have a very gay time, but as it is I am too old, gray and wrinkled for these youths."

Those were strong, derogatory remarks to make about herself, especially to a man she once fancied. Part of Sophia's reason for leaving LeMars was to avoid feeling old as a spinster aunt, but now she was quick to blame her age for a drying up of invitations and visits, though there were other plausible reasons why the "youths" were not including her as much as they had at first. By now, men such as Austin Frick and his roommate, Lieutenant Raycroft Walsh, knew that Sophia was educated, independent, and rather proper, which were not necessarily traits valued by single Army men looking to have a good time. Nor did it help Sophia's popularity that she was the sister of a commander who irritated Frick and his friends as too strict and moralistic—for example, reprimanding Frick even for gossiping, such as when he told "a scandalous story about an officer's wife on this post and some Lieutenant," as Ben put it.[3]

Unfortunately for Sophia, as the sister of the commander, her social world was small, limited to officers and their wives or girlfriends. In contrast, Ben never lacked for company. He interacted with multiple people throughout the day. "I think he likes it, though he has been very busy," Sophia told Roy.[4]

Ben had left the island only twice, once in April to see his former boss, William Kenly, in Manhattan, and one afternoon in July he accepted a last-minute invitation to take a boat to Greenport, a village on the Long Island mainland. Both excursions would come back to haunt him, but in the summer of 1912, leading the summer drills gave Ben an opportunity to shine.

Ben took military preparedness seriously, having fought in the Philippines and lost a brother there, and the summer exercises were his first opportunity to show officers from other forts how he was improving discipline at Fort Terry. In the evenings, he was able to play the role of host to visiting officers because a more senior officer who lived on Plum Island, Lieutenant Colonel Sidney Jordan, had been on sick leave since February.

Yet it was not only Sophia who regarded the summer drill season with less zeal than Ben. Some soldiers seized the opportunity to stay up late and drink in the virtually empty barracks. One morning, on his way to breakfast from his tent, Ben noticed bunks without blankets in the tent where Master Gunner Harry King and Master Electrician Byron Brown were supposed to have slept. A sergeant in the adjacent tent confirmed that the two had not shown up, and Ben spoke to Brown, reminding him of the order to sleep in camp. Ben said he would check back that night to make sure the bunks were in use by their assigned occupants.[5]

Brown was already on Ben's problem list for poor appearance—"one of the slouchiest, dirtiest looking men on the post"—and Ben had told him to stop visiting Captain Ellis's quarters when

Ellis was away, for Ben believed Brown was seeing the housekeeper, "who was colored."[6]

"I have had trouble with Brown," Ben would later acknowledge, attempting to explain Brown's damaging contributions to the case against him, for Brown was keeping his own problem list, and it included the post commander.

DESPITE SOPHIA'S HURT FEELINGS, she continued to make an effort socially, especially after the summer frenzy was "all over with." In mid-September, she went to a "hop"—but she was one of the few who did: "There were more in the band than on the floor dancing and if it had not been for four young lady guests on the post we couldn't have had a dance."[7]

Where were the men if not at the hop? They had better things to do—such as private parties in their homes or at the officers' club. An officer could also take a boat to Fishers Island to socialize at Fort Wright. Close to New London, Fort Wright offered men a better chance of meeting women, and the atmosphere was casual. Captain Robinson helped set that tone.

In October, Sophia conceived of a remedy for her isolation. If the "youths" were not extending invitations to her, she would send out her own invitations—to a Halloween party. She busied herself making pumpkin lanterns and lampshades with black cats and witches. The wife of one of the captains helped her make yellow silk pumpkin pincushions to put on the table for favors. "They have turned out very attractive," Sophia wrote to Roy a few days before the party, "so I feel encouraged that the rest will go well." She planned "a few games and jokes and then refreshments."[8] (There would be no men wearing women's clothing at the Koehlers' Halloween party. For that, Fort Terry's officers would have to wait another year.)

Preparing for the party helped lift Sophia's spirits, as did relief from "the strenuous days" of entertaining military personnel, and her ability to "play an occasional game of golf" thanks to fine autumn weather. Something else contributed to Sophia's better frame of mind:

Roy had done her a favor from three thousand miles away, visiting a lonely former neighbor of the Koehlers' who had moved from LeMars to Tacoma, Washington, about 150 miles from Portland. Receiving word that Roy had completed the requested mission, Sophia thanked him and sent a dollar, writing, "I wish next time you go to see her you would take her some candy for she is very fond of it."[9]

Sidney Jordan, the lieutenant colonel, returned from sick leave on the day of the Koehlers' party. Jordan's title was now executive officer of the post, which caused some ambiguity given Ben's role, but Ben and Jordan got along well and Jordan considered Ben an "excellent officer," as well as "perfectly fair and reasonable" in his treatment of the men under his command.[10]

Jordan thought that Ben "did more than anyone else . . . to keep up the social end of the post and get the officers together," and Jordan was happy to let Ben continue in that role. The Koehlers hosted the single officers for Thanksgiving dinner, but for a few of the guests, the plates of turkey paled in appeal compared to the pretty young woman in the room: the Koehlers' cousin, Margaret Gund, who had just arrived to spend the holidays on Plum Island.[11] At least four lieutenants called on her in the next few days, including Frick and his roommate, but the handsome, athletic Thomas Humphreys won out. Humphreys was friendly with Ben and a stickler for discipline himself. It was he who had complained about Barrett and Palmer taking his movie seats.

As Humphreys would later explain, "After Miss Gund arrived here, the bachelors on the post paid her attention and every time that I ever went there I always found some person, Lieutenant Frick, Walsh and Steese, or somebody like that . . . And finally as I went more frequently the others did not go so frequently."[12] When he could, Humphreys saw Margaret in the afternoons, sometimes taking her for a stroll. He would return in the evening, staying "as late as it was proper to stay."[13]

In mid-December, having won the competition for Margaret's affections, Humphreys was chosen for something less satisfying: an order to join another fort. Humphreys asked Ben if he needed to leave immediately. Ben told him, "No, take your time and turn over properly and then go down. Those orders do not mean they shall be obeyed right on the spot.'"[14] Ben's charitable interpretation of the order enabled Humphreys to extend his time with Margaret for close to a week. He departed on the evening of December 20.

After Humphreys left, Sophia and Margaret gave a holiday party for the Sunday school children and then observed Christmas on a quiet island, many of the soldiers having left on passes or furloughs. Ben would soon have all the company he needed in the person of William Kenly, who arrived on Plum Island in time to celebrate the siblings' New Year's Day birthdays.

CHAPTER ELEVEN

# *Living with a Man*

WILLIAM KENLY DREW people in. Of Scottish descent, he had fair skin, wide eyes, and a mouth quick to smile. He could be stern, but usually his face looked kind and free of tension, more like a contented father observing his children than a military man.

Kenly had served in the Philippines with Ben, whom he regarded as a brave man whose "exceptionally fine" actions included "sav[ing] [a] battalion from being annihilated."[1] Bonds formed in combat were strong, and when Kenly was called back to the Philippines in 1906, he arranged for Ben to relieve him of command of a field battery in Kansas for nine months. The next year, after Kenly was promoted to major and assigned to head Army recruiting in New York City, he asked that Ben be placed on his staff. As a result, in 1908, Ben had headed to a new stretch of coastline, the New York Bight on the Atlantic Ocean. There, Ben managed the bustling recruitment office in Brooklyn, one of the largest recruitment centers in the country.

Kenly was eight years older than Ben, though the two had overlapped at West Point. Like Ben, Kenly was short, but unlike Ben, Kenly was married—to the daughter of a colonel—and had two children. That did not keep Kenly from seeing a great deal of his new staff member.

Nearly every weekday, Kenly inspected the Brooklyn office where Ben worked. He usually ate lunch with Ben at the Army's Hamilton

Club. Occasionally, Kenly spent the weekend at Fort Hamilton, where Ben lived. Sometimes, Ben spent weekends with Kenly and his family in the Bronx.[2]

In 1910, Ben's situation changed again—markedly. Kenly promoted him to command "the eastern half in what I consider the most important part of the district in Manhattan," and Ben and his boss started living together.[3] Kenly's wife and children were away on an extended trip.

Sharing an apartment was Kenly's idea, as he would later explain: "[W]hen I came back from, I think, Fort Schuyler or Fort Totten, I am not sure which now, where I had been living with my family during the Summer,—this was about September or October, 1910, at my suggestion we hunted up an apartment and finally found one on West 27th Street between Sixth Avenue and Broadway, at a place called the Beverwyck."

The two men "had our breakfast together practically every morning," and Ben indulged the cultural interests that LeMars had nurtured in him by accompanying Kenly to plays in the nearby theater district.[4]

The relationship between Ben and Kenly began in the wartime Army—what the psychiatrist William Menninger would describe as "in a technical, psychiatric sense . . . fundamentally a homosexual society" in which "the satisfaction the soldier derived from the comradeship and fellowship of his associates—his male friends—[was] a disguised and sublimated homosexuality."[5]

This "sublimated homosexuality" was officially encouraged, Menninger said, as a substitute for actual sex, and the close friendship between Ben and Kenly does not require a sexual component to explain it.[6] Nor should one impose what historian Carroll Smith-Rosenberg calls "twentieth-century categories" on a relationship that began in the 1890s in the all-male world of a military academy.[7]

Come the early 1900s, male bonding was socially encouraged outside the military as well—largely as an antidote to the perceived feminization of American life. Pro-interventionists had cited the need for masculinity training to justify war in Cuba and the Philippines, and back home, men were being encouraged to spend more time with one another in clubs and gyms. Membership in men's fraternal organizations swelled at the turn of the twentieth century, allowing "men to reinvent themselves as men, to experience the pleasures and comforts of each other's company and of cultural and domestic life without feeling feminized."[8] It was also the era when "[r]ough sports became popular on college campuses, endorsed by educators and students alike as the optimal way to build character. Prizefighters, cowboys, soldiers, and sailors became popular heroes, heralded as paragons of virility."[9]

Part of the hand-wringing over male "virility" was a reaction to the greater visibility of homosexuals in American life. In the words of George Chauncey:

> The fairy became one of the most prominent and volatile signs of the fragility of the gender order, at once a source of reassurance to other men and the repository of their deepest fears. On the one hand, men could use their difference from the fairy to reassure themselves of their own masculinity . . . But the fairy also provoked a high degree of anxiety and scorn among middle-class men . . . His womanlike manner challenged the supposed immutability of gender differences by demonstrating that anatomical males did not inevitably become men and were not inevitably different from women.[10]

The preoccupation with manliness in the early 1900s included concern over the amount of time that boys were under the influence of women.[11] Camps and clubs were recommended as a solution, including the Boy Scouts of America (founded in 1910)—"the most important organization developed to rescue boys from their mothers and reunite them with a virile ideal."[12] Michael Kimmel observes that the Boy Scouts "yoked the development of manhood to a nostalgic re-creation of the frontier."[13] This was necessary, according to Boy Scouts cofounder Ernest Thompson Seton, to counter conditions in modern society that produced the sissy—"more effeminate than his sister, and his flabby muscles are less flabby than his character."[14]

For Kenly, the closeness that men developed in a military academy was natural, something to be revered. In his efforts to exonerate Ben, Kenly would later speak of having shared with Ben "all the intimacy that any two men can possibly live and who have been brought up together in a military academy, which means you wander around in your underclothes."[15]

Kenly would point to Ben's personal habits as evidence that Ben never showed any "symptom of anything that could be objected to." Reflecting a supposition that a man inclined to engage in sex with other men would be uninhibited with his body, Kenly thought it noteworthy that Ben was "rather sensitive and super-modest." Kenly, not Ben, was the one who walked around the apartment bare-chested, coming "out of the bath as men do carrying my kimono over my arm in the most careless way imaginable."[16] Kenly could not recall that Ben "ever did that at all in the same free, entirely careless way that I did."[17]

That Kenly could speak candidly about his own "free, entirely careless" behavior while living with Ben shows his confidence that no one would perceive him as a "homo-sexualist." Kenly was a married man with children. He apparently did not worry that others might see his marriage as a cover for a relationship with Ben that went beyond fraternal intimacy. Kenly was adamant that over the course of knowing Ben for fifteen years he had "never seen a single symptom of anything that was not manly."[18]

Kenly was 50 years old. His attitudes about male intimacy were a holdover from the nineteenth century, archaic to younger men such as Worcester and Frick. Not only was sexuality in general a more public topic when Worcester and Frick became adults, but so was concern with "unnatural" sexuality.[19] As Chauncey observes, "[t]he overtness of the fairy's sexual interest in men . . . raised the possibility of a sexual component in other men's interactions. Once that possibility was raised, the very celebration of male bodies and manly sociability initially precipitated by the masculinity crisis required a new policing of male intimacy and exclusion of sexual desire for other men."[20] It was like a hall of mirrors. The "manly man" was the socially acceptable man, the type of man a male wanting to be considered manly wished others to believe him to be, and wished, therefore, to be surrounded by. That required the making of distinctions based on more than anatomy.

Categorizing men as "normal" versus "perverted" helped, especially in the Army—the biggest male club of them all. Language and labels could provide a sense of order, for "as long as no homosexuals were enlisted, soldiers could play at being lovers (and even consummate the roles) without ever having to acknowledge those feelings."[21]

By the time Kenly visited Plum Island for New Year's, it was apparent to those who were looking that Ben demonstrated no romantic interest in women. It seems that someone in Frick's circle had seen Ben and Kenly together in New York City and formed a suspicion about the nature of the men's intimacy less influenced by the aura of West Point brotherhood than the gender-policing goal of detecting, rejecting, and punishing homosexuals.[22]

Ben had no way of knowing what others were saying about him, but after the holidays, he learned that without consulting him, Frick and a new doctor had gone around him to ask Jordan for permission to hold a dance. Ben was perturbed because he, Frick, and the doctor made up the hop committee, responsible for deciding when dances would be held, and Ben considered himself the committee's senior member. Frick blamed it on a misunderstanding, saying he thought Ben had resigned from the committee.[23] Jordan spoke to Ben, who assured him he would "smooth the matter out," and a dance was scheduled for later in the month.[24]

But there was more to it. In the fall, Frick had told Ben a story reflecting a classic double standard toward women. Frick said he'd had sexual intercourse at Fort Wright with a woman from New London who was now dating a Fort Terry officer. According to Ben, Frick asked him to tell the officer that the woman "was not a suitable person for an officer to marry."[25]

Ben declined to convey the message, but when he learned that the woman attended the January dance, as did the daughter of an officer whom Frick had invited, Ben reprimanded Frick.[26] This moral parsing reflected a paternalistic frame of mind. Ben would not intervene with a man dating a possibly unchaste woman—letting the man make his own judgment—but he objected to Frick's allowing the woman to socialize with an officer's daughter.

For his part, Frick was not interested in what Ben's reaction said about his adherence to chivalric values. Frick only knew that, for at least the second time, Ben had not interpreted his sexual gossip the way he intended it—man to man—and Frick saw that he could not get away with much with Ben in command. Frick groused about Ben behind his back, and come spring, his complaining would incorporate a new rumor about Ben's proclivities. First, however, a different island beckoned, providing a welcome distraction for Sophia as Plum Island turned chilly—for more reasons than winter temperatures.

AFTER DECADES OF KILLING and enslaving the Taino people of Puerto Rico, the Spaniard Juan Ponce de Leon chose a ridge in San Juan overlooking the bay as the location for a fort and trophy house. It was to this white stone mansion with tiled floors and high ceilings, completed by Ponce de Leon's son-in-law in the 1520s, that Sophia traveled by ship in February 1913.

Casa Blanca had a throne room and shady verandas. There were fountains, a swimming pool, and a stone wall that kept the ridge under the mansion from sliding into the sea, fighting gravity for four centuries—a fitting legacy for Ponce de Leon, who had successfully and ruthlessly battled whatever stood in his way.[27] Everything about the place offered a stark contrast to the Koehlers' shingled house on Plum Island, but it wasn't the grandiosity of conquistador architecture that drew Sophia. She came to see the current occupants of Casa Blanca—her brother Louis and sister-in-law Maude Anthony Koehler.

It was almost incredible that Louis had such a fine assignment, on the order of Sophia's cat actually leading nine lives. Louis now commanded the only regiment of native Puerto Ricans in the regular Army, the Regiment of Infantry of Porto Rico, as the island's name was then spelled.[28] It was a testament to Louis's strong record and popularity that his career had not been derailed by the enemy he had made in the Philippines, Leonard Wood, for Wood now worked at the top of the Army's hierarchy in Washington as its most senior general and chief of staff.[29]

Before the year 1913 was out, the charges against Ben would give Wood a chance to cage the cat and penalize two men named Koehler, so it was fortunate that Sophia visited when she did. In December, Wood would add to Casa Blanca's history of ruthlessness by evicting Louis and Maude and sending them to a post in the Texas desert. Neither Louis nor Sophia knew that in February, as Louis drove his sister through valleys lined with coconut palms and banana trees, where "everything was new and interesting" and she "loved the place."[30]

At that point, Sophia's only complaints were an uncomfortable bed, sour oranges, and the children she saw in public wearing no clothes. War and men's grudges seemed far off, and Louis could be forgiven for feeling that way, too. It had been seven years since his run-in with Wood, long enough for most men to move on.

# CHAPTER TWELVE

# Ladies "Wearin' Pantaloons"

WHEN MORO WOMEN IN the southern Philippines wore trousers, silk shirts, and headbands, the results could be deadly. The women were sometimes armed like men, too, with swords called *kris*. If an American soldier realized his adversary was female and hesitated—out of scruple or surprise—that was all to the martial advantage of the Moros.

U.S. soldiers wrote a song about this unnerving battle tactic. One verse asked, "If a lady wearin' pantaloons is swingin' wit' a knife, Must I stop an' cross-examine as ter sex?"[1] Another stanza answered "no"— even though orders from Washington ostensibly forbade the killing of women and children.

When the Army sent Louis to the Philippines in October 1905 to lead a cavalry unit on Jolo, a southern island in the Sulu archipelago, he knew conditions were dangerous well beyond the Moro strategy of using western notions of gender-appropriate behavior against a western enemy. Edgar's death remained a painful reminder of Filipinos' skill at surprise attacks and superior knowledge of their country's terrain—even as American leaders continued to disparage their abilities, calling them "robbers" and "fanatics" and portraying them as animalistic and undisciplined.[2] Yet Filipino men were also depicted as effeminate, caring for children and cooking while their wives worked, indicating their supposed unfitness for self-government and "the need for U.S. intervention to put the Philippine gender order right."[3]

Married to a suffragist whose famous aunt, now 85, was still campaigning for the right to vote, Louis likely had little patience for the ways in which womanhood was transmuted into an epithet against the Filipinos, but he did care very much about the poor accommodations for his men and horses that he discovered upon his arrival.[4] In seeking to solve that problem, he encountered a bigger issue: the dual role the United States was playing, trying to rule a foreign nation and subjugate its people through force at the same time.

In the north, the American-led government was well in charge by 1905, due in large part to an alliance with "a small group of elite landowners, bolstering the power of an oligarchy that continues to dominate political life."[5] But in the south, many Moros were resisting American rule—just as they had resisted the Spanish, who never succeeded in converting the Moros from Islam/Mohammedanism to Catholicism, as in the north. Local traditions had prevailed for centuries under a loose federation of villages headed, at least ceremoniously, by a sultan.[6]

By the time Louis arrived in 1905, it had been three years since Roosevelt proclaimed the war over in the north.[7] In contrast, of the over 51,000 inhabitants of Jolo and its surrounding southern islands, a mere 1,270 were "civilized," and the rest were "wild," according to Secretary of War William Taft, who had served as the first civilian governor of the Philippines and would become U.S. president in 1909.[8] One definition of "civilized" was whether the Moros accepted American "reforms," such as uniform criminal laws that weakened village autonomy. While some Army officers had managed to forge alliances with smaller, more vulnerable village chiefs, the dominant American approach was authoritarian and frequently deadly.

The man responsible for the aggressive approach was Leonard Wood, who arrived in the Philippines in 1903 at a time when he sought promotion to major general. Leading campaigns against Moros served Wood's interest in shoring up his military credentials and trying to counter the view that the best thing he had going for him was his friendship with Roosevelt.[9]

Wood left his comfortable headquarters in Zamboanga, a beautiful town on the island of Mindanao, to lead "Krag and howitzer onslaughts," according to his biographer, Jack Lane.[10] The results were horrible for the Moros, with many killed and hundreds of villages destroyed.[11] Over time there would be scores of attacks led or ordered by Wood, in what another writer calls a "reign of terror."[12]

In 1904, Congress approved Wood's promotion to major general after "one of the most explosive debates of Roosevelt's administration."[13] Even Taft questioned the bloodshed. "Could not the suppression of the more undesirable Moro customs be effected by peaceful means rather than force?" Taft wrote, receiving a reply from Wood that the "only way to deal with these people is to be absolutely firm."[14]

Wood obviously did not consider "these people" to be his people— the same way he felt about other nonwhite groups, and even many whites.

From the perspective of ancestry, Wood possessed the rare insider credential of descent from four Mayflower passengers, but West Point and the Naval Academy had rejected him.[15] The son of a doctor, Wood had better luck with medical schools, graduating Harvard Medical School in 1884, but "what he really desired," according to Roosevelt, "was the chance to lead men in some kind of hazard."[16] That chance arrived when the Army sought a doctor to join the campaign to capture Geronimo.[17] Wood signed on as a "contract surgeon" and came out a highly praised soldier with a commission as captain.[18]

Like others of his day, Wood subscribed to the conflict model of human relations embedded in social Darwinism, and he believed in inherent differences between whites and other races. He also saw gradations among whites. There were the "right sort of white men"—such as himself—and all the others. Somewhat paradoxically, Wood thought in 1886 that what made a white man the "right sort" was his ability to defeat Native Americans on their own terms, living and fighting in the heat and desolation of the desert. As Wood wrote in his diary, "I saw General Miles at Fort Bowie and had a long talk with him. I told him I believed the right sort of white men could eventually break these Indians up and compel them to surrender. I have been selected as medical officer of the expedition."[19]

Apaches served as scouts for the men set on taking Geronimo dead or alive, and Wood wrote of how the scouts made fire from dry sticks (something Wood had never seen before), killed deer with precision when Wood's shots missed, and noticed subtle signs on the landscape, undetected by the soldiers, that revealed the "hot trail" of Geronimo's party.[20]

Wood noticed such tasks being performed, knew that they contributed to his group's objectives, and observed that he and other whites could not do the same tasks as well or at all, but he did not allow those observations to change his belief in the Native Americans' inferiority. General Nelson Miles had told Wood to assess whether Native Americans were physically superior to whites, and if so, what made them that way. Wood recorded facts that might have formed the beginning of such an analysis, if there was any chance of it being conducted objectively, but there wasn't. From the start, Wood set out to prove the absence of such superiority.

After Geronimo surrendered, Wood and a few soldiers became separated from the other troops and encountered a group of Apaches who until that day had been among the pursued. "They were all fully armed and could have seized us at any time as hostages," Wood wrote, expressing surprise that the opposite happened: The Apaches told them "our camp is your camp" and fed them "the best they had."[21] Once again, such behavior is recorded, but nowhere is a value judgment expressed as to the honorableness or worth of people who would behave in such a way to their enemies-just-turned-captors.

One day, "a young Indian girl gave birth to a child" while marching with Wood's party. "The command halted perhaps an hour for this purpose and then took up the march, the girl carrying her young baby," Wood wrote. "She looked pretty pale, but otherwise seemed to pay little attention to the incident."[22] Was it a lack of "attention," or unusual strength that enabled the woman to march an hour after giving birth? Surely the woman whom Wood married four years later—the niece and ward of a Supreme Court justice—remained prone for more than an hour after bearing the couple's children.

The best that Wood could say about Native Americans was that, like General Lawton, leader of the final Geronimo campaign, he preferred them to Mexicans, referring to the latter as "civilized Indians, with only a moderate strain of white blood."[23]

Yet Wood's fully white commander, the "fighting giant" Lawton, got so drunk one evening that he threatened a junior officer with a "heavy coffee cup," prompting the junior officer to pull out a gun.[24] Was that the behavior of a superior person? Wood protected Lawton, interceding on his behalf lest the full story be told. That served Wood's interests at the time, but years later, in Cuba, Wood chafed under Lawton's command and wound up getting Lawton's job after word of a drinking binge by Lawton reached McKinley.[25] The accusation that Wood had reported the drinking to McKinley "followed Wood throughout his life."[26]

The "ideological complex of aggressive Anglo-American manhood and nationhood" appeared not only in the words of public figures such as Wood and Roosevelt, but in popular war songs and poetry in the late twentieth century, though there was an imperfect "racial and ethnic inclusivity within some aspects of military culture."[27] Black soldiers had served in the Indian Wars, earning them a modicum of recognition as "manly" fighters, and a place in the war against the Spanish. Yet even though blacks fought bravely in Cuba and sustained high casualties—including the all-black Tenth Cavalry under Wood's command—their participation and sacrifice were largely trivialized as the acts of loyal slaves, not those of heroic men entitled to respect after the war.[28]

Efforts by women during the Spanish-American War as nurses and organizers of supplies also went mostly unrecognized or were characterized as proving women's value as "angels" and muses to men, rather than their worth as citizens.[29] The glorification of men's actions in the war set back women's suffrage for years, "call[ing] out a fresh crop of assertions that women ought not to vote, because they cannot render military service," as suffragist Alice Stone Blackwell put it.[30] Not one state passed women's suffrage from 1896 to 1910, a period known as the doldrums in suffragist history.[31]

There is no doubt that Wood possessed "extraordinary physical strength and endurance," as Roosevelt wrote. Wood had taken great risks in the Geronimo campaign, including a mostly solitary trip of nearly one hundred miles to send a telegram to Miles.[32] While feverish and swollen from a tarantula bite, he had fought and marched long distances[33] and after it was over, Lawton singled out Wood for a Medal of Honor, "a bitter pill for the other officers who had campaigned for years against the Apaches."[34] In the Geronimo campaign, Wood also learned the importance of influence with Washington insiders, a lesson taught well by Miles, who gave virtually no recognition to his predecessors and their years of more peaceful dealings with the Apaches that laid the groundwork for their surrender.[35]

After the campaign, Wood secured an appointment in the Surgeon General's office in Washington. He became doctor to Presidents Cleveland and McKinley and friend to Roosevelt, who saw Wood as he wished to be seen, as "one of the two or three white men who could stand fatigue and hardship as well as an Apache."[36] Following the Spanish-American War, Wood became military governor of Santiago and then, through a power play, all of Cuba. He led reforms such as improvements in sanitation, impressing people in Washington as an able administrator, while denigrating the Cubans as "stupid and downtrodden."[37]

To Roosevelt, Wood was a man of "high ideals," but the Koehler family would come to see him quite differently.[38]


SHORTLY AFTER ARRIVING IN Jolo in 1905, Louis antagonized Wood by complaining about Hugh Scott, Wood's former chief of staff in Cuba, who was now in charge of Jolo Island both as commanding officer of its military post and civil governor.

It was too much for one person to handle, Louis concluded, and in the spirit of his outspoken father-in-law, he said so. When Scott ignored Louis's requests for improved accommodations for his men and horses, Louis accused Scott of "inattention to duty and incompetency."[39] As Taft put it, Louis "insist[ed] that Major Scott should be in his office at certain times and should discharge his duties as military post commander with the same degree of promptness that he would have done had he not the additional duties of civil governor."[40]

Louis's complaint challenged Wood indirectly, for he, too, held dual roles as military head of the Department of Mindanao and civil governor of Moro Province. That may have seemed efficient to some, but Louis thought it put soldiers at risk.[41] Louis had married a modern woman, yet his military training was old-school, and he had received enough positive reinforcement to trust his judgment.

"[O]ne of the ablest of soldiers," was how a brigadier general characterized Louis, having observed him in the Philippines during skirmishes, including one that resulted in his receiving a Silver Star.[42] "You and your lamented brother [Edgar] could meet any proposition of a military character," the general wrote. "[A]ny C.O. [Commanding Officer] is to be congratulated who is so fortunate to have you with him."[43]

Scott and Wood saw Louis in a different light, as an upstart—but just as the lava had disappeared from the southern Philippines, leaving behind hollow craters where Moros could seek refuge, so did Scott disappear, creating a different sort of abyss for Louis. It was mid-November when Louis made his complaint. Scott waited six weeks to respond, mailing charges against Louis on December 31 as Scott left Manila for the United States.[44]

Wood did not go along with an inspector's recommendation that Scott be investigated.[45] On short notice—Louis said it was two hours—Wood ordered Louis to Jolo's capital city in mid-January to stand trial, during which not only Scott but several other key witnesses failed to appear. Louis was denied his choice of counsel, and the captain assigned to represent him said he did not receive notice until after the court-martial.[46] Louis defended himself against an Article 61 charge that he had prejudiced good order and discipline by making his complaint.

On March 3, the War Department announced that Louis was acquitted of making "malicious, vexatious, and groundless" charges, but convicted of filing charges against a superior that were "captious and unnecessary."[47]

Talk about splitting hairs. "Vexatious" means "annoying." "Captious" means "difficult to please." Louis was acquitted of being malicious and annoying but convicted of being difficult to please for having filed a complaint found to be trivial and unnecessary. No wonder soldiers called Article 61 the "Devil's Article."[48]

Substantively, the conviction was virtually meaningless, yet it was a conviction nonetheless.[49] Wood seized the opportunity to censure a West Point graduate with combat experience far more extensive than his own. Wood publicly declared that Louis was "seriously wanting in those clean-cut and well-defined conceptions of a soldier's duty which should be found in every officer of the Army."[50] Wood admonished Louis to "cultivate those habits of true soldierly subordination, which the evidence in this case showed him to lack."

Louis was fuming, but his ruminations were cut short by an order to fight. The target was a contingent of Moros called Tausugs living in the deep bowl of a 2,100-foot-high crater. What happened on March 5-8, 1906, in the center of Jolo Island, was no skirmish. It was an event that some historians equate with Wounded Knee.

It was First Battle of Bud Dajo, the most horrific battle in the Philippine War.[51]


WANTING IN DUTY? THOSE were Wood's words about Louis, but on the morning of March 5, Louis quickly took command of more than 130 soldiers after Captain Tyrell Rivers was shot in the thigh leading a reconnaissance up the west trail of the crater. Until nightfall, Louis and his men continued to scope out the trail, which was blocked by Moro fortifications.[52]

Inside the crater, a huge earth form with a circumference of eleven miles, were some 850 Tausugs, many of them women and children. Their numbers had been growing for months, ever since a small group hid there to escape Wood's hunt for a wanted Moro and the destruction of their village. The Tausugs subsisted mostly on rice and sweet potatoes, which they were able to grow thanks to a source of water. Scott requested the departure of the Tausugs, even getting the sultan to ask nicely, but Wood's patience ran out. "This is a ridiculous little affair from every standpoint and should be brought to an end . . . A couple of columns should take the place some night and clean it up," he had ordered.[53]

On March 6, separate columns of Americans and allied Moros attempted to scale the south and east trails, encountering rolled boulders and sniper fire. One American bled to death, and all three columns stopped for the night. On the east, the Moros beat drums and gongs and sang taunts all night long.

Early the next morning, the south column attacked, prompting 150 Tausugs to charge down the crater with swords and a few guns. The combat was ugly, fast, and close. "In the space of ten-fifteen furious minutes, all 150 of the charging Tausugs are killed and one out of every three men on the American side are casualties. The remainder crawl up the last 100 yards of the last steep slope to capture the South summit amidst only desultory resistance," according to the author of several books about the conflict.[54]

Later in the day, Wood arrived at the base of Bud Dajo, and Navy soldiers and Army infantrymen used ropes and pulleys to hoist heavy machine guns up the slopes.[55] When told to charge, the men hauled the guns to the top of the crest and fired. In ten minutes, all of the Moros in the trenches died, some four hundred of them, leaving alive "only about 100 Tausug defenders . . . surrounded and inside a lone cotta [fortress] at the top of the West trail, the highest point on the mountain."[56]

The next morning, the Americans finished what they had started. They seized the cotta, killing another 67 Tausugs, for a total Tausug death toll of between 700 and 850, two-thirds of them women and children by some accounts. American casualties were far lower: eighteen dead, between fifty-two and seventy wounded.[57]

• • •

"WOMEN AND CHILDREN KILLED IN MORO BATTLE," *The New York Times* announced on March 10, 1906, shocking American citizens who had little idea their troops were still engaged in so much fighting—much less killing women and children.[58] The last line of the headline was also shocking: "President Wires Congratulations to the Troops."

It took a couple of days for Roosevelt—and others in Washington— to realize that the press reports of the battle were not sitting well with the American public, notwithstanding the *Times*'s description of some Moros as "savages and head hunters . . . on the warpath."[59] Secretary of War Taft wired Wood: "It is charged there was wanton slaughter Moros, men, women, and children, in the fight Mount Dajo. Wish you would send me at once all the particulars with respect to this matter, stating exact facts."[60]

Wood blamed reporters for supplying "sensational features," telling Taft that "the Moros, one and all, were fighting not only as enemies, but religious fanatics, believing Paradise to be their immediate reward if killed in action with Christians. They apparently desired that none be saved." Wood also blamed the Moros' cross-dressing, saying, "Moro women wore trousers and were dressed, armed much like the men, and charged with them. The children were in many cases used by the men as shields while charging troops. [W]e have begged Moros again and again to fight as men, and keep women and children out of it."[61]

But if Wood was suggesting that firing machine guns at civilians living in a crater was an act of "manliness," opponents of the Philippine War in the United States had been arguing the opposite: that men were being "unmade," not "made" through the war. Unlike the quick and decisive Spanish-American War, fighting to subjugate the Filipinos had dragged on. One frame was that American soldiers were being degraded through the prolonged association with an "inferior" set of people, sexually, morally, and in battle tactics such as those exhibited at Bud Dajo.[62]

Mark Twain was among the critics who expressed outrage at what he called a "slaughter" and "massacre." Twain castigated the artillerymen—"Christian butchers"—who fired "from a safe position on the heights above" at the Tausugs penned in the crater "like rats in a trap."[63]

Those "butchers" included a second lieutenant named Philip Worcester, newly graduated from West Point, who "energetically" led the hoisting of a machine gun up the south trail, according to battle commander Joseph Duncan, and who received credit for the "efficient and enterprising manner" in which he used the gun—"Worcester's gun," as a major called it.[64]

In contrast, Duncan praised Louis for his restraint. Louis had kept his men from going over the crater's lip and attacking the Moros. Said Duncan, "A harder and more thankless position can hardly be conceived and he is recommended for suitable reward."[65]

Throughout March 1906, members of Congress called for an investigation, until some of the same subterranean processes that had created the Mount Dajo volcano erupted across the Pacific in a place where Americans, not "savages," dwelled. The earthquake and Great Fire of April 1906, and all the tragedy they wreaked on San Francisco, swept the killing of Muslim Filipinos off the front pages and out of the speeches of politicians for a very long time.

In 2016, the Battle of Bud Dajo resurfaced in American and Filipino newspapers when Rodrigo Duterte, the first Philippine president from the southern island of Mindanao, demanded an apology from President Obama 110 years after the fact.[66] The indignation felt by southern Filipinos over their treatment by the United States in 1906 apparently never went away.

Nor did Louis's anger over Wood's rebuke recede following Bud Dajo. The "suitable reward" he wanted was for Wood to eat his words that Louis was "wanting . . . in duty."

Louis could not know that his insistence on justice for himself would wind up harming his younger brother. Nor could he know that Philip Worcester—the gunner approved by Wood to receive a Silver Star for "conspicuously efficient and gallant service during the action against hostile Moros"—would become his brother's chief accuser.[67]

A year after Bud Dajo, Worcester and Ben met at Fort Monroe in Virginia, where Ben, a captain, was heading a company and Worcester, a lieutenant, was attending a summer training school. Bud Dajo gave them a bond, Worcester being a veteran of the same controversial battle in which Ben's brother had led a column, and the two men interacted cordially over the course of a few months.[68]

At that early point in Worcester's career, before Ben became his boss on Plum Island and criticized his behavior, Worcester acted deferentially to the higher-ranked Captain Koehler.

Meanwhile, the other Captain Koehler, Louis, was engaged in challenging authority at the highest levels.

# CHAPTER THIRTEEN

# The President Disapproves

Louis wanted his conviction nullified, but Army rules did not allow appeals from court-martial verdicts. The feisty Louis improvised, writing directly to the secretary of war.

"I believe that I have been injured in my character and reputation as an officer and soldier by unfair, unjust and illegal acts at the hands of my Department Commander, Major General Leonard Wood," Louis wrote to Taft, contending that Wood's handling of his court-martial for complaining about inadequate accommodations had "but one object, namely, the unwarranted protection of Major Scott and the unfair and biased effort to do me all the injury possible."[1]

From lack of counsel and witnesses to the jury's substitution of charges that hardly made sense, Louis described the case's "many irregular and unusual features" that left him "feeling that I have not been given a fair trial but have been the victim of prejudice, bias and even malice" and "helpless and at the mercy of a superior who would make use of every unfair advantage to harm me and to protect his own personal friend." Louis asked "for a full and complete review of the case . . . with a view to the setting aside of the findings, sentence and reprimand."

Another captain helped Louis write the appeal. Tyrell Rivers, still recovering from his thigh wound, encouraged Louis to send it, although other officers advised him to hold back.[2] As the more cautious officers warned, the letter was received in Washington like a cannon blast. In July, the Army ordered Louis to stand trial again, this time for using disrespectful language, being insubordinate to Wood, and making derogatory statements about his superiors.

In Kansas and Missouri, political figures took note of the punitive action against a favorite son, "one of the most brilliant of the younger officers of the army," according to the *Washington Post*.[3] A senator wrote to Taft, as did a representative, explaining that "Captain Koehler's friends are not only numerous here, but influential—among our leading citizens. The interest, therefore, taken in the Captain's cause is lively and sympathetic."[4]

The writer expressed confidence that Taft, as secretary of war, would handle the matter fairly, but Taft did not directly control the process. That fell to Wood, recently elevated by Roosevelt to commander of the entire Philippine Division. Wood delayed the trial until he felt confident that he had found jurors who were not partial to Louis.[5]

Finally, in December 1906, the second court-martial took place. Four officers testified in support of Louis, including a major general who disputed Wood's testimony. Even the prosecutor in Louis's first trial, a captain, testified that Louis had been a victim of prejudice. Louis's counselors, also officers, accused Wood of "tyranny," all of which was reported in the Philippine papers. In the United States, the *Leavenworth Weekly Times*—now published by Louis's brother-in-law, Daniel Anthony Jr.—wrote of the "sensational disclosures that have greatly stirred military circles in the Philippines."[6]

After the trial, the jury's undisclosed verdict went to Washington. In February 1907, a paper reported that Louis was likely to be dismissed, but at the end of March, a year after Louis had written to Taft, the truth came out. Despite the care with which its members had been chosen, the jury acquitted Louis of all charges. A panel of the Army's most senior officers found that there was nothing wrong with Louis having accused Wood of "prejudice, bias, and even malice."[7]

It took months for the verdict to be released because Taft, Roosevelt, and the Army's senior lawyer had been considering what to do. Here was Roosevelt's friend and political ally being castigated by offi-

cers under his command in a proceeding the government itself had
ordered. Not only that, but if Roosevelt approved the verdict, he would
have to order Wood to undergo a court-martial for "perverting his
power." As Taft explained to Roosevelt:

> [I]f you approve the finding you necessarily affirm or approve the state-
> ment derogatory to General Wood contained in the appeals, and if you
> do so approve those statements, then it would become your duty as
> Commander-in-Chief to order General Wood before a court-martial
> for perverting his power as department commander to accomplish an
> unjust and unfair purpose against his subordinate officer.[8]

Court-martialing a highly controversial major general, a favorite of
Roosevelt, would have ignited a firestorm of press interest and greatly
embarrassed the president. Laying the groundwork to avoid that result, Taft opined that there was not "any evidence in the record to
sustain the bringing of such proceedings," and Roosevelt ordered that
"the proceedings, findings, and acquittal in the case of Captain Lewis
M. Koehler, Fourth Cavalry, United States Army, are disapproved. I
entirely concur in all that the Secretary of War says of Captain Koehler, and of General Wood, and of the poor showing made by the
court which last passed on the case."[9]

Roosevelt and Taft surely wished they could convert the jury's "poor
showing" into a finding of guilt, but fortunately for Louis, in this situation an Army rule cut in his favor. The president could not "change
a finding of acquittal to one of conviction," Taft explained. Instead,
Roosevelt "set aside the proceedings as if they had not been
commenced."

All that time and effort, and now, with Roosevelt's signature, it was
as though the second court-martial had never taken place—except
that it had, with two major consequences. First, Louis succeeded in
rehabilitating his reputation, for Taft wrote in his official letter that
"Captain Koehler is an officer with an excellent record for coura-
geous service in the field and attention to duty generally. He distinguished himself at the battle of Mount Dajo." This was reported

throughout the country, for the president's intercession to "save" Wood was big news.[10]

Second, it was now a matter of public record that officers had called Wood malicious and tyrannical under oath and that a jury of senior officers had agreed with them.

Louis nearly succeeded in making a defendant out of a notorious user of the court-martial process against others, and according to an attorney and friend of the Koehler family, "General Wood manifested a very decided antagonism toward [Louis] from that time on."[11]

Roosevelt not only rescued Wood from a court-martial but soon gave him "the highest assignment next to that of Chief of Staff." Wood became head of the Department of the East, an appointment, according to the *Washington Post*, "taken by those who are familiar with recent history as one of the President's answers to the criticisms of his friend Gen. Wood in the Koehler case."[12]

Years later, Wood would seek to change the provision that had protected Louis, proposing legislation to allow the Army chief of staff to convert a court-martial acquittal into a conviction—exactly what Taft advised Roosevelt could not be done in Louis's case.[13] The bill did not pass, but by then, Wood had found another way to strike back at Louis. One of Louis's Army brothers had died serving his country, but the other was very much alive and, in 1913, also quite vulnerable.

Wood and Ben Koehler both grew up wishing for a military career, and both earned commendations from General Lawton—a man known for stinginess with praise as much as for excess with alcohol— but the ways in which the two men approached their own careers could not have been more different. Unlike Wood, Ben never made currying influence a priority.

While Ben would become known as an officer exhibiting fairness, especially to enlisted men, Wood had a reputation for sabotaging rivals, such as the time he was accused of planting an unfavorable article about a general whose job Wood wanted, leading the general to say publicly that he would never speak to Wood again.[14]

For most of Ben's career, the differences in the men's approaches to their jobs had not mattered. Ben liked being in the field. He was willing to put his faith in Army leaders to deploy him where they wanted. But in his second full year of commanding Fort Terry, Ben's lack of strategic self-protection would leave him exposed to an ambush of a very different sort than the unseen gunman who had killed his brother.

# CHAPTER FOURTEEN

# Hatched on Plum Island

SOPHIA RETURNED TO PLUM Island in March 1913 after a long trip from Puerto Rico by ship, train, and steamer. She had been away for six weeks and immediately faced a domestic problem: the need for a new housekeeper. Sophia took over the cooking and cleaning until, at the end of April, "Ben finally made me come to New York to try to get someone."[1]

Sophia stayed in William Kenly's apartment while interviewing candidates, choosing a woman named Emma Jones. "Whether she will be a treasure or not remains to be seen," Sophia wrote to Roy. "It's all such a lottery—for there is no way here of finding out much about them."[2]

Indeed, how very difficult it was to know a person fully. A man or woman could seem to be one way and really be another. In less than a year, this would be one of the Army's main arguments against Sophia's brother.

WHATEVER ELSE PEOPLE WOULD soon accuse Ben of doing—or being—no one could dispute that he spent much of his leisure time in the large garden behind his house.[3] He grew vegetables and flowering plants for placement "around the trees in front of the officers' line down to the Company barracks."[4] He also raised chickens and gave away their eggs.

His first summer on the island, Ben had tried hatching pheasants from eggs that he purchased and placed under hens, but the hatchlings did not live. In the spring of 1913, Ben arranged for mature pheasants to be delivered. Lieutenant Colonel Jordan was so impressed he offered to contribute money so that Ben could buy more pheasants, raise them in his coop, and release them.[5]

The pheasants would play a supporting role in the case against Ben, for Worcester's top sergeant, Edison Kirkman, would tell the Army inspector that Ben received a call from Jordan about the pheasants the same night Ben invited him to his house in December 1912 or January 1913. That was the night, according to Kirkman, that Ben told him to "cut the women out entirely," stripped naked in front of him, "took hold of me by the arm, felt of my breast and told me I was built like a woman," and "went down around my privates . . . and felt of them and . . . taken them out."[6]

Kirkman never set foot in his house, Ben would say. Nor was there any call about pheasants, Jordan would add.[7]

In May, Ben thought the time had come to invest in a larger animal, a horse, but "[o]ne of the first times I ever rode my horse I came near having an accident, on account of the saddle slipping."[8] After that, Ben told John Barrett he wanted "to saddle my own horse," for, as a civilian employee put it, "Sergeant Barrett was not very much of a horseman and in regard to bridling a mule even he would have trouble."[9] However, Barrett would tell the Army inspector that he frequently saddled Ben's mount, which was when Ben made his sexual overtures.[10]

The stable was one of the few locations where it would not be unusual for the post commander to encounter enlisted men with no one else around. That made it a good place for a grope—or a made-up story about a grope.


FOR SOPHIA, SPRINGTIME BROUGHT pleasures that compensated for the extra housework: "[Fort] Terry has been quite gay ever since I came back," she wrote Roy, "partly owing to there being guests on the post and due in part to the Turkey Trot fever that has just struck the place."[11]

Turkey trot fever was spreading through the nation. The fast, ragtime music was right for turn-of-the-century America, but dances also provided a forum for men to demonstrate their interest in women at a time when, George Chauncey writes, "single-sex (or homosocial) gave way to mixed-sex (or heterosocial) socializing," and "[m]iddle class men increasingly conceived of their sexuality—their heterosexuality, or exclusive desire for women—as one of the hallmarks of a real man."[12] In a few months, Frick would put a different slant on the "gay" aspects of Fort Terry's turkey trot craze, claiming that Ben declared, "Frick, let's dance," at a party and grabbed his genitals.[13]

In July, Ben took action regarding the sport he had not played as a boy: baseball. Complaints reached Ben about Frick's way of rescheduling missed games. As a result, Ben relieved Frick of his job as athletic officer. Ben also relieved Sergeant Brown of the unauthorized pigs and a dog he had brought to Fort Terry, ordering them removed to the mainland.[14]

Around the same time that Frick lost his athletic position, he gained a new company captain, Worcester, who had reason to empathize with Frick, having been a post athletic representative himself (at Fort Totten in 1910). Worcester arrived at Fort Terry after a couple of months working on Fishers Island where Frick, a frequent visitor, had been complaining about Ben to Robinson and others. Frick brought Worcester into those conversations, and on August 1, Worcester moved to Fort Terry to take command of the 88th Company, which included Frick and Kirkman.

Late summer meant Army–Navy maneuvers and also a lot of beer: sixty-four gallons per week for one group of soldiers authorized by a permit issued by Jordan. After an inebriated private fell from a second-floor window and broke his hip, Ben asked Sergeant Harvey Kernan for a list of the members of the group that had arranged for the beer "with a view of withdrawing their permit."[15] That was not a popular idea and Kernan did not furnish the list, but he would show up on the list of Ben's accusers later in the year.

The busy summer season was in full swing. Still, the Koehlers usually ate lunch together at home. Curiously, on the days when Robinson visited Plum Island, he would decline Ben's lunch invitations, "saying he would not have time," but several times he showed up at the Koehler household in the middle of the meal. Robinson "would sit there until the boat went," according to Ben, and it was time for Robinson to return to Fishers Island.[16]

Robinson's behavior puzzled Ben, as did a visit by Sergeant Elvin Byers, who served with Frick and Kirkman. Byers, whom Ben barely knew, said he had come to pick up plants for a captain, yet Ben had already made arrangements for the captain to receive the plants.

Also in July, a former sergeant, James Ward, wrote Ben and asked to meet with him in New York City. "I told him that I had something very important to say to him," Ward later explained. "If he would come down to New York I would tell him what I had to say."[17]

Ben was going into Manhattan anyway so he agreed to the meeting, but Ward sent a telegram saying he had been called home and could not see Ben after all. As a result, Ben heard none of the "very important" information that Ward claimed to have.

How much Ward would have shared with Ben cannot be known, but the information was this: In July, at Frick's urging, Robinson had gone to New London to see Colonel Richmond Davis, district commander of several Long Island Sound forts, including Fort Terry, to report "that Major Koehler was a degenerate."[18] Robinson had no direct proof. He had a description of an allegation by a second lieutenant named Thomas Jones, a friend of Frick's, regarding inappropriate conduct by Ben, the details of which are not known. Conveniently, Jones had left Fort Terry and was not available for questioning.[19]

According to Davis, he reacted by telling Robinson, "I want you to get any information possible in connection with this report, it is a very serious matter and we should find out definitely about it but no action is possible unless we get absolute facts."[20]

If Ben had grabbed Frick's genitals at a dance in April 1913, or tried to kiss him in August 1912, as Frick would later say, those incidents would have come a lot closer to "absolute facts" than hearsay involving a departed officer—but in July 1913, Frick did not mention any improprieties he had experienced directly. Apparently, Frick was testing whether he could trigger an investigation of Ben without involving himself—but Davis wanted more than hearsay.

Davis's instructions to "get any information possible" likely accounted for Robinson's showing up at the Koehler household, as though Robinson's feigning unavailability would cause Ben to use his lunch hour for assignations with men rather than dining with his sister.

Robinson's role at this point is curious. He did not know Ben well. The two disagreed in their assessment of people, such as Barrett, and men that Robinson socialized with, such as Frick, were telling him rumors. Robinson may genuinely have believed the rumors. He may have thought that proving Ben's "degeneracy" would be as simple as surprising him during lunch.

It was not that simple. No information came back to Davis, who said nothing of the matter to Ben. Ben had no idea that others were calling him a degenerate and making that allegation to Davis, his new boss, Sidney Jordan having left Plum Island in May.[21]

Should Davis have alerted Ben? Perhaps. On the one hand, if Ben were a sexual predator and learned that people had gone to his superior to say so, he might have denied it to Davis, continued the predation, and acted in a more self-protective way, perhaps even threatening harm to anyone who spoke about it. Or he might have stopped the predation. If Davis thought there were any basis to the charges, including misinterpretation of innocent acts, the modern view would be that, at the very least, he had an obligation to discuss the issue with Ben and tell him to cease any objectionable behavior. On the other hand, if Ben was innocent, shouldn't Davis have asked him why men were saying those things? Warning Ben that he was being talked about as a degenerate would have allowed him to protect himself against false accusations. He could have avoided being alone with certain people—as adults who work with youth are often advised to do today—and he could have documented the issues he was having with various subordinates.

As it was, Ben was left in the dark. Somehow Ward, a former sergeant, knew that "there was an investigation going on" by Robinson,
yet Ben remained ignorant.[22] Had he not been so trusting of the
Army, and so self-confident, Ben might have done more to inquire,
such as following up with Ward after Ward canceled their meeting.

Ben did register the strangeness of Robinson coming to his house
unannounced, behavior that resumed in the fall when Robinson re-
appeared and sat so quietly that Sophia "said she could not understand why Captain Robinson came there because he is not an
interesting talker." It made no sense to Ben because their "official
business was transacted at other times."[23]

In October, Ward visited Plum Island and gave Ben another hint that
something was going on behind his back. According to Ben, Ward told
him he had overheard Frick and Sergeant Charles Moody discussing
him "on the boat" and "talking about plotting; he didn't say what."[24]
According to Ward, "I told him I heard something was coming off; I
would give him a chance."[25] In any event, Ben discounted Ward's talk
because Ward was working for a supply company and "immediately
following his telling me this he asked me to intercede with him in doing
business with the Post Exchange," which Ben declined to do.[26]

Again, it appears that Ben missed an opportunity to find out more.
Instead of probing what Ward was trying to tell him, he dismissed it,
believing he knew Ward's motives.

Perhaps there was a bit of arrogance underlying Ben's presumption
about Ward, but Ben had plenty else on his mind; for in October his
workload increased significantly. Colonel Davis began a new assignment, and the Eastern Department chose Ben to assume Davis's duties
until a permanent replacement could be named.[27] That meant Ben
now had responsibility for three other forts in addition to Fort Terry.
Having received this strong vote of confidence from above, Ben could
only hope that his promotion to lieutenant colonel was not far off.

BEN DID NOT BEGIN to learn how much more there was to Ward's
half-hearted attempts to warn him until five weeks after the Worcesters'

party. The year 1913 had begun with a visit by Sophia to see Louis in Puerto Rico, and it was ending with a trip by Louis to New York. Ben left Plum Island on Friday, December 5, to see Louis for the weekend.

On Sunday, after saying goodbye to Louis, Ben took the train from Manhattan to New London. During the three-hour ride, he had plenty of time to reflect on how fate had taken two Iowa brothers and placed each in charge of an island. As the differences between Plum Island and Puerto Rico well demonstrated, islands' detachment from the mainland allowed them to develop in unique ways. Some of the differences had obvious sources, such as climate and currents. Less noticeable causes could be understood after scientific study, but life is complex, and much of what makes populations of plants and animals—including humans—on one island different from those on another defies understanding.

Ben was about to experience this. He was about to see what shocking result could be brought about by a unique mixture of egos, malice, and masculine insecurity in a subpopulation of humans living on a North Atlantic island.

Ben boarded the two o'clock steamer at the New London dock. The boat was due to arrive at Fort Terry at four o'clock, but first it made a stop at Fort Wright on Fishers Island.

There, surrounded by water and very far from Iowa, a colonel of the U.S. Army placed Major Benjamin M. Koehler under arrest.[28]

# CHAPTER FIFTEEN

# A Hurried Investigation

T**HE PRESUMPTION OF INNOCENCE** offered Ben cold comfort as he
stood facing Colonel Stephen Mills on the Fishers Island dock. As
the winter sun began its descent over the Sound, Mills told Ben "that
he had various charges against me of an immoral nature and asked
me if I wanted to resign," virtually announcing a verdict and
sentence.[1]

The Sixth Amendment of the U.S. Constitution provides criminal
defendants the right "to be informed of the nature and cause of the
accusation" against them, but it was different in the military—and to
a large extent still is. Another section of the Constitution makes it that
way, giving Congress the power "To make Rules for the Government
and Regulation of the land and naval Forces."[2]

Yet Congress had not made any rule banning homosexual overtures in the military when Ben felt his world quake on December 7,
1913. Rather, military officials were accustomed to applying the broad
provisions Congress had adopted more than a century earlier, proscribing "conduct unbecoming an officer and gentleman" and "prejudicial to good order and discipline," as they saw fit. The acquittal in
Louis Koehler's case was a rare exception.

And so, when Mills confronted Ben, he did not specify "the nature
and cause of the accusation" even when Ben asked "if he could give
me some idea of what it was."[3] Mills simply proposed that Ben make a

quick exit from the Army and leave the only life he had known since entering West Point twenty years earlier.

Ben replied that he had no intention of resigning—an offer, unjust as it was, that likely would not have been made to an enlisted man. Rebuffed, Mills asked for Ben's sidearm and told him that "he had authority to place me in arrest, which he did, and I asked him to notify Major Moses that he would be in command and I took the boat and came back to Fort Terry."[4]

Ben's life and work were so intertwined that his thoughts went immediately to the sudden chain-of-command gap at Fort Terry. Who would fill the gap on short notice? Ben assumed it would be his old friend and classmate, Andy Moses, the man who had stood a few feet away from him in the West Point graduation photo published by *The New York Times*.

Though neither Ben nor Moses had yet fulfilled the *Times*'s "embryo general" prophecy, both had done equally well—until now. Like Ben, Moses was a major in the Coast Artillery Corps. In March 1913, the Army had given him an assignment similar to Ben's, to bring discipline to Fort Wright. Remarkably, after sixteen years of very different postings, the two West Point friends found themselves working as commanders of coastal garrisons ten miles apart on the same steamer run. For nine months, Ben and Moses had seen more of each other than since the academy, but their satisfying parity and renewed camaraderie came to a sudden halt with Ben's arrest. Now, until the Army made other arrangements, Moses would be in charge of two forts, not one.

Ben lived in limbo in his house, his routines ruptured, not knowing the details of the charges against him. He would not let that sort of uncertainty hang over men of lesser rank, as he had shown when he ordered the release of a private, Edward Shanley, who had been detained in the guardhouse on orders of a lieutenant for more than twenty-four hours without charges being lodged.[5]

Ben's home was more comfortable than a metal cell in the guardhouse, but he was a prisoner nonetheless, and far longer than a day had passed without his knowing what he was accused of doing. All he knew was that a powerful man—the inspector general of the Army's Eastern Department—had traveled from Governors Island to accuse him of immoral acts, ask for his resignation, and arrest him.

Ben would soon learn that while he was in New York with his brother, Mills had been on Plum Island conducting an investigation, the Eastern Department having chosen a time when it was known that Ben would be off the island to question his subordinates.

Mills believed what he heard. After interviews with Ben's accusers, he did not return to Governors Island to discuss the evidence with the top brass who had dispatched him to Plum Island. Mills did not think it necessary to ascertain the accusers' discipline histories or check their stories against a calendar to see if Ben had even been on the island on the dates given. Nor did he think it necessary to hear what Ben had to say. There was no discussion with officers who saw him every day, who would have told Mills that the accusers were some of the people that Ben most often reprimanded. There was no call to Colonel Davis to ask why he had dismissed the statements made to him in the summer.

There was, it can only be said, a rush to judgment: After two days of interviews, Mills had decided that Ben was guilty. Mills probably requested Ben's resignation without telling him why because Mills believed that Ben had committed the acts described.

Who was Mills and how did he have so much power? A member of the old guard, he attended West Point when Ben was still a boy idolizing Grant. He had served as chief of staff in the Philippines, whose people he described in a 1906 essay as a "treacherous, barbarous foe."[6] Now he was one step away from holding a top job, inspector general for the entire Army.

Mills was a strong defender of the status quo, as he showed in his 1906 essay, the point of which was to blast a West Point professor who recommended that the Army, no longer able to rely on the frontier to provide training and adventure, should make adjustments to attract and retain talented individuals. Army recruitment was fine, responded Mills. The professor was out of touch, and how dare he make comments so offensive to the enlisted man? Replying to Mills's attack, the professor wrote that he was "much impressed by its discourtesy and its violence."[7]

Ben might have used the same words to describe how Mills treated him. He had to have wondered whether the case of Samuel Silverman had predisposed Mills against him, harking back to when Ben worked for William Kenly. One time, Ben accepted a man he considered "exceptionally intelligent," who spoke French and German and "understood what he read" in English, but the recruitment depot disagreed and rejected the man for inadequate language abilities. Ben defended his decision, saying the applicant's weakness was simply poor pronunciation, but the depot prevailed.[8]

What happened regarding Samuel Silverman was quite different. Silverman, a former private, had sought to reenlist but the discharge certificate he presented to Ben bore a handwritten note: "should not be reenlisted owing to hopeless deficiency in target practice." Nonetheless, Silverman told Ben he had been assured that the notation would not bar his readmission.[9]

Ben valued shooting skills as much as anyone, but there were plenty of non-artillery jobs in the Army, and he regarded that sort of "mutilation" of a discharge certificate as a violation of the rules.[10] Plus, Silverman could have lost or destroyed the certificate and no one would have ever known about the comment.[11] Ben referred Silverman to the depot at Fort Slocum, but the staff there saw the notation and rejected him.

Pressing the issue, Ben wrote to the Army personnel office in Washington to ask if there were any records in Silverman's file that would cut against his reenlistment. The answer came back no, so Ben sent Silverman back to Fort Slocum. Again, the depot rejected him, and a depot officer reported the matter, requesting instructions on how to proceed.[12]

Ben refused to back down. Asked to explain himself, he asserted that "injustice was done to this soldier" by the note and "a further injustice has been done this soldier in rejecting him at Fort Slocum."[13] Ben said his actions had Kenly's approval.[14]

The adjutant general, Fred Ainsworth, rebuked Ben, saying that

"this whole transaction was marked by a suppression of facts that mis-
led this office and that cannot be too strongly condemned." If Ben
wanted to challenge the alteration of certificates, he should have presented the "facts fully and clearly." Not having done so, Ainsworth
wrote, was "reprehensible."[15]

Ben's defense of his actions revealed strong self-confidence, but-
tressed by his close relationship with Kenly, who afterward praised
Ben and recommended his promotion to major. Kenly wrote to Ben
that "the zeal and interest you have shown in your official work as well
as your performance of it have at all times been of the most satisfac-
tory and commendable character."[16] The Army listened to Kenly, not
Ainsworth, and promoted Ben in less than a year.

Ironically, the man who came down so hard on Ben became one of
Leonard Wood's targets. Wood helped engineer Ainsworth's depar-
ture in 1912, but not before Ainsworth's criticism was placed in Ben's
file and printed on his "efficiency reports."[17] Not only that, but the
Silverman incident had occurred while Mills was chief of staff in the
Eastern Department.

In the military, behavior viewed as "zeal" by some could look like
defiance to others. Ben had purposely taken a risk to prove a point,
suggesting he thought he knew better than the men in Washington
about unfair practices and rule violations. Perhaps it was that self-re-
gard, buoyed by regular praise from his immediate superiors, that
had kept Ben from seeing the quiet mutiny building around him at
Fort Terry.[18]

THE INSPECTOR GENERAL'S OFFICE recognized the sensitivity of alleged officer misconduct—for both the officer and the Army—and
had uncovered some instances of large-scale bad behavior at various
posts, including embezzlement and corruption.

What brought the inspector general's attention to Fort Terry was
unprecedented: alleged homoerotic behavior by a domestic post's
commanding officer with a strong war record and long service.[19] The
unusual nature of the case explained why Mills considered his involve-

ment necessary, but even if "discourtesy" and "violence" were not reg-ular features of Mills's temperament, it was a shock for Ben to be confronted by such a stern representative of the Army hierarchy on his way home from a rare visit with Louis.

Ben learned right away that the inspector general's sensitivity to-ward officers only went so far. He would have to wait until he was summoned to Governors Island by the Eastern Department's com-mander, Major General Thomas Barry, to learn the details of the "im-moral acts" for which he was being asked to resign. That is when Ben learned the identity of the men who had complained—or, as Sophia would describe them, the "scoundrels."

# CHAPTER SIXTEEN

# Long Walk from Quartermaster Dock

THE RIVERS OF BEN Koehler's adolescence had flowed in one direction, unlike the currents around islands, which moved in more unpredictable ways. Yet even a "Nebraska boy" could see from the ferry as it cut through Buttermilk Channel that Governors Island was no wild place.

Unlike Plum Island, where the shoreline remained natural, encircled by boulders, bluffs, and sandy beaches, Governors Island lay within a newly built wall of cement bricks intended to block waves. On this island, man tried to tame nature. The vast quantities of water being funneled into narrow places did not make for a stable environment—open sea to harbor, harbor to channels, channels to rivers—and yet many humans had decided to live where those water bodies intersected. Hence, the seawall.

The same geologic event created both Governors Island and Plum Island—the retreat of the last ice sheet—and the islands shared a similar history of European occupation. In 1637, the Dutch governor of New Netherland had obtained a deed to Governors Island from the Manahatas tribe in exchange for two ax heads, a string of beads, and a handful of nails.[1]

After that, the islands' fates diverged. Plum Island went to seed—literally, as a place for farming—while Governors Island became a trophy for the rich and powerful. The most centrally located island south of Manhattan, and at sixty-nine acres one of the largest, Governors Island offered splendid views of what came to be known as upper New York Bay. The island served as a reserve for the British governor once the British displaced the Dutch as the rulers of New York.

Time brought new rulers, and after the Revolutionary War, when tensions heated up once again between the former colonists and Great Britain, engineer Jonathan Williams of the U.S. Army Corps designed a star-shaped fort in the center of Governors Island, replacing a deteriorating Revolutionary War earthen fort. With a dry moat and twenty-six-foot-high walls of granite and brick, the imposing Fort Jay (then Fort Columbus) was completed in 1809, yet none of its many cannons fired in the War of 1812. Like Fort Terry, the value of Fort Jay and the two other Governors Island forts—South Battery and Castle Williams—was said to be their deterrent effect.

During the Civil War, Castle Williams housed Confederate prisoners. Deaths approached 20 percent due to overcrowded cells and primitive sanitary conditions. Meanwhile, Confederate officers roamed with relative freedom within Fort Jay. Many knew their captors, having been their military academy schoolmates. Inside Fort Jay, honor and class trumped enemy status.

By the time Ben disembarked in December 1913, Governors Island was an administrative center more than a military one. Castle Williams still housed prisoners, mostly deserters, whose escapes supplied the newspapers with colorful copy. The shape and size of the island had changed, too. Using nearly five million cubic yards of landfill from tunnels being excavated in Brooklyn and Manhattan for the new subway system, engineers had more than doubled the size of Governors Island.

That winter morning, the walk from Quartermaster Dock up the hill to headquarters must have seemed unusually long to Ben, the clicks of his heels on the cobblestones sounding ominously like a countdown to a reckoning. With all he had dreamed of and worked for hanging in the balance, he may well have wondered whether he had more in common with the prisoners in Castle Williams than the officers whose homes lined Colonels Row.

. . .

GENERAL BARRY BELIEVED THE evidence against Ben was strong.
That was Mills's conclusion, and Barry had been relying on Mills's
advice for more than a year, ever since Barry had been relieved as superintendent of West Point and tapped for the prestigious job of leading the Eastern Department. Every day Barry and his family woke up
on Governors Island in a large brick house overlooking Buttermilk
Channel. The house had a white Greek Revival roof, polished wood
floors, and a central staircase curving to the second floor. Its previous
occupants had been Leonard Wood and his wife.[2]

Wood now worked in Washington, having been appointed chief of
staff by President Taft. Barry reported to Wood, but his relationship
with Mills went much further back. Classmates at West Point, Barry
and Mills had known each other for forty years when they were presented with the shocking charges coming out of Fort Terry. Barry also
knew Ben, and he had approved of Ben's assuming Colonel Davis's
duties while a replacement was sought. It was a difficult spot for Barry,
and he asked his chief of staff, William Haan, and an officer from Fort
Totten, Edwin Sarratt, to question Ben about the charges.

"I didn't see the charges, but they would ask me whether I ever
knew a certain man, giving his name," according to Ben, who said that
Sarratt and Haan had a "little memorandum" on which they based
their questions.[3]

The meeting lasted two hours. No lawyer accompanied Ben, but he
did not need an attorney to understand one fact clearly: The only
commissioned officers among the accusers were Worcester and Frick.
Just about everyone else making a claim of unwanted touching served
under them or socialized with them. They were, as Sophia would
write, members of a "clique." Ben and Sophia knew that, but Barry,
Haan, Sarratt, and Mills did not.

In addition to their claims of groping, some of the men who spoke
to Mills had portrayed Ben and Sophia's home as a place where Ben
invited soldiers to drink, fraternize, and, they implied, engage in sexual relations.

Ben denied the allegations, but it was one man's word against the word of many others. How could he prove anything sitting in a room on Governors Island without dates or details? Just as Mills had done, Sarratt and Haan asked Ben to consider resigning, and Barry told Ben the same thing.[4] They all mentioned their concern about publicity if Ben did not leave quietly.

"They put it in that way," Ben later said, "that there was nothing to be gained; if I won it would be the publicity and if I did not the publicity would hurt my family, and they thought as long as I was a bachelor that I ought to consult my family or their interests."[5]

Why did it matter that Ben was unmarried, and why was his bachelor status called out? Wasn't the most important issue regarding Ben's resignation the impact it would have on Ben himself, whether or not he had a conventional family as Barry, Haan, and Sarratt did? Would each of those men have asked his wife to decide whether he should give up the profession he loved, in the prime of his career, without an opportunity to rebut the accusations against him? And while it was true that publicity would be embarrassing for all concerned, if Ben was acquitted, the publicity would be far worse for the Army, which was the employer of multiple people who in that event would be found to have lied.

The choice presented to Ben made sense only if the accused man knew he was guilty. Then, he might deserve to lose everything for which he had worked and should not drag his family through a public disgrace. Then, the man ought to give great weight to the interests of his spouse, or in Ben's case, his siblings. Yet Ben was proclaiming his innocence. It may be inferred that Barry, Haan, and Sarratt, like Mills, believed otherwise.

Military law might salute the presumption of innocence, but nothing prevented senior officers from believing that Ben was guilty. They had seen McKinley depicted as short, paunchy, old, and female back when he was accused of insufficient manliness for opposing war with Spain. Now, a short, paunchy man in his forties was sitting in front of them accused of a much more scandalous kind of unmanliness. A less than virile appearance did not help either McKinley or Ben, but it had been understood that McKinley's accusers were operating in the arena of politics, whereas Ben's accusers were specific people, specific *Army men*, telling of acts they said actually happened.

Come 2017 and 2018, the #MeToo movement and hearings on the nomination of Brett Kavanaugh to the U.S. Supreme Court would make sexual predation a household topic in America, and some Kavanaugh defenders would claim that untruthful allegations of sexual misconduct were being used for political purposes. Indeed, the planting of doubts about the credibility of *women* as accusers of men grew throughout the twentieth and twenty-first centuries, requiring state legislatures to intervene by passing rape shield laws and spawning a field of analytical philosophy known as testimonial injustice. By 2019, the idea that an accuser of sexual misconduct might be lying was so topical, even in a homosexual context, that *The New York Times* reported on a male artist's lawsuit alleging that his ex-lover was attempting to extort money by "threatening to portray their consensual sexual relationship as a case of sexual harassment."[6]

It must be remembered that in 1913, such a backdrop of suspicion about sexual accusers did not exist, especially when the accuser purported to uphold heterosexual values against an alleged homosexual. After World War I, in 1919, Sherwood Anderson would publish a story about an unmarried teacher beloved by his students who was beaten and run out of town after a "half-witted boy of the school . . . imagined unspeakable things" and made "[s]trange, hideous accusations" against him.[7] In 1934, Lillian Hellman would write a play about a teenage girl who made false claims about "unnatural" acts by two women who ran a school, resulting in one's suicide and the other's broken engagement.[8]

No similarly popular literary treatment comes to mind from pre–World War I America questioning the veracity of an accusation of homosexual advances. Historian Jonathan Katz has reported on an early legal case, in 1846, in which a police officer said he was wrongly accused of sexual advances by a man he arrested.[9] After a hearing, the police officer lost the case and his job. A 1910 textbook on criminal law included "threatened prosecution for the crime of sodomy" as a criminal tactic a person might use against another, describing a case in which one man threatened another with prosecution for sodomy if money was not paid.[10]

For the most part, however, the Army was in new territory. The Articles of War listed rape as a crime but only in times of war, and there was no mention of sodomy or attempted sodomy. While the *Manual for Courts-Martial* recommended dishonorable discharge and five years' hard labor as punishment for a soldier convicted under a state sodomy law, Ben was not accused of having had anal or oral sex with anyone.[11] He was accused of groping and making lewd comments, and no policy determinations regarding those acts had been made as to the boundaries between legal and illegal conduct, and no rules had been promulgated to curb arbitrary decision-making. It was unclear whether Ben's alleged acts were considered a problem in and of themselves—because of assumed impacts on the victims and Army morale and discipline—or because they indicated a man *acting* like a homosexual, who might therefore *be* a homosexual, contrary to prevailing standards of masculinity that posited heterosexuality as "normal."

British physician Havelock Ellis wrote in the early 1900s that same-sex attraction, which he called "inversion," "is a psychological and medico-legal problem so full of interest that we need not fear to face it, and so full of grave social actuality that we are bound to face it."[12] Other doctors may have agreed, especially ones interested in the new field of psychology, but there is no evidence that the Army undertook to "face" the issue of homosexuality by seeking to determine, in any methodical and thoughtful way, whether a man's sexual interest in other men truly presented a "problem" in the context of military service, rendering him less brave, less honorable, or less efficient than a heterosexual man, and if so, why, when, and how.

At the local level, around the same time that Ben was being asked to resign, anti-vice crusaders in New York City were relying on "a patchwork of laws against vagrancy, disorderly conduct, solicitation, obscenity, prostitution, and being a public nuisance" to harass and prosecute people whose sexual practices they wanted to stop.[13] Like immigration officials, the anti-vice campaigners were stuck with old laws that did not line up with their present moral outrage. But if the broad wording of the Articles of War offered the Army more flexibility on the surface, below the surface was a most uncomfortable situation for Barry, Haan, and Sarratt: Ben's case pitted presumptively credible men against a man who until very recently had been considered enormously credible, too. Ben was one of them—or had been.

The pressure placed on Ben to resign instead of defending himself showed a paramount concern with fixing a problem quickly and avoiding adverse publicity by an institution that placed a strong premium on conformity. Unlike the Bureau of Immigration, the Army was an actual institution with an image to protect, such that "If the Bureau of Immigration failed to detect perverts, it might look ineffective; when the military failed, it looked queer."[14]

The reaction of the Eastern Department's senior officers to the conundrum Ben presented—an excellent officer by objective measures now said to be a sexual deviant—reflected an unspoken and largely unexamined discomfort with homosexuality that would take many forms over the course of the twentieth century, reaching an apex of ugliness and hostility after World War II[15] before morphing into the 1990s policy of Don't Ask, Don't Tell, which persisted until 2011.[16]

The problem in Ben's case was that the "telling" had been done only by others. Ben denied that he had made advances toward any man, but in Haan's and Sarratt's reference to Ben's bachelor status, one can discern that his not having married was perceived as doing its own telling, silently admitting what Ben verbally denied. Ben's marital status was the same it had been since he graduated West Point in 1897. What had changed was the cultural importance placed on marriage as a signifier of a man's heterosexuality.

Rather than wait for a court-martial, Ben offered a strategic compromise. He agreed to resign, but only after a leave of absence. He asked for two months so that he would have time to see Louis, his most important confidant, in Puerto Rico. Ben was appearing to go along, but it was actually a form of resistance for he believed he could revoke the resignation and request a trial before the leave ended.[17]

That evening, in the apartment he had once shared with Kenly, Ben wrote two documents: an application for leave and a resignation to take effect "upon expiration of so much leave."[18] He submitted them the next day, December 14, and Barry approved the arrangement.

Having bought himself some time, though little peace, Ben left Governors Island for the long trip back to Plum Island, that wild place where Sophia had expected to be happy. There, in the quiet house he shared with his sister, which others were now portraying as a meeting place for homosexual liaisons, Ben waited for the Army's next move.

CHAPTER SEVENTEEN

# *A March, then a Brawl*

O THERS AT FORT TERRY also waited to see what the Army would
do, none more so than Philip Worcester.

It was gutsy for a new captain to have sought an audience with the
Eastern Department's leadership to assert that the major to whom he
reported was a serial groper of men. Now Ben had been arrested and it
was the talk of the post.[1] Worcester knew that some officers were shocked.
He knew that others, such as Frick, Ellis, and Robinson, were not.

A few weeks earlier, on the day before Thanksgiving, when many
people were leaving Fort Terry and his departure would not raise
notice, Worcester had traveled to Governors Island to join Robinson
for a meeting with Haan. Providing what Davis had said was lacking,
Worcester claimed to have personal knowledge of Ben's sexual interest in men, saying Ben had grabbed his genitals at a party. Worcester
maintained that others would tell of similar experiences.

This time, the Army opened an investigation immediately, sending
Mills to Plum Island the week after Thanksgiving. To anyone who
asked, Mills said he was looking into a recent fight at the officers'
club.[2] Ben had closed the club as a result, which was an unpopular
decision, but Worcester's issues with Ben ran far deeper.

One of the most significant disputes arose from a march that began on October 1, when the six Fort Terry companies sailed to Fort
Mansfield on Napatree Point, a sandy spit of land forming the south-

western part of Rhode Island near the border with Connecticut. The men were to hike forty-three miles over the course of two weeks.

October was a beautiful month to be walking along the Rhode Island shore. The soldiers passed bushes turning gold and dunes covered with beach grass swaying in the breeze. The surf of Block Island Sound rolled in, calm one day, rough the next, the mounds of moving pebbles sounding like billiard balls on the break every time a wave washed over them. There were shorebirds, monarch butterflies, and unusual saltwater ponds. Further landward, oaks and maples displayed hues of crimson, orange, and yellow.

On the last day of the march, October 14, many of the men had something on their minds besides fall foliage. After returning to Fort Mansfield, they found the energy to walk into Watch Hill, a seaside resort where a soldier could buy a beer—or several. There was a "general drunk that day, nearly all intoxicated."[3] Two brawls broke out involving Edison Kirkman, Worcester's first sergeant.[4]

Worcester intended to mete out punishment back at Fort Terry, but first his own actions came into question. Seas were choppy during the return trip, and Worcester's company, riding in one of the less stable vessels, docked at New Harbor, more protected than North Dock but further from the buildings. After disembarking, Worcester told a sergeant to "march the rest of the men back to barracks" while he "got in the Post Exchange wagon and rode up to the house."[5] Ben later stated that he reprimanded Worcester for being the only officer who did not march with his company to the barracks.[6]

Worcester would claim he had "no recollection" of the reprimand, though he recalled quite well Ben's disagreement with him over the proper punishment for the fights at Watch Hill.[7] Worcester termed the first fight "just a rough house" and accepted Kirkman's statement that he had "not entered into it at all."[8] Worcester brought no charges against Kirkman but ordered three privates to appear before a hearing officer on summary charges, less serious than a court-martial. The men lost pay and the right to leave the post for three months. Kirkman was the main witness against them—a lying witness, according to one of the privates punished.[9]

Regarding the second fight, Worcester wanted Private Edward Shanley tried by general court-martial "[b]ecause I had the charges of disobedience against the first Sergeant in addition to abusive language and assault on Sergeant Kirkman in the case of Shanley."[10]

Shanley denied that he was to blame for the second fight. He said Kirkman disliked him for reasons Shanley did not understand, and while everyone else was getting intoxicated on the last day of the march, Kirkman "passed the remark that he was looking for us, and stayed sober enough to get us."[11] Shanley said that Kirkman brandished a knife, and Shanley punched him.

Ben told Worcester he thought summary charges were sufficient for Shanley.[12] So did Major Moses at Fort Wright, whom Ben consulted when Worcester challenged his decision.[13] In the end, Shanley did face summary charges and not a court-martial. Kirkman again testified as the main witness, and in November, Shanley received the same punishment as the men in the first fight. The outcome left Worcester angry and he began insinuating to others that Ben was protecting Shanley due to a personal relationship.[14]

Worcester may have looked up to Ben during the summer of 1907 at Fort Monroe, but in the ensuing six years, Worcester had developed into a different sort of man than Ben.[15] Whether it was riding in a wagon instead of marching with his men, challenging his superior's decisions, or giving raucous parties, Worcester's assertiveness reflected newer ideas about manhood, "defin[ing] his identity not just in the workplace but through modes of enjoyment and self-fulfillment outside of it," in contrast to the older standard of "self-restraint and self-denial."[16]

Yet Worcester held old-fashioned military credentials, too, which enhanced his credibility with higher-ups. He had a Silver Star from the Battle of Bud Dajo, in contrast to Austin Frick, who lacked combat experience and a West Point degree.[17] Indeed, by Ben's standards, Frick showed himself to be a coward during a mining exercise at sea when a private under Frick's control became entangled in cables and drowned. Ben said he did not blame Frick for failing to save the private but for failing to try. "I told him if my dog fell overboard I would try to save him," was how Ben put it.[18]

In the midst of the dispute over Shanley, the Worcesters held their Halloween party, where Worcester not only cross-dressed and acted out lesbian-like behavior with Lieutenant Smith but also performed a skit with an ensign named Montgomery from the naval base in Newport. "I went in front of young Montgomery," Worcester would recount, "who was a sailor and did the motions of a hitchkick in front of him and he got up and sat down alongside of me."[19]

It is unclear whether the skit was intended to portray flirtation between a sailor and a woman or between a sailor and a man acting like a woman. Why Worcester chose to dress as a woman is also unknown. He did not say why he did so, though he suggested that he coordinated the idea of female costumes with Smith.[20] Smith was a friend of Ben's who would later strongly support his innocence, so if Worcester sought to mock Ben as effeminate through his choice of costume, Smith almost certainly did not share that objective.[21] Of course, Smith and Worcester may have had different motives for their female attire, or no conscious motive at all. Along with Captain Ellis's appearance as the cross-dressing Buster Brown, they may simply have been reflecting the era's preoccupation with sexuality and gender roles.

In the early 1900s, newspapers in America reported "with unusual frequency the arrests of men who dress in women's clothing and women who dress in men's clothing," observed a German sociologist. Some of the stories were "quite remarkable," the sociologist noted, such as one about a "man who simply could not stop dressing as a woman [and] was forced to wear a sign on his waist with the legend: 'I am a man.'"[22]

Men at Fort Terry had other reasons besides press accounts to know about the gay subculture. In Manhattan and Brooklyn, "fairies," sailors, and male sex workers congregated along the waterfront, places an Army officer might pass on a day of leave or on his way to take a ferry to Governors Island.[23]

When Worcester boarded that ferry right before Thanksgiving, his irritation with his boss had only increased since the Shanley dispute and closure of the officers' club. Something else had happened that Worcester saw could affect his future: a possible academic ethics violation.

Worcester might party hard but he also had a strong intellectual side. Before West Point, he had studied at the Massachusetts Institute of Technology, and he had returned to West Point as a teacher six years after graduating. This was thanks to Louis Koehler's foe, Hugh Scott, who was then the West Point superintendent and unsuccessfully recommended Worcester for a teaching position in 1909 and again, successfully, in 1910.[24] Worcester joined the chemistry department in August 1910, the same month that Barry relieved Scott as superintendent.[25]

It was far more pleasant to teach at West Point than toil and drill as a cadet: more control inside the classroom, more freedom outside of it. The Army gave Worcester time to savor that freedom, renewing his assignment for three years. Worcester married Mabel in November 1912 and she joined him on campus, but when classes ended in June 1913, so did his teaching job.[26] The Army promoted him to captain, assigned him to the Coast Artillery Corps, and ordered him to trade the verdant Hudson Valley for the sandy soils of eastern Long Island.

If Worcester hoped to return to West Point, it would not help if he was reported for plagiarism, which Ben had threatened to do just days after the Shanley dispute. Ben made this threat after being told by Captain Hudson Patten that in a military tactics course Patten was teaching, Worcester had not provided his own answer to a hypothetical problem but had copied from a textbook.[27] Ben called it "the same thing as cheating" and said he would report the matter to Colonel Davis's successor.[28]

That was when Worcester sprang into action, speaking to Robinson, lining up the meeting with Haan, and proceeding to Governors Island. Worcester must have felt confident that he would be well-received by the men in charge, having spent "considerable time" on Governors Island in 1912, and having impressed Barry, now commanding general, as a "very good instructor of cadets" when Barry headed West Point.[29]

Events unfolded so fast that Ben never had the chance to report the alleged plagiarism.[30] Davis's post remained unfilled when Mills arrested Ben, a mere eleven days after Worcester went to Governors Island. Now, Ben had his own future to worry about. His problem was not hypothetical, like the one in the tactics course, and there was no approved solution from which to copy—not for Ben, not for his family, and not for the U.S. government.

# CHAPTER EIGHTEEN

# *Orders*

S HOULD HE INSIST ON a trial or resign? Those were Ben's options after he returned to Plum Island. How quickly and radically his life had changed.

In the next two months, Ben planned to travel to Puerto Rico to obtain Louis's advice, stopping first to see his siblings in the Midwest. He and Sophia started to pack.

According to one press report, the telegram arrived as Ben headed to the dock, his belongings loaded in a wagon.[1] Whether or not the timing involved such drama, Ben received word on December 18 that there would be no leave of absence and no opportunity for him to make a choice between resigning and standing trial. The choice had been made for him—in Washington. He was now forbidden to leave the island and slated to be court-martialed. General Barry had been overruled.

Barry and the general's family also received a shock in the form of another order issued the same day. It reassigned Barry not to Washington, where he had expected to succeed Wood as chief of staff, but all the way to Asia, where he would take command of the Philippine Department in early March.[2] The ink dry on those orders, Wood signed one more, directing Louis and his wife to vacate Casa Blanca in Puerto Rico by December 28. A fort on the Mexican front would be their next home.[3]

Revenge against Louis Koehler united all of these actions. Wood was punishing Louis not only by cutting short his assignment in Puerto Rico but also by directing the court-martial of his brother.[4] Barry needed to be sent halfway around the world because he had shown sympathy for Ben and might do so again. The stated rationale for Barry's reassignment, that he had seen less foreign duty than other generals, was quickly challenged as false.[5]

For the Army men, orders were orders. Daniel Anthony Jr., now a member of Congress as well as a publisher and attorney, felt less restraint. He protested Wood's action involving Louis, saying the transfer order "was most abruptly and inconsiderately made" and caused his sister much distress.

Louis, one of the last people to see Ben before his arrest, had returned to Puerto Rico in mid-December after his trip to New York only to receive a cable from Ben saying he was in trouble.[6] Louis boarded a return ship and did not learn of his transfer to Texas until he arrived in Manhattan.[7] The order had been mailed to Puerto Rico, where Maude "nearly worked herself into a condition of nervous prostration packing their effects to get ready to move in the short time allowed," according to Anthony.[8]

"Now Mr. Secretary here is the real point to all this," Anthony continued. "Major Koehler was in this country on leave and called at the department about the 10th of December. If a change in commanding officers in Porto Rico, was at that time contemplated, and it was in fact then under discussion, he should have then been notified."

The link between Ben's case and Louis's transfer was clear to Anthony, who observed that "[t]he order was issued on the heels of the order to try the Major's brother at Ft. Terry."[9]

On December 26, Louis told a lieutenant colonel what was obvious: Even if he immediately sailed back to the Caribbean, he would not make it in time to move to Texas by December 28.[10] Wood then delayed the date of the transfer to January 15, ending after seventeen months an assignment that Louis thought would last four years.[11]

At least the brief delay allowed Louis to visit his siblings on Plum

Island, where he counseled his younger brother not to be afraid to stand up for himself and assert his innocence.[12] Louis had done that in 1906. Ben could only hope that the result would be as favorable for him as it had been for Louis.

# CHAPTER NINETEEN

# *All Hail Washington*

WHILE LOUIS MADE HIS way to New York to help his brother, their siblings in Nebraska also learned of Ben's arrest. The timing was terrible, right before Christmas. People's minds were elsewhere. They wanted to be with their families, not react to a sudden problem and confer about strategy.

In Washington, officials in the Woodrow Wilson administration were preparing to observe the president's first Christmas in office—a bad time for an Army sex scandal, though no time would have been favorable for appeals on behalf of an allegedly homosexual Army commander. Economic issues, not individual rights, were the first-year priorities of Wilson, a Virginian who had been president of Princeton University and then served as New Jersey governor.[1]

The people who tried to come to Ben's aid did the best they could under the circumstances. A Missouri senator, James Reed, asked for a slowing down of the proceedings, which, to be sure, had moved along at a fast clip.[2] Reed served on the Senate's banking committee and socialized with Henry Koehler, who had come a long way from the Blue Hill National Bank and now worked as a senior officer at Kansas City's oldest bank.

Reed addressed his letter to Wood, a holdover from the Taft administration who had vastly more inside knowledge of Washington than many members of the new administration, and certainly more knowl-

edge about military matters than the new secretary of war, a lawyer
from New Jersey named Lindley Garrison.

Wood responded to Reed in a conciliatory way on Saturday, December 27:

> I have just received your letter concerning the Koehler case, and have
> also had a telegram from the Secretary of War on the matter.
> The Secretary directed that the proceedings be delayed until I hear
> from him, which will be done.[3]

The same day, Wood wrote the Army's administrative head that
Garrison wished to "delay convening the court until further orders,"[4]
although Garrison was not in Washington at the time. He was spending
his first Christmas as secretary of war in the largest reinforced
concrete building in the world, a hotel in Atlantic City, New Jersey.

Wood had called Garrison in the morning, the first of several calls
that day concerning Ben.[5] Wood was known for self-discipline and
long hours, so it would not have struck his colleagues as odd that he
was working on the Saturday after Christmas. The Koehler case was
shocking, and now that Christmas was over, important people were
reacting. Others did not need an additional explanation for Wood's
intense focus on the case, such as the unfinished business with Louis
Koehler, and likely few people in Washington recalled the details of
that seven-year-old case. The newsworthy aspect had been Roosevelt's
rescue of Wood, not much else—unless you were Leonard Wood and
remembered the whole drawn-out affair, especially the last name of
the officer who instigated it.

At the end of the day on December 27, Wood wrote Garrison a
letter marked "Confidential" about the new Koehler case. Even though
Wood had revoked Ben's leave of absence and slated Ben for court-martial, Ben's resignation was still being debated as potentially best for
the Army. Wood argued for a trial:

> I am afraid that if we should permit a case of this kind, which has been
> formally acted upon by Colonel Mills, the department inspector, rec-

ommending trial, to go without trial, even though the department commander recommended resignation for the good of the service, we should find ourselves in a sea of trouble afterward.

Papers like the "Appeal to Reason" are bound to get hold of cases of this kind; and it would give them abundant ammunition with which to continue their attack, which has been to the effect that the autocratic officer strives to protect those of his own kind, but has no bowels of compassion for the enlisted men.[6]

Wood's clever rhetoric may have come across as reasonable and persuasive to Garrison, but it was highly misleading. What, exactly, did Wood mean by "a case of this kind," a phrase he used twice? He could not have meant all cases in which the inspector recommended trial, or, more narrowly, all such cases against officers, because then Wood would be arguing for no independent judgment by the Army and executive branch, which was what had saved Wood from a trial. Nor could he have meant a case involving alleged sexual overtures by a post commander against subordinates. It was simply untrue that Ben's case was representative of many the secretary of war would have to deal with, such that he should set a strong precedent.

More likely, what Wood truly meant by "a case of this kind" was any case involving a man named Koehler, which interpretation he disguised through a generalization that converted Ben from a person into a vague concept. In a few months, Garrison would write in *Harper's Weekly* that all Army personnel matters were "of serious consequence to the individuals concerned . . . and are entitled to be considered and decided strictly upon their merits"—but here was Wood urging Garrison from the outset not to apply that approach to Ben Koehler.[7]

The second disservice Wood did to Ben was to place him in the category of the "autocratic officer" with no "compassion for the enlisted men." Any degree of research would have shown that Ben was the antitype of the autocratic officer portrayed by Wood. Ben was known "for a square deal," according to one private.[8] He overruled officers when he thought they were not treating enlisted men fairly, as he did with Worcester regarding Shanley's punishment, and the time he released Shanley from the guardhouse when the officer who put him there failed to file charges promptly.[9] Ben had refrained from court-martialing Byron Brown even though "strictly speaking, he should have been tried."[10] He had also let John Barrett keep his house and had disciplined officers whom he liked. "Any time that I would not come up to my duties around the Company and so forth, proper action was taken," according to Lieutenant Humphreys, the man who had dated Ben's cousin. "I never knew him to let any personal feeling carry any weight officially."[11]

"More sympathetic relations between officers and enlisted men" was the ideal Garrison said he considered "nearest to his heart."[12] In Ben's case, Garrison was being manipulated by Wood to view in a false light an officer who had often acted in conformity with that ideal.

In a third disservice, Wood's remarks that the press would attack the War Department if it did not try Ben were wholly speculative. For the most part, they would prove incorrect. Like General Barry, Wood undoubtedly wanted to protect the Army from adverse publicity—and newspapers already knew about the case, the Eastern Department told Washington—but negative publicity could also flow from siding with Ben's accusers if a jury found that those accusers were liars in uniforms.

The Army did shine one slender ray of fairness in Ben's direction on December 27. The judge advocate general, the Army's top lawyer, pointed out that Mills's certainty about Ben's guilt might not be matched at a trial, for "the case came with more force before the inspector than it would before a court-martial. Much of the testimony elicited by him would be irrelevant or hearsay and properly excluded by the court-martial. Many of the witnesses would stand discredited by their own admissions."[13]

The memo's author, Major General Enoch Crowder, manifested decorum. With his spectacles, well-groomed hair, and mustache, he looked polished and erudite, though he grew up poor on a farm in Missouri. He made much of that aspect of his past and how he had "inherited" a "hopelessly dependent family"—obliging him to provide for his parents, see to the education of his brothers and sisters, and monitor their financial affairs throughout his life.[14]

Crowder relied on the story of his burdensome but benevolent service as family caretaker to explain something atypical about his life: Like Ben, he was single. Crowder "frequently has expressed regret at being a bachelor . . . but by the time he finished caring for his folks the time had passed for him to start a home of his own," wrote the author of a profile of Crowder.[15] Even though Crowder was born sixteen years earlier than Ben, he seemed to know that a sympathetic explanation for his not having married would be to his lifelong advantage.[16]

While Ben may have avoided the gender police in San Francisco thanks to his uniform and shooting skills, he had not created a narrative the way Crowder did to explain his bachelorhood. As events were demonstrating, the lack of such a narrative allowed other people to explain it for him. Crowder wrote, "It is suggested by the hearing held by the inspector, if not established, that certain enlisted men have procured their discharge by purchase in order to escape the approaches of Major Koehler." Yet this highly prejudicial "suggestion" was not made to the inspector by anyone who had bought his discharge. It was classic hearsay, an unverified story about a former private who had once gone to the Koehler home to fix a typewriter. The story was conveyed to Mills by Elvin Byers, a sergeant friendly with Worcester, Frick, and Kirkman, and the same man who had made the curious visit to Ben's garden in July asking for flowers.[17]

Crowder wrote that Frick's claims against Ben seemed particularly strong, though he had not "had time to make a critical examination of the evidence taken by the inspector." Even if Crowder had done so, the so-called evidence did not include Ben's responses, nor assessments by other officers that Frick was considered untruthful and had complained about Ben to the point of being Ben's "enemy."[18]

Instead, Crowder jumped to a biological explanation: mental illness. "I have no doubt that his counsel at the trial will be prepared to represent that he is so diseased mentally as to be criminally irresponsible," Crowder wrote, intoning a theory being advanced by some that when educated middle- or upper-class men engaged in male-male sex it was due to insanity, whereas moral depravity was deemed a sufficient explanation for nonnormative sex by working class men and newer immigrants.[19]

Crowder did acknowledge that a jury might acquit Ben, but as far as Crowder was concerned, that would not mean Ben would resume the life he loved. "If . . . we should have a trial and be confronted with a finding of not guilty," Crowder wrote, "I am afraid we should have to consider separating this man from the service through retirement."

Crowder did not say why Ben might have to leave the Army if acquitted. Was it so obvious that it need not be stated, or so unclear and bound up in assumptions, stereotypes, and male angst that it could not be stated? If the underlying idea was that a man *accused* of homosexual conduct was tainted and unwelcome, that pointed to another unfairness Ben was up against: use of the court-martial process not to determine his guilt but to confirm it. And if the jury did not go along, here was the Army's top lawyer saying a verdict of acquittal would be ignored and another way found to oust Ben.

The only Army interest Crowder actually spelled out in his memo was "protection of the service from scandal," which, he agreed with Barry, might be a reason to let Ben leave the service quietly through resignation. Crowder was not sure. He could not "without a further study of the case commit myself to a definite recommendation."

Wood attached Crowder's memo to his letter to Garrison but attempted to minimize Crowder's indecisiveness. "I had a further talk with General Garlington [the Army's inspector general], who says the case should go to trial, and also a talk with General Weaver," Wood wrote. "Weaver feels, as you and I do, that this case should be brought to trial. General Crowder, I think, feels the same way, but he is a little bit stirred up with the possibilities of the medico-legal expert, etc."

Wood inserted the words "who says the case should go to trial" in handwriting after the letter was typed.[20] He apparently thought it added weight to cite Garlington's pro-trial position, though the fact that Ernest Garlington still had a job, much less influence, was remarkable considering his leading role in an earlier miscarriage of justice.

In 1906, a white bartender was shot and killed in Brownsville, Texas. White civilians accused the black soldiers of the 25th Infantry stationed at nearby Fort Brown. The soldiers' white commanders swore the men had been in their barracks at the time of the shooting. Nonetheless, Garlington, investigating for the Army, blamed them all because none would—or could—identify the shooter. Garlington recommended the dishonorable discharge of 167 black soldiers, and President Roosevelt went along.

A congressional investigation in 1907–08 revealed much damning evidence about Garlington's biased investigation.[21] In words that Ben Koehler could have uttered, Garlington was accused of having "already made up his mind that the soldiers were guilty."[22] Consistent with that reputation for prejudging guilt, Garlington—without hearing anything Ben had to say—opined that Ben "would be a menace to any community in which he might live and no actions of the War Department should operate so as to shield his real character from the public."[23]

Those were the top men in whose hands Ben Koehler's fate rested: Wood, who had suffered the biggest humiliation of his career at the hands of Ben's brother; Crowder, a self-pitying single man who had an interest in differentiating himself from another single officer alleged to be a "pervert"; and Garlington, a person who would ruin the lives of 167 black soldiers because none had identified the killer of one white man.

Having carefully edited his letter, Wood sent the Army's recommendations concerning Ben to Atlantic City for the secretary of war to consider in his concrete bunker by the beach.


OFFICIALS IN WASHINGTON WERE not the only ones who mistakenly thought Ben wished to resign. Henry Koehler, Ben's banker brother, also thought so. On December 30, without Ben's knowledge, Henry penned a most ill-advised letter to President Wilson's secretary in which he blamed alcohol and New York City for any misconduct on Ben's part. Here was a family member writing at length over the holidays, but it would have been better if he had never written at all. Henry's three-page letter contained one prejudicial statement after another. The letter could not have been reviewed by an attorney, which prudence would have warranted in a communication about an officer facing expulsion and imprisonment.[24]

Henry began by thanking the secretary for agreeing to bring "to the attention of the President the resignation of my brother." Henry wanted to convey "the facts," including his view that Ben's recruitment duty reflected disapproval of his service in the volunteer army in the Philippines.[25] Perhaps for Henry three years in New York City could only be punishment, but the Army valued recruiting, and Ben had advanced in rank thanks to William Kenly, a respected senior officer whose partiality to Ben may have protected him from exactly what was now unfolding.

New York itself was also to blame, Henry wrote: "His family feels that he became dissipated in New York city [sic]; and, if there is any truth in these charges, which he strenuously and which we strenuously deny, it may have some connection with that service and the excessive use of liquor, which his family claims has temporarily upset his mind." Henry Koehler was not the only Midwesterner who regarded New York as a sinful place, but he was almost certainly the only Midwesterner writing to the office of the president about how New York had ruined his brother because the Army kept him there too long.

Henry claimed to "strenuously deny" the charges against Ben, though he did not qualify his statements that Ben was drinking too much and that his mind was "temporarily upset." The word "temporarily" itself raised questions, given that Ben had left the recruiting job in 1911 and it was now nearly 1914. If "excessive use of liquor" had started in New York, was Ben's mind "upset" then, in which case it was not a temporary malady, or had Ben's mind only started to become "upset" at Fort Terry because the drinking continued? Either scenario had damaging ramifications. In times past, a star general such as Henry Ware Lawton might be forgiven an attachment to alcohol, but in 1914, an Army administrator did not need to be a teetotaler like Wood to believe that an officer with a drinking problem should not

command a post. One of the few Articles of War that had been updated provided for expulsion of an officer who abused alcohol.

Henry's statements were simply beyond the pale. Ben had been the
best man at Henry's wedding, but that was back in 1902. Now the two
were hardly in touch. Henry knew nothing about Ben's life, his drinking habits, or the drinking practices of Army men—notwithstanding
the rules. Henry went so far as to recommend that Ben "should not be
tried until he has been sent to a sanitarium for examination and
treatment."

Henry wrote that Ben "claims his innocence and his defense is conspiracy," but for reasons not stated, Henry reached the same conclusion as Crowder—that "if he is successful in defending himself against
these charges his usefulness in the army would be terminated."

What would any reader of Henry's letter have thought, learning
that Ben's own brother believed an acquittal should lead to Ben's ter-
mination from the Army?

Henry ended his appeal by pointing out that Ben "is one of three
brothers given by our family to the army, one of whom, Capt. Edgar
F. Koehler, lost his life . . ." For that and all of the other reasons cited
in his letter, Henry wrote that "we . . . feel that his family is entitled to
this consideration"—acceptance of the resignation—"but the Secretary of War, Mr. Garrison, for some reason refuses to follow the usual
custom regarding my brother's resignation."

Accordingly, Henry had decided to contact the president, who, he
pointed out, might remember meeting him when "I had the pleasure
of acting as his escort in Kansas City . . . through the Woodrow Wilson
for President Club No. 1, of which I am a charter member."

Whether the words of his fan in Kansas City ever reached Wilson is
unknown, but the president's secretary shared Henry's letter liberally,
including with the War Department.


OTHERS WITH GREATER TACT and Washington experience also
weighed in. Iowa Representative George C. Scott requested a copy of
the charges and urged acceptance of Ben's resignation.[26] An official

replied that the charges were "confidential."[27] In truth, they had not been written yet.

Representative William Borland, from Missouri, also wrote urging acceptance of Ben's resignation,"[28] and a Kentucky senator wrote of "a considerable sentiment in the country favoring the reception of the resignation of Major Benjamin M. Koehler. From what I can learn of the case, it seems to me that he should be spared a Court Martial."[29]

The most illustrious person to write was Secretary of State William Jennings Bryan.[30] A lawyer and former member of Congress, Bryan had been the Democratic presidential candidate three times, losing to McKinley in 1896 in a campaign that attacked Bryan's masculine fitness. While McKinley's Civil War service was said to prove his "vigorous manhood," a *Harper's* cartoon pictured the much younger Bryan in a cradle holding a rattle, prompting Bryan's supporters to cite his athleticism and broad shoulders as proof that "there was 'nothing soft, yielding or effeminate about him.'"[31] Bryan was close to Ben's brother Barthold, known as "Bat," who had become an influential behind-the-scenes politician in the Nebraska city of Geneva. Bryan sent a cable to Garrison:

> May I ask you to make a personal examination into the case of Major B. M. Koehler of Nebraska, who desires to resign from the service. General Barry of Governor's Island has twice recommended the resignation. Major Koehler is a member of one of our prominent Nebraska families and he desires the resignation accepted in the interest of the honor of the family. If you can not [*sic*] act favorably upon this request will you please suspend action until I can see you upon my return?[32]

By mid-January 1914, despite Henry's misguided letter, the appeals to Washington started having some effect. Garrison spoke to Crowder about accepting Ben's resignation. His main concern, according to Crowder, was "the principle of uniform treatment of officer and enlisted man." Crowder assured Garrison that the punishment of separation from the Army was the same whether it was achieved by an officer's resignation or an enlisted man's dishonorable discharge.

Crowder said he was "inclined to suggest acceptance of resignation for the good of the service"—less publicity than a trial—even though he believed a conviction was likely.[33]

Garrison was not so sure. Bat Koehler had come to Washington to discuss Ben's conspiracy claim, which caused Garrison "much embarrassment," but his reasoning led him in circles. If the charges "are false, then we should not bring Koehler to trial upon the charges, but should proceed against each and every one of the affiants, to the end that they may be convicted and punished of the heinous offense committed by them in making these grave, false charges against their superior officer."[34]

Yet Garrison went on to say that the only way to find out if the charges were true or false was to put Ben on trial, and then, if he was acquitted, "each and every person who participated in this matter" could be court-martialed on charges of false swearing and conspiracy.

Bat traveled to Plum Island, heard from Ben and Sophia about the "scoundrels," and came away a believer. He returned to Washington and met with Charles Sloan, the Nebraska representative, and Nebraska Senator Gilbert Hitchcock, who rallied to Ben's side. As Hitchcock wrote Garrison, Bat was "confident and he has to some extent convinced me that a conspiracy has been entered into against Major Koehler—and that he is brought face to face with this terrible charge without having been given an opportunity himself to be heard."

Hitchcock requested that Garrison "send another inspector to make a [sic] investigation and report his findings to you before a court martial is ordered." Hitchcock also asked Garrison to meet with Bat to hear "what he learned while on his recent visit to his brother."[35]

Garrison did not take the meeting, but he did take action:

I sent instructions to the Commanding General of the Eastern Department to have the officer named by General Crowder to make a re-investigation, especially with a view of ascertaining the motives and truthfulness of the witnesses. I have suggested to him that this officer should ascertain from Major Koehler himself, or his counsel, any lines that they desire to have investigated, for the purpose of reaching a proper conclusion upon the matters just mentioned. This is, of course, as far as I possibly can go in this matter . . ."[36]

The "re-investigation" was the first good news Ben had received since his arrest. He began to think seriously of beating the charges and immediately requested that Kenly, now a colonel, be appointed as his counsel—a role that did not require a legal background.[37] Kenly had protected Ben before. Ben understandably hoped he would do so again.

Ever since Ben's arrest, Sophia had kept the news from Roy, who had once again tried to see Sophia over the holidays. A storm hit Plum Island on Christmas Eve and shut down the boats, but Sophia made it into New York a few days later. She told Roy she would wait for him but changed her mind. Instead, Sophia sent a note to be held for him at his hotel and headed home: "I am sorry not to see you but I can't wait any longer. Margaret Gund is here with me and is ready to leave and I have been away nearly a week so feel that I must get back. Ben expected to get in the city Friday but has not come nor sent me any word so I am getting anxious to get back. Wish you could come to [Fort] Terry but suppose it's out of the question."[38]

Roy, ever the busy salesman, sent candy and nuts to Sophia instead of seeing her, without any understanding of why a week without hearing from Ben would make Sophia anxious when her brother had spent years on another continent at war and now lived nearby in peacetime.

In late January, feeling optimistic, Sophia divulged what was going on, why she and Ben "had a very unhappy Christmas," and why "We were sorry you couldn't get to Terry—We needed cheering up—but I am afraid you would have found us very blue and discouraged."[39]

"We have been terribly worried since the seventh of December so I haven't had the heart to write," she explained, telling Roy of the "scoundrels," the "clique," and their allegations, which she termed "a lot of lies—needless to say these men have no character."

"We think the inspector is now convinced," she wrote. "We at least feel more hopeful but it will be ten days probably before we hear any-thing definite." She reported, too, that many of the enlisted men had come to see Ben "all anxious to testify for him and some willing to risk the guardhouse in order to testify for him."

Why would a soldier be put in the guardhouse if he testified on behalf of the post commander? In that offhand statement by Sophia lay an essential key to the case: the power of a company captain such as Worcester to punish subordinates who did not do as requested. That sort of abuse of power was one reason why "autocratic officers" had a bad name, but some officers considered it a perquisite of the job. If there was an autocratic officer who needed reining in at Fort Terry, Sophia would have identified Worcester, not her brother.

Would the new inspector see it that way? Ben and Sophia could only hope so.

# PART THREE

# CHAPTER TWENTY

# The Meaning of "Start"

F AR FROM NEW YORK, in Russia, Major Charles Hagadorn headed to the St. Petersburg train station in November 1913. His whole body ached, which he blamed on the cold weather. After two months as military attaché at the American Embassy, Hagadorn was grateful to have received a cable from the War Department approving his request for reassignment due to poor health.

The major's bags were checked to Berlin, where he planned to transfer to a steamer for the Atlantic crossing. His ticket was purchased, but before he could board the train another cable arrived, this one from Leonard Wood on behalf of President Wilson. The cable instructed Hagadorn to remain in St. Petersburg and apply to the Embassy for permission to return to the United States—unless he had already started on his way.

Hagadorn paused, then boarded the train, concluding that the purchase of a ticket and surrendering of his luggage constituted a "start" to his trip.

Wood disagreed. After Hagadorn arrived home, Wood ordered that he be court-martialed on Governors Island. Reminiscent of Louis Koehler's first trial, the jurors struck the word "willful" from their verdict, and by Christmas, Hagadorn stood convicted of having "fail[ed] to obey" a lawful command from the president.[1]

Hagadorn's poor health was borne out by significant weight loss, said to be over 40 pounds. General Barry, the reviewing authority, declared that no further punishment was warranted, commenting that it must have been Hagadorn's illness that caused him to misinterpret the word "start" as applying to his luggage and not his person. Wood had made his point about the supremacy of orders, and Hagadorn could go on working for the Army in a milder climate.

Whether the prosecutor, Captain James J. Mayes, regarded the outcome as a victory did not really matter. It was his duty to present the evidence in the strongest way possible. If the officers on the jury wanted to show mercy and return a lesser verdict, that was out of his hands.

Mayes believed, correctly, that his job as an assistant judge advocate was secure. Enoch Crowder, Mayes's boss, regarded Mayes highly, and that was demonstrated with the next assignment given to Mayes and approved by Wood and Garrison. Mayes would be able to spend the holidays at home, but come mid-January 1914, he would be required to travel to Plum Island. Eastern Long Island was cold in winter, to be sure, but not nearly as cold as St. Petersburg.

IF THE HAGADORN COURT-MARTIAL was straightforward, turning on the meaning of one word in the context of virtually undisputed facts, the Ben Koehler case presented a morass by comparison. Many people were making allegations involving different acts at different times, all of which the accused man steadfastly denied and attributed to a conspiracy.

Conspiracy cases are difficult, even for experienced attorneys. Much of a conspiracy involves planning carried out through words, and it is easy for people to lie about conversations and avoid the existence of documentary proof. This was especially true before computers, social media platforms, and mobile devices.

Mayes was not an attorney, and it was not his job to prove a conspiracy. Rather, his instructions were to "ascertain from Major Koehler, or his friends or his counsel, the motive which they allege prompted the witnesses to make these false statements concerning the alleged occurrences" and also "to ascertain whether it is possible that so many men could have been actuated by bad motives into making false statements."[2]

Those were some of the instructions, at least. They came from Secretary of War Garrison, who wrote that he wanted to be "sure of the facts before proceeding," and asked that "before any definite action is taken upon the report of Captain Mayes, it is sent to me."

Garrison included an additional instruction: Mayes "must proceed with extreme care, because, if he reaches the conclusion that these witnesses were actuated by bad motives and did make false statements, I propose having each and every one of them court-martialed for so doing." That could apply to some or all of the witnesses, depending on what Mayes found: "If . . . bad motives have actuated these various witnesses, or any of them, and they have, under the influence of such motives, made false statements, then their conduct is reprehensible to the highest degree and they must be court-martialed."

Those sentences sent a clear message that veered from Ben's interest in exoneration. While Garrison observed that the charges were "of a very grave character," he did not say that "extreme care" had to be followed to avoid ruining the reputation and career of an innocent man. Rather, "extreme care" was needed because the consequence of finding merit in Ben's assertions of innocence would be more work for the judge advocate—up to a dozen court-martials instead of one—not to mention adverse publicity and embarrassment for the Army.

Garrison's umbrage at the possibility of lying soldiers may have been genuine, but how objective did he expect an investigator to be when Garrison was dictating that the outcome of agreeing with Ben Koehler would be twelve times Mayes's workload?

Yes, a portion of the typed instructions said to investigate, but as Mayes had just recently learned in the Hagadorn case, words could be interpreted in different ways. The word "start" could mean "go" or "stay," depending on one's perspective. And so, the person on whom Sophia and Ben were pinning their hopes was dispatched to Plum Island with a warning that if he concluded that any or all of the witnesses were lying, he had better be sure—and prepared to spend many more hours trying cases on Plum Island.

Mayes had his reasons for wanting Ben Koehler to be guilty, and Sophia had hers for wanting her brother to be cleared. She wrote with optimism to Roy after Mayes had conducted his interviews, but before the Army had disclosed the findings. Sophia wanted to believe, and apparently did believe, that Mayes was "convinced"—that he had seen right through the "clique" to the underlying truth, in her opinion, that Ben was being framed.

Sophia had no idea that Mayes had been told to take "extreme care" to do the opposite. Nor did she know that the new adjutant general of the Army, George Andrews, had already ordered the case to proceed to trial "upon charges to be prepared at Headquarters of the Eastern Department."[3]

Under these circumstances, even if Mayes thought the complaining witnesses were lying, it would take a person with strong independence of mind—not to mention someone willing and able to rise above his self-interest—to convince the Army to drop the charges against Ben and court-martial "each and every" complainant instead.

Did Mayes have that in him?

# CHAPTER TWENTY-ONE

# *Unthinkable*

A DVOCATES FOR PEACE WERE "murderers of soldiers," James Mayes wrote in an essay on military training, one of Wood's favorite causes. The essay won a prestigious award, earning it prime placement in 1910 in a national military journal published on Governors Island, as well as coverage in *The New York Times.*[1] Mayes's promotion to captain followed.

Mayes's damning words were not necessary to his thesis that Congress should fund military training centers on college campuses—which it would do in 1916 by creating the Reserve Officers' Training Corps—but they provide a window into his mind-set:

> [W]hen war comes, as it always has and always will, thousands of brave but ignorant volunteer soldiers die in foul camps, victims of peaceborn ignorance. The preachers of unpreparedness are not there to die. The pity is that they stay at home and start a new eternal peace crusade as soon as a new treaty of peace is signed, using the ghoulish evidence of their own crimes to awaken revulsion against war.[2]

Concerning the nexus between the strength of men and strength of the nation, there was no doubt where Mayes stood. "Real soldiers," he wrote, "are never found preaching eternal peace." A person who preached peace was "ignorant" and cowardly. Mayes sounded like

Roosevelt, who "blamed the 'silly, mock humanitarianism of the prat-
tlers who sit at home in peace' for costing the lives of American men
in the Philippines."[3]

Ben Koehler had proven himself in battle, and he supervised peacetime drills diligently in the interest of preparedness. If he and Mayes
were to have met at a conference on military training, they might well
have found like-mindedness on that subject. As Colonel Davis wrote
of Ben in 1913: "Attention to duty, professional zeal, and intelligence
and judgment shown in instructing, drilling, and handling enlisted
men, excellent."[4]

But Mayes, formerly of the 10th Infantry, was not meeting Ben as a
fellow officer dedicated to military ideals. No evidence exists that
Mayes requested the file containing the glowing reviews of Ben's performance, and maybe those reviews were irrelevant. A man could appear good at his job and still act inappropriately in private.

Mayes's award-winning essay had shown that he held strong views
about gender roles. Too many teachers, he had complained, "are either women or men who ought to have been women." Such "[e]mas-
culated specimens" were "one great source of popular indifference to
military needs."[5]

Still, what happened after Mayes visited Plum Island and spoke to
Ben, Sophia, Worcester, and many other people there was a shock—a
shock hastened by Wood, who directed on February 7 "that the report
of the inspector on the Koehler case be expedited."[6] The next day,
Mayes submitted his report.

After the first investigation by Stephen Mills, twelve people claimed
improper advances by Ben. After Mayes's reinvestigation, the number
grew to sixteen. Far from clearing Ben, the second investigation expanded the case against him. It would emerge that Worcester had
done his best to make sure that Mayes left Plum Island not the least
bit inclined to recommend a court-martial of any of the accusers, but
only of the man Worcester and Frick claimed was a degenerate masquerading as a real soldier.

# *Confusion*

M AYES'S REPORT QUICKLY REACHED Secretary of War Garrison, along with a comment from General Barry. "In Koehler case, your endorsement renews recommendation that his resignation be accepted," Garrison cabled back to Barry. "He withdrew his resignation, and the record now is as if he had never offered it. In view of this, do you still wish to make the recommendation which is contained in your endorsement. Please reply immediately."[1]

Barry did reply immediately, at 2:12 a.m., in a manner sympathetic to Ben: "When Major Koehler was informed his resignation would not be accepted and that he must stand trial he had to withdraw his resignation in his own protection."[2] In other words, when Barry's agreement to a leave was overruled, Ben withdrew the resignation consistent with his claim of innocence.

Barry noted his "belief that Koehler would resign if again given the opportunity." He told Garrison he had summoned Ben. In a second telegram, Barry said Ben "will be here tonight will telegraph result of conference with him soon as practicable after seeing him."[3]

No, Garrison replied, chiding Barry that he was "misinformed as to facts" and that Ben "was never informed by my authority that his resignation would not be accepted." Rather, in Garrison's view, the withdrawal of the resignation was the doing of Ben's "brother and others [who] came to the Department, and stated that they under-

stood that he had offered his resignation without proper consideration of what he was doing, and that . . . the charges against him were
the product of conspiracy. They asked me to postpone consideration
of the acceptance of his resignation until they could communicate
with him. After communicating with him, as they afterwards informed
me, he withdrew his resignation."[4]

The situation looked different from Washington than in New York.
Apparently, Wood never told Garrison that the initial resignation was
connected to a leave, which was overruled, nor did Ben's brothers
know that, so Garrison was the one "misinformed as to facts." But he
was also the one with cabinet-level authority—and growing impa-
tience, judging by his words. He had ordered another investigation
and that was that. The Koehlers had gambled and lost.

Garrison made it clear that no matter what Barry thought was best,
the War Department wanted a trial: "His first resignation having been
withdrawn . . . and the new investigation having been undertaken in
view of his assertion of innocence[,] I am convinced that there is no
other course now open than a settlement by judicial determination."
Koehler might offer to resign, "but I do not think it wise for it to be
done at the suggestion of any one in military authority."

This left Barry and his chief of staff confused, and they consulted
Ben when he arrived at Governors Island. As Ben put it later, "They
had a telegram from the Secretary of War which they said they did not
seem to understand; it was something about my resignation. They
asked me whether I still considered my resignation as being in the
hands of the Secretary of War."

"What was your reply to that?" Ben was asked.

"That I [did] not, that I had previous to that time telegraphed withdrawing it."[5]

Looked at from today's perspective, Garrison was declining to endorse a quiet deal with an alleged harasser. This is a stance one wishes
the Catholic Church had taken later in the century, rather than reas-
signing priests accused of sexual predation against minors, allowing
the priests to commit the same offense again and again.[6] The same
could be said of academic institutions that elevated protection of their

football teams, fraternities, and fundraising over the interests of female students who came forward with charges of sexual assault—from unwanted touching to gang rape.[7] And as women joined the armed services in significant numbers, far too many would be ignored, ostracized, harassed, or discharged after reporting sexual assault, leading some to take their own lives or die from other trauma-related causes.[8]

Some progress has been made to address these injustices, and much more work is necessary, but back in 1913 and 1914, the law did not even recognize "sexual misconduct" and "sexual harassment" as wrongs. The available categories were rape, sodomy, and assault, and a sex crime accusation by one employee against another was highly unusual. Surely Mayes was no specialist in investigating such a charged situation. The male-male context only added to the strangeness, especially since the men who claimed Ben made advances, all adults, did not say they had suffered emotional or physical harm as a result.[9]

Yet what is the same then as now is the general paucity of physical evidence in non-stranger sexual assault cases. Based on what people told him, Mayes concluded that four accusers held grudges against Ben due to reprimands—not enough, in his view, to show a conspiracy to lie. It would emerge that Mayes had undercounted the grudges, but his opinion that bad motives did not explain the charges was accepted by Garrison, who, having entertained the possibility of a dozen liars in the Army, undoubtedly welcomed the findings.

In January, Senator Hitchcock had aroused Garrison's emotions, prompting Garrison to write that "If . . . bad motives have actuated these various witnesses, *or any of them*, and they have, under the influence of such motives, made false statements, then their conduct is reprehensible to the highest degree and they must be court-martialed."[10]

By early February, Garrison seemed to have forgotten his own words. He let Wood hurry Mayes. Then he reacted in one day to the report's findings. More time may or may not have affected the outcome, but here was a second investigation involving Ben that was rushed. Possibly, with a more careful review, Garrison might have asked himself or others why four men with grudges was not enough to make the case suspect. Now, contrary to Garrison's earlier statement, bad motives by "any" of the accusers changed nothing.

Garrison may have had no personal animus against Ben, but he had no firsthand knowledge of him either. He knew only what people were telling him, and that ran the gamut, with one man consistently recommending a trial—Wood, who once wrote, "When I fight, I can't fight softly. I try to hurt my opponent. I try to hurt him as much as I can."[11]

Unfortunately for Ben, his last name alone placed him in Wood's "opponent" camp, and there was no countervailing weight. Wood had headed the Eastern Department when Ben served in recruitment, but they had not worked together, and reports of Ben's success in turning Fort Terry around would not have made their way to Wood and Garrison. Ben's staunchest advocates, Kenly and Moses, did not stand in Wood's inner circle, nor did Ben's length of service earn him points with Wood, who was just as likely to believe that long tenure made an officer an impediment to reform. Add the claims of numerous men that Ben had groped them, claims that Mayes had not only ratified but expanded, and Ben had a great many strikes against him in Washington, fair or not.

In January, Louis had encouraged Ben to fight the charges, but a month later, after the second investigation went against him, the prospect of fighting the Army did not inspire as much hope. Ben may well have been willing to resign on February 10, when he met with Barry and Haan, accepting that he was being outmaneuvered—from below and above. Instead, he returned to Plum Island without options, knowing that Barry, the general who exhibited the most concern for him, was about to move to the Philippines.

What Ben and Sophia did not know, and perhaps even Garrison did not fully appreciate, was that the men running the Army never thought the second investigation might lead to Ben's exoneration. General Crowder had endorsed further inquiry to sharpen the government's trial strategy.[12] The adjutant general had instructed that it be used to help write "definite charges" against Ben.[13]

Mayes did exactly that—and Ben naively helped him do it. When Mayes handed Ben a list of charges, Ben reviewed the two pages on the spot and pointed out errors. A date was wrong here, he was off the island there. Ben thought Mayes would withdraw those charges. Instead, when Ben and his counsel received revised charges, several dates had been changed—"by months and years"—and some claims had no dates at all.[14] Through his voluntary statements, Ben strengthened the case against him and forfeited what would have been strong alibi defenses at trial.

Identifying mistakes in the charges was an example of Ben's continued belief in the Army's good faith. Even as powerful people in Washington rushed to confirm his guilt, he still thought Mayes had an open mind and that the Army wanted truth and justice.[15]

# An Old Nemesis Returns

THE DREADED PUBLICITY BEGAN on a Monday.

"It is reported that the general court-martial of Major Benjamin M. Koehler at Fort Terry, Plum Island, next Tuesday afternoon will be one of the most sensational ever known in army circles," wrote the *Sun* on February 23.[1]

Ben's trial had not started, but already it was attracting attention with three media magnets: New York location, high-ranking officer, and undisclosed "immoral practices."[2]

The *Sun* characterized Ben as "a bachelor, an excellent disciplinarian and very popular with the enlisted men at the fort," adding that "[h]is sister lives with him." The article stated that "no details of the coming trial have been made public by Government officials," yet quite a bit of Ben's personal history appeared, most of it accurate, including his service in the Astor Battery.

The *Sun*'s tone was decidedly pro-Koehler, contrary to Wood's prediction. Far from casting Ben as an "autocratic officer," the article's description of him as "very popular with the enlisted men" appeared near the top, and his "troubles" were blamed on a decision that irked officers, not enlisted men—the closing of the officers' club. The *Sun* mentioned the possibility of a "plot": "[D]ays passed without [the club] being reopened. The officers keenly felt the loss of their favorite lounging place. A delegation waited on Major Koehler and pleaded with him to reopen the quarters, but without avail. From that time, it is alleged, 'the plot thickened.'"

The article also portrayed the Army as unfair in its handling of Ben's leave, reporting that "all his household goods were packed and labelled for Iowa. A big van was loaded and was ready to leave when a telegram was received relieving Major Koehler of his command and placing him under arrest."

With reporters being told little officially and banned from Plum Island, inaccuracies and exaggerations were bound to occur. The *Sun* article likely arose from conversations in New London over the weekend when soldiers on leave spoke off-the-record to the reporter.

Toward the end of the story, an ominous statement appeared: "It is also predicted that more than one officer at the fort will have to 'walk the plank' before the affair is ended." Left unspecified was whether the plank-walkers would be on the accusers' side or Ben's.

The article closed by stating that on Tuesday, a special government "transport" would bring the members of the jury to Plum Island, to be led by Colonel Henry Kirby of the 3rd Infantry. Known as the Old Guard, the 3rd Infantry was then and remains the oldest active duty regiment in the Army. Its motto well fit the case: "*Noli Me Tangere*"—"Touch Me Not."

*The New York Times* also reported on the case, under the restrained headline "Army Board to Try Major B. M. Koehler." Its story showed no sympathy for Ben and read like a press release from Wood, which in effect it may have been.[3] The *Times* wrote that when the charges were presented to Koehler "he forwarded his resignation," which "Maj. Gen. Wood received . . . and forwarded to Secretary of War Garrison." The *Times* went on to say, prejudicially, that Wood and Garrison decided that "in a case in which the charges were of so serious a nature, and in which so much evidence was offered, the acceptance of the resignation was out of the question."[4]

Journalists could rely only on what people were telling them, and no one was telling them that Ben had already been arraigned nearly two weeks earlier.

The pace at which the proceedings unfolded is stunning by today's standards. On February 11, one day after Ben met with Barry and Haan on Governors Island, he was back on Plum Island being formally charged with multiple counts of misconduct.

Even Barry was kept in the dark. While he was telling Ben to undertake a ten-hour round trip to discuss resignation, the Army was sending officers from throughout the East Coast to Plum Island for Ben's arraignment—further evidence that, at least as far as Army leaders were concerned (if not Garrison), the point of the Mayes reinvestigation was always to sharpen the prosecution's case—not probe whether an injustice had been done.

Ben might have thought things could not get much worse, until he saw Lieutenant Colonel Delamere Skerrett walk into the small library room where the proceedings were being held. Years ago, Skerrett had criticized Ben for speaking his mind about deficiencies during a Fort Monroe target practice, leading to ill feelings.[5] Here he was showing up to serve as a juror with the power to vote to dismiss Ben from the Army and send him to jail.

Outside the steam-heated building, snow covered Plum Island, a blizzard having struck a few days earlier. The island was not a place where anyone would want to be sent in the middle of winter, certainly not majors, lieutenant colonels, and colonels who lived as far away as Maine and Virginia, all high-level personnel, as the *Times* explained: "The importance of the case may be judged from the personnel of the court, which includes the commanding officers of every important Coast Artillery fortification in this section of the United States, the commanding officer of Plattsburgh Barracks, and two of the artillery district commanders of the North Atlantic Coast Artillery Division."[6]

To have traveled such distances and arranged for coverage at their posts, these men required advance notice. It is likely that Wood chose the date of February 11 for the arraignment before Mayes's report was even received, necessitating the February 7 "hurry up" order so as not to disrupt the plans of so many top officers or have them arrive before the report's completion.

Less than three weeks after Sophia had written that "we think the inspector is now convinced" of Ben's innocence, Mayes stood on Plum Island intent on proving the opposite.

Representing Ben was Harry J. Hawthorne, now a colonel stationed at a post in Boston Harbor. Told that William Kenly was unavailable to serve as his military counsel, Ben turned to Hawthorne, another old friend who had credited him with saving lives in the Philippines. Now Hawthorne was being asked to save Ben's military life. Though not a lawyer, he was an expert in military law with credentials considered impressive at the time, including a Medal of Honor for the Battle of Wounded Knee (now the Wounded Knee Massacre).[7] On Hawthorne's recommendation, Ben also hired an attorney in private practice in Boston, Samuel H. Hudson. Not too many Army men could afford that, but as to Ben, the *Sun* wrote, "it is said that he has plenty of money."[8]

Before Ben entered his pleas, Hudson's challenged Skerrett for bias. Skerrett, stationed in Brooklyn, claimed to have no memory of criticizing Ben, but Hudson argued that Skerrett had "expressed himself in such harsh, unfriendly and critical terms as to indicate to [Koehler] a pronounced prejudice against him" and had acted coldly toward Ben ever since.[9] Hudson said the stakes were too high—Ben's life, as he knew it—to seat anyone "who has in the past had unfriendly or troublesome dealings with the accused."

"I consider myself entirely able to conduct my share of this trial without any bias," Skerrett replied, but without calling a recess, Kirby announced his decision: Skerrett would be excluded.[10] The defense had won its first motion. It was back to Brooklyn for Skerrett.

Next, Hudson took issue with there being two sets of charges based on the same alleged acts. One set was under the article proscribing conduct "unbecoming an officer and a gentleman," and another was under the article prohibiting actions to "the prejudice of good order and military discipline"—the second set based on the New York statute making assault in the third degree a misdemeanor punishable by a five hundred dollar fine, one year in jail, or both.

Hudson said Ben had "accumulated a reputation that is as dear to him as any member of this court" such that "dismissal [from the Army] under the specifications of the first charge would be far and away worse to him than any punishment under the State Laws of New York for assault."[11] Hudson asked that the second set of charges be dismissed as redundant.

This time Kirby called a recess, giving Ben—now called "the accused"—his first taste of waiting for a ruling from men who used to be his colleagues. When court resumed, Kirby denied the motion. Ben then pleaded not guilty to charges described by *The New York Times* as "among the most serious any officer in the history of the army has ever been called upon to plead to, involving, as they do, allegations that are [of a] scandalous nature."[12]

There were seventeen specifications, or counts, under the first article and sixteen under the second article. All in all, Ben uttered the words "not guilty" thirty-three times.[13]

At day's end, Kirby adjourned the court until the last week in February, when the jurors would return and testimony would begin. First up would be the star witness for the prosecution: Philip Worcester.

The very week that Theodore Roosevelt, the proponent of "soldierly virtues," was launching canoes into a tributary of the Amazon on his famous trip down the unmapped River of Doubt, a professional soldier with many years' experience would begin to have his courage tested—as well as his "manhood," to quote Sophia—in a far different but also uncharted way.

Plum Island was closer to home, less isolated, and less dangerous than the River of Doubt, but to the men sent to Plum Island in the dead of winter to hear seamy allegations about one of their own, riding rapids in Brazil may well have seemed more appealing.[14]

# "Any Such Tendencies"

B EFORE PHILIP WORCESTER SWORE to tell the truth on Thursday, February 27, the Army needed to decide who would hear him speak. Would reporters and curious civilians be allowed in the Fort Terry library, or would the court-martial be held in secret?

The presumption that American criminal trials should be open to the public predates the Constitution, having been brought to the colonies by the same Brits who traded fish hooks for Plum Island. But this was a military tribunal, given wider latitude by the U.S. Supreme Court.[1] As head of the Eastern Department, at least for a few more days, Barry was considered the trial's convening officer. He and Kirby decided to keep out the press and public.

The next morning, when Mayes called Worcester to the stand, those present included only the jurors, Ben, the counselors, and the court reporter who was transcribing the proceedings. Guards stood at the government wharf in New London and the landing on Plum Island.

*The New York Times* printed Ben's denial of the charges and said he was in "good spirits."[2] This was despite the elimination of a second officer from the jury, one favorably disposed toward Ben—Sidney Jordan, who now commanded Fort Strong in Massachusetts. He had not arrived with the other jurors, notifying Kirby that he was ill. Kirby decided that the trial should proceed with eleven jurors rather than twelve.[3] While Mayes would likely have challenged Jordan as too partial, the defense would not have the opportunity to find out.

Unlike in a civilian trial, there were no opening statements in which the prosecutor and defense counsel told their respective versions of the truth, pitched their strongest evidence, and tried to take the sting out of adverse testimony anticipated from the other side. This cut against Ben, for many accusers would testify before he and other defense witnesses took the stand.[4] Without an opening statement, Hudson had no chance to tell the jurors to watch for signs of fabrication, such as inconsistencies, inability to provide details, or failures in recollection that seemed surprising. Setting up a skeptical perspective would have been especially valuable to Ben given his claim that the charges were based on lies. Ben would not, contrary to Crowder's prediction, plead mental illness, or "temporary upset" from alcohol, as his brother Henry had put it.

Mayes made fast work of the direct examination, concentrating on the Halloween party. "Did anything unusual between you and Major Koehler occur at that party?" he asked Worcester.

"Yes, sir."[5]

Worcester began with a preamble of how he was "dressed up as a girl," presumably to minimize the costume's shock value. He told of the cobweb game and dinner in the basement. Then he got around to answering Mayes's question:

> I cannot tell about the exact time but approximately about 10 o'clock I passed in through this doorway into the little laundry room, which was being used as a smoking room and as I went by Major Koehler, who was sitting on the edge of the table right near the door, he reached down—I think with his right hand, and grabbed me in what I consider rather an insulting manner by the testicles and I jumped away.

Worcester said he left the room quickly, and a "few minutes later when I came around again he grabbed me very suggestively by the buttock—I think it was the left buttock."

Hudson interrupted, saying, "any conclusion like this 'very suggestive' we object to." Mayes countered that the suggestiveness of the act was not Worcester's opinion, but "something that the man himself may know." As Mayes elaborated: "[B]y the very nature of these actions the character of them is a matter within the knowledge of this man as much as the act itself. An act which verges on an approach or suggestion cannot be described actually by physical description, but it is something that the man himself may know, is within his positive knowledge rather than his opinion . . ."

In response, Hudson set up an alternative defense, that Ben may have touched men innocently, but his intentions were misperceived because of rumors about his "tendencies."

> [A]ccusations such as have been made in this case are most peculiar and if a rumor gets abroad that a man has any such tendencies as have been charged in this case the most innocent act will be misunderstood and will be to the man himself suggestive. A man accused of these offences may meet a man and put his hand on his shoulder. The man draws back. That means something.

Hudson may have accurately described the suspiciousness that had crept into male-male dealings, but whether his words would help his client was another matter. He seemed to be saying it was reasonable for people to believe Ben had "such tendencies." He went on to say that a single word could be interpreted differently if spoken by a man suspected of homosexuality: "I can imagine a man accused of such an offence to walk up to me in the morning and say 'How do you feel?' I would say that 'feel' means something else; I draw back."

If Worcester had heard rumors about Ben, Hudson argued, then Worcester was not reliable concerning "what Major Koehler meant" by touching him. Mayes replied that just as a person can reliably sense a physical threat, "That applies with equal force to this case, where it is a threat against his dignity and sense of manhood."[6]

After conferring privately, the jurors sided with Hudson. "The witness will be instructed to confine himself to facts and to leave out suggestions," directed Kirby.

Worcester resumed testifying and said that "about an hour later I was in another part of the main cellar talking to the Major. It was in a rather dark part of the cellar behind one of the brick pillars supporting the floor, and again he reached and grabbed me by the testicles."

This time, according to Worcester, he spoke up: "I remember asking him what he meant by such an act or words to that effect, if he thought that I was that kind of a person that he could do that to, or words to that effect. I remember we had several rather heated words."

Worcester claimed that Ben "remarked that he was doing it just in fun, he was just fooling, and he moved off in the direction of the smoking room. I can't quote exactly what I said. I was very mad and sputtered out to him that I was not that kind of a person and would not stand for it, or words to that effect."

According to Worcester, Ben left "about half an hour later without saying anything to me."

HUDSON HAD WON A ruling that would apply throughout the trial, but it was not necessarily in Ben's interests to cut off speculation as to why Ben might have done what Worcester said he did. Kirby instructed Worcester "to leave out suggestions," but Worcester managed to make the same point by saying he told Ben he was "not that kind of person." Embedded in that statement was the idea that Ben was making an "an approach or suggestion," as Mayes put it, as well as presuming Worcester's willingness to participate. The testicle grabs were not objectionable because they hurt, or because Worcester had trouble rebuffing them, but because they were "a threat against his dignity and sense of manhood," to quote Mayes.[7] The implication was that Ben had propositioned Worcester, just like what was happening on New York City's streets.

But what sort of proposition was it? Surely Ben was not "suggesting" that he and Worcester have sex in a house full of guests, including Sophia. Was it a way of asking Worcester to consider sex at another time? If so, in an era when hiding one's homosexuality was all-important in the middle-class gay world, why would Ben, if he were gay, choose Worcester, with whom he had differed and who was therefore likely to decline and tell others of the overture?[8] And why would Ben come on to Worcester when he was tired and anxious to leave, and when Worcester was dressed and behaving in a manner that Ben considered distasteful?

Mayes was not going to ask those questions, and Hudson, having argued that Worcester should not be allowed to speculate about what Ben "meant," closed the door on his own ability to ask them when the time came for cross-examination. Yet Hudson could not prevent the jurors from speculating on their own, nor could he count on them to parse the fantastical from the plausible without help. If the prosecution's theory was that Ben had tried to use his authority to coax subordinates to have sex with him, it might be wise for Hudson to call that out and plant doubt in the jurors' minds that a person would keep trying the same strategy when it repeatedly failed. And if Ben was not "suggesting" sex or trying to use his position to obtain it, then the motivation for the acts described by Worcester had to be something else. Was Worcester saying that Ben found the act of holding another man's testicles pleasurable in and of itself? Was it a power thing? Was Ben simply unable to contain his impulses—or was the entire account a lie?

Hudson was likely wary of Worcester's answers if he posed those questions, but it is also probable that Hudson—an older, traditional man from New England—lacked sufficient knowledge of the incipient gay world even to conceive of them. Non-fairy, middle-class homosexuals sought to hide their interest in men from all but those whom they trusted. By that standard, the acts Worcester described defied rationality—for Ben had no reason to trust Worcester—but only an unusual lawyer would have been able to ask questions in 1914 arising from knowledge of how a rational homosexual would have acted. Like Crowder, Hudson most likely believed that "rational homosexual" was an oxymoron.

Hudson hailed from a state with one of the country's most restrictive Comstock Laws, which criminalized discussion of contraception and printed material about sex in the interests of "moral purity."[9] He and the jurors were undoubtedly influenced by a socio-legal climate that made discussing sex taboo, but by avoiding exploration of the reasons for Ben's supposed "suggestion," Hudson ceded territory to the imaginations of the jurors and what they knew, or thought they knew, about male "perverts." The record now contained Worcester's assertion that Ben grabbed his testicles and then said he was "just fooling."

Why would a man do such a thing? The jurors, married men, could only wonder. Often separated from their wives, they presumably had a reasonably uniform conception of how a "normal" man dealt with desire when it could not be satisfied through spousal sex—by adultery, masturbation, or abstinence, the first two being understood to require secrecy and discretion. But the unmarried Ben Koehler was accused of coming on to men, a big unknown for most people in 1914. Hudson had left the jurors free to throw up their hands and say "Who knows how such people might behave?"

Hudson did not want Worcester to opine about Ben's motives, but he had many other questions for the lead witness, who admitted that the first time Ben supposedly groped him, "I was where others may have seen me," including the private supervising the furnace and "some other person smoking in the room at the time." The jurors would have to wait to find out whether or not either person would testify that they had observed what Worcester described.

Hudson pressed Worcester for details, asking, "How was Major Koehler standing or what was his position when this first thing occurred?"

"As I remember it there was a small table just inside the door and he was sitting on the corner of the table with his right leg thrown over the table. Of this I will not be positive. I remember he was near the corner of the table."

"As you passed by him he grabbed you by the testicles?"

"Yes, sir."

Hudson imitated the body position Worcester had described and asked if it was correct.

"Yes, sir. I think he was sitting on the table but of that I can't be positive."

"You have so described it?"

"Yes, sir I said as far as I could describe it."

"Well, an incident of this kind would impress your memory, wouldn't it?

"Not to remember such details as that."

"A most extraordinary action on the part of Major Koehler, you construed it, did you not?"

"Decidedly so."

"Then you would remember a detail like sitting on the table?"

At that point Mayes objected that Hudson was arguing with the witness. Of course, Hudson was trying to show that Worcester's lack of precise recollection made his account suspect, but Hudson went along with the objection and began a different line of questions. There was no gain in coming across as too aggressive, both because the trial was only beginning and because this was no ordinary jury. Hudson's client was being judged for failure to be a gentleman by men who themselves had taken oaths to behave as gentlemen. It behooved Hudson to appear polite—even though the subject matter was anything but.

"Now did he actually grab your testicles?" Hudson asked.

"Yes."

"So that he held them in his hand?"

"Yes, sir."

"Which hand?"

"I don't know sir. My impression is that it was his right hand but I can't be sure."

"You know how you were passing by the table?"

"Yes, sir."

"You cannot tell whether it was the left hand or right hand?"

"No, sir."

Hudson returned to the subject of Worcester's costume. "Now could anyone see through the dress when you were in a certain light to see the outline of your body?"

"I think they could sir."

Hudson was gearing up to ask whether Worcester may have misinterpreted a playful gesture invited by the dress, but Worcester swerved instead of going along.

"Were you personally friendly?" Hudson asked.

"Personally I had at that time come across so much information that I rather suspected he was a moral degenerate, yes."

"From rumors you had heard you had formed an opinion of Major Koehler?"

"No, sir, not of rumors but of things that had been told me as facts which I finally brought up to the Commanding Officer of the Department."

"You mean other things you had been told?"

"Yes, sir."

"Whether they were facts or not is an opinion."

"Yes, sir."

Hudson then had the chance to pose his theory of misinterpretation: "Now entirely apart from anything you hear, if you were dressed as a woman in the way you described to the court and some other officer, as you had passed, had made a reach for you in the way you have described, would you consider it of any great significance?"

What was Worcester to say but yes—which is what he did say: "I certainly would if he grabbed me by the testicles."

Hudson would not let go of his theory.

"Couldn't that be done innocently and as a joke by one man to another, a man dressed as a woman, the way you have described?"

"Not by that movement, you know in the vernacular what is called goosing, or reaching for the legs."

Worcester said no matter who had done what Ben did to him, he would have reported it to a higher level "or knock[ed] him down."

Hudson may have thought that accusing a West Point graduate of misinterpreting levity was more palatable than calling him a liar, but if Worcester was the mastermind of a plot, if he was prepared to lie and enlist others to lie, asking him whether he might have misperceived his target's actions wholly missed the mark. It only allowed Worcester to repeat and fortify his characterization of events.

Hudson was more successful showing that Worcester had trouble recalling details. When asked about the second incident, Worcester said, "[W]e were standing there talking to one another and he grabbed me by the testicles," but Worcester could not remember the subject matter, how long they talked, or anything that Ben said before the first or second incident "until I said 'What do you mean by that?' the last time."

"[A]nd just what did he say? Give us the exact words."

"I can't give his exact words. I remember they were to the effect that 'I was just joking' or 'I was fooling.'"

Notably, Worcester said that party guests "were all sitting around the other part of the cellar" when the second act took place, again bearing on the believability of Ben's having accosted Worcester with other people so close by.

After questioning Worcester about his imitation of a hoochie-coochie dancer, Hudson asked whether Worcester was called to Ben's office to discuss the dancing and the party.

Mayes objected, complaining that Hudson was "virtually trying this witness for any conduct of his which Major Koehler may have objected to." Yet conduct to which Ben objected was exactly what Hudson needed to prove to support the conspiracy defense. Hudson argued that he should have latitude to show "that Major Koehler's discipline of these various witnesses . . . might be . . . a reason for their hostility to him and their testimony to put him in the worst light possible."

Mayes countered that Hudson could ask whether Worcester received a reprimand "but we cannot go into the subject matter which prompted that reprimand."

Hudson tried a different approach. "Was there any kissing at this dance?" he asked.

"Not that I know of," Worcester answered. Immediately, Mayes objected. A juror asked Worcester to leave the room.

More sparring took place, for so long that one juror asked to be reminded "to what question he is objecting." Mayes's reply left no doubt about his view of the case: "The question which started all this was 'Was there any kissing at this dance?' It does not make any difference whether there was any kissing or not so far as one man grabbing another man by the testicles. It is absolutely immaterial."

Hudson steered back to Worcester's motives, saying that if "there was general conduct there that was unusual and then this man was criticized after or reprimanded after by his superior officer, wouldn't that be a ground for maliciousness afterward on the part of that man?"

Now Kirby asked everyone to leave except the jurors. When the session reopened, he told Hudson to proceed, but it proved to be an empty victory, for just as Worcester claimed to have no memory of being criticized during the party, the same held true after the party.

"I have absolutely no recollection of this dance ever being mentioned to me or the other affairs of that night ever being mentioned to me by Major Koehler," he said.

If Ben did call Worcester to his office to reprimand him for his attire and conduct, as Ben would testify, putting that criticism in writing would have been a good idea—but that was only glaringly obvious in hindsight. At the time, just a few months after Worcester's arrival on Plum Island, Ben had no idea of what was building in Worcester's mind, as the rest of Worcester's testimony would reveal.

# A Clever Witness

WORCESTER TOOK FULL RESPONSIBILITY for reporting Ben. "I considered it my duty," he testified, "to bring this matter up to higher authority, in order that the Army should remain clean."[1]

"Clean." That was a zinger, sure to make an impact on a group of officers who had pledged allegiance to "good order and discipline" and collectively bore responsibility for upholding the moral standards of thousands of men. The answer had followed a question from Mayes: "What prompted you in making this report? Animus toward Major Koehler or a sense of duty to the military service and society?" It was a softball question, and Worcester swung well.

Hudson had made a decision earlier not to allow Worcester to speculate as to Ben's intentions, but he apparently decided he had to let Worcester talk about more than the party and Ben's reprimands if he wanted to elicit elements of a conspiracy to lie. Mayes was able to ask on redirect about Worcester's motivation because Hudson had opened the door to that question.

It started when Hudson asked if Worcester had reported "the action of Major Koehler to anyone" after the party.

"No, sir."

"Why not?"

"Because when this happened it thoroughly convinced my mind that the stories I had heard about the Major were true . . ."

Yet instead of reporting Ben right after the party, Worcester said he did something else: "I put a letter in to Lieutenant Putney, West Point, to corroborate certain stories and he agreed that these stories were true."

That was the first reference to Edward Putney, formerly of Fort Terry, who now taught in the West Point chemistry department where Worcester had worked. Like Lieutenant Thomas Jones, whose name had been used in Captain Robinson's report to Colonel Davis, Putney was a phantom who would never appear at the trial but whose existence would hang over it.

Hudson moved on, asking Worcester, "How long before this dance had you heard anything relating to improper conduct on the part of Major Koehler?"

Worcester answered that Frick said something to him "about the last of June or the 1st of July" when Worcester had just arrived on Fishers Island after his three years of teaching.

"Did you hear it from anyone else from that time up to the time of this dance?"

Worcester responded that "due to the Shanley incident I talked with Captain Robinson," but the answer did not make sense. How did speaking to Robinson reveal impropriety by Ben? There was no allegation by Robinson that Ben accosted him, and the dispute over Shanley's punishment did not come to a head until mid-November 1913, after the Halloween party.

Worcester realized his mistake right away. "Up to the time of the dance, sir?" he repeated.

"Yes, sir," answered Hudson.

Then Worcester provided a different answer: "Lieutenant Putney from West Point wrote me a letter."

That was not right either, Worcester realized, for he had testified a few minutes earlier that he contacted Putney after the Halloween party. Once again, he changed his story.

"No, I am getting the time wrong. I guess Sergeant Kirkman was the only man up to that time."

Hudson wanted to be sure he understood: "Sergeant Kirkman and

Lieutenant Frick were the only men then who had ever spoken to you about Major Koehler along the lines that I have discussed?"

"Anything definite. Sergeant Byers intimated something to me."

That "intimation," it turned out, also concerned "the Shanley incident." According to Worcester, Byers told him, "You will never try Shanley . . . he is one of the Major's pets."

"What was the Shanley incident?" Hudson asked.

Worcester spoke about the drinking and fights after the Rhode Island march, casting Ben as practically indifferent.

[T]he day we left for Fort Terry I was walking along the street and met Major Koehler that morning and I said I had a fight in the Company and he sort of laughed and said "Yes?" and asked me who was in it and I told him. He said "Oh, yes, a drunken row, I guess." He said "Shanley is a pretty good man; just summary court charges." Or words to that effect. I looked into the matter and thought the man should be tried by general court. That is what I mean by the Shanley incident.

Worcester went on, saying Ben told him Shanley "is a good man and it will come out that he was drunk and it will break up our having beer at the smokers of the post."

This portrayal of Ben as overly fond of alcohol would be echoed by Frick and other prosecution witnesses—just as it had been presented in Henry Koehler's letter—consistent with a rising stereotype of gay men as intemperate. A psychoanalyst writing in the early 1900s opined that "[t]he homosexual component-instincts, which education has taught us to repress and sublimate, reappear in no veiled form under the influence of alcohol."[2]

Through all this Ben sat mute, eyes downcast, knowing he had challenged the beer permit for the Army–Navy games and closed the officers' club after a fight related to drinking.

Worcester had taught cadets and knew how to prepare and deliver lectures. He exhibited characteristic self-assurance on the stand, but every now and then, Hudson pressed him sufficiently that Worcester recast a prior answer in terms more favorable to Ben.

For example, when first describing what happened after he disagreed with Ben's decision to try Shanley on the same charges as the
other privates, Worcester said Ben "showed me a letter and he said
that letter gave him the authority not to forward those [general
charges] and he returned it to me with the incident closed. So the
man was tried by summary court." But later, Worcester admitted that
Ben had left it up to Worcester to decide whether to appeal to a higher
level. It was Worcester, not Ben, who "considered the matter was
closed."

Yet Worcester had insinuated to Colonel Mills, and was now insinuating on the stand, that Ben rejected stronger charges against Shanley because of a sexual relationship with him. Worcester said his belief
that "the Major was protecting Shanley . . . was the reason these things
and other things excited my suspicions. Then soldiers came to me and
gave me statements which convinced me that I was right in these suspicions. That is what I told Colonel Mills."

Citing the Shanley incident as the reason for his "suspicions" suffered from the same defect as Worcester's initial answer, that "due to
the Shanley incident I talked with Captain Robinson." The timing was
off. If Worcester's testicles had been fondled by Ben on November 1,
why were his "suspicions" about Ben not "excited" until two weeks
later?

Hudson did not ask that follow-up question, and it takes repeated
readings of the transcript to see how much Worcester was jumping
around in time and yet purporting to tell a chronological narrative of
consecutive events and growing suspicions.

It was, Worcester maintained, a "mere accumulation of circumstances" that made him think Shanley was a "favorite" of Ben's. "Favorite" here was code for "lover," unlike when used to refer to
Worcester's favorite, Kirkman, his first sergeant, who had asked to
transfer into Worcester's company. Worcester had not brought charges
against Kirkman for the fights, and he thought Shanley deserved
harsh punishment because of insubordination toward Kirkman.
Worcester criticized Ben for telling him that Kirkman had been
accused of enticing two young girls into a building when Kirkman

denied any involvement, after which Worcester "made up my mind that Major Koehler was not telling me the exact facts."

Apparently, the issue was not having a favorite; it was whether the favoritism could be perceived as sexual. Worcester, deft at innuendo, said he saw Shanley "coming out of the Major's house one evening and wondered why he had gone there without asking my authority."

Worcester denied that the disagreement over Shanley's discipline gave him any motive to sabotage Ben, saying it "opened up to me what I thought was a line of information that Major Koehler was not straight. That was my only idea in taking the matter up."

And while Worcester admitted that he had ridden home in a wagon after returning from Rhode Island, rather than marching with his company to the barracks, he denied that Ben reprimanded him for it—"never had a word to say to him about it."

He testified similarly when Hudson asked about the alleged plagiarism in the course taught by Captain Patten. At first, Worcester claimed not to know what Hudson was talking about. Hudson pressed on, asking Worcester "[w]ere you not accused by Captain Patten of copying the problem and its solution from a text book used in the Leavenworth school?"

"No, sir, I was not accused of anything in the matter."

"Were you not criticized for doing it?"

"During the second recitation Captain Patten said 'Some of you officers are following the Leavenworth course too closely' . . . but Captain Patten did not accuse me of anything at all, he just made the statement . . ."

"Did you and Major Koehler have any discussion about the way in which that problem was solved?"

"No, sir, we never had a single word about it," answered Worcester. "The matter was never brought up."

A different story emerged on redirect. Asked by Mayes whether an official report had been made about the copying, Worcester answered, "No, sir, the first I heard of it was when Captain Patten told me of his conversation with Major Koehler."

That was an important admission, confirming that Worcester did know Patten had told Ben of the matter. Surprisingly, Hudson did not come back to the point during recross. It does not appear that Hudson ever grasped the significance of Ben's intention to report the alleged plagiarism as a powerful impetus for Worcester to seek Ben's ouster before he could do so.

Hudson might have asked Worcester about his past teaching at West Point, suggesting a reason why Worcester would want to conceal a possible violation of academic ethics, but likely Hudson did not know about Worcester's teaching background. Preparation for the trial had been so rushed that Hawthorne and Hudson did not request their own client's official military records until the first day of the trial—and did not receive them until much later.[3]

All Hudson asked was "have you any feeling of hostility to Major Koehler?" Predictably, the answer was "No, sir." Worcester claimed that Ben and he "were great friends" the summer after Bud Dajo at Fort Monroe, where "Major Koehler was very nice to me . . . in an official manner."

AFTER NEARLY THREE HOURS of testimony, a juror asked for the court to be cleared. Another agreed. It turned out they were hungry. Kirby asked Hudson how much longer he intended to keep Worcester on the stand. "It is getting pretty near our lunch time now," he pointed out.

Hudson promised to be brief, but he wasn't going to give up his next set of questions. They were important, revealing the extent to which Worcester was involved in what other men had told Mills. Worcester acknowledged that while Mills was sitting upstairs in the Post Exchange building, Worcester sat downstairs calling prospective witnesses by phone, including Kirkman, Barrett, Byers, Brown, and Robinson. In all, he identified twelve men he told to come talk to Mills.

Serving as gatekeeper, Worcester was the last person to speak to the men, many of whom were under his command, before they gave their accounts to Mills. At first Worcester denied that he "discuss[ed] what

they were to tell Colonel Mills," but again he backtracked, saying he
told Kirkman "to tell what he told me"—certainly an ambiguous statement. It could just as easily mean that Kirkman was to repeat a lie he
had rehearsed as to tell the truth. Worcester also admitted discussing
others' testimony before they spoke to Mills: "After the first part of the
investigation I went over to see Master Electrician Brown and Sergeant Griswold at their quarters respectively and I asked them if they
had anything to testify and they told me what they had to testify and
then I went to Colonel Mills and told him that these men had things
to testify and he called them the next day."

Ben could only hope the jurors were not too hungry to pay attention. Here was Worcester admitting that he had sought out and
screened witnesses to speak to Mills, and (as Sophia had written to
Roy) Worcester had the power of the guardhouse behind him to persuade men to fall in line. He also had the power to deny furloughs,
passes, and promotions.

Worcester's dialogue with the witnesses continued after they spoke
to Mills. Some men told him what they had said to Mills, and Mills
"came down himself and discussed some of the things," giving Worcester the opportunity to check compliance with his instructions.

At that point, Hudson switched gears, eliciting an acknowledgment
by Worcester that he attended two social functions with Ben in November, a dinner in New London and a beach picnic. "I could not get
out of either one of them," Worcester said.

Then, as though a clock was counting down final minutes in a
match, the pace sped up. Hudson and Mayes alternately rose to their
feet for quick rounds of redirect and recross, both trying to score
points. An important new detail flew by. Asked by Hudson why, after
the party, Worcester had not inquired of other officers "whether Ben
had done anything of that kind" to them, Worcester answered, "I was
not discussing what he had done to me with anybody until I told Captain Robinson that day."

It seemed that all roads came back to the conversation Worcester
had with Robinson in mid-November. Only then, Worcester was now
clearly saying—when he was fuming over his inability to get Shanley

court-martialed and he was worried about a possible accusation of plagiarism—did Worcester assert that he had been groped on November 1.



DESPITE THEIR RUMBLING STOMACHS, the jurors had a few questions of their own. Kirby wanted to know whether the social events with Ben took place after the Halloween party. Worcester admitted that they did.

Kirby asked whether Worcester could have "walked away" when he saw Ben in the cellar after the first grope and before the second grope. "Yes, sir," Worcester answered. Kirby also asked why Worcester invited Ben to his party if he had "any reason to believe and did . . . believe that the accused was a moral degenerate."

The question showed that Worcester's jumbled timeline had succeeded in muddying the record. Worcester sidestepped, saying, " It appeared to me from the stories that were coming to me that he was, but I was not in a position at that time to make any difference with him on this post and I waited my time to do it until I had a chance to take it up to General Barry's authority."

Kirby asked Worcester to demonstrate how Koehler "is alleged to have grasped you by the testicles." The court reporter did his best to capture the moment: "He grasped me in this way (Witness illustrates by grasping himself in the crotch) and squeezed the testicles and in the buttock it was up in under that way, with a squeeze (illustrating)."

While Worcester had told Mayes in December that Koehler touched his breast, and that allegation was spelled out in the official statement of charges, when now asked whether there was any touching of his breast, he answered, "no."

Kirby wanted to know, given that Worcester described himself as "incensed" at being touched, why Worcester had not said anything to Koehler the first time. Worcester replied:

I was in a quandary as to what to do. I considered myself insulted, but in my own house with a party going on and a lot of ladies present I did not like to make any stir or commotion and . . . I decided when this thing happened the second time to make no scene, but to wait until such time as I could co-ordinate that occasion with these other things I had heard and lay them before the proper authorities, which I did at Governors Island.

That was some answer. A man has his genitals grabbed by his boss. He is angry, but what goes through his mind is when he can report the matter to a general five hours away.

Now Hudson made a request: Would the jury visit the basement of Worcester's house and require Worcester to wear his Halloween costume—"including everything"?

No, Kirby responded after the jurors conferred. They were not interested in the house or "having him dress in that dress . . . At present there does not seem to be any necessity for it."

Why was there no necessity to visit the scene or make Worcester "dress in that dress"? The court broke for lunch, with both sides free to speculate as to the answer. Was it because the jurors were so convinced that Worcester was telling the truth—or that he was lying?

# *Ungrateful Guest*

After lunch, when Second Lieutenant Austin Frick took the stand, he had to be asked to remove his dark glasses. Afternoon light was streaming in through the library windows, amplified by the sun's reflection off the snow.

"It will not be a hardship for you to remove them, will it witness?" asked Kirby.

"No sir," answered Frick.

"Then just keep them off please."[1]

Frick would refrain from wearing his sunglasses for more than two hours as he gave testimony portraying Ben as a bawdy, queer man with so little self-control that he tried to caress Frick in the bathroom with Sophia downstairs, and fondled Frick's genitals in a room full of people.

Two and a half months had passed since Ben's arrest, time to get over the initial shock, but still, it must have been especially painful to listen to Frick's words. Unlike Worcester, Frick was no latecomer to Plum Island. When Ben and Sophia arrived, in the autumn of 1911, Frick had been at Fort Terry since the previous spring. At first, he seemed grateful for their company, especially Sophia's, livening up her life with cards, bowling, and tennis and making her feel young. Frick came for Thanksgiving dinner and vied for the attention of the Koehlers' cousin. He also helped the Koehlers entertain visiting officers, sometimes serving as bartender. He had invited Sophia and Ben to be his guests at the officers' club as recently as September 1913.[2]

Frick was always affable, Ben would testify. "[I]t is Lieutenant Frick's nature, no matter what you say to Lieutenant Frick, he will pretend to be very friendly."[3]

Not on the witness stand.

Frick testified that at the end of the Koehlers' first summer, in August 1912, target exercises ran late one night and Ben invited Frick to eat dinner at his house. Ben showed him upstairs to the bathroom and, Frick said, as he washed his hands, Ben "came up to me and put his arms about me and attempted to pull my head towards his shoulder." Then, in the bedroom, while Frick brushed his hair, Ben "reached up again and brushed his face against mine and put his arms around me."

Inserting a dig at Ben's height, Frick said that "being somewhat taller than he it was rather difficult for him to reach up and reach my cheek as long as I moved around at all."

As they headed to the stairs, Frick continued, Ben again pressed his cheek against Frick and said, "'Do you know what is the matter with Russell?' referring to Mr. Russell who was just relieved as Ordnance officer here. He said 'He was fucked to death.'"

Hudson objected, and Mayes told his witness, "Just limit your testimony to acts."

Frick went on to say that Ben walked with him back to camp and asked, "Do you care to come to the tent and have a drink?" but Frick declined.

Mayes then inquired about a dance at Captain Ellis's house in April 1913—one of the dances that Sophia had said made life "quite gay" after her return from Puerto Rico.[4]

"Did anything unusual occur between you and Major Koehler during the dance?" asked Mayes.

"Decidedly so," replied Frick, repeating one of Worcester's pet phrases. "[T]he Major proposed that we dance a rag together or our present day turkey-trot. We were dancing in the middle of the room and people all around us. The major reached down and grabbed me in the crotch, grabbed my penis and testicles and squeezed my testicles so hard that I had very much the sensation of being struck."

Frick said he stopped dancing "as soon as I could near the edge of the crowd" but did not say anything to Ben. "I simply did not know what to say."

"Did you consent at all to this action on his part?" asked Mayes.

"No, sir, I stopped dancing and got out of the whirl of the dancers as quickly as I could."

During cross-examination, Frick so exasperated Hudson that Hudson apologized to the jury "for a little temper." Frick was fuzzy on details yet did his best to score points. He cast his visits to the Koehlers as involuntary—"primarily [because] he was my Commanding Officer" or because Frick had been summoned "to come down and mix a cocktail or mix a drink" when there were guests, including some of the jurors.

The night he ate dinner with the Koehlers, Frick had said he rode his bicycle to the house and walked back to camp pushing the bike, but in response to a question from Hudson, he claimed not to remember whether it was raining or whether he walked, rode his bicycle, or took the buckboard.

He did, however, remember that he said "nothing" after the upstairs overtures.

"Made no comment at all?" asked Hudson.

"No, sir."

"And then you went downstairs and sat down at the table?"

"Yes, sir."

"And finished your dinner?"

"Yes, sir."

Nor, Frick said, did he make any comment when Ben grabbed him at the dance. Unlike Worcester, Frick claimed that Ben's grope hurt, but he did not yell or cry out and did not say anything about it until "after Colonel Mills came."

Meanwhile, Frick was engaged in finding out what other people were saying, or were willing to say, about Ben's "moral character," as Hudson phrased it. Frick said he first heard something negative in

1912—the content went unspecified—and then talked about Ben in April 1913 at a dance at Fort Wright.

"[W]ith whom did you talk?"

"Lieutenant Putney and Sergeant Byers. No discussion, just simply they asked me the question if I had heard certain reports. I said that I had."

In addition, Frick acknowledged discussing "the rumors or talk about Major Koehler" with Walsh, Robinson, a retired sergeant, and "then Captain Worcester." Frick also said he asked a sergeant named Archer "if he knew anything irregular about the Major."

"Did you give those names of the persons you talked with to Captain Worcester before the arrival of Colonel Mills?" asked Hudson.

"I did," answered Frick.

Before the trial, Colonel Hawthorne had invited the accusers to speak to him one on one. It was voluntary, they were not under oath, and no court reporter was transcribing their answers—as would occur today in pretrial depositions—but the sessions gave Ben's counsel an idea of what the defense was up against. Frick had apparently told Hawthorne that he spoke to ten men before Mills arrived, but now Frick claimed not to remember what he had said to Hawthorne.

"He asked me so many questions I don't remember what I told him on any of them."

Hudson turned to Frick's "trouble" with Ben, a word Frick said was too strong. "I think we had one misunderstanding, but not what I consider anything in the sense of trouble."

"Have you had more than one misunderstanding?"

"Not that I would consider a misunderstanding."

"Well, have you had more than one difference?"

"I suppose I have."

Mayes objected to further inquiry, but Kirby overruled him. Obliged to answer, Frick minimized his "differences" with Ben, just as Worcester had: the dispute over the hop committee, Frick's dismissal as athletic director, his failing to try to rescue the private who fell overboard, his gossip about others' sex lives, and the times Ben found Frick "studying" instead of carrying out instructions. "I personally liked Major Koehler," Frick maintained, though he admitted Ben was "quite nettled" about being excluded from the hop committee's decision to hold a dance.

When it came to Frick's having allowed an officer's daughter to socialize with the woman Frick told Ben he had slept with, Frick again gratuitously portrayed Ben as a drinker.

"I did not consider it a reprimand. I was told I had made a mistake," said Frick. "The fact of the case is the statement was given to me while the Major was drinking a high ball sometime after this night in which he grabbed my person."

Hudson returned to the supposed overtures in the Koehler house, asking Frick a variant of the question he had refrained from asking Worcester: "What did you think he was trying to do?"

"I am not sure," Frick answered. "I don't know; I am not used to doing things like that."

"What did you think when you went in to the room he was trying to do?"

"I was still more puzzled, really panicky."

"You did not say anything to him in criticism of it at all?"

"It is not wise to criticize your Commanding Officer at any time much, especially not to his face."

At that point a juror interjected, "I wish he would answer that question."

And Frick did: "I said nothing."

Another juror offered some help, asking Frick, "Did Major Koehler attempt to kiss you in his quarters?"

Frick answered coyly: "I interpreted the fact that he pressed his lips against my cheeks that that was the intention."

Yet Frick had earlier said that Ben was too short to reach his cheeks. Frick stood at five foot eleven. Ben Koehler was five foot three. Hudson might have pointed out the discrepancy, but perhaps he thought it was obvious. Nor did he ask Frick why, if he was the one prodding Robinson in July 1913 to report Ben to Colonel Davis based on supposed advances to an absent lieutenant, Frick did not mention that he himself had twice been victimized by Koehler.

With all the damning statements coming out of Worcester's and Frick's mouths, a lawyer could do only so much, and Hudson had to give the jurors some credit. While Enoch Crowder had pronounced Frick's claims particularly strong after reading the Mills report, Hudson had to hope that seeing Frick in the flesh would cause the jurors to think otherwise.

# An American Dreyfus?

T HERE WAS NO LEAVING Plum Island over the weekend for nearly everyone involved in the trial—and no coming ashore by curious reporters—but the absent media gave the defense a boost, comparing Ben to one of the era's most famous victims of persecution.

"LIKEN HIM TO DREYFUS" read the headline in Sunday's *Washington Post*, referring to Alfred Dreyfus, the French Army captain who was convicted of treason in 1894 in a hurried court-martial. Dreyfus was heckled with cries of "Jew" and "Judas" in a public degrading that included the breaking of his sword and mutilation of his uniform, then imprisoned on Devil's Island, retried after a national outcry over faked evidence and anti-Semitism, and exonerated in the early 1900s.[1]

Dreyfus's lawyer called the conviction the greatest crime of the century. French novelist Émile Zola famously wrote an article entitled "J'Accuse" portraying the French military and government as heinous. He accused them of violating usual procedures, ignoring evidence of the true seller of military secrets to Germany, and intentionally sacrificing truth and justice in order to obtain a conviction, knowing that hatred of Jews lay just below the surface in modern France and that a large portion of the public would welcome the chance openly to hate a Jew, especially for something as egregious as treason.

Dreyfus was a hard-working and soft-spoken family man, an assimilated Jew from Alsace who never stopped declaring his love of France—

not when people spat at him when he was degraded in front of the Eiffel Tower, and not after years of imprisonment, enforced silence, and separation from his wife and children. He went on to serve again in the Army, rise in rank, and receive the Légion d'honneur.

Historians say the Dreyfus Affair marked the birth of the liberal intellectual in western society—the first time writers, artists, and academics played a major, successful role as political advocates. The first Jewish prime minister of France, Léon Blum, credited the affair with enhancing acceptance of Jews such that he could hold such a high office.[2] "A country that tears itself apart to defend the honor of a small Jewish captain is somewhere worth going," Blum's father is said to have quipped.[3]

Writers still find relevance in the case, such as Louis Begley and *New Yorker* contributor Adam Gopnik, who in a review of Begley's book about Dreyfus wrote that the "Dreyfus affair matters . . . because it was one of the first tests of modern pluralist liberalism and its institutions—a test that those institutions somehow managed to pass and fail at the same time."[4]

They failed by accusing and convicting Dreyfus; they passed by admitting error and allowing Dreyfus to rejoin the military. Samuel Hudson had to hope that the same would come to pass for his client, for there were definite similarities between the two men and their cases.

Like Ben Koehler, Dreyfus was a military academy graduate and artilleryman. Both men were short and wanting in charisma. Neither was a charmer, in contrast to the key witnesses against Ben, the gregarious Worcester and likable Frick. Gopnik describes Dreyfus as having a "cold and correct demeanor," and the same could be said of Ben, at least some of the time, such as when he wore his uniform to a costume party, told men to button their collars on hot days, and closed the officers' club. Ben's English-molded propriety put some people off.

And just like Dreyfus, Ben had supporters who claimed the military justice system was failing him. "Koehler's friends . . . liken his case to that of Dreyfus and hold he is being made the victim of a plot," wrote the *Washington Post*.

But while Dreyfus's many advocates—the so-called Dreyfusards—
pointed to anti-Semitism as the factor fueling the persecution of
Dreyfus, Ben's supporters did not have a name for what was happening to him.

One "man who knows Maj. Koehler" hinted at what might be called
homophobia today when quoted as "tell[ing] this as an example of the
charges": "Maj. Koehler, who made personal inspections among the
company quarters, frequently would discover that a young recruit was
melancholy. He would take a fatherly interest in the youth, encouraging him by cheering words and by advice. His interest in those new
soldiers is misinterpreted purposely by his accusers."[5]

Surely there were married officers who took "a fatherly interest" in
new soldiers in 1912 and 1913, but no one was accusing them of homoerotic behavior. The idea that "fatherly interest" by an unmarried
man in other men could be "misinterpreted" as homosexuality aligns
with Michael Kimmel's "central thesis about American manhood at
the turn of the century; that masculinity was increasingly an act, a
form of public display; that men felt themselves on display at virtually
all times; and that the intensity of the need for such display was increasing. To be considered a real man, one had better make sure to
always be walking around and acting 'real masculine.'"[6]

Though he had fought in the Philippine War, Ben did not spend
his time at Fort Terry "walking around and acting 'real masculine.'"
There would even be debate by the lawyers about Ben's hobby of growing flowers and what that said about him, as though no married man
in the early 1900s ever liked to look upon a rose—including the officers who planted Ben's flowers in front of their houses.

Were people ready to "tear the country apart" over the alleged mis-
treatment of a possibly homosexual man who wasn't even claiming
that identity for himself? They were not, and the consequent lack of
an ideological rallying cry left people speculating about the possible
reasons for a "plot" against Ben.

One explanation offered by the *Washington Post* was that "Koehler
offended his brother officers, closing the Officers' Club at Fort Terry,

by requiring hard work of them and in other ways." Yet the paper also reported that at Fort Terry, Ben had "won the esteem of those with whom he has come in contact."

"Personal hatred," was the explanation provided in the *Washington Times*.

It is impossible to know where the press was getting its information. Both Washington papers sent reporters to New London, in view of extreme interest in the case in the nation's capital arising from the charges of a plot within the Army, the nature of the charges, and the involvement of congressmen, senators, and cabinet members. For its part, *The New York Times* appears to have been in daily contact with Wood and/or Garrison.

Yet whether or not they knew the details of the allegations, reporters were not printing them (at least not yet), merely referring to them as "scandalous," "immoral," and "reek[ing] with immorality and degeneracy."[7] According to the *Washington Post*, the utmost secrecy was being enforced: "Passes on the government boats are refused. Attempts to land from private boats are frustrated. Soldiers are denied the privilege to leave the island, and civilians are kept there veritable prisoners for fear they may talk. Two local photographers who were known to have photographs of interest at this time, it is alleged, are detained at the fort."

Even a prominent attorney was denied access to Plum Island. Daniel Anthony Jr. and Bat Koehler urged the national chair of the Democratic Party, William McCombs, to look into Ben's case, and McCombs sent his law partner, Frederick Ryan, from Boston to speak to Ben. While the Army let Ryan cross the Sound from New London, he was blocked from disembarking. Instead, Ben and Hawthorne conferred with Ryan in the captain's cabin. The lawyer then turned around and headed home.[8] It does not appear that he played any further role in the case.

For a time, however, it looked like the veil of secrecy might be lifted on orders from Washington. This development caught everyone by surprise late Thursday.

. . .

IN THE DREYFUS CASE, government secrecy infuriated both sides. For
failing to make the accusation of treason public when first lodged,
anti-Semites accused the French military of "protecting a traitor Jew,"
while the Dreyfusards accused the government of using secrecy to
hide its unfair legal tactics.[9]

In Ben's case, the press wanted access, and Garrison and Wood
wanted them to have it.

After Garrison received the Wednesday telegram from Barry stating that the court-martial would be closed, he replied the next day
that while he "sympathized" with the desire "that the unpleasant details" of the case not be made public, that did not outweigh the "undesirable attitude of holding the sessions . . . in private." He went on
to explain: "I am a firm believer that the administration of justice
should be open and in sight of the people, and I have never favored
trials not so open to the public. Much less harm is done to what is
essential by having justice administered in plain sight . . ."

Garrison ordered "that the trial of Major Koehler be open to the
public," and as for the "unpleasant details," he was prepared to trust
the media: "Newspapers must be guided by their own sense of decency as to what is proper to publish, and it is not our business to act
as their guardians in this regard."[10]

Garrison's words sounded stirring, anticipating arguments that
First Amendment advocates would make later in the century in support of media access to official proceedings. His message was also
complimentary of reporters' judgment—but it was written before trials became true-life dramas for public consumption, before the "media circus" of the Lindbergh baby trial, the O. J. Simpson case, and
other legal spectacles. It is possible, however, that underlying Garrison's order was a desire for, or indifference toward, Ben's public shaming. If Wood wanted revenge and the investigations had convinced
Garrison of Koehler's guilt, did Wood and Garrison agree that Ben
deserved as much public censure as could be delivered?

Barry had no choice but to relay Garrison's order to Fort Terry, where a soldier handed it to Kirby after Frick finished testifying.[11] Kirby read the telegram and fumed. As adamant as Garrison was in favor of opening the trial, Kirby was equally opposed. He discussed the order with Mayes and Hudson, and he telegraphed Barry that he wished Garrison would change his mind.[12] Kirby may have agreed that publicity would hurt the Army, but his main concern was "decency," or so he said. He did not believe the public should read about testicle-grabbing in the papers.[13] Mayes agreed, quoted as saying that "any degree of secrecy was preferable to the exposure of disgraceful conditions affecting a whole garrison."[14]

Kirby also knew that the person with the biggest stake in the trial was Ben, and the telegram that went back to Governors Island Thursday night said, "the accused now requests that in his interest the action of the Secretary [of] War be reconsidered." Kirby cited legal authority to support his request, which Barry's chief of staff relayed to Washington that night.[15]

Until the matter was decided, Ben's court-martial stood in recess. There would be no testimony on Friday. Garrison was getting some attitude from little Plum Island.

The pushback worked. Garrison replied that he did not mean to "control" the court's discretion in "passing on any motion of the accused requesting exclusion of spectators." He gave the jury the right to make the decision—"bearing in mind that unless the administration of justice will be furthered by the exclusion of spectators, courts-martial should be open to the public."[16]

Kirby did not need the lecture. He knew what he wanted. On Saturday morning, the parties gathered in the headquarters building. Hudson rose and on behalf of Ben made a formal request that the public and press be excluded. Mayes agreed, and a majority of the three colonels, five lieutenant colonels, and three majors on the jury voted to keep the trial secret.[17]

According to *The New York Times*, "it was generally believed that Major Koehler wanted the trial open to the public, and the news from Washington this morning that he was opposed to an open session caused surprise."[18] The *Washington Post* reported that Kirby had pressured Ben to make the motion and that "Koehler's friends say they see in the secrecy surrounding the court-martial an attempt by high ranking officers to center all accusations on the major."[19] Other papers reported that Ben's Nebraska brothers were "fighting" to keep the trial closed.[20]

The Dreyfus case echoed. As much as Ben stood to lose in reputation from national publicity describing the details of the accusers' testimony, in Dreyfus's case secrecy had favored the government, hiding the paucity of the prosecution's evidence from public scrutiny. An open trial, making visible the government's prosecution of a perceived homosexual of high status who denied the charges, might have brought people concerned with social justice and individual rights to Ben's cause, possibly accelerating the creation of a political movement in opposition to such discrimination. Overall, it was hard to say whether an open or closed court would have served Ben best.

Another similarity between Dreyfus and Ben Koehler concerned the central role played by their brothers. Dreyfus's most tireless supporter was his brother, Mathieu. Likewise, Ben had relied on Louis in deciding to fight the charges. There was a key difference, however, between Louis Koehler and Mathieu Dreyfus: Mathieu was a private citizen, not an employee of the same military that had charged his brother with crimes.

Louis had already been expelled from Puerto Rico, and it was alleged that Wood had "retired from the service" members of the jury who acquitted Louis in 1906, setting up Wood to be court-martialed but for Roosevelt's intervention.[21] So it mattered that Wood would soon become the direct superior of Kirby and the other jurors by returning to his old job as commander of the Eastern Department.[22]

When Roosevelt first gave Wood that top position back in 1907, only weeks after nullifying the Louis Koehler proceedings, there were "many officers who did not think that the War Department's intentions would get out so soon after the Koehler affair," according to *The New York Times*.[23] Indeed, sources had told the *Times* that Roosevelt made the appointment precisely to show support for "his friend Gen. Wood" after the Louis Koehler verdict cast Wood as a tyrant.

How ironic, then, that Wood should return to a position he may have obtained as a result of one Koehler brother to influence the fate of another. As head of the Eastern Department, he would have even more power over the jurors hearing Ben's case than Worcester had over his company soldiers. He would have the power to change their assignments—to send them all the way to the Philippines—and end their military careers, to deprive them of pretty much anything a military man could want.

Wood was also said to have made it clear to his soon-to-be subordinates what he wanted from them: a conviction of Ben Koehler.[24]

Kirby and nearly all the other jurors had stood up to Garrison regarding a closed courtroom. Would they do so to Wood? And, after fourteen more accusers presented their sordid stories, would the jurors be so inclined? Would they believe in Ben Koehler's innocence with the passion of a Dreyfusard?

# Irregularities

J AMES WARD LIKED TO talk. On his way back to Baltimore after
testifying on Saturday, he stopped to chat with a reporter waiting
in New London. Ward declined to reveal his testimony, but when
asked, "[A]t Fort Terry did you form a personal enmity for Major Koehler?" he admitted, "There was a grudge." [1]

That may have been his most honest statement all day.

Ward, the former sergeant who had made the tepid attempts to
warn Ben in July and October, testified that Ben "used to come in my
room occasionally in the morning before I got up and talk with me
on the subject of women and the like of that and once he opened the
fly of my trousers and took out my penis and handled it."[2] He gave an
approximate date, early August 1912, conceding that he was not sure,
may have given Mills a different date or no date, and did not recall
being asked for a date by Mayes.

Ward first said he did not try to thwart Ben because Ben was his
commanding officer, but later, under cross-examination, he said he
"sort of moved away a little bit." The same was true of his testimony. It
moved away from its original presentation. By the end, the incident
may have occurred around noon, not in the morning before he got
up, and he was fully dressed and standing, not lying in bed, though
he couldn't remember where he was standing.

A former schoolteacher at the post, Ward was the first witness to allege that he and Ben actually spoke about sex: "I told the accused that I didn't care for any relations like that. He must have misunderstood me because he said well, he would do anything at all."

Ward initially placed this exchange in his room at the same time as the grope, then said, "I believe it took place in his own home, in his office," and finally said, "I withdraw that, this happened over in the Post Exchange." There was another inconsistency. If Ward did not feel free to resist Ben's unbuttoning his pants because of Ben's rank, why did Ward feel free to tell Ben he did not "care for any relations like that"?

The bigger mystery was why Ward would be warning Ben of a plan by others to bring him down if Ben had already made an advance on Ward. "I told him I heard something was coming off," Ward testified. "I would give him a chance."

If Ward had been groped, why would he want to give Ben a chance? And wouldn't the warning be more like "people are planning to report you" than "something is coming off"?

Hawthorne, not Hudson, was questioning Ward, and due to his persistence, Ward provided information about how the gathering of stories proceeded after Davis told Robinson in July that more information was needed before action could be taken. Ward described Frick as a good friend and said that when Ward visited Plum Island in July, Frick spoke to him about testifying against Ben. As Ward put it:

> Lieutenant Frick called me aside and asked me if I knew anything about a certain individual, mentioning no names, and I said "Of what nature?" and he said "Now you know who I mean," and I said "no." "Well" he says "I mean irregularities of high standing at Fort Terry." Then I grasped his meaning and I said "yes" and he said "You know something about this?" I said "Yes." He said "Would you be willing to get up and testify to what you know?" I said I would be willing.

It is understandable that Frick, like Worcester, would have used such circumspect language—"irregularities of high standing" and "[y]ou know something about this?"—allowing the members of the group to create their own stories, so that when Mayes asked Ward whether Frick told him what to say, Ward answered, "No, sir." Yet if Ward had previously mentioned an advance by Ben, there would have been no need for artifice. It would have been natural for Frick to refer to the incident directly and ask Ward if he was willing to testify about it.

"Had you ever spoken to anyone or had any one spoken to you about the alleged misconduct of the accused prior to the time Lieutenant Frick approached you concerning a pending investigation?" Kirby asked.

"No, sir," said Ward, "only as to common gossip of the post."

In other words, if Frick had no reason to believe that Ben had made an advance on Ward, the more it looked like Frick was fishing or planting a suggestion in Ward's mind.

It was after the conversation with Frick, Ward said, that he wrote to Ben, inviting him to New York because he had "something very important to say to him"—the meeting Ward wound up canceling. "Major Koehler was a member of my lodge and that was the reason I put him wise to himself," Ward said. That association did not keep Ward from telling Mills, Mayes, and the jury a dubious story to go along with his friends, but months earlier, it apparently made him feel some moral pangs—just as he told a reporter, but not the jurors, about his "grudge."[3]

What was the source of the grudge? The jurors would have to wait until Ben testified to hear about that.


HARRY WILSON HELD NO obvious grudge against Ben, nor was Ben his boss. A former deckhand on the *Nathaniel Greene* steamer, Wilson testified that one morning, Ben, who had never taken any notice of him, came into the empty civilian cabin where Wilson was washing windows, "put his hand on my back or shoulder and said I was quite a stocky young fellow and his hand went down a little further and I picked up my bucket of water and went out of the after cabin . . . and wiped the windows off and he asked me to come over and see him, so I came over to Fort Terry and he showed me around his place and his chickens."[4]

"He went down around my privates," Wilson elaborated, encouraged by Mayes to "speak plainly to the court."

"Did he squeeze your privates in any way when he touched them?" asked Mayes.

"Only pressing, that was all . . . He didn't grab them in any way," answered Wilson.

Grabbing would have been difficult, considering how Wilson said he was dressed, wearing underwear, trousers, denim overalls, and a sailor's jumper.

Like Ward, Wilson placed the incident as occurring during the busy month of August 1912, though he couldn't say what day "because I never gave it a thought again at all."

Wilson was not one of the original accusers. His charge was added as a result of Mayes's investigation, prompting Kirby to ask, "How could Captain Mayes have known that you had anything to tell him about the accused if you had never spoken to any one prior to that?"

"I don't know sir, only I knew that Sergeant Moody told me that somebody wanted to see me."

"Had you ever told Sergeant Moody about this?"

"No sir I never told anybody."

"When did Sergeant Moody tell you that Captain Mayes wanted to see you?"

"I believe it was two nights before I went up to the place where he was at."

"Up to that time you had never said one word to anybody that you knew anything against Major Koehler."

"No, sir."

Charles Moody was another friend of Frick's and a member of Robinson's company on Fishers Island. He served as provost sergeant on one of the boats, where he sometimes slept, along with Frick, and that was how he knew Wilson. Wilson said that Moody delivered a subpoena to him in New London to testify, and Frick's roommate, Walsh, followed up with a second subpoena when Wilson said he was too ill to honor the first.

Kirby asked why Wilson had not reacted more strongly when the

grope happened. "You could have shoved him away and been perfectly in your rights?"

"I suppose I could in a way. I might have got discharged from my
job, or something like that for instance."

"Had he anything to do with employing you?"

"No, sir."

Kirby also wanted to know why Wilson had visited Ben's home "[i]f
you felt that you had been improperly treated by the accused."

"I went over to see the hens, sir."

Later in the trial, the jury would hear from Ben that the first time
he ever saw Wilson was in mid-June 1913 when Ben was pulling lettuce
from his garden and Wilson showed up "and asked for a pass to see
the fortifications."[5] The jury would also hear from the captain of the
*Nathaniel Greene* that due to Wilson's unreliability he was "mighty glad
to get rid of him" when Wilson quit after a year. The captain would
have fired Wilson sooner, he said, except that Wilson's father-in-law
was the boat's cook "and a cook is a hard man to hold."[6]


BY THE END OF Saturday, four witnesses had testified. How many were
among the four that Mayes reported to Garrison had a motive to lie?
Surely, he must have counted Frick, who acknowledged several "differences"—or maybe he didn't, because Frick said he "personally liked
the major." Did he count Ward, who reported his "grudge" to the press
but not the jurors? Did he count Worcester?

However credible Mayes thought his witnesses, the early verdict of
the press was not favorable. "It is said that the case, as so far developed
against Koehler is so weak as to lend color to the stories that he is a
victim of personal hatreds," wrote the *Washington Times*.[7] Another reporter wrote of the "hard grilling" Worcester had received.[8]

That had to make Ben and his counsel feel good as they prepared
not for a day of rest but for an unusual Sunday session of court.[9] They
didn't know that there was a back channel and that what they were
hearing in court was not all that was being said.

# CHAPTER TWENTY-NINE

# A Fake Letter Makes the Rounds

Ben Koehler, an artilleryman, knew how to shoot at moving targets. Samuel Hudson, an attorney, did not—yet that is what he was being called upon to do at Fort Terry.

So far, except for the Halloween party, there had been a notable lack of precision regarding the timing of the alleged gropings, despite a requirement that "the time and place" of an offense should "properly be averred" to "enable the accused to understand what particular act or omission he is called upon to defend."[1]

Early in his testimony, Ward had said "the approximate date of this occurrence was October, 1911," referring to times when Ben "used to come in here after school hours and talk with me [about] mostly women and men, that is, so far as sexual relations were concerned."[2]

Hawthorne objected because August 1912, not October 1911, was the date of the Ward claim in the specifications. Kirby sustained the objection, so Ward, prodded by Mayes to "[c]onfine your descriptions to anything that did occur about August, 1912," modified his testimony, changing the date to August 1912. As he had been relieved as a teacher by that point, he also changed the location to the Post Exchange, where he was then working as acting steward and sleeping in an office.[3]

Wilson, too, had been evasive. Asked "Can you fix the day more exactly in the month of August when this took place?" he said, "No, sir, I could not just tell you the day."

"Could you say that it took place in the last half of August?"

"Not exactly sir, no sir."

"Could you say it took place in the first half?"

"I could not give you any accurate statement on it . . ."[4]

Despite the vagueness, the month of August 1912 kept coming up: Frick's dinner with the Koehlers, the unbuttoning of Ward's pants, the pressing of Wilson's cloth-covered crotch. The next witness, Private Leonard Davis, would also describe an incident in August 1912.

Why were so many of the allegations clumped together in that month?

For one thing, August was the camp and battle practice season when Ben was often out of his house and office, mixing with soldiers, but when Davis first spoke to Mills, he told of an advance by Ben during the August 1913 battle practice. Mayes put that date in the initial charges, but when he showed the charges to Ben, Ben had pointed out that during the 1913 battle practice, he was in a different location than Davis described.

In response, Mayes did not drop the Davis charge. He just changed it. Davis's August 1913 date became August 1912. Ben also had an alibi for an October claim, so Mayes learned the value of keeping all dates as uncertain as possible, to preclude additional alibis.

The imprecision made it difficult for the defense to prepare, as Hudson complained to the jury, labeling the initial charges "very misleading," causing "extra work which would not otherwise have been necessary . . . for example, where it is stated in the specifications a thing occurred in 1913, considerable work was undertaken to meet that date, when a little later we were told it was not in 1913 at all, it was 1912."[5]

At least the identities of the twelve original complainants and four post-Mills accusers were certain, and all the "immoral acts" were alleged to have occurred after Koehler's arrival on Plum Island, though with no more detail than "at Fort Terry." For the most part, the defense had to wait for each accuser to take the stand to find out where on the 840-acre island, inside or outside its many buildings, Ben's gropings and lewd comments were alleged to have occurred.

Just as the sea makes a clear boundary around an island, Hudson and Hawthorne regarded the sixteen accusers and 840 acres of Plum Island as the boundaries of their case. It was a breach of those boundaries when Worcester and Frick intimated to the jury some special knowledge on the part of Lieutenant Putney, who had left Plum Island and was unavailable for cross-examination. Hudson and Hawthorne did their best to reign in such references to people, locations, and times outside the record, but some damage was inevitably done. The bell that had sounded would keep reverberating in the background, suggesting to the jurors that there was even more to Ben's alleged bad acts than they were being asked to rule on.

Such innuendos served the prosecution, presenting Worcester as the officer who, in the interest of keeping the Army "clean," had finally stood up to a man who had been getting away with predatory sex acts for years against people too intimidated to complain. Moreover, the innuendos of past bad acts weakened Ben's claim of a Fort Terry conspiracy. If Ben had victimized others who were not present, then those present did not look like members of a closed conspiracy so much as men standing on the exposed tip of a large, submerged iceberg.

Imagine Mayes's interest, then, when he was shown an unsolicited letter claiming that Ben's "acts of degeneracy" went all the way back to his days in San Francisco:

If you make an investigation you will find that Major Benjamin M. Koehler's acts of degeneracy extended back to the time he was captain of the ninety-second company of Coast Artillery, when several fine young fellows were forced to desert to avoid his brutal treatment following repulsion of said acts, and one poor lad committed suicide out of fear. Personally, he attempted a crime against nature on me, getting down on his knees before me, unbuttoning my trousers, and when I repulsed him and walked out of the house he made life miserable thereafter for me. I sincerely pray to God that in justice to the poor, unfortunate, enlisted men you will see that this vile scoundrel is given his just deserts.[6]

The name at the end of this inflammatory letter, accusing Ben of causing a suicide and several desertions, was A. J. Searcy—typed, without a signature. The letter included no details about the purported author: no rank, dates of service, or ID number. The sender's address was given as "General Delivery, N.Y.C."

Remarkably, the letter bore a date of February 28, 1914—the very day the testimony of the first witnesses was called "weak" by whoever was talking to the press. Apparently, someone eager for a conviction decided the testimony needed buttressing, for A. J. Searcy had never served in San Francisco, nor did he live in New York City. He had been a Confederate soldier in the Civil War—in Gould's Texas Cavalry. He was 72 years old and had lived his entire life in Texas.[7]

The Searcy letter was a fake, but by whom?

Addressed to "the Honorable Secretary of War, Washington, D.C.," the letter had quickly made its way to Enoch Crowder, Mayes's boss. Crowder was a thorough lawyer regarding legal issues in Cuba—his main interest—but less so regarding an alleged male degenerate whom he had already concluded was guilty. The same day he received the letter, Crowder sent it to Garrison and recommended that it be forwarded to Mayes in New York. Far from expressing skepticism about the author's identity, Crowder referred to the letter as "evidence":

> While the charges upon which Major B. M. Koehler, Coast Artillery, is now being tried do not allege the acts of degeneracy referred to in the attached communication, I think the letter should be referred, through channels, to the trial judge-advocate, Captain James J. Mayes, Infantry, for his information. It is possible that the accused officer may set up such a defense as to make the evidence of Searcy competent and admissible in rebuttal.[8]

Garrison wrote "OK act accordingly" and signed his initials on Crowder's cover note, which was dated March 3, a mere two business days after the letter's date.

Thus, a forged letter accusing Ben of "brutal treatment" causing grave harm and making the author "miserable" after an attempted "crime against nature" went to the secretary of war and the prosecutor without any hesitation expressed about its reliability. Such striking claims—calling Koehler "vile"—had to have colored Garrison's view of Ben Koehler and fortified Mayes in the belief he already held of Ben's guilt.

Hudson and Hawthorne, if shown the letter, would surely have suspected it of being a fake. They would have discussed it with Ben, and Ben would have responded with whatever proof he had. If there had been desertions and a suicide by men from the 92nd Company under his command, presumably records existed to confirm or refute that, and to evaluate the circumstances—not to mention the records showing the true background of A. J. Searcy.

All of this might have been investigated had the letter and its toxic contents not remained a government secret, retained for posterity in Koehler's file but never given to his counsel. That, too, resembled the Dreyfus case, in which a secret dossier prepared by the French military, including documents that "emphasiz[ed] suspicions despite the lack of proof," were shown to the court on the last day of trial and "brought the board to their unanimous verdict."[9]

There is no definite proof that the Searcy letter was shown to Kirby or the other jurors, but the placement of the letter in Ben's official personnel file directly following other court-martial documents suggests that the letter may have been in Kirby's possession. And, as Crowder predicted, Mayes would indeed seek to introduce evidence of purported actions by Ben in San Francisco.

Without doubt, the letter was read by Garrison, whose job would be to review the jury's verdict and make a recommendation to President Wilson concerning the final ruling and sentence. For that reason alone, the letter should have been scrutinized and its authenticity investigated, or it should have been given to Ben's team for a response. Instead, ex parte "evidence" was forwarded to Garrison without any vetting, apparently not raising any concerns on his part, either. Garrison well knew that Ben alleged a conspiracy. Would not an intelligent, objective person—especially a lawyer who claimed to respect the administration of justice and all that was "essential" to it—have considered that a typed letter with no identifying information about the author, written in the midst of the trial, might be part of that conspiracy?

When it came to "B. M. Koehler," as Crowder referred to him, it seemed that anything would be believed.

More troubling than negligence in failing to investigate the claims in the Searcy letter is the possibility that a senior officer in Washington helped create the letter. On Plum Island, Frick and Worcester had reason to be concerned about their testimony, but they did not have access to correspondence in Army files in Washington, D.C., related to Civil War soldiers, including the 1909 letter from the Texas Commissioner of Pensions requesting "the military record of A. J. Searcy" in connection with Searcy's application for a "Confederate pension granted by this State."[10] Adjutant General Ainsworth had confirmed Searcy's service from 1862 to 1864 in Texas.[11] Those letters were placed in two different Army files, and both sets of papers were missing from their boxes during an inspection (by the author) in 2017. Copies were then obtained from the State of Texas.

While the letters' absence in 2017 does not prove their absence in 1914, there would be little reason for the documents to go missing accidentally, not just from one location, but two. Was this early case of identity theft engineered by an officer of high rank, possibly even Wood?[12] Or did someone at a lower level, friendly with the accusers, pull the records and give the Searcy name to Worcester or an ally, who proceeded to type and mail the letter?

No matter who created it, the Searcy letter is the clearest evidence of a malicious effort to fabricate evidence to try to secure Ben's conviction.

. . .

MEANWHILE, ON PLUM ISLAND, Ben's counsel had their hands full with the witnesses who were using their actual names, though Kirby gave Hawthorne a little help drilling Private Davis.

Davis testified that one August day in the battle command station, Ben asked Davis his name, ordered others out of the building, told Davis to call a gun battery to get coordinates for target practice, unbuttoned Davis's pants in a phone booth, fondled Davis's penis, and "said something about quite a long one, 'Suppose it is any bigger than mine?' Had his own out, turned around and he said 'I guess we better quit before some one comes in' and put it away."[13]

Kirby's interest was piqued. He had several questions.

"Major Koehler was in front of you and he took your tool in one hand and his own in another, is that true?"

"Yes, sir."

"What followed that? Just simply stood there holding penises, is that all?"

"He moved his hand around, of course."[14]

Davis's testimony was unique in that he said he found some pleasure in the encounter—but Kirby did not let that go unchallenged.

"What pleasure did you get out of it, where did the pleasure come in?"

"Well, I can't explain the pleasure at all; I can't describe the feeling."

"Did it cause an erection on your part?"

"It caused an erection, that was all."

"Cause any emission on your part?"

"No."

"Any on his?"

"Not that I know of; I could not say anything about that."

"Just simply stopped off suddenly or how?"

"Just stopped off, and walked over to the other part of the Station."

"Did you button up your own trousers?"

"I buttoned up my own trousers."

"Did he put your penis back in your trousers, or did you do it?"

"He done it."[15]

The man most concerned about keeping salacious details from the public was asking questions likely to produce those details, but Kirby may have sensed that fairness to Ben required probing the uncomfortable subject matter.

So, when Davis said the act gave him pleasure, after saying he did not consent to it, could have moved away, but did not because he was so surprised and intimidated, Kirby made the man squirm a bit on the stand. Kirby's attitude can be gleaned from one of his final questions: "Do you understand what you mean by an oath?"[16]

There were other reasons to be skeptical of Davis, especially the change in date from August 1913 to August 1912.[17] That revision required a lot of explanation because other details in the story did not easily match up to the earlier date. Plus, Davis could not say to whom he spoke when he supposedly called the gun battery, which conveniently meant no one could confirm or deny that a call took place. That would dovetail with Ben's testimony that there had been no call, and would be no reason for a call, because the kind of coordinates Davis said he obtained could not be used in the command station.[18]

Davis did make one remark that rang true. Asked about rumors he might have heard, he said they "were not very definite . . . I just heard them in a faint way . . . I could not say what they were about except that he was not what he should be."[19]

That seems to have been Ben's main deficiency as far as Worcester and his allies were concerned: For a host of reasons, Ben wasn't the commander they wanted.

# CHAPTER THIRTY

# A Little Shutter and a Green Shade

EXCEPT IN THEIR OWN minds, jurors in civilian trials may not question witnesses, one of many ways in which the court-martial system that had its grips on Ben operated by its own rules. The system was broken, abused by superiors, and led to "brutal injustice" against countless men, according to an article in the nation's most widely read magazine that happened to be circulating as Ben girded for more witnesses to portray him as perversely attracted to men, sex-crazed, lewd, undisciplined, dishonest, and alcoholic.

With a soldier on the cover, the February 28, 1914, edition of *Harper's Weekly* prominently featured "The Honor of the Army" by Charles Johnson Post, a former soldier. The "court-martial can—and does—punish with a merciless severity," Post wrote.[1] Commenting on the article, the magazine's editors opined that "the United States Army system is not fit for a democracy," urging readers to "grapple with and settle the question of what kind of army life, army discipline, army training is needed in our modern democracy."[2]

The article's thesis both helped and hurt Ben's interests. Post gave examples of courts-martial of enlisted men ordered for no good reason, while the "same—and greater—offenses against officers [are] gently silvered o'er." He wrote of the "power, fantastically used and abused" whereby officers punished subordinates who failed to comply with their wishes. At the same time, the article echoed Wood's advice to Garrison that the Army could be perceived as more concerned with officers than enlisted men.

*Harper's* well demonstrated why Wood might worry about that perception, for Post's article linked Wood to the overly punitive state of the Army and high rate of desertions.

On the adverse influences of Wood as chief of staff, Ben might have agreed, though the *Army and Navy Register* called the Post article a "libel of the Army," disputed the desertion figures, and wrote that relations between officers and enlisted men were not nearly as bad as Post maintained.[3] Ben might have agreed with that statement, too, having shown a willingness to take the enlisted man's side against an officer, as he had done for Samuel Silverman and Edward Shanley.

Edison Kirkman, the sergeant whom Worcester had declined to punish for fighting with Shanley, took the witness stand on Sunday, reminding Ben and his counsel that court-martial procedures could be used to stack the deck against an officer, too.

For one thing, the Army's case was being presented by a prosecutor without formal legal training who allowed his witnesses to say pretty much whatever they wanted. That proved especially true with Kirkman, who clearly relished the role of raconteur. Hawthorne handled the defense on Sunday and had to pick his battles, objecting to the most egregious violations of the rules of evidence, but not all of them, lest he come across as nettlesome. While Kirby sustained a number of objections, the rulings often came late, after the witness had answered. Kirby was a far cry from an experienced judge who could discern an improperly phrased question at once.

Sometimes, it was Kirby who asked a question Hawthorne considered improper. After Kirkman testified that Ben fondled his penis in December 1912 or January 1913 in the Koehler home, Kirby asked whether Ben "approached you in connection with immoral or unnatural practices prior to the night . . . when you visited his quarters."

"Yes, sir," Kirkman answered, and Kirby asked for details. Hawthorne objected that he "would like to have the court keep this inquiry with the limits of [the] specification."[4] Another juror agreed, and Kirby dropped the question—but not before harm was done.

Kirkman had referred to a past overture, and the lack of details gave Ben no opportunity to refute them.

The rushed schedule also worked against Ben. Holding court on Saturday and Sunday left his counsel virtually no time to rest or review the prior days' testimony. Hawthorne was already feeling sick and asked, successfully, that the proposed Sunday nighttime session be canceled.[5]

Ben continued to be hurt by the rule that deprived his counsel of an opening statement. The sixth accuser was now testifying, and there would be ten more before the defense witnesses could speak. On Sunday, that seemed like a long time. During Kirkman's colorful testimony, Hawthorne managed to sneak in a preview.

Kirkman testified that the evening he visited the Koehler house, when Sidney Jordan supposedly called about the pheasants, Ben invited him upstairs while Ben changed into evening dress for a meeting with Jordan, stripped to his underclothes, "and asked me how did I think he was built, his shape . . . Then he faced around . . . and he had an erection on and he asked me what did I think of it . . . I says 'You ought to get married.' He says, 'I don't care for women anyway.'"

Kirkman continued: "I called his attention to a window just opposite and he went over and pulled one of those small green shades in front of the window, and he came back again and this time he opened my pants and taken my privates out and I had taken them loose from him and put them back. I told him he better go down stairs . . . so he did."

Downstairs, in Ben's office, according to Kirkman, Ben "pulled a little shutter down over the glass door and turned the lights out," proceeding to put his arms around Kirkman, take out his "privates" and ask Kirkman, "if I was not interested in him and his work of that kind. I told him no, a man didn't appeal to me with any interest. 'Well,' he says 'I guess if I slept with you all night I probably would.' I said 'If you did I would have to be half drunk.'"

Kirkman said Ben then invited him to take a trip so they could spend the night together, "that there would be something doing before morning," to which Kirkman said he replied that he had no civilian clothes, but some were on order, and Ben said the trip could await the clothes' arrival. According to Kirkman, Ben asked for a kiss, which

Kirkman declined to give, at which point Ben hugged him, "tried to bite me on the neck and told me to come to his quarters again any show night, I was entirely welcome, he was sorry he didn't know me better before that, we had missed a number of good times."

On cross-examination, Hawthorne wanted to know if Kirkman had ever been inside Worcester's house, and Kirkman said he had been there "quite often."

Mayes objected, and Hawthorne gave the reason for his question: "The knowledge of the witness of the accused's quarters we believe to flow entirely from his knowledge of the quarters of Captain Worcester. We believe his whole story to be a pure invention and is laid by him in surroundings with which he is quite familiar . . . ; hence his remarkable detailed knowledge of the interior of the accused's quarters."

Kirby sustained the objection, but Hawthorne had gotten his point across.

Kirkman gave conflicting reasons for being in Ben's house and was not sure whether it was before or after Christmas. Later, the jurors would learn that Kirkman first told Mills the date was November 1, when Ben was attending the Worcester party. Mayes and Kirkman could not change the date of the party, but they could and did change the timing in Kirkman's story.

Kirkman provided titillating testimony, sex terms and all, saying Ben asked him:

> . . . how many different ways I had ever connected with a woman . . . asking me if I had ever heard of any man keeping a boy and used the expression of corn holing him. I asked the Major what he meant by that and he explained he meant going up his rectum. I told him I had heard of it, and he asked me if I had ever been tampered with the French Style and I asked him what did he mean by that and he told me a person going down on another.

Kirkman admitted that at times he used "some obscene talk myself" but it wasn't "of that nature"—meaning male to male. Anything "of that nature" was "not pleasant by any means."

And so it would go all day Sunday, not pleasant for anyone, least of all Ben, who was said to look "ten years older than he did a week ago," having "worried greatly since he was placed under arrest."[6] For now, all Ben could do was worry and listen, unable to contradict or point out, for example, how unlikely it was that he would propose to travel with a man he found as irresponsible as he found Kirkman, or follow Kirkman around the house with Sophia at home, trying to fondle and kiss him after rebuffs. Had Worcester not already spoken of Ben's low opinion of Kirkman? Was anyone listening?

Next up was Elvin Byers, a member of Kirkman and Frick's company and former first sergeant to the absent Lieutenant Putney. Byers described an advance made by Ben on July 15, 1913—a precise date, for a change—and now the reason for the curious visit to Ben's garden became clear. Byers said he went to the garden with two men to pick up flowers for an officer, and that after the other men took the plants, Ben invited him to tour the garden and "suggested we sit down in the grass," where they spoke of sex, erections, and gonorrhea for about an hour.[7]

Ben was "talking about fat women and such stuff as that," said Byers. "He didn't see what a man wanted with a fat woman, or words to that effect." Then, Byers said, Ben placed his hand on Byers's ankle, and "I was laying on my left side and I think he was in the same position. I was on his left and I turned around and looked at him and I noticed he had an erection, had his hand on his penis, and had an erection, and he said 'Guess we better take a walk.'"

That would have been an uncomfortable if not impossible position for a man who was five foot three, lying with one hand on his genitals and one hand on the ankle of another man who rested three feet away. Kirby asked Byers to "illustrate the manner in which you allege the accused grasped your leg," which Byers purported to do, grasping his own leg around the ankle. He acknowledged that he was wearing his uniform and leggings at the time.

Corporal Isaac Spears, also a member of Kirkman's company, told of Ben following him into a hotel restroom in Greenport, Long Island, and placing his hand on Spears's hip while they urinated into adjacent urinals, separated by partitions, even as a soldier stood on Spears's other side. A few minutes later on the hotel porch, Spears said, Ben "asked me how I would like to do business with a fat boy." He gave the date as August 1912 and admitted that he spent most of the afternoon drinking in the hotel bar. Spears said he probably drank eight to ten beers.[8]

Ben would testify that he went to Greenport with a group that included Spears, then a private, in July 1912, but he had no memory of seeing Spears in the restroom and only recalled talking to Spears on the sidewalk near the boats—not about "business with a fat boy."[9]

Next to be sworn was Sergeant Charles Moody, whose testimony prompted argument. The specification read that "on or about the 15th of October 1913," Ben touched Moody while on the steamer *Brennan*, where Moody worked as provost sergeant, but on the stand Moody talked about "two different occasions that I seen Major Koehler or that I spoke to him on the 'Brennan,' and I don't remember whether this was that particular time or not."[10]

Hawthorne objected to the sudden addition of a second incident, and Mayes countered that Ben should simply "defend his conduct at any time he may have been on board that boat, on or about the 15th day of October." Kirby overruled the objection and permitted Moody to continue.

Moody said both incidents occurred in October, after he heard other men make "common talk" about what Ben "was referred to." One time, Moody said, Ben asked "what makes you so fat" and "if I was getting much, and I don't just remember my answer, but he says 'Maybe you ain't getting it in the right way.'" Another time, according to Moody, Ben pinched his leg and said, "if one man goes down on another man it is nobody's damn business," then grabbed him by the arm and breast while the boat's captain, standing nearby, looked out the window.

Moody's testimony shifted when Hawthorne asked the questions. The captain's looking out the window morphed into the possibility that the quartermaster was the one steering, in which case the quartermaster should have been the one at the window. The grabbing of his arm and breast shifted to "pinching."

Hawthorne succeeded in getting Moody to concede that he "might" have told Mills the incidents occurred "between August and December or something like that," but it was Mills who chose the date of October 15. "I never gave no certain date," Moody acknowledged.

Moody also conceded that he never mentioned the incidents to anyone before Worcester came to see him on the *Brennan*: "As near as I remember, it was on the boat and he asked me if I had ever had any dealings with Major Koehler."

One can read between the lines that Worcester expected "yes" for an answer.

When Moody finished testifying, Kirby ended the session. It was 6:40 p.m., a long day for all, and a terrible day for Ben Koehler.

"Be like the promontory against which the waves continually break," wrote Roman Emperor Marcus Aurelius in his *Meditations*, a favorite of military men, "but it stands firm and tames the fury of the water around it."[11] Waves were breaking all around Ben, literally and figuratively. He tried to stand firm, but according to *The New York Times*, on Monday he broke his silence and "in conversation . . . declared that he would clear himself and confound his enemies."[12]

In March 1890, six of the eleven Koehler siblings gathered in LeMars, Iowa, to observe their mother's birthday. FRONT, FROM LEFT: Edgar, Margaret, Ben, Sophia. BACK: Lizzie, Henry, Rudolph. *Courtesy Mary Elke*

Sophia in 1894, the year before she graduated high school. *Courtesy Mary Elke*

Ben, standing behind Peyton March, both lieutenants leading the Astor Battery in the Philippines, 1898. *Courtesy Mary Elke*

Sophia and Ben, now a captain, in 1902.
Location unknown, but likely the Presidio in
San Francisco. *Courtesy Mary Elke*

Fort Terry on Plum Island, circa 1913. Officers' houses are on the left; the
guardhouse is the small building to the right of the road; a large barracks
building #54 is at the far right. The parade ground is the grassy expanse in
front. *Courtesy Bolling Smith, Coast Defense Study Group*

When soldiers from other forts visited for summer drills, they slept in tents on
the parade ground. *Courtesy Bolling Smith, Coast Defense Study Group*

A wagon called a buckboard, drawn by horses or mules, provided the primary means of transportation at Fort Terry—as well as the setting for one of the claims against Major Koehler. *Courtesy Bolling Smith, Coast Defense Study Group*

Philip Worcester, date unknown. *Photo by Michael Belis*

Louis Koehler, circa 1915. *Courtesy Mary Elke*

*Major Benjamin M. Koehler Who Is on Trial at Fort Terry*

Ben Koehler walks behind Samuel Hudson, his lawyer, and Colonel Harry Hawthorne, his military counsel, on the day photographers were allowed on Plum Island during the court-martial. *Leavenworth Post*, March 16, 1914.

TO RIGHT—LIEUTENANT THOMAS O. HUMPHREYS (witness for defence), MAJOR BENJAMIN M. KOEHLER, LIEUTENANT STEESE (witness for defence) and COLONEL HENRY KIRBY (president of the Court Martial).

*Schenectady Gazette*, April 15, 1914. Left to right, Lieutenant Humphreys, Ben Koehler, Lieutenant Steese, and Colonel Kirby, the jury president.

# ARMY SENSATION IN TRIAL OF KOEHLER

Major's Court-Martial at Fort Terry Involves Captain and Two Lieutenants.

## FIST FIGHT IN CLUBHOUSE

Investigation After the Affair Leads to the Arrest of Koehler.

The Sun,
February 23, 1914

---

# KOEHLER WITNESSES ESCAPE IN ROWBOAT

## Three Soldiers, in Fear of Court-Martial Grilling, Decamp from Fort Terry.

## RUSHING TRIAL OF MAJO[R]

[S]essions Even Held on Sunday—Koehler, Charged with Serious Offenses, Alleges a Plot.

*Special to The New York Times.*

The New York Times, March 7, 1914

---

# ARMY BOARD TO TRY MAJOR B. M. KOEHLER

Former Commander of Fort Terry Faces Serious Charges.

## HIS RESIGNATION REFUSED

General Court-Martial Will Begin Sessions at Fort Terry, New London, Wednesday.

The New York Times,
Feb. 23, 1914

---

SATURDAY. **New-York Tribune**

# KOEHLER ON STAND DENIES CHARGES

Accused Major Plans to Show Conspiracy to Drive Him from Service.

## TWO PROSECUTORS TO SIFT EVIDENC[E]

Judge Advocate Calls for [As]sistance and Officer Is Sen[t] from Governor's Island.

[From a Staff Correspondent of The Tr[ibune]]
New London, Conn., March 6.—[...]
Benjamin M. Koehler, of the coast [artil]lery, whose court martial is be[ing con]ducted secretly at Fort Terry, [took] and, took the stand in his own defence to-day. No other witnesses were called. The weather to-day aided Colonel Henry Kirby, president of the court, in [...]

---

## LABOR AGAINST ASIATICS

A. F. of L. Wants Japanese [Denied?] Citizenship.

[...] their domestic [...] for imperial government [...] factors in the assimilation of a [...] immigrants.

---

# DAMAGING CASE AGAINST KOEHLER

Prosecution Continues to Get Evidence Against Accused Officer.

## MAXIMUM PENALTY IS 99 YEARS IN JAIL

Prisoner, Showing Strain of Trial, Must Face Testimony of Thirty More Witnesses.

[From A Staff Correspondent of The Tribune]

---

# TWO WOMEN TESTIFY IN KOEHLER'S DEFENCE

## Photographers at Fort Terry Snap Accused and Members of Court.

[NEW] LONDON, Conn., March 5.—Photo[grap]hers invaded Plum Island to-day by [permi]ssion of the War Department, and [fini]shed for pictures of the persons [promi]nent in the secret court-martial of [Majo]r Benjamin Koehler. They were put [in c]harge of a tall sergeant, who per[mitt]ed them to snap the members of the [cour]t and the accused as they crossed [the] grounds for the morning session, and [agai]n again at noon.

[M]ajor Koehler and his lawyers after [the] experience in the morning returned to [the] court at noon in one of two hacks, [dra]wn by army mules, which are Plum [Isl]and's only rapid transit.

The court-martial hopes that all tes[tim]ony will be in by Saturday night. The [cou]rt was surprised to-day by the unex[pec]ted return of First Lieut. Roy R. Lyon [of] the 109th Company, Coast Artillery, [Ca]pt. Philip M. Worcester's and Lieut. [Pat]rick's company. Lieut. Lyon was sent [in] October with eight men to survey Con[nec]ticut farm lands for military maps [a]nd was to have been gone until May. A [f]ew minutes after his return it became [k]nown that he was to be a witness, prob[a]bly in Koehler's defence.

The court heard two women witnesses [i]n the morning, the first who have ap[pe]ared. Mrs. H. M. Ewing, wife of Pro[v]ost Sergeant Ewing, and Mrs. James [H]alt, wife of a corporal of the 125th Company, gave testimony that will do much to discredit certain witnesses for the prosecution. Both have helped Miss Koehler, the Major's sister, in keeping house for him.

The Sun, March 4, 1914

Ben and Sophia's farm in Hawarden, Iowa, as it looked in 2016.
*© Marian E. Lindberg*

Ben at the Hawarden farm, 1925.
*Courtesy Mary Elke*

Sophia with her son, Louis, in 1920 in
Portland, Oregon. *Courtesy Mary Elke*

One of the former Fort Terry barracks #54, 2017. © *Marian E. Lindberg*

The view from Eldridge gun battery, 2017. East Point is in the distance.
© *Marian E. Lindberg*

The largest of the barracks (#55, with 218 beds) viewed from the beach in 2017. © *Marian E. Lindberg*

Plum Island Light was built in 1869 to help boaters navigate Plum Gut, the unpredictable body of water between Orient Point and Plum Island. The granite building is listed in the National Register of Historic Places. © *Marian E. Lindberg*

# So Much Talk about Fat Boys

S OME MEN CHOSE TO flee into the breaking waves to avoid testify-ing. "KOEHLER WITNESSES ESCAPE IN ROWBOAT," read the headline in *The New York Times*.[1] "RISK LIVES TO FLEE FROM KOE-HLER TRIAL," dueled the *Sun*, reporting that on the afternoon of Monday, March 2, three enlisted men "took their lives in their hands and fled across icy, tide swept Plum Gut."[2] The soldiers "are said to have been actuated by fear of a grilling on the stand," word having spread of the defense counsel's "particularly severe examination."[3]

The men had reason to fear worse, for Garrison's threat to try any-one "spreading scandal and making false charges" was reported in Monday's papers.

The three soldiers rowed to the nearest spot on Long Island, Orient Point, where they "abandoned their skiff and were last seen running in the direction of Greenport"—a distance of nine miles.

That wasn't the kind of running away Charles Post had in mind when he wrote in *Harper's* about high numbers of desertions, and the man now in charge of Fort Terry, Captain Patten (who was scheduled to testify for Ben), seemed rather blasé about the episode. Patten didn't threaten the scared soldiers, telling the *Times* that a charge of desertion would depend on how long they stayed away.

The identities of the fleeing men are not known. They were not among the sixteen accusers; for by the end of the day on March 2, all sixteen would finish testifying.

"No time is being lost," as the *Times* put it.

Outside the courtroom, a record-breaking blizzard was hurling sleet and snow, causing deaths, breaking telegraph lines, and stranding thousands in New York City, but for the jurors stuck on Plum Island, the raunchy stories continued without interruption.[4]

Harvey Kernan, who worked in the hospital tent during the drill season, began the day's testimony with an account that Ben showed up one evening holding a flashlight and asked him, "Would you like to have one like that?" which Kernan took as a reference to penis size. According to Kernan, Ben then advised him to "marry a big Swede girl, she could hatch one," and ran his hand over Kernan's back.[5]

Under cross-examination by Hudson, Kernan made a series of revealing admissions including that Mills "insisted that I give an opinion of Major Koehler's character" that Kernan "did not wish to give."

"I knew absolutely nothing based on facts," Kernan said.

Apparently, Kernan had told Hawthorne in his informal, pretrial interview that there was only "ordinary conversation" from Ben, but Kernan now claimed not to remember all he had said to Hawthorne, though he did recall that it was Worcester who told him to speak with Mills, even though Kernan had never told Worcester anything about an advance by Ben.

When Mayes resumed his questioning, Kernan returned to his original story about Ben's having put his hand on Kernan's back, though he subsequently went along with Hudson's theory that he may have considered Ben's actions improper because of gossip he had heard.

Kirby picked up on the theme of misinterpretation. He asked, "When Major Koehler showed you an electric flashlight saying 'Would you like to have one like that?' what did you understand him to mean?"

"I understood a penis that size."

"Why did you understand a penis?"

"From the nature of one or two talks and from the nature of the gossip that I had heard."

"Did he say anything at this particular moment to draw your attention to the fact that it was a penis that was meant?"

"No, sir."

"When he asked you this question 'How would you like to have one like that?' or words to the same effect, what reply did you make?"

"I said if I did I would not have to work any more, or something of that nature."[6]

On that peculiar note, Kernan stepped down from the witness stand.

"GIVE US THE EXACT words," Hudson asked the next witness, John Barrett.

"Why, he asked me this day if I woke up with a hard-on and I told him yes, sir. He said to me 'You want to get a fat boy and leave the women alone.'"[7]

"Fat boy" proved a recurring phrase among the accusers. Had instructions circulated to use it as a reference to Ben's stockiness? A "fat boy" was the opposite of the era's masculine ideal, for social directions writ large held that muscular bodies were manly, "allow[ing] men to emphasize their difference from women at a time when women seemed to be insisting on the similarity of the sexes."[8] Team sports, magazines devoted to bodybuilding, and popular men's novels with cowboy-type heroes fueled a "preoccupation with physicality," writes Michael Kimmel. This gave bodies "a different sort of weight than earlier. The body did not *contain* the man, expressing the man within; now, that body *was* the man."[9]

Edgar Koehler's obituary had lauded his body, describing him as "manly" and "look[ing] every inch the soldier, being tall, good looking and well proportioned."[10] The repetition of "fat boy" by Ben's accusers suggested that, in contrast, his body was perceived as defective. Worcester and Frick likely chafed at taking orders from and being disciplined by a man who did not *appear* to be as manly as they. Journalists also noted Koehler's appearance, describing him as "short, heavily built, with a large nose and bronzed face."[11]

Barrett was the soldier whom Ben had removed as provost sergeant and opposed as stable sergeant, the man allowed to stay in his cottage after the movie dispute in early 1912. Like other witnesses, Barrett's recollection of the timing of Ben's alleged bad acts was all over the place, starting as June to December 1913 when Barrett spoke to Mills, then becoming September or October with Mayes, and ultimately landing in the specifications as "on or about October 1."

Mayes had since learned that Ben and most of the troops, including Barrett, were on their way to Rhode Island on October 1, so, while Barrett was on the stand, Mayes tried to shift the location of the alleged improprieties to Rhode Island. The previous witness had changed one incident to two, and this witness wanted to shift locations.

Kirby sustained Hudson's objection to the "surprise . . . suggestion that this accusation occurred in another place," so Mayes had Barrett testify to other actions that supposedly took place at Fort Terry in September, even though Barrett had told Hawthorne there was only one day when improprieties occurred. Now he spoke of multiple offenses at the stable, including Ben's grasping Barrett "underneath the arm," "by the buttocks," and "by the testicles," and comparing their penis sizes to that of a mule.

Like Moody and Kernan, Barrett said he was summoned to speak to Mills by Worcester.

"I would like to know how Captain Worcester learned that you had had any unusual experiences with the accused," a juror asked.

"I don't know, sir."

Barrett did know, and acknowledged, that Patten had recently demoted him to private for gambling with a private he supervised, Walter Ensley, who was next up for the prosecution.

Before his transfer to stable duty, Ensley had reported to Worcester's friend, Captain Ellis. The specifications alleged that Ben groped Ensley when Ensley was driving the buckboard. In the first part of his testimony, Ensley said the incident happened in August 1913. However, under cross-examination, he got tripped up by his prior statements about background events. He solved that dilemma in the same way as Moody, by announcing that there were actually two gropings, one during target practice and one during the Army-Navy maneuvers.

Hudson could not contain his disbelief.

"Did you mean by that that exactly what you related took place twice?"

"Yes, sir."[12]

Ensley had said that while he was sitting in the front seat holding the reins, Ben reached up from the rear seat—one to two feet behind the front seat—and unbuttoned Ensley's pants and held his penis while removing one of Ensley's hands from the reins and placing it on his own genitals. Later, Ben exposed his penis. All the while, the mules kept walking.

Apparently realizing that it seemed incredible for this same set of actions to have occurred twice, Ensley proceeded to deconstruct his own testimony and break the incident into two parts. The first part, he said, happened in broad daylight. The second part, when Ben exposed his penis, happened on a second trip, which Ensley placed at a little after midnight.

"How do you know that he exhibited, showed his penis?" Hudson asked.

"I seen it through the light, sir."

"What light?"

"Street light, road light."

"You looked around to see it, did you?"

"I seen it, yes, sir, I looked around."

"What caused you to look around at that particular time?"

"I just happened to look around."

After lunch, Ensley embellished the answer when a curious juror asked again, "How did you happen to see it? That is the thing—did he tell you to look around at him?"

"He says 'Look at this,'" Ensley went along. The lights had been out "and they lit up again in a few minutes" just when Ben took out his penis and Ensley looked back.

Another juror questioned the penis-holding part of Ensley's story, asking, "How could he do that when you were on the front seat and driving and he was way back on the rear seat?"

"He was leaning over, sir," answered Ensley after a long pause.

"He was leaning over?"

"Yes, sir."

"Could he sit down and lean over and pull your hand back clear to his person? Are you sure of that, that is what I want to know? Now tell it in your own way. Are you sure of it or not?"

"He was sitting down, yes, sir; he was not standing up."

Throughout his testimony, Ensley took such long pauses before answering questions that Kirby grew frustrated, chiding him, "Don't sit there and think so long; you certainly ought to know what you know." It turned out that Ensley was already familiar with senior officers' ire. He conceded that Ben accused him of taking whiskey from his house.

"Did he seem to be quite angry with you?" Hudson asked.

"Yes, sir."

"And it was on that occasion [that] he told you not to go near his house again?"

"Yes, sir, he said not to enter his quarters no more."


MAYES TOLD GARRISON THAT only four accusers had issues with Ben, but clearly the count was higher: Worcester, Frick, Ward, Kirkman, Barrett, and Ensley so far. Moody also could be added to the list if it was true, as Ben would testify, that he declined Moody's request to transfer to San Francisco.[13]

Sergeant Jacob Campbell held no obvious grudge against Ben. He did, however, work in Worcester's company. Even though he had never told anyone about improper actions by Ben, Campbell said he received a call to speak to Mills—from whom, he could not recall.[14]

Hudson asked him, "Did you not state to Colonel Hawthorne that you were very much surprised that you had been called before Colonel Mills, as you considered that nothing that had taken place between you and Major Koehler was exceptional?"

"I believe I did, sir."

Campbell also admitted telling Hawthorne that Ben "never done anything to me that I ever remember that I considered wrong."

Nonetheless, Campbell testified in response to Mayes's questions that Ben "kind of squeeze[d] my arm" on or about November 15, 1913, in the Post Exchange, where Campbell worked. "One or two different times I believe he taken hold of my leg with his hand," Campbell added, and a little while later this became "Two or three times that he slapped my leg and felt of my arms and generally on my legs here at my thigh."

Campbell was also the soldier who testified that Ben spoke to him about "Pacific sporting houses." At first, he said he could "not remember it just word for word," but the "gist of the conversation" concerned "the different kind of women that a man could meet, and the different ways and manners that a man could get satisfaction in a sporting house."

"I would like to know," asked a juror, "did the accused mention different ways of accomplishing sexual intercourse?"

"Yes, sir."

"Just describe some of the methods he mentioned."

"Do you mean the different ways?"

"That he said it could be done."

"No, sir, I don't believe he just exactly described to me how this intercourse could be accomplished, but he just described to me the different ways that a man could get the satisfaction. That is, I don't know just exactly how to explain it, sir."

"What did he say—just use his words as near as you can remember."

"Well, he told me that you could get screwed or you could get sucked or you could get a fat boy, or anything you wanted. That is the words the Major used to me."

Faced with Campbell's sudden recollection, Hudson asked, "Did he say that this was the custom on the Pacific coast?"

"Yes, sir."

"Then it was describing a general custom, not anything that he—?"

"No, sir, not any of the experiences that he went through, that is he didn't say they was."

Hudson stopped there. The jury heard nothing more about Ben's time in San Francisco—not a word about his "great shot" that shattered a moving target three miles off the coast that had so impressed people back in 1903.


As the prosecution's case neared its end, the accusers had less and less to say and the jurors asked fewer questions. Were they tired, zoning out, or becoming inured to the accusations, like spectators at a bullfight getting used to seeing blood by the sixth gored bull?

Private Henry Fairey, the next witness, never spoke to Mills. Fairey's boss, Barrett, told him to see Mayes and "tell him what you know." This was what Fairey said he knew: "I couldn't say the date, but about the latter part of August [1913], I was in the corral and the Major came in to get his horse . . . I went in to help him put the saddle on and he pinched me in the leg."

Mayes asked if there was lewd talk, and Fairey disappointed him: "He just said something about women, pretty nice to be with a nice girl, or something that way."

If Fairey had put it differently in an earlier discussion, he was perhaps having second thoughts, like the men in the rowboat who had fled—though it seems Fairey was another accuser with grounds for a grudge. According to Ben, Fairey had requested a recommendation for a promotion that Ben declined to provide, telling Fairey that he was too young and inexperienced for the job.[15]


Of all the claims, perhaps none was more outlandish than that of Sergeant Charles Byers, who claimed that while Ben's good friend Major Andy Moses sat a few feet away, Ben felt Byers's "privates" while they crouched on the floor in a small room inspecting old ammunition.

Byers (no relation to accuser Elvin Byers) worked as quartermaster sergeant at Fort Wright. Byers reported to Robinson and served in the same company as Moody. He admitted that he and Moody discussed what they would tell Mills in advance of their interviews.

Byers said he had seen Ben only once before, at maneuvers. When the incident was alleged to have occurred, in October 1913, Ben had traveled to Fort Wright to inspect condemned ordnance in his position as acting commander of the district.

First, Byers claimed, when he passed items, Ben "would take hold of my hand in place of taking hold of the article and feel over my hand." Then, Ben "felt down on my legs into my privates like that, and he done that two or three times and I got up from behind the desk and he put his hand up from behind up on the backside of my leg." Throughout the inspection, which lasted five to ten minutes, Moses was sitting at a nearby desk calling out the names of the articles.

Kirby wanted to know whether Moses could see what was taking place.

"He was in such a way that he could not see the accused," Byers answered.[16]

Moses's ability to observe what Ben was doing with his hands would become a matter of considerable dispute, but not before the last complainant took the stand.

That honor fell to Harry King, one of the men Ben had criticized for not sleeping in camp. For two years, King had served in the junior position of master gunner. At the end of 1913, he obtained a commission as second lieutenant at another post.[17] Now, on Monday afternoon, as the blizzard stranded one hundred thousand rail commuters in New York City, King returned to his old post with a train story of his own: that Ben spoke to him about sex when King returned to Plum Island in spring 1912 after a furlough.[18]

Ben was also heading back to Fort Terry after his visit with William Kenly, and King apparently saw the two men together at Grand Central Terminal, though that wasn't what King spoke about on the stand. Instead, he testified that he was retrieving his checked luggage when Ben "came up behind me . . . and I believe he swung a suit-case into me from behind and asked 'Where are you going.'" King said the two sat together on the train—at Ben's invitation—and that Ben asked King if he had "got enough to last me for a while," which he understood to refer to sexual intercourse. Then they talked about "women in general, and a man's connection with women and so forth . . . sexual intercourse I should judge, although I don't know that anything was said directly about that, but that was the understanding I had all along."[19]

Later, when Ben testified, he would deny sitting with King, describing an entirely different train car, which might explain why King could not remember anything else Ben said to him—beyond reference to "women of easy virtue"—on the three-hour trip.[20]

King's charge, brought solely under the "conduct unbecoming" article of war, highlighted the elasticity of that provision, especially considering that, according to King, Ben's remarks concerned heterosexual sex. Was the Army saying it was a violation of the articles whenever an officer spoke of women and sex? Surely, any such policy could only be selectively enforced, as conversations went on all the time without being overheard. More aptly, it seemed that speech a "normal" man might get away with—like Frick and his sexual gossip— was being cast as improper when allegedly uttered by the wrong sort of man. The innuendo was that an officer who spoke to enlisted men about sex was likely to grope them, too.

The account King gave put him first in the chronology of victims, though he was the last to come forward. King never spoke to Mills. He said a telegram sent to his new post in Queens told him to go to Governors Island to meet with Mayes, right before Mayes finalized the charges.

Later testimony would suggest that Byron Brown, King's best friend at Fort Terry, persuaded him to join the campaign against Ben and gave King's name to Mayes. King provided ample motive for his willingness to do so. Contrary to his inability to describe the train conversation, he exhibited a clear memory of the times Ben disciplined him. Once, King was carrying a load of blankets. It was hot, and he had his uniform open at the collar. Ben, riding by on his horse, stopped to tell King to button up. Later, after King had left to take the officer examination, Ben criticized him for failing to report to headquarters when he returned to Fort Terry for a visit.[21]

The jurors had no questions for King. He left the stand, unceremoniously ending the prosecution's main case. When the trial resumed the next afternoon, witnesses for Ben would finally begin to testify.

Hudson and Hawthorne had their work cut out for them. While the accusers had fudged details, proposed some unbelievable scenarios, and revealed animosity toward Ben, there was no denying the strong, cumulative impact of so many stories of penis grabs, erotic fixation, and ribald talk.[22] Could the jury be persuaded that all sixteen men were lying?

Hudson needed to shatter many targets as well as prove a conspiracy. It wouldn't be easy. Nor would it be as private as before. Major Sarratt had arrived reportedly to investigate the prior day's rowboat escape. Leaks to the press were also being investigated, and photographs of Ben were being offered for sale—all causing "panic," according to the *Sun*.[23] The *Sun* was beginning to print details of Ben's supposed advances, exaggerating the testimony against him to such an extent that plainly a source on the prosecution's side was intentionally misleading the reporter.[24]

As if that wasn't enough, reporters and photographers would be allowed on Plum Island on Wednesday. The order came from Wood, who had installed a temporary replacement for Barry over the weekend: a Mississippi-born brigadier general named Robert K. Evans, who had gone to West Point with Mills. Wood let it be known that he would replace Evans in about two months.[25] Apparently, Wood still had a few things he wanted to accomplish in Washington, such as sending the press to Plum Island.[26]

Although the courtroom would be off limits, that would not stop the journalists from trying to find out what scandalous acts Ben Koehler was said to have done that warranted so much secrecy and concern.

# CHAPTER THIRTY-TWO

# Psychology Makes an Appearance

WHEN REPORTERS FINALLY GOT a look at Ben, they saw signs of a broken man, not the confident commander who spoke his mind, cantered with purpose from one inspection point to another, and signed his name elegantly with large swirls around his initials.

Ben's "head is cast down and he looks like a man under a heavy nervous strain," wrote the *Sun*. "He lifts his head only when one of the lawyers addresses him."[1]

Armed guards kept the press from entering the library, but people coming and going outside in the cold air were fair game. Since the start of the trial, privates had been gawking at high-ranking jurors striding two-by-two along Officers Row to and from court. On Wednesday, March 4, reporters and photographers were also on hand to observe the power parade.

Captain Patten met the newcomers at the dock and explained the rules: Ben and his counsel would make no comment, and the "fortifications" were off limits.[2] Patten then handed the "picture men" off to a "tall sergeant, who permitted them to snap the members of the court and the accused as they crossed the grounds for the morning session."[3] In one photo, Ben, wearing a bulky overcoat with its hem nearly to his ankles, stood a few feet behind Hudson and the much taller Hawthorne, holding his right hand on his chin. According to the caption, he did so "to keep the photographer from getting a view of him."[4] At lunchtime, Ben and his counsel traveled in the buckboard, not on foot.[5] One photo session was enough.

The day the media arrived, Ben had not yet taken the stand. A "heavy nervous strain" was understandable given the upsetting testimony of his accusers, ranging from men he had felt friendly toward, to those he had disagreed with, to several he barely knew. Nor was Ben blind to the challenge of disproving so many stories. On top of that, there had been an unpleasant legal argument the previous afternoon.

A number of the accusers had described being alone with Ben: Barrett and Fairey at the stable, Ward in his room, Kirkman in Ben's house, Ensley in the buckboard, Davis in an empty building, Wilson on a boat. In the absence of eyewitnesses, a reasonable defense strategy was to show that Ben's general practices differed from the scenarios presented by the accusers. For example, on Tuesday, the captain of the *Nathaniel Greene* steamer, William B. Proctor, testified that Ben "[a]t all times . . . rode with me in the pilot house," and not "down below with the servants" in the civilian and wives' cabin where Proctor said "an officer would not go," but where Wilson claimed Ben interrupted his window-washing to press on his groin.[6]

Yet evidence of customs and practices only went so far. Mayes could counter that Ben may have deviated from his routine. Indeed, that fit the picture of a sex-crazed man too undisciplined to stop himself when the urge struck.

Hudson had a tactic for that. If he could not disprove specific acts through eyewitnesses or alibis, he would show an absence of impropriety at other times when it theoretically could have happened. He tried the strategy first with George Krouchonoskie, one of the soldiers punished by Worcester for fighting with Kirkman.

Having established that Krouchonoskie frequently found himself alone with Ben while serving as an orderly, Hudson asked whether he ever knew "Major Koehler to say anything in your presence that would not be the words of a gentleman?"

"No, sir, I did not."

"Did you ever see him do anything that was not the act of a gentleman or an officer?"

"No, sir."[7]

At that point, Mayes objected and asked for a ruling on whether this line of questioning would be permitted. In the ensuing argument, both sides ventured beyond law into psychology, for there was little relevant legal precedent in 1914 for the case they were trying.

Hudson and Mayes were pioneers of a sort, discovering the difficulties inherent in adjudicating allegations of sexual misconduct, and though some of their concepts and words appear crude by today's standards, they staked out arguments still repeated to this day in one form or another. The fact that the case involved alleged male-male predation is historically significant. But the atypical context is also interesting analytically, elucidating difficult testimonial issues free from the freighted, misogynistic backdrop that underlies a male defendant's claim that his female accuser is lying, exaggerating, misremembering, or misinterpreting, because such claims often invoke or rely on the stereotype of women as too emotional, unreliable, or vindictive. Here, the accusers said to be lying were men.

How can legal proceedings adequately protect the accuser in a sexual misconduct case from the possibility that the defendant is lying while protecting the defendant from the possibility that the accuser is lying? What role, if any, should character play, and how should character be proved? These remain difficult issues, though Mayes sought to make them seem simple.

He called the sort of "negative testimony" Hudson was trying to elicit from Krouchonoskie "absolutely immaterial." Mayes said, "They can hunt up all the men who have ever been alone with him and whom he has not offended," but what would that prove? "Now, an offense is not committed every time an opportunity is presented. If that were true rape would be an hourly occurrence."

Surely, Mayes had no idea how often rape was committed, but his point was a good one, if unartfully worded. In response, Hudson again complained about the "the difficulty in meeting charges of this nature when the dates are uncertain," making it "necessary for the defence to introduce evidence from men who are closely connected with the accused, and to ask those witnesses if their more or less intimate relationship with the accused was such that there would be an opportunity for him to be familiar with them in the way that has been testified . . . , and then to ask the witness if the accused was ever familiar with him."

Mayes grew more heated, claiming to know about the behavior of "degenerates." "It is inconceivable that even a hopeless degenerate would attempt an act of sexual perversion at every opportunity," he argued. "They do not do it. The fact does not eliminate their guilt when they do attempt it."

Though Mayes offered no support for his psychological thesis, it certainly sounded persuasive, but again Hudson offered a smart response, putting his finger on the fundamental contradiction in the prosecution's case: How could a man be as unable to control himself as the sixteen accusers described Ben, and at the same time, able to control himself when he chose?

As Hudson put it: "A man whose mind is perverted to such an extent as charged will have a tendency to become familiar with men in the way that they attract him." Hudson, too, was more than willing to offer up psychological theories without support. How did he know that a "pervert" could resist an unattractive person but not an attractive one?

In what was surely the first and perhaps the only legal argument to involve "fat boys" in a major Army court-martial, Hudson went on to note the "evidence in this case of a fat boy" and to suggest that testimony from an "attractive looking—if you will pardon that reference— an attractive looking fat boy" that Ben had not been "indiscreet or perverted" with him despite opportunities "might impress the court and it might have considerable weight in determining his tendencies and his guilt in other cases." Hudson apparently did not grasp that the witnesses were suggesting that Ben referred to himself as a desirable fat boy, not that he sought a fat boy.

Had Hudson been looking around Fort Terry for an "attractive looking" fat boy since arriving, one he might put on the witness stand?

The back-and-forth continued between Hudson and Mayes about the correct way, under legal precedent, to prove Ben's good character. For Hudson, it all came back to unfairness in the way the case had been presented:

> We are entitled, it seems to me, to every bit of evidence under the circumstances here where no man ever sees the offence committed and where a date may be changed to a month or six weeks in the trial and we get a specification of a certain date and have to rush around to get the evidence to control it and are met with the elasticity of the law, and it seems to me it is simply a question of how much weight that witness will have in court.

For Mayes, it was a question of rules. The right way to establish character was through reputation, not specific instances of good conduct. But when he started to cite legal texts, Hudson asked, "Are any of these authorities to decide a case against a perverted mind?"

"I think not," replied Mayes.

"That is the distinction," responded Hudson.

"I would like to hear the distinction," Mayes shot back.

Ultimately, Hudson had to admit he had "not examined the cases as to charges against a pervert" and had no relevant legal authority to offer.

He returned to the argument that if Ben's "mind was [as] perverted" as described, comparing penises to flashlights and mule organs, with "a constant tendency to vulgarity or obscenity," then he would act on an opportunity "if the personality is attractive." Showing his own tendency toward racism, Hudson then stated, "Now, if we had an ugly negro here who had been a servant in his house, a most repulsive looking man, and [we] attempted to ask that question we should expect the court might rule immediately upon it, but if the court looks at the individual who is testifying and who has had this opportunity and thinks that this is the kind of man this man might have been unmoral with, then that kind of evidence, it seems to me, is clearly admissible."

Mayes argued the reverse, that "the laws [*sic*] concerning secret crimes goes further the other way and presumes that their secrecy will make their proof difficult, and it is for that reason that in a case of secret crimes a conviction may be had upon the testimony of one witness." That, he contended, "even strengthens the general principle that character may not be established by specific instances, or by the method employed here."[8]

In the end, the jurors agreed to give Hudson the latitude he sought. Krouchonoskie's answer that he never witnessed improper conduct by Ben remained in the record, and Hudson would be able to ask subsequent witnesses the same question.

It was a legal victory for Hudson but not an emotional win for Ben. There is an old saying that it isn't news when a dog bites a man; it's when a man bites a dog. The court seemed to be agreeing with Hudson that it was as noteworthy when Ben Koehler did not molest a soldier as when he did. This frame reached its most astonishing point when Hudson called a former recruitment aide to Ben in New York City, Sergeant John Cashman, to testify that Ben never did anything improper the many times he sat in a room full of Army applicants who were "[a]ll naked, nothing on at all," while Cashman checked them for "defects." Sometimes an applicant would come in late and it would be just Ben, Cashman, and the applicant in the room.

"Did Major Koehler ever request you to leave the room while those men were there?" Hudson asked.

"No sir, never," answered Cashman, who said he "always respected Major Koehler as an officer and a gentleman."

"Major Koehler was the same as anybody else," he continued. "I never found any difference between Major Koehler and anybody else."[9]

# *Female Advocates*

Despite all the talk of fat boys, three women presented some of the strongest testimony in Ben's behalf: Emma Jones, Katie Ewing, and Sophia.

Jones, the housekeeper Sophia had selected in the spring of 1913, testified with precision and confidence—despite efforts by men in the room to portray her as unreliable by asking irrelevant questions they would never have asked a man, such as what she did on her last birthday and what she had served for dessert the day Elvin Byers showed up unannounced.[1]

Jones said Byers came alone that day, not with two others as he claimed. She recalled seeing Byers and Ben leave the garden after no more than fifteen minutes, the time it took her to wash the lunch dishes—not over an hour, as Byers said—and walk together toward the tennis court, where work was being done that she presumed Ben was going to inspect.

Ben's gardener, Ralph Lones, also disputed Byers's story, saying he could see Ben and Byers the whole time, and they never sat on the ground.[2]

John Smith made a helpful witness, describing his boss and friend as "very particular" about social etiquette and responsible for "very high" discipline at the post. Lieutenant Smith said he accompanied Ben nearly every time Ben rode. Ben saddled and bridled his own horse and urinated, as Smith did, in a corner with his back turned, not in the place John Barrett had described. Smith also bolstered Ben's defense to Worcester's claim. Describing the dress he wore at the Halloween party as more "modest" than Worcester's costume, Smith said Ben "looked me up and down and sort of laughed at me and made a motion with his thumb toward me," just as Ben would say he did to Worcester—a poke in the stomach, not the genitals.[3]

Smith said John Fuller, not Ensley, usually drove Ben in the buckboard. Fuller took the stand and agreed, recalling each time Ben had summoned the buckboard during maneuvers and target practice. Fuller testified that he did not think Ensley had ever driven Ben.[4]

Lieutenant Colonel Jordan, having recovered from his illness, made the trip from Massachusetts to Plum Island to testify to Ben's being an "excellent officer, capable and efficient and interested in his work." Jordan said he used to see Ben several times a day and Ben never did or said anything "unrefined or ungentlemanly"—nor did Jordan call Ben about pheasants, as Kirkman had said.[5]

Not until the tenth defense witness took the stand, however, was there testimony about a conspiracy, and it was Ben's bad luck that the witness with the most direct evidence of a plot happened to be a woman, Katie Ewing. In 1914, the majority of U.S. states did not allow women to serve on juries, and some of the same specious notions used to support their exclusion—undue emotion, lack of objectivity, home and family as their primary sphere—meant that female witnesses faced an uphill battle to be believed. This had been evident from the grilling given to Emma Jones, who was not only a woman but African-American.[6]

Hudson took Ewing through her background, hoping its military orientation might elevate her standing in the jurors' minds. She had been "born and raised in the Army"—at Fort Monroe, where her father was a retired soldier and tailor. She married a sergeant and they moved to Fort Terry. She had lived on Plum Island nearly as long as the federal government owned the place. Her first husband died, and she married a sergeant named Ewing. Over the years, she worked as a domestic employee, a hospital matron, and in the dining hall.[7]

That set the stage for the bombshell she delivered: When she and a friend were crossing Long Island Sound on a steamer, she overheard Elvin Byers and Charles Moody conversing through an open window. "Tell the court what you heard," Hudson prompted.

> Both of them stood outside about 3 feet from where I was standing. Sergeant Byers said to Sergeant Moody "So Koehler is over there yet?" and Sergeant Moody said "Yes, his trial has been ordered" and Sergeant Byers said "I am sorry that I had anything to do with it." Sergeant Moody said "You don't want to talk like that, you have taken an oath and so have I and you have got to stick to what we have said. We have got to stick tight."

This was testimony of critical importance, an account of one accuser speaking to another about an "oath" and the need "to stick tight." Mayes did all he could to limit the damage.

"Might not that mean that he would not be influenced by anybody in his testimony?" he asked Ewing on cross-examination.

"I don't know just how anybody else would take it," she answered, "but I took it just the way I have repeated it."

There was no doubt in her mind as to the import of what she heard: "I thought from the way those men acted it was just spite work."

Ewing already had a low opinion of Byers. She said he had asked her out even though she was married, and on the steamer, after Byers realized he and Moody had been overheard, he came inside, offered the women whiskey, and suggested he and Ewing "go over [to New London] some night and stay over all night and have a good time."

Ewing had told all this to Mayes, but Mayes still put forward Byers's claim that Ben grabbed his ankle while fondling his own penis as they lay on the grass. Ben had to hope that Ewing's testimony would matter more to the jury. One juror, however, strained to minimize its significance, asking Ewing whether Byers said "anything he said was not true" when he remarked that he was sorry he "had anything to do with it."

"No, sir."

"He didn't say why he was sorry?"

"No, sir."

If Byers was speaking to a co-conspirator, he did not need to say why he was sorry. It would have been understood, as it was by Ewing. "We had heard this rumor around the post and I said those two men were implicated in it, that is the way I looked at it," she said.

The jurors asked more questions about another part of Ewing's testimony: a child-snatching by Kirkman, who had told the elaborate story of Ben taking him upstairs and undressing in front of him and inviting him on a trip.

Ewing testified that a young girl was under her care one summer evening, playing outdoors, when a soldier rushed in and told her that Kirkman had pulled the girl into one of the barracks through a window. Ewing hurried over and found the girl in Kirkman's lap, struggling to get loose. There was another man in the room and a bottle of whiskey on the table.

"Do you think it was whiskey?" asked a juror.

"I don't think it was wine," Ewing replied. This was one witness who did not hesitate before answering.

She grabbed the child and left, and testified that the girl's father, a widower, was so furious that he threatened to go over and "shoot" Kirkman, but Ewing calmed him down. "You don't know the character of those men like I do," she quoted the girl's father as saying. "They must have broken into that building to get in because they were supposed to be in camp."

This was the incident, Ben would testify, that caused him to form a poor opinion of Kirkman, though Worcester and Kirkman both denied any recollection of it. Worcester and Kirkman were apparently willing to wager their word against that of a woman, and at least with Mayes, they succeeded. It remained to be seen whether the same would be true with the jury.[8]

Several other witnesses testified to Kirkman's poor reputation. "Whenever he is in a little trouble in the Company he brings somebody else into it and lies and gets out of it himself," asserted Edward Shanley. Shanley also explained that he served as Ben's orderly occasionally, which was why he went to Ben's house—bringing envelopes to Sophia, cigars to Ben. It was true, he said, that another time he did not tell Worcester where he was going—because he wanted time off to see a sick brother, a request he was sure Worcester, his captain, would not approve.[9]

Shanley testified that he sought Ben's advice "on account of men around the post telling me that Major Koehler would do all he could for a man that was in trouble and would help him out and advise him what to do." According to Shanley, Ben said he could not grant the leave due to protocol—only Worcester could—but he would speak to Worcester about it. Shanley believed Worcester was so biased against him that he just dropped the request.

Shanley did not want to stick around Fort Terry to learn what his testifying for Ben would mean for his future. He had spent all the time he cared to in the guardhouse and did not want to be a "man in trouble" again. When Shanley stood up from the witness chair, he no longer worked for the Army. He had secured an honorable discharge effective that day, signed by a lieutenant who would testify for Ben later in the week. Shanley would not have to sneak off the island in a rowboat, but his departure showed that the *Sun*'s prediction—that some men would "walk the plank"—was coming to pass.

The same held true for Krouchonoskie. Like Shanley, Krouchonoskie secured his discharge the day before he testified.[10]

Corporal Clayton Zerphy of the 88th Company told of a different sort of plank-walking. He had declined to give incriminating information about Ben to Mills and paid for it by being denied a furlough in December 1913 for the holidays. He testified that both Elvin Byers and Richard Ellis—Worcester's friend and successor as captain of the 88th Company—linked the punishment to Zerphy's failure to go along with the plot. As Zerphy testified, Byers told him, "'Corporal, you are not getting any furlough.' I said 'Why not?' He says 'The Company Commander is not satisfied with the evidence you gave Colonel Mills.'"[11]

Zerphy said Byers told him that if he changed his story, Worcester and Ellis would make sure he got his furlough. Zerphy did not do that. He signed up for a five-day pass instead of a longer furlough, only to find that his name was crossed off the pass list, so he spent the holidays at Fort Terry. In addition, Zerphy said that Byers and Ellis, who had previously recommended him for a new assignment, changed their minds after he refused to incriminate Ben, and they told Captain Patten they did not want Zerphy to get the assignment. (Ellis was not around to hassle Zerphy any longer, having been ordered to move to Fort Slocum.[12])

Zerphy's testimony—corroborated by a clerk who overheard his conversations with Byers and Ellis—provided strong evidence as to how Worcester, Ellis, Byers, and others pressured men to "stick tight" against Ben. Other defense witnesses had undercut elements of the prosecution's case, but Ben's classmate Andy Moses came the closest to providing direct refutation of a charge. Moses testified that he sat no more than three feet away from where Ben was inspecting ordnance with Charles Byers. It was an "absolute impossibility," Moses said, that Ben could have touched Byers in the thigh and crotch without Moses seeing it.[13]

Mayes chipped away at this certainty, getting Moses to concede that he could not "swear" the touching did not happen, because there were occasions when Moses glanced down at the list of inspection items. Nonetheless, asked if Ben could have "put his hand on the thigh of the Sergeant and on the same side each time run his hand up along the thigh to his testicles without your seeing it," Moses responded confidently: "I think not, that is my belief, that he could not have done it without my seeing him or noticing him."

Moses also said that it was he who decided not to forward Worcester's appeal after the Shanley matter. This, Hudson argued, put to rest Worcester's insinuation that Ben was "protecting" Shanley due to "improper relations going on."

Moses had known Ben the longest of anyone in the room, for more than twenty years, and he swore that he had never known Ben to do anything "suggesting vulgarity or coarseness."

One by one, other men took the stand to say the same thing, from noncommissioned corporals to lieutenant colonels, testifying to Ben's good character and behavior as a gentleman. "WITNESSES GIVE

THE ACCUSED GOOD NAME," read a typical headline as the record grew thick with praise for Ben.[14] According to the article, "As a large number of persons in different parts of the country have indicated a desire to testify in behalf of Major Koehler, it is expected that the trial will extend through another week at least."

Mayes continued to object to such "negative testimony" as worthless. So what if Ben had never made a lewd remark or sexual advance to some men, if he had made so many to the accusers? Mayes told the jury it could all be explained by the concept of the double life.

Many a gay man or woman has lived a double life, residing in a kind of two-room house, maintaining a job and family relationships as an ostensibly straight person in one room, while socializing in same-sex situations when and where a safe room for that purpose presented itself. But there was no evidence that Ben had lived that sort of life, going to clubs or bathhouses on the sly, having gay friends or a gay partner. Even if his relationship with William Kenly came close to the latter, no evidence was introduced at the trial, or even an insinuation made, that there was any sexual aspect to their association.

Rather, in Ben's case, the double life was presented to the jurors as a two-room house with the second room a dark dungeon. There was the visible part of his life, which Mayes dismissively termed a "halo of innocence" created by the defense—and then there was the secret room supposedly containing uncontrolled and erratic sexual obsession in both word and deed, grabbing men's penises on a dance floor, in a phone booth, in a wagon, and during an inspection with an esteemed fellow officer seated nearby. The ways in which Mayes and the witnesses portrayed Ben recalled the spin tactics American hawks had used against the Spanish when trying to justify war—portraying them as lustful, dissolute, rapacious—and later against the Filipinos, when it suited the speakers' purposes to characterize the native people of the Philippines as animalistic, deviant, and lacking in self-discipline.

Yet if Ben had done the acts with which he was charged, they were the acts of a man not trying to hide his "unmanly" sexual orientation but almost defiantly daring to be caught, or so incapable of squelching sexual urges that he could not stop himself.

And so, Hudson was right to point to a conflict between the prosecution's portrayal of a man who lacked restraint and Mayes's thesis that Ben artificially created an image of wholesomeness through intentional self-control with other men.

Moreover, if Ben was sexually attracted to men at a time when keeping that quiet would be in his professional interest, why would he have taken risks with the people he had most antagonized, people highly likely to resist and report him? There were six companies of soldiers at Fort Terry. Why would Ben focus his overtures on men currently or formerly in the two companies associated with Worcester and Frick— the man Lieutenant George Gorham described as Ben's only "enemy" at the post, who had vowed to "get" Ben several times?

Gorham and a post doctor also contradicted Private Leonard Davis's account that Gorham had walked up to the battle command center to seek a medical leave from Ben, a point Davis had inserted to try to shore up the date change of his charge from 1913 to 1912.

As the favorable defense testimony continued, despite another blizzard on Friday, it seemed like more and more of a stretch for the jurors to see Ben as the man described by the accusers. One of Ben's supporters was quoted as saying that if Ben was convicted, it would be like "Samson falling, bringing down the pillars of the temple with him."[15]

At the same time, the concept of a secret life was powerful. It could remind each juror of a darker moment or impulse in his own past, preying upon the human ability to imagine that the impossible just might be possible, even in the absence of corroborating evidence.

Which was the reality? A gentleman or a sex fiend?

Of course, Sophia was going to say the former, but how convincing would she be? She would lead off the next week's testimony on Monday morning. Ben would have to wait all weekend to hear the third woman on his witness list defend his honor.

At least there would be no photographers when court resumed. Reporters could stay, but the experiment with having "the picture men" on Plum Island had ended after one day. Kirby was said to enjoy having his photo taken in his gold and scarlet Coast Artillery cape, but no one else much liked having cameras around. When the photographers were returning to New London, a captain "took up their passes and told them they would not be allowed on the island again while the trial was in progress."[16]

It was a small act of defiance from a small island where, it was said, "the whole garrison is in a state of nerves."[17]

# Details, Details

SOPHIA KOEHLER RADIATED PRECISION. "Or words to that effect" was not her style. Looking poised and self-assured, she recalled dates, times, and conversations.[1] Methodically, she eviscerated Frick's claim that Ben tried to kiss him upstairs in the bathroom of their house.

She distinctly remembered the night her former friend stayed for dinner, the only time he ever dined alone with "Brother" and her. Ben did not meet Frick at the dock after target practice, as Frick had testified. Ben arrived home around five o'clock that evening in August 1912 and remained home. The doorbell rang around seven thirty. It was Frick.

"Brother went to the door and let him in and they came into the parlor where I was and Mr. Frick made his report," Sophia testified. "He had been out on the target and he asked what Brother wanted him to do for the next day and Brother gave him directions."[2]

She overheard Ben say, "I know your dinner is over and ours is late." He invited Frick to stay and dine with them. "Then I spoke up and told him we would be glad to have him," she recalled.

Ben remained downstairs with her the entire evening, except for a few moments when she went into the kitchen to tell the cook that a third person would be eating. There was no awkwardness between the two men. Frick ate and left within a half-hour, saying he was tired.

In the months afterward, Sophia said, Frick returned to the house for bridge games that included his roommate, the Halloween and Thanksgiving parties, and to visit Margaret Gund during her five-week stay.

"Did you ever notice any appearance of coolness on the part of Lieutenant Frick and your brother during that period of the card games?" Hudson inquired.

"I did not."

Mayes asked no questions of Sophia, but Kirby posed several.

"Did Lieutenant Frick visit the second floor of your house that evening?" Kirby asked.

"To my knowledge, no," answered Sophia.

"Before or after dinner?"

"Not to my knowledge."

"Well, could he have gone up and remained any length of time without your knowledge?"

"I think not."

"Do you know positively that he did not after dinner?"

"Yes, I do know that."

"Do you know whether or not your brother went upstairs at any time while Lieutenant Frick was in the quarters?"

"No, he was [sic] not."

"Are you positive about that?"

"I am positive about it."

Sophia was also positive about her "disgust" for Worcester's Halloween costume in 1913. She recalled sharing her opinion with Ben the day after the party. Contrary to Worcester's testimony that Ben had not criticized him, Sophia testified that Ben said to her, "I told Worcester he was positively indecent."

Sophia described the beach picnic with the Worcesters and two other couples in mid-November, two weeks after Ben's testicle-grabbing at the Halloween party supposedly occurred. Worcester had testified he could not "get out of" the event. Sophia disagreed. The picnic was spontaneous and "very informal," planned in the afternoon by Sophia and two officers' wives due to unusually warm weather.

There was no reason why Worcester could not have stayed away, So-phia stated. The women mainly cared about Mabel Worcester's atten-dance because she could be counted on to bring plenty of good food, and Worcester accompanied his wife, arriving before Ben. The group sat in a favorite spot, on a wrecked ship deck that had washed ashore. The men collected wood while the women cooked over three fires. "Brother fixed the coffee," Sophia said. Then they lit a "great bonfire" and stayed on the beach past dark. The party lasted three hours.

"Did you notice whether Captain Worcester was cool or quiet during the evening, or was he his usual self and manner?" Hudson asked.

"No, he practically entertained the crowd while we were sitting around the fire," Sophia answered. Ben and Worcester sat next to each other. This was about eight days before Worcester traveled to Gover-nors Island to tell his story and make the Army "clean." Either Worces-ter was a very good actor at the picnic, or he had not yet decided to turn on Ben, consistent with the theory that what motivated him to act when he did was Captain Patten's telling Worcester in the days after the picnic that Ben intended to report the alleged plagiarism.

Indirectly, Sophia also contradicted Harry King's claim. She said she was certain Ben ate lunch on the train the day he came back from New York in April 1912. King had described the men sitting side by side in a row, but Sophia said Ben would have ridden in the dining car.

She also testified that she had never left Ben alone in the house at dinnertime, undercutting Kirkman's claim that he came over one eve-ning and found Ben alone. She also said there was no shutter on the home office door, as Kirkman had testified, just black strips applied in rectangles to give the sheet of glass the appearance of individual panes.

Some bitterness crept into Sophia's words when Hudson asked how she could be "so certain" that she had never left Ben alone in the eve-ning. "Because the occasions are very rare when we are invited out and we are always invited together," she answered. A sense of being socially shunned also allowed her to recall the timing of a visit by

Lieutenant Colonel Jordan and his wife. She felt "hurt," she said, that "they did not come sooner to call on Miss Gund."

When Sophia finished testifying, Ben felt the best he had since the trial began. Many noticed the change in his demeanor. On his way home for lunch, he "greeted the reporters with a cheery good morning," wrote the *New York Herald*, and later in the day visited parts of the post for the first time in weeks.[3]

"Major Koehler is now convinced that he will be proven innocent," the paper went on, quoting "one of his friends," who said Ben had "good reason for such a belief after hearing the evidence that has gone in during the last two days of court sessions."

In a few weeks, in his closing statement, Mayes would advise the jurors to discount everything Sophia had said. She was Ben's sister, maybe a graceful and intelligent one, but a biased woman nonetheless. Out of courtesy, he said, he had asked no questions, but what was the point of asking them, anyway? Everyone knew that a sister was going to give testimony favorable to her brother.

But for now, Ben felt vindicated by Sophia's words. He was not the only one to credit her testimony with importance. An unidentified juror was quoted as saying her "story, calmly told . . . convincingly contradicted much of the evidence which the foes of Major Koehler have relied upon to bring about his conviction."[4]

Next, Colonel Hawthorne switched roles and took the stand as a character witness. He testified that he did not see how the man he had known since the Philippines could possibly have committed the acts alleged. He and Ben had endured all manner of hardship, pestilence, and violence during a three-month campaign in the Philippines, and Ben had been nothing but strong and dutiful—and, when the men slept side by side, Ben had kept his hands to himself, Hawthorne said in response to a question.[5] Again, Mayes objected: What mattered was only whether Ben had committed the acts with which he was charged.

Fair or unfair, no one knew that better than Ben Koehler, whose opportunity to speak finally arrived after Hawthorne resumed his seat as adjunct counsel.

Fifty witnesses had now testified. Finally, on the afternoon of March 9, some three months after his arrest, Ben's turn arrived. He swore to tell the truth to the jury of his former colleagues, and then, in a corner of the sprawling Fort Terry compound that used to be his to command, he tried in his own words to recover all he had lost.

# The Accused Speaks

B EN GAVE A "STIRRING refutation" of the charges according to some newspaper reports, but that was hyperbole. No journalists heard him speak. For the most part, Ben kept his answers short and to the point and delivered them in a colorless, matter-of-fact way.

He gave clear denials but spent as much time referring to a custom, habit, or other reason why an accuser's claim could not be true. Having had months to think about it, he may well have decided that the best way to defend himself was with objective evidence such as customary practices. He was, after all, a man devoted to rules, and he conferred on the conventions of the fort and his daily routines an almost independent existence, as though they could speak for themselves and exonerate him.

Like Sophia, Ben's recollections were specific. Regarding what happened in the basement of the Worcesters' house during the Halloween party, Ben first described how he "encountered Captain Worcester in the pathway . . . jumping along towards me with his hands up to his face, sticking his stomach out."

"When he came up like that at me I did not like that and struck him in the stomach," he said, the court reporter noting "witness indicates by making a gesture with his thumb."

"What did he say?" asked Hudson.

"He said 'Don't do that.' I said 'Worcester, suck up your stomach. It looks as if you were in a family way,' and I said 'You have not enough clothes.'"[1]

Kirby asked, "Did you come near enough to him or touch him in any way to make him think you had done the thing he has charged you with and testified to before this court?"

"I don't see how I could," responded Ben, "because I said he approached me in a dancing way with his stomach protruding. As most everyone knows, when you make a move like that, a person will immediately cover their stomach."

"You didn't catch him anywhere about his privates, grasp him at all, or touch him there."

"No sir."[2]

And so it went regarding all the accusers. There was no reason to accompany Frick upstairs, Ben said, because "it was customary for the gentlemen [playing cards] to know where the toilet was if they wanted to use it."[3]

Regarding Davis, Ben described why it was "necessary to keep two men" in the battle command station to refute Davis's claim that Ben had asked everyone to leave except Davis.[4] Ben also said the station equipment did not fit Davis's description.[5]

Ben did not recall ever being driven in the wagon by Ensley, whom he rarely saw because Ensley usually drove the commissary and laundry wagons.[6]

Yes, he owned a flashlight, Ben said, but he did not need to carry it in camp as Kernan had described. Electric lamps lit the sleeping tents. Ben recalled that his tent stood close to the road, and he would "turn on my light when I went away in the evening and leave it on until I came back."[7] He visited the hospital tent to sign papers as it had the nearest desk, and once seeking "rhubarb and soda" for a headache. There was usually another soldier there, and he denied stroking Kernan's back "unless it was accidentally, when I took hold of his chair."[8]

"Very frequently he would be studying," Ben recalled of Kernan. "I asked him one time what he was studying—arithmetic or something, and he said he was studying for Sergeant First Class, and I asked him whether he was a married man. He said no, that he intended to be."[9]

That was the discussion about marriage as Ben recalled it, which in Kernan's telling concerned "big Swede" girls who could "hatch one."

It was not only the accusers who seemed inclined to twist Ben's words. One juror did so after Ben testified that he never spoke to Campbell about Pacific sporting houses, but he did recall Campbell asking him about "the 606 treatment, and I told him it got its name from the number of applications [on animals] the man that invented it had made in inoculation for syphilis."[10]

"Is that a usual question, or is it unusual for a soldier to ask an officer a question of that kind?" the juror asked Ben.

"Why, I don't think it is; it is spoken of in the papers, it was written up in the papers."

"Why should he have asked you about it?"

"I don't know sir."

"Can you explain it at all?"

"No sir. As I say, there was some one else present. I had been talking to Mr. Arthur about dogs just before that."[11]

Why did Ben need to explain a sergeant's asking him about medicine for venereal disease, an issue of considerable concern on Army posts at the time? Wasn't open communication between an enlisted man and his commander a desirable thing? Roosevelt had written of his pride at being described as an officer "as ready to listen to a private as to a major-general."[12] Apparently, there was a different standard for a man accused of homosexuality. Once again, Ben's "fatherly interest" in a soldier was being misinterpreted, this time by a juror, who seemed to see in the conversation an obsession with sex and overly familiar relations with an enlisted man rather than an officer doing his job in a non-autocratic way.

The accusers' portrayal of Ben as a man who improperly touched other men, invited them to his house, and discussed sex had obviously raised questions in at least some jurors' minds. One wanted to know why Ben had "felt muscles of the noncommissioned officer in charge of the caretaking detail at Fort Michie." This was not in the specifications, but Ben answered: "I don't remember of doing it . . . There was something came up one time, as I remember, about their wanting a boat to come over here and I don't know whether it was in this connection I said 'I don't think you could row a boat against the tide with your muscle.'"[13]

Even a teasing gesture like squeezing a man's biceps was suspect when Ben did it.

Kirby expressed surprise that Ben had once let a former sergeant from out of town stay at his house. The man might reenlist, and Kirby reminded Ben that "it is not customary for a Commanding Officer to be familiar with soldiers that are under him."

In his response, Ben showed the most emotion of his testimony. The man had been his first sergeant in the Philippines. Ben said, "He came over to see me, my family were there, and I considered that man is equal from what I know about him in his knowledge and his ability. I think he has had more service and done good work for the Government than a great many officers, and I have very high respect for that Sergeant."[14]

Ben then referred to Louis, Ben's model for what was right: "My brother, who is in the service, when his Sergeant-Major came to Washington with his horses he took him down to . . . Congress and he introduced him to Dan Anthony, who took him into the Senate and introduced him to a lot of Senators and went to luncheon."[15]

But while both Louis and Ben may have shared an egalitarianism progressive for their day, Louis was a married man and sixteen men had not accused him of sexual advances. Apparently, that cast everything Ben had ever done in a different light.

In *The Stranger*, Albert Camus wrote brilliantly about the reenvisioning of a criminal suspect's past. In the novel, the protagonist's dalliance with a woman after his mother's funeral was portrayed by the prosecutor as showing the cold-heartedness of a murderer, when it could just as easily have been a grieving man's desire for distraction and relief. In 1914, when "the masculinity crisis required a new policing of male intimacy,"[16] in George Chauncey's words, an act of kindness such as Ben's opening his house to an ex-sergeant could be converted into an improper, homosexual overture.

Louis's name resurfaced in connection with the confusion over

Ben's resignation. Ben testified that when Louis sailed up from Puerto Rico after Ben's arrest, Louis encouraged him to fight the charges, unlike Barry and Haan, who had pressured Ben to resign.

In hindsight, if Wood had let Ben take the two-month leave, events might have played out more simply and less prejudicially. There would not have been confusion in Washington regarding Ben's resignation. He would have returned from leave and most likely announced his decision to go to trial. Secretary of War Garrison would not have received letters asking him to accept a resignation that had not really been tendered, and Captain Mayes might never have done a reinvestigation that added claims and gave Mayes considerable control over the accusers. In addition, Bat Koehler might not have irked Garrison with his intervention, and Henry Koehler might never have written his damaging letter.

As fully as Ben embraced Louis, he distanced himself from Henry and Bat, saying whatever they had done in Washington, it was not "by my authority." He stated, "There was one brother whom I had been in correspondence with that did not know anything about it, had asked some Senator to accept my resignation and when my other brother came on and I heard about it I told him to stop it, but I do not correspond with that brother at all. I don't know where he got it from."[17]

Had Ben ever seen the letter that Henry wrote blaming alcohol and too much time in New York City for Ben's undoing, he would undoubtedly have been appalled.

Ben finished his testimony in the same way that it began—blending denials and explanations in response to a series of questions from Kirby.

"Did Master Gunner Harry L. King, now 2d Lieutenant, sit in a seat any part of the time between New York and New London with you?" Kirby asked.

"No sir."

"You positively deny that?"

"That I positively deny."[18]

Kirby asked what was on many jurors' minds: Why would so many people have ganged up against him? How did Ben account for the testimony of people such as Spears, Moody, Ensley, and others who did not have obvious grounds for animus against him?

Ben did not give the strongest answer:

Not except Sergeant Byers at Wright, belongs to the Company that Sergeant Moody does, and Sergeant Moody has been, as I say, connected with Lieutenant Frick and Lieutenant Frick and Captain Worcester have been connected through Sergeant Byers of the 88th Company with men in the 88th Company and . . . Sergeant Barrett has control over men in the stables who have been caught stealing, both of them at different times, without reporting it, both Fairey and Ensley, and gambled with them.

"How about Davis?" Kirby asked.

"I don't know," Ben responded. "Davis is connected through Electrician Sergeant Brown. That is all I know about Davis. I have had trouble with Brown. He is a married man; he has been keeping company with a colored woman."[19]

The answers were a bit abstruse. If there was a weakness in Ben's testimony, it was his inability to give the jurors a single, compelling reason for a conspiracy. Sophia's explanation in her letter to Roy was stronger and more concise: There was a "clique." Ben had rubbed the clique's leaders and members the wrong way, and they thought life at the post would be better without him—though the rest of the post knew he was innocent.

Ben was not Sophia. He had difficultly explaining the situation in a narrative way. He may have been a problem solver when it came to maintaining buildings and grounds, and a compassionate man to others in trouble, as Shanley testified, but now Ben was the man in trouble—and nothing he had learned in LeMars, at West Point, or by shooting at Filipinos and floating targets had prepared him for handling this sort of trouble.

It was understandable that a senior Army officer would regard words only as utilitarian instruments, a means by which actions were carried out and information exchanged.[20] Oratory was the domain of politicians. Why should Ben have known how to use words in his legal and moral defense? Yet in a proceeding animated by so much that wasn't being said—presumptions about masculinity, ideas about how homosexuals behaved—brilliant words were needed, based on extraordinary self-awareness and understanding of the times.

Ben's capacity for compassion and fairness made him different from an autocratic officer—different from some of the jurors, as reflected by their questions—befitting a member of Susan B. Anthony's family by marriage. If Ben was sufficiently self-aware to portray his actions as reflecting a more egalitarian worldview than that of the jurors, he risked coming across as arrogant, or worse—feminine. It was a no-win situation at a time when men concerned about their own manliness and appearing masculine to others were satisfied to have the homosexual be that "category of person who could represent men's unacceptable feminine impulses."[21]

As it was, when questioned about something that seemed odd to a juror, Ben frequently answered, "I don't know."

Ben was being asked to describe why other people would band together to try to destroy him. What a difficult task for anyone to do, especially someone with Ben's factual bent of mind. His approach was to describe the accusers' relationships with each other. He did not try to describe their interior feelings and motives. Psychology was a new field, certainly not a prominent part of a late nineteenth-century West Point education.

Still, despite any weaknesses in his testimony, a dispatch from New London printed in Ben's hometown paper favored Ben's position: "The evidence introduced so far, it is said, is not sufficient to convict Major Koehler of immorality," wrote the *LeMars Semi-Weekly Sentinel.*[22] Whether he was convicted or acquitted, according to the article, Ben planned to file charges against "certain officers at Fort Terry."

The source of those statements is unclear. They were neutral comments, so it did not much matter—unlike the egregiously false report making its way to the Secretary of War.

. . .

WOOD'S VENDETTA AGAINST LOUIS had so far remained offstage—remembered by some, whispered to others, but not openly discussed. That changed overnight when the *Sun* incorrectly reported that Sophia had testified about Louis's old case: "She told of serious charges that her elder brother Major Lewis M. Koehler of Iowa brought against fellow officers about ten years ago, causing a feud in the army."[23]

Few people knew what witnesses were actually saying in the library, but that did not stop the *Sun* from relaying what its source claimed, that Sophia "gave names and circumstances to link the case with the present trial and to make the alleged feud the motive actuating the accusers of Major Benjamin Koehler easily understood . . . Miss Koehler referred the court to the records of the War Department."

Two days later, the *Sun* made the connection explicit, writing that Sophia "is understood to have recalled on the witness stand that her other brother, Major Lewis M. Koehler, had once had trouble with Gen. Wood." The paper said that "friends" of Ben "have implied that his trial was a revenge taken by enemies his brother made seven years ago."[24] The *Washington Post* went even further, writing, "The plain implication in the reports from Fort Terry is that Maj. Gen. Leonard Wood is responsible for Maj. Benjamin Koehler's court-martial, and that he brought it about to retaliate against Maj. Lewis M. Koehler."[25]

The *Herald* also chimed in, quoting "a high officer of the army" as vowing that the connection between the two cases "will be one of the biggest sensations that the army has ever known."[26]

In Washington, Garrison rushed to defend the chief of staff. "If there is any conspiracy against Maj. Benjamin M. Koehler, it began with me and ended with me, for I handled the case myself, and I alone am responsible for the court-martial," he told reporters, completely mischaracterizing the nature of Ben's defense.[27] Ben was not alleging a conspiracy from above, but from below. In fact, he was being targeted from both levels, but in the courtroom, all his ammunition had been aimed at the conspiracy from below.

Garrison went on to say that Wood had nothing to do with the case, and that "the charges were presented to me from, I think, eighteen different witnesses . . . I directed Capt. James J. Mayes to make a personal investigation of the charges. He investigated the motives of the accusers and found only four who had possible ulterior motives."[28]

Even if the difference between sixteen and eighteen accusers was not material, Garrison made it sound as though he had personal familiarity with the case. Yet he had not sat in the courtroom nor received briefings about the testimony. He knew nothing of the mounting evidence of grudges by many more than four men and the use of pressure to gain the cooperation of others, not to mention the holes, inconsistencies, and sudden changes in so many complainants' testimony. He had not heard Katie Ewing state that she overheard two accusers talk of an "oath" and the need to "stick tight," nor Clayton Zerphy tell of being grounded and losing a promotion due to his failure to implicate Ben. He had not heard Ben's denials and explanations, nor Sophia's strong rebuttals. And the assertion that Mayes had objectively "investigated the motives" of the accused was ludicrous. Mayes had put words in the accusers' mouths, arbitrarily choosing dates for their claims and using Ben's alibis against him.

Garrison's remarks, published in numerous papers around the country, immediately caused a stir in the capital—"no end of surprise here," as the *Washington Post* put it. "There was much conjecture over whether or not the Secretary's statement could be taken as grounds for a new trial in case Maj. Koehler was found guilty."[29]

Daniel Anthony Jr. raced to Garrison's office from Capitol Hill and told him the statements were prejudicial. Anthony followed up with a letter saying he had received a communication from Fort Terry "which states that none of the witnesses in the trial or the defendant or the counsel made use of the name of General Wood. So, if this is correct the newspaper story to that effect must have been a fiction and you were imposed upon with misinformation."[30]

Even the *Army and Navy Register* castigated Garrison, calling his statements "astonishing, to say the least, in view of the fact that the trial of Major Koehler was then in progress." In an article entitled "Interference with Army Trial," the paper also took aim at Wood. Reporting on his "alleged previous persecution" of Louis, the paper wrote that in Washington "considerable skepticism was expressed" as to Garrison's claim that Wood "is innocent of all complicity" in court-martialing Ben.[31]

The *Register* reached well beyond Ben's case to report general criticism of Garrison's reliance on Wood "as his exclusive source of information and inspiration concerning military matters." The *Register* noted that a member of Congress had recently written that a good relationship between Congress and the Army, and the passage of meaningful Army-related laws, "will have to wait until the advent of a chief of staff in whose character, judgment, and professional ability Congress shall feel that it can confide fully and safely."[32]

Garrison was wrong about Wood's name having surfaced in Sophia's testimony, and wrong about the number of witnesses with animus, but he was the one with power. Fuming, he sent an order to Kirby: Expedite the case. As the *Post* reported, "It is believed that Secretary of War Garrison has not been pleased with the continued notoriety."[33] Papers reported that Ben might not be allowed to call any additional witnesses, by order of the secretary of war.

For Ben, who had been feeling hopeful after his and Sophia's testimony, Garrison's sudden intrusion and the surfacing of Wood's name were dispiriting reminders that forces well beyond Plum Island had the capacity to influence his fate. Hudson and Hawthorne could fight all day long to keep the boundaries of the case tight, to exclude hearsay from other times and other places, but now it looked like that was only part of the battle Ben needed to wage. A man he had never met, a lawyer with little understanding of the military, seemed to be dropping bombs from the nation's capital.

Garrison's statements and order came at a bad time for Ben's side. Hudson had rested the defense's case Tuesday morning, March 10, reserving the right to call additional witnesses after Mayes presented rebuttal witnesses. Now, Hudson and Hawthorne would have to listen to more than a dozen additional witnesses for the prosecution knowing they could do little in response without contravening Garrison's directive to expedite the case.

The Army had already interfered with Hudson's witness list, telling Colonel Richmond Davis, who was on his way to testify from his new posting in San Francisco, to turn around when he was "half way across the continent."[34] Davis was told to submit sworn written answers instead, which could be read to the jury—a blow for Ben as a live witness makes a much stronger impression. Davis would not only have spoken of his high regard for Ben as his most recent superior but also would have gone into the whole matter of Frick and Robinson trying to trigger an investigation back in July. That would have raised the obvious question of why Frick had not at that time spoken of his own experiences with Ben if they had actually occurred. The order telling Davis to turn around likely came from Wood. Having told Major Hagedorn not to "start" from St. Petersburg, he was certainly capable of telling Davis to "stop" in the American Midwest.


On Tuesday afternoon and all day on Wednesday, Mayes called people to the stand to try to undo gains made by the defense. Several were additional members of the 88th and 100th Companies who swore to the fine reputations for veracity of Frick, Kirkman, Barrett, and others.

Mayes was especially worried about the damage done to the two Byers claims. Regarding the Charles Byers claim, set during the ordnance inspection, Mayes had asked a captain at Fort Wright to take photographs of the desk at which Moses sat and to create charts and diagrams purporting to show that Moses did not have a clear view. The captain, George Cocheu, took the stand to introduce the exhibits. Asked by Kirby when he had first heard "rumors of immoral character" about Ben, Cocheu said he "heard a rumor which came to me—well, I should say through about 4 or 5 hands early last summer and I didn't believe it and dismissed it from my mind."

"Up to that time you believed he was everything that he should be?"

"Yes, sir."[35]

To fortify the Elvin Byers claim, Mayes called Byers back to the stand and produced two privates who testified that they had come with Byers to Ben's garden to pick up plants, though they could offer few details. The issue was tangential, bearing only on Byers's credibility, but Mayes wished to give the jurors a basis for discounting the testimony of Ben's gardener and Emma Jones who said, among other things, that Byers had come alone.

Mayes was also concerned about Davis's claim involving the supposed fondling in the battle command center. Lieutenant Gorham had fixed part of Davis's story at a different location. Now Mayes countered by putting Master Electrician Byron Brown on the stand. He said Davis told him of the molestation the very day it occurred.

Hudson fought hard to keep out that hearsay, but Kirby overruled him. Brown's resulting testimony was quite damaging:

> He [Davis] says . . . Major Koehler rubbed up against him either with his foot or his knee, and kept rubbing him and he got passionate and turned around to the Major and his face was red and then they went further down to the space between F Prime 5 Booth and F Prime 6 and there Major Koehler took out his privates and played with them and he went to the door and looked out and he seemed to be afraid there might be someone in the Stoneman Secondary Station, and he states that he didn't know what he wanted to do, could not seem to find out.[36]

The best Hudson could do was show that Brown had originally told Mills and Mayes that the conversation took place in August 1913, and he was now saying it was August 1912 after admittedly discussing the matter with Davis.

Brown had many reasons to resent Ben's authority, including being told to stop visiting Ellis's house, ordered to give away his dog, and being criticized for his appearance. While Brown had brought no claim of his own, that was probably because he, Worcester, and Frick knew it would be met with disbelief. Instead, Brown played a supporting role. Not only did he prop up Davis's account but it appeared he was responsible for setting up Harry King's train car claim.[37]

One juror questioned Brown intensely, zeroing in on gaps in his testimony and referring to his account as a "story," but there was no way of knowing whether the other jurors regarded Brown with the same suspicion. If they did not, it was bad for the defense, for here was a witness testifying to a conversation about Ben's advances that supposedly happened in 1912, undercutting the thesis that everything was fabricated in November 1913.

The final rebuttal witness called by Mayes showed the impact of the fake Searcy letter. Needless to say, the Texas Civil War veteran Searcy would not be testifying, but another man apparently was willing to claim that Ben's bad acts went back to his time in San Francisco. This strategy was just what Crowder had suggested when he forwarded the Searcy letter. The man was Sergeant William J. O'Brien, a company mate of Sergeant Moody.

"How long have you known Major Koehler?" Mayes asked him.

"I first met Major Koehler when he was Captain of the 92nd Company."

"Where was that Company stationed?" asked Mayes.

"Presidio, California, San Francisco."

"Did you ever know Major Koehler to do or say anything unbecoming an officer and a gentleman?"[38]

Hudson objected immediately. Mayes argued that he was permitted to bring in the testimony of prior acts outside the specifications because the defense had "built and fashioned a sort of halo of innocence surrounded [sic] the accused by means of that negative testimony. Now, I want the opportunity to prove that that halo does not fit." He told the jurors he had "five witnesses on this line and I have two or three in process of getting here."

Hudson countered that whether the halo "fit" was for the jurors to decide. "[I]t is a question for the court, no matter what other men think he is and has been, whether a man can live a double life and do the things that they say this man does and still be what his friends and associates think him to be."

It was only fair, Hudson went on, to limit the case to the specifications "when you consider that we must make our defence up over night on serious charges and now if the judge-advocate presses that question and he introduces witnesses, why it seems to me the court should give us additional time to prepare evidence. We have got 17 and any one of them is sufficient to disgrace this man forever, if sustained, disgrace his name and drive him out of the service."

The request for additional time was a smart move. The jurors had already spent more days than they cared for on Plum Island. Kirby asked a few questions and then the jurors conferred privately. It was a little after five o'clock in the evening when they announced their decision. No, they did not care to hear five to eight additional witnesses any more than they cared to make Worcester wear "that dress." Hudson's objection, an important one, would be sustained.

O'Brien and the other surprise witnesses would not testify, but one wonders what O'Brien would have said had the court's ruling gone the other way, for a review of his Army personnel records shows that just like A. J. Searcy, O'Brien had never served at the Presidio.[39] His answer to Mayes made it sound as though he spent time in the 92nd Company under Ben, but that was not true. He had only passed through California on his way to the Philippines, and that was in 1908, long after Ben had left San Francisco. His present address was not Plum Island or Fishers Island, even though he served in the 146th Company under Robinson. O'Brien was on duty with the militia in New York City, where a man so inclined could type a letter for a friend and send it by general delivery to Washington, D.C.

Having been deprived of his highly questionable final witnesses, Mayes rested his case.

EARLY IN THE WEEK, before Sophia and Ben testified, the jury was said to be torn: Five members believed the evidence was inconclusive, five leaned toward conviction on at least some counts, and one was in doubt.[40] If Jordan had not been excused as a juror, seven votes would be required to convict, but now six would do.

While Hudson had kept out the testimony of O'Brien and others willing to puncture Ben's "halo of innocence," the jurors had been

told that up to eight people had such stories, which was highly prejudicial. Hudson might have responded to the prosecution's latest witnesses in a number of ways, but Garrison's order to expedite hung
over the room like a theater curtain starting to descend. As a result,
Hudson called only three additional witnesses on Thursday—actually,
three people and a piece of furniture, for he arranged to have the
desk at which Moses sat during the inspection loaded onto a boat and
carried into the courtroom from Fishers Island.

First, a corporal told an unflattering story about Private Davis, and
then Ben returned to the stand. Again, he spoke of what he considered facts and details. He might have done better to speak of his manhood, how he defined manliness, and what it meant to him—for by
now, those were the issues swirling in people's minds.

Ben's attentiveness at the post had been impeccable, and the explanations he offered seemed mundane compared to the drama of the
accusers' stories. For example, Elvin Byers, when recalled in the rebuttal phase, had said he had reason to believe Ben was having "improper
relations" with Shanley because Shanley "had told me that Major Koehler had been down to the Pumping Station to see him several times
early in the morning," and "in a smiling way," using words Byers did
"not remember," Shanley had implied that the trips were "not for inspection, but merely to visit him."[41]

Ben met that claim head on, saying he visited the water plant "on a
great many occasions," though not early in the morning, "[o]n account of in the summer of 1912 we had at one time 10 extra Companies here and it was a question of our water supply holding up,
everybody was prohibited—it was a post order—to use water for any
other purpose than drinking. No hose was allowed to be used and
frequently I went there to see how much water they were pumping . . .
Since then we have duplicated the plant so that it can run both night
and day." Shanley was on duty at the plant because the regular engineer "went away on a drunk and disappeared for two weeks and then
was relieved from the position."[42]

Ben denied serving alcohol to soldiers, contrary to the picture
painted by the accusers, especially Byers, who had acknowledged be-

ing the source of the claim in the Mills report that enlisted men went to Ben's quarters "who had no business there in an official way" and "seem[ed] to be intimate" with Ben. When Hudson asked about the basis for the allegation, Byers said it was his "opinion," his "thought," and finally admitted, "I had no reason for knowing at all."[43]

For a man overheard saying he regretted having anything to do with the case, Byers had certainly played a big role in it, though he admitted his role did not start until Worcester came to him "about the 10th or 12th of November" and "asked me to make a statement of what I knew about Major Koehler and I told him.

Byers was also the source of stories told to Mills about the private who had bought his discharge, and an ex-sergeant named Swicgood. Byers had testified that "[o]n several occasions Major Koehler would ring up the 88th Company office and have Sergeant Swicgood sent to his quarters." The calls came at "8 or 9 or 10 o'clock in the evening, and I could not understand why the Sergeant would be called there for official business at that time of night." Once, Byers asserted, Swicgood came back late "practically intoxicated."[44]

Not true, Ben told the jurors. Swicgood visited because "[h]e was Captain of the baseball team of the 88th Company and they had a great deal of trouble that year about playing their games . . . and Sergeant Swicgood was concerned."

"Did you ever give this Sergeant any liquor in your house?" Hudson asked.

"I did not."[45]

As to the ex-private, Calkins, also in the 88th Company, Ben explained, "I had a typewriter which my sister uses and . . . I had it unpacked and I asked the Sergeant-Major for some one to come down and put it in condition." Calkins was sent, Ben said, and "When I came home in the afternoon I offered to pay him for his trouble. He said no, he didn't want any pay and I told him he could go out in the kitchen and get a glass of beer if he cared to."

What Ben said next explained a great deal.

"Later on I understood that he bought out and as a reason for buying out he said I was bothering him, interfering with him, and I learned that this man was in the service because he had gotten into trouble at Lincoln University." The trouble was:

> that he had gotten some girl in the Indian Agency in the family way and that he enlisted solely to hide his whereabouts and I remember his asking—he saw in the Register I suppose, that I came from Nebraska, whether I know anything about Nebraska, and I said I had lived there and had several cousins there and nephews and nieces going to the University. My sister graduated from the University, and that is all I know about Calkins.[46]

The implication was that Calkins left the Army due to concern that Ben would disclose his whereabouts to people in Nebraska, and that was the nature of the "bothering" that was communicated to Putney, also in the 88th Company, sometime before Putney left Fort Terry in summer 1913. Whether it was Calkins, Putney, Byers, or someone else who gave the story its sexual overtone is unclear, but this had to be the reason Worcester wrote to Putney in November. Worcester testified that Putney "agreed that these stories were true," but Putney could have had no more knowledge of what happened in the Koehler house between Ben and Calkins than Byers did.

A juror asked who told Ben about Calkins's getting "a girl in the Indian Agency in a family way."

"I don't know whether it was the Sergeant-Major that was here or whether it was Sergeant Byers himself, the explanation for his going away," answered Ben.[47]

"Are you in the habit of talking with enlisted men about such things?" the juror rejoined in another display of how almost anything could be seen as a point on the "map of perversion," when applied to a man suspected of homosexuality.[48]

"No, sir, I am not," answered Ben.

No one asked Ben whether, when he learned of it, he had made any effort to counteract the assertion that he had "bothered" Calkins. Ben may have felt secure enough that he did not think it mattered what a private who had enlisted to avoid paternal responsibility might give as

his reason for buying his discharge. But perhaps on the morning of
March 12, 1914, Ben was wondering if he should have taken the matter
more seriously. Without naming Calkins, newspapers had reported
that his allegations started the case—and also that he may have been
coached to say what he did and then told to disappear.[49] Ben's supposed bothering of Calkins likely constituted the reports that Frick
said he discussed with Putney at the Fishers Island dance in the spring
of 1913, and the rumor that Cocheu said reached him at Fort Wright
at the beginning of the summer "through about 4 or 5 hands."[50]

During his second appearance as a witness, Ben spoke of the many
times he had reprimanded Brown and gave an explanation for Ward's
"grudge": that Ben had cost him seventy-five dollars a month by not
being "for him" to become Post Exchange steward and then, after
Ward left Fort Terry, Ben declined to "meddle[] with the Post Exchange" to get Ward more business. Ben said Ward was "not particularly friendly" after that.[51]

There remained the bell that was still ringing as a result of the
mysterious reference to Lieutenant Thomas Jones, and Ben was ready
to stop the reverberations.

"Anything else you have heard here during the trial that you can
recall as a reason for hostility?" Hudson asked.

"Well, there was a rumor about Lieutenant Jones over at Fort
Wright," Ben answered, but Hudson cut him off, saying, "Leave out
anything except what has been testified to here."

Perhaps it would have benefited Ben if the jurors heard what he
had to say about Jones, but Hudson was not going to let that happen.

Kirby gave Ben another chance to "explain, if you care to explain
it at all, why all these people came in here and testified to these things
against you?"

Ben did care to explain, or at least he cared to try:

> I don't know unless I can see a connection between Lieutenant Frick
> and Sergeant Moody on the boat. Lieutenant Frick used to sleep on
> that boat and knew Sergeant Moody very well and he also used to serve
> with Sergeant Byers. They belonged to some lodge or union or some-

thing where they had meetings and I think that, as I say, I have ridden on the boat before; Sergeant Moody was the first man, first Provost Sergeant that has ever come in that office and has ever spoke to me. I didn't invite him in and since this thing came up I think he just made it an occasion to say that he had a conversation with me.[52]

"This thing" was how Ben referred to creation and coordination of the stories against him—not the most articulate word choice. He now saw a reason why the dates of the allegations fell when they did: "I think that when this thing was brought first to Colonel Davis' attention, Ward told me when I came back, he didn't tell me what the thing was at all, but I can see now that they tried to get as many things around that time as they could. Then, later when it was not taken up by Colonel Davis— most of the occurrences took place in October. That was Sergeant Moody and Sergeant Campbell of the Post Exchange."

In those answers, Ben again focused more on the *what* than the *why*, and the strain he had been under came through. For example, he should not have said "most of the occurrences took place in October" but rather "they made up a series of occurrences that supposedly took place in October." That is what he meant by referring to Moody and Campbell, who claimed Ben's advances took place in October (Moody) and November (Campbell).

"I have seen Sergeant Campbell, but I had no conversation at any time with him in the Post Exchange," Ben said.[53]

Ben seemed to have difficulty putting himself in the position of someone who thought he was capable of committing the offenses alleged and intuiting what words would be necessary to dispel that mindset. He had denied the charges, offered benign accounts of events spun as improper by the accusers, and provided all sorts of practical explanations for why the alleged overtures could not have occurred. Peers had testified that the allegations were impossible. Jurors had been quoted calling the evidence insufficient, and Ben had worked closely with several of them who, as far as he knew, held a good opinion of him up to the trial.

And so, Ben may have been lulled into believing that the jurors were on his side and that he did not need to be more forceful in answering Kirby's questions of *why*. Most notably, he refrained from calling his accusers liars—a strong statement to make about fellow Army men, especially Worcester and Frick, who had taken the same officer oath that he had.

Perhaps Hudson could have better prepared his client, and as Ben flailed in his answers, Hudson stepped in, asking, "Have the visits of Captain Robinson to your house and your relationship with him any significance in your mind?"

"Yes, they have now," Ben said. "[H]is visits were for no other purpose than to observe my actions."[54] But from the jurors' standpoint, that could cut both ways. If Robinson had reason to suspect Ben's "actions," making an effort to observe them was not evidence of a plot. Ben needed to say more, like how ludicrous it was for Robinson to think he would find Ben doing something improper during his lunch hour, how it showed the exaggerated nature of any rumors going around, how all Robinson ever did find was Ben having lunch with his sister, and how that was Ben's actual life—far duller than the accusers implied.

Much more could have been said in general about the ways in which strange actions by the accusers and their helpers, and the nature of the claims themselves, were best explained as parts of an orchestrated scheme. The claims were carefully spread out: 1912: April (King), August (Frick, Ward, Wilson, Davis, Spears); 1912–13: December–January (Kirkman); 1913: April (Frick), July (Elvin Byers), August (Fairey, Ensley, Kernan), September (Barrett), October (Charles Byers, Moody), November (Worcester, Campbell). Yet Moody and others had testified that they only heard "common talk" about Ben. If Ben had really accosted so many men, was it believable that when discussing rumors about Ben's sexuality, not one would have mentioned to another that he himself had been the victim of an advance?

Perhaps Hudson was waiting to make those points in his summation. For now, he asked a few more questions, while the jurors stayed silent, not asking for clarification, making it impossible for Hudson and Ben to know what impact Ben's answers were having. It may have pained the jurors to see what had become of a fine officer, who was at times sounding virtually incoherent as he attempted to explain "this thing" at Fort Terry threatening to ruin his life.

After Ben finished, his old friend Andy Moses returned to the stand to reiterate that "Major Koehler was directly in front of me" during the ordnance inspection.[55] Kirby asked Moses to sit at the desk and point to where Ben, Byers, and the inspection items were situated. And so, the phase of the case called the sur-rebuttal assumed a surreal quality, with a focus on whether the desk's wings blocked Moses's sight, and whether Moses's insistence that he could see Ben's right hand the whole time implied he had a particular concern with what Ben might do with that hand.

To be sure, everyone was tired after weeks of confinement in a small room on a cold island dealing with sordid matters, the collapse of a man's career, and the jurors' concerns with their own futures once Wood became their boss. One can understand the temptation to fixate on small, tangible details like desk height and width, as though the answers to the Ben Koehler dilemma might be as clear as units of measurement. Instead, what the scene revealed was a suspicion and demonization of a suspected gay man that had come to lack any rationality. If Ben was going to use the occasion to grope the functionary who would be assisting, why would he have invited Moses to attend? Ben had never met Charles Byers, whose role was to carry a few pieces of equipment during a process that lasted at most ten minutes while Moses called out descriptions and discussed each item with Ben. Did the jurors really think that gay men were so unable to control themselves that, under those circumstances, Ben would rub a stranger's thigh and grab his testicles?

After Moses finished, Hudson followed up on a surprising fact he himself had revealed the previous afternoon: that Ben's personnel file had just arrived. Overnight, Hudson had reviewed the file and now he summarized Ben's reviews, especially the laudatory statements about Ben's performance in battle. Mayes asked if the jurors wanted to pause and review the documents.

"I don't think the court wants to inspect them," Kirby said, but another member immediately spoke up asking whether copies would be appended to the record.[56]

Kirby asked Mayes whether he accepted the oral summary Hudson had just made. Mayes said yes.

"I don't think they need to be appended to the record at all," Kirby said. "Anything further?"

In this manner, the strongest evidence of Ben's manhood as Roosevelt had defined it—courage and skill in battle—and the rest of his seventeen years of service were converted into an endnote, becoming three pages of a thick transcript beginning on page 1076. The commendations from Lawton, MacArthur, and other Army luminaries would not go to the jurors in formats they were used to seeing and could pass around. There would be only a summary.

Hudson told Kirby that he was still trying to locate Kenly, but otherwise he would not defy Garrison's order and seek to bring in additional witnesses who wanted to testify for Ben. Yet while the jurors sat listening to Ben's last words under oath, a drama of a different sort was building outside the courtroom, a flare-up of tensions between the United States and Mexico. Would a new war set Ben Koehler free? "Mexican Crisis May Save Koehler from Court-Martial," declared one paper.[57]

The United States had been on edge over the "Mexico situation" for at least a year. Now a battle loomed in western Mexico between Emiliano Zapata's loyalists and Victoriano Huerta's government, which concerned the United States for a variety of reasons, including the interests of U.S. corporations. On March 10, a band of Texans crossed the Rio Grande to exhume the body of a Texas rancher whom Mexicans had allegedly tortured and hung. Wilson's administration was on the defensive, for the Texas governor and others blamed Secretary of State Bryan for an insufficient response.

At noon on Thursday, March 12, Kirby told the jurors to head back to their posts and await further instructions. Some of the jurors took the possibility of war very seriously. "We will meet again in Mexico," one was quoted as saying to another as they parted at the New London train station.[58]

Turning to James Mayes, the same juror was overheard saying in stirring words, "This is not the first time I have known an upheaval such as we are about to have to save a man."

# CHAPTER THIRTY-SIX

# *Manliness*

THE MEXICAN REVOLUTION DID not cause the United States to wage war in March 1914 or forget about Ben Koehler. Two weeks after the jurors' emotional partings in New London, they were back in their seats at Fort Terry.

Far from helping Ben, the two-week delay only added to his anxiety. "Major Koehler showed plainly the strain he has undergone," wrote a reporter. "His face was thin and drawn."[1]

That was Ben's demeanor when William Kenly arrived, not as an old friend paying a visit but as the last witness. Finally, the issue of Ben's manliness would be directly addressed.

Kenly described his long relationship with Ben, including their living together, and stated adamantly that over the course of knowing Ben for fifteen years he had "never seen a single symptom of anything that was not manly."

> I am trying to impress on the Court that I am saying these things without any reservation whatever—no suspicion, no symptom of anything that could be objected to, and I say it because I have an idea that the allegations against him would indicate something else, and therefore I feel that I cannot be strong enough in what I wish to convey. I have considered him a normal, manly man and in all respects an honorable gentleman always.[2]

As best as can be determined, Kenly was the closest Ben ever came to having a love interest other than family members, and yet it was Kenly who gave the most heartfelt testimony that Ben was not the sort of man to be sexually attracted to men. Listening to his former mentor from the position of the accused, Ben could only hope that, if he was acquitted, he and Kenly would be able to revive their close friendship.

The next day, Hudson worked on preparing his summation. Kirby granted the extra day due to the late arrival of the final section of the transcript.

While Ben endured the biggest trauma of his life, time proceeded gaily for others at Fort Terry. Enlisted men and officers danced the tango at a full-dress ball the night before the closing arguments. Others attended a play. Ben, on the other hand, stayed in his house with Sophia. That gave rise to a rumor that he had escaped to New London, which Captain Patten termed "absurd."[3]

Too bad for Ben that other rumors about him had not been as easily dispelled. At three o'clock on Thursday, March 26, when court reopened, Ben sat in his usual place, more interested than anyone to hear what Hudson would say about the circumstances that had put him there.

Hudson's closing argument could have been a powerful early shot in the fight for gay rights, but it wasn't. Hudson could have implored the jurors not to let typecasting and unsupported fear of homosexuality hijack their judgment, but he didn't. He was no Clarence Darrow, the eloquent defender of unpopular clients and causes. While Darrow challenged convention, Hudson adhered to it. In the ensuing two hours, he would not speak directly to the jurors about prejudices and preconceived notions, as Darrow did throughout his career.[4] Hudson had never before defended a man accused of "degeneracy," and his own disdain of homosexuality pervaded his closing statement.[5]

Hudson went so far to say that if Ben had really done the "vile" things he was accused of—"charges that a well-bred dog should not be charged with"—he would have ended his life back in December—"blown his brains out"—after Mills first confronted him.[6]

Following a multi-week trial with more than sixty-five witnesses, that Ben had not committed suicide was hardly the strongest argument in defense of his innocence.

Hudson wanted the jury to conclude that the charges were so vile Ben could not have committed them. But by repeating the prosecution's message over and over that the actions described were egregious—"this vileness, this filth"—he only fanned the flames of homophobia, giving the jurors more reason to be alarmed that a gay officer might be in their midst. Hudson seemed to say that Ben's self-presentation formed a basis for that belief: "He is an officer who is very considerate of his men and has done many kindnesses for individuals at this post. That is just what he has done, a good many kindnesses, and is a little bit too refined for this testimony. He likes flowers. He likes to look neat. There are men vile enough to think that a man that likes flowers is effeminate and something worse."[7]

Yet not all the accusers were vile, Hudson went on to say. As to Jacob Campbell, who claimed Ben spoke to him about Pacific sporting houses and once squeezed his arm, Hudson said, "no viciousness can be charged." Campbell "has been unduly affected by rumor" and "wanted to be on both sides of this case," repeating "stories that other men had told him" while also stating that Ben "had always acted like a perfect gentleman."[8]

Of Charles Byers, the soldier involved in the ordnance inspection, Hudson declared: "This is a man I could not call a liar if I wanted to. He is the cleanest witness here, and he tells the story as if he believed it . . . Now that man believes he was touched; there is no doubt about that, and he is a good, clean-looking man, to my mind."[9]

To Hudson's mind, appearances counted for a lot. Clean-looking men were the ones to be believed. Ben's neatness might make him seem effeminate. The "attractive-looking fat boy" was the one Ben could not have resisted, and "a man cannot say that there is anything in that man Moody attractive enough to excite the passion of any man under conditions such as existed."[10]

At the time, male "perversion" was explained as a man's having the same attraction toward men that a "normal" man felt toward women.

Hudson went along with that paradigm, creating a portrait of male homosexuality based on ideas about female attractiveness to straight men.

But why concede that any accusers genuinely believed Ben had behaved as alleged? While Hudson did argue that "no man" would have insulted Moses's "intelligence by trying to do anything like that in his presence," why was Hudson going out of his way to say Byers believed he was telling the truth?[11] Ben had a strong rebuttal to Byers's claim, a credible eyewitness who said it did not occur. Hudson would have done better to argue the opposite, that a "clean" appearance might make a person seem honest but could also camouflage a good liar.

Instead, Hudson made an extraordinary statement: "Koehler is poison to a man like that."[12] Others recoiled from the "poison," too: "[T]here must have been a lot of men here who would see this man come along the street and would shun him almost because that offense means a good deal to a man, especially a young man with a mind that is easily worked upon."[13]

It was true that young men had become some of the most assiduous policers of other men, but it did not serve Ben's interests to make it sound as though rumors about him were so widespread that large numbers of people shunned him. Hudson should have been stressing that the majority of people at Fort Terry respected Ben. He should have been arguing that it was only a small minority—the "clique"—who thought otherwise, or claimed to think otherwise, for self-interested reasons. Instead, Hudson gave credence to a perception of Ben as different—and marginalized—due to his appearance, marital status, mannerisms, and hobbies.

Humans respond to stories, and in a closing argument, a lawyer is selling a story, a narrative that plausibly explains the evidence and leads ineluctably to the outcome the lawyer seeks. Hudson's story began: "Early in the Winter after [Ben] came here . . . there began to be a rumor circulated about him and his tendencies."[14] Hudson offered a few theories as to the rumor's source: talk by Putney and Byers, the sighting of Ben with Kenly, speculation about the Astor Battery.[15] The rumor flourished, Hudson said, because "the conditions in an Army post are even worse than they are in other places where men are isolated and away from the refining influence of families and women, good women, and children and other associations; . . . gossip spreads more quickly and . . . exaggerations become almost facts in a very short time." Then, "[a]fter this little stream was started in the early winter of 1912 it seems that everybody threw filth into it until it ran along and overran its banks and the result was this call for disinfection."[16]

While that introduction portrayed a climate of anti-homosexual vigilantism, even if Hudson failed to call it such, his words did not negate the merits of a motive to "disinfect" the post by ousting Ben if the rumors to which "everybody" contributed had some factual basis. The story fed into the accusers' strategy of making the claims seem like a natural unfolding of events over time, instead of fabrications concocted in November 1913 and backdated, then altered as necessary on the stand in light of conflicting evidence. Moreover, the testimony indicated that "everybody" consisted primarily of Frick and his friends, who did much to create the rumors, talking among themselves at Fort Wright in the spring of 1913.

Frick and Worcester may well have propounded the idea of Ben's being homosexual to justify lying and encourage fealty to the plan of ousting him, along the lines of "we know he is homosexual, and even though we don't have proof, we can say we do and it will be in the Army's best interests." People who believed Ben was failing to uphold male norms may even have felt entitled to punish him.[17] But Hudson erred in letting the jurors think that the case was about a group of men overreacting in their zeal to rid the Army of a suspected homosexual. Not only did the jurors likely agree with that objective, but the thesis was not sufficient to explain the testimony. Nearly all the witnesses said that while some touching by a man might be accidental, they were sure it wasn't accidental when Ben did it.

Hudson accounted for that in part by saying that Mills pressured men into giving damaging testimony and, at trial, they were reluctant to step back and tell the truth because "the uniform of the Judge Advocate impresses these soldiers, and the fact that they told something before makes them think they ought to stick to it and they are doing the best they can."[18]

Another explanation, of course, was outright falsification, but far from calling Worcester a liar and mastermind of a plot, Hudson said: "I don't want to criticize Worcester, except that he is unfortunately immature and inexperienced, had this idea and it got the better of him."[19]

Worcester had not testified to the "idea" of Ben being a homosexual, but to Ben's intentionally grabbing his genitals—twice. So, when Hudson added to his narrative and told the jurors that "[w]hat really started this result . . . was the Halloween Party and nothing else," it wasn't going nearly far enough to characterize what happened there as Worcester's misinterpretation of innocent touching.[20]

Lieutenant Smith had testified that Ben "made fun of my costume" and poked him with his thumb, supporting Ben's testimony that he did the same to Worcester. Hudson made that point weakly, saying, "Smith was treated in the same way practically by Major Koehler, but he didn't say anything" whereas Worcester "resented Koehler's action when he poked him." Hudson did not explicitly say that it made the most sense for Ben to have touched both men in the same way. He simply called it "a startling thing" for Worcester to have "concluded that this man was a degenerate" based on Ben's acts at the party, where Worcester "acted in a way that invites any familiarity and it was not so much the familiarity as it was a reprimand or a suggestion that he had better dress properly."[21]

A "conclusion" is the product of reasoning; a lie is something else altogether, but Hudson was apparently unwilling to call a captain with a Silver Star a liar.

As a result, Hudson utterly failed to knit the evidence together to show how the portrait of Ben as sexually predatory against men, impulsive, and lewd was the intentional creation of a small group led by Worcester and Frick, who wanted Ben gone and used a strategy of false accusations, surmising that the homosexual label could be made to stick.

To be sure, Hudson referred to the lack of precision in much of the testimony, asserting, "If a man is inhuman with you . . . and he was your superior officer you would remember the day, the hour and the minute, the weather and everything else."[22] Frick was "a man you are justified in disbelieving," Hudson argued, Ben's sole "enemy" at the post, "harsh" and continual in his criticism of the commander.[23] Kirkman was a "knave" who used "the old criminal trick" in his testimony of incorporating arcane factual details—such as the supposed call from Jordan about pheasants—to "try to give credence to his story."[24]

Spears, "with ten drinks of beer, all in two hours, is not the man to hurt anybody's reputation."[25] Davis told a "hideous, vile story unbelievable by anyone" about an encounter in a phone booth, refuted by Gorham, who "made that man [Davis] out a false liar without a doubt."[26] As to Wilson, the window cleaner, Hudson said, "Now if you will believe him . . . I should be very surprised."[27] Ensley, the wagon driver, "contradicted himself half a dozen times" such that "no one can believe him, but who put him up to that?"[28]

Hudson needed to answer that question convincingly not just for Ensley but for all the accusers. Who put all of them "up to that?"

He suggested a partial answer: that Brown, whom Ben had reprimanded several times, persuaded Davis and "young King" to testify.[29] He also cited Ward's account of Frick asking whether Ward "knew anything."

"That shows . . . that Lieutenant Frick was not only active in talking about [Ben], but was active in getting the men to talk about him," Hudson said.[30] Talk, however, did not necessarily equal fabrication.

Why didn't Hudson accuse all the accusers of lying? He may have been reluctant to offend the jury, but the bigger problem was that he lacked a coherent theory—a story—to explain it. He failed to point out, and perhaps to realize, that the accusers included not only men with grudges but also men who feared punishment—including the guardhouse, as Sophia had written to Roy. Hudson hinted at this by noting that "nine witnesses have either been in the 100th Company or the 88th Company or both," the units commanded by Ellis and then Worcester.[31] But Hudson did not say why that mattered—that those relationships gave Worcester and his friend Ellis authority to penalize the men for not incriminating Ben.

Hudson did not even mention Zerphy's grounding by Worcester

and Ellis. He made no reference to Ewing's testimony about Moody's talk of an "oath" and "sticking tight."[32] He let Moody off the hook, saying he did not put Moody, Campbell, and Charles Byers "in the same class with the rest of these fellows."[33]

Nor did Hudson remind the jurors of Worcester's key role as gate-keeper for the Mills investigation and the ability that gave Worcester to check whether witnesses went along with the party line—as Zerphy said he was penalized for not doing. Hudson pointed out that both Shanley and Krouchonoskie had resigned, but he did not associate their leaving with fear of being punished for having testified on Ben's behalf.

Hudson noted that Worcester chose a time when there was a power vacuum to go to Governors Island, but he failed to link that timing to Worcester's desire to prevent Ben from telling Davis's replacement about the alleged plagiarism. Indeed, the plagiarism incident was one more critical piece of evidence that Hudson did not mention. That and ire over the Shanley dispute were a more forceful explanation of what "started it all" than rumors and resentment at being criticized about a Halloween costume.

The record contained ample evidence that the claims were concocted after the Shanley incident. Why, for example, would Frick rely on information from the absent Jones to trigger an investigation in mid-1913 if Frick had been approached twice by Ben, and why, in mid-November, would Worcester write Putney for corroboration of "certain stories" if Worcester had been accosted on November 1? Instead of asking those questions, Hudson weakly stated that "thirteen of these alleged offences occurred before Colonel Davis left this post, and he never heard of one of them or if he did he did not think it was serious enough to take action."[34]

In January, Ben's supporters had promised Garrison proof of a plot. Mayes found no plot, and now, after all the time and money spent on a trial, Ben's own lawyer seemed to be saying he could not deliver on the promise. "This conspiracy or whatever it is" was how Hudson phrased it.[35]

Evidence of conspiracy existed, but Hudson simply did not marshal that evidence for the jury. He was under immense time pressure, unfamiliar with Army practices, and convinced that the best strategy was the theory of misconstrued accidental touching. Hudson may have been so wedded to that theory that it blinded him to the evidence of outright evil—a scheme to lure the Army to oust a strict commanding officer using panic over homosexuality as the bait.

In the end, rather than exhorting the jurors to see through the scheme and rise above musings about Ben's "tendencies," Hudson played into the hands of the schemers, allowing it to seem that Ben's perceived homosexuality was a major concern of many at the post. While Worcester, Frick, and a few of their allies likely did consider Ben not their kind of man, making it even more distasteful to take orders and criticism from him, the evidence was strong that they were in the minority, for many other Fort Terry witnesses testified about their respect for Ben.

Hudson told the jurors that Ben's denials deserved weight. Ben was "not dead morally yet," Hudson said. Ben would not be "dead morally" until and unless the court convicted him "and no one has called him a liar."[36] Yet Hudson could not undo Ben's "credibility deficit," to use philosopher Kate Manne's phrase in her discussion of "testimonial injustice as hierarchy preservation."[37] Before the allegations, Ben would have been considered eminently credible in a courtroom as a white male and Army officer, but as an accused "degenerate," he forfeited that presumption in the eyes of some jurors, as their snarky questions showed.

Ironically, Hudson cast Ben's friendship with Kenly as one of the strongest points in Ben's favor. Kenly, Hudson opined, "is an ideal man and a man cannot be under his influence for three years and not get something that is manly and he cannot leave a man like that and become a beast in six months."[38]

It could be asked why Ben needed to "get something manly" through friendship with "an ideal man" unless there was some question of his leanings before then, so it was not the best choice of words by Hudson. He went on to say that if Ben had changed so much after working with Kenly that he began to accost men at Fort Terry six months later, if Ben could be at once so disciplined with and esteemed by many people, yet "let himself go" with others, "the only explanation of this man's conduct if any of these stories is true, that it is insanity."[39]

There was Hudson finally uttering the word that Crowder predicted would be Ben's main defense, but Hudson was arguing the opposite—that Ben was not insane: "We have introduced men who have associated with this man from time to time ever since he came to this post and men who knew him before in order to show you that there is no insanity in this thing."[40]

In other words, if insanity was the only explanation that could account for the erratic behavior described, and Ben was not insane, then he could not have done the things alleged. That was Hudson's point, but he did not lay it out articulately. Unfortunately, his phrasing introduced the idea that insanity might, indeed, explain the mismatch between the accusers' testimony and the numerous witnesses who said Ben had never said or done anything improper.

Even in Hudson's closing endorsement of Ben, however, there lurked hints that Hudson was still trying to persuade himself that Ben was "manly."

> The man himself is a marvel to me. Charges of this kind two or three months old, staying with them night after night . . . staggering under the load of these gross accusations, he comes into the Court every day and appears to me like a man who was perfectly indifferent to criticism because he knew he was innocent. But he is going further than that; he is meeting men he has known all these years and he is facing the grossest, vilest, dirtiest thing that one man can possibly say of another and very few can possibly think of another and his face is like a man's.[41]

"His face is like a man's." Hudson wasn't challenging a cultural obsession with masculinity and how one proved it; he was intoning it. And so, Hudson ended with reference to Ben's "bravery" in war and "record for gallantry." The commendations from Ben's superiors had been reduced to three pages, but they did show the ultimate paradox in the case: A man who had aced the last era's highest test of manliness—success in military combat—was now being portrayed as the lowest form of man, "inhuman," in Hudson's words.[42] No wonder Hudson wanted to remind the jury of the days when the Army considered Ben one of its "desirable men."

"Now gentlemen," Hudson closed, "I thank you very much for your attention, and I only have this to say: This man has fought for his flag; it is a flag that the whole people respect and it is a flag that you love. Everything that that flag symbolizes today ought to be taken into consideration in his case so that truth will conquer malice and vilification."[43]

Which truth Hudson meant was hard to say. The jurors could be forgiven for not knowing. Were they supposed to rule on Ben's manliness or on his being an assaulter?

JAMES MAYES KNEW HOW to use words succinctly to cut and deride. "So unique as to suggest its desperation," he proclaimed his adversary's "ornate summary," before pouncing on its weakest spots.[44]

"The conspiracy failed," Mayes declared. The defense offered only "[a] motive . . . from reprimands and so forth to these witnesses . . . There is not one single reprimand testified to here which would justify any animus on the part of either the officer or non-commissioned officer which would cause them to do such a thing as this. It is incomprehensible."[45]

Mayes asserted, incorrectly, that most testimony about reprimands had come from Ben, and if he was "the officer that he has been held up to be by the testimony of the defense," there would be more documentation of disciplinary measures if they had really occurred.[46]

Mayes was masterful at lumping all testimony on a subject into one category and then dismissing that category in a few sentences. He made it all seem very simple, whereas Hudson had made the case seem rather complicated. And what did the jurors most want? They had been living on or traveling to and from Plum Island for more than six weeks. They wanted to be done.

Turning Hudson's argument as to the "vileness" of the charges on its head, Mayes said, "They say these charges are incomprehensible. The idea of a man making them is more incomprehensible if they are not true. No man is going to risk trial for perjury and come here and testify before this Court that these charges are true if they are not true."[47]

They might risk it, however, if they thought punishment for not perjuring themselves would be more immediate and certain—but Hudson had failed to make that point. Moreover, there was testimony that Mills had insisted some men give evidence against Ben.

Mayes also went beyond the record to remind the jurors of his attempt to produce evidence of offenses by Ben going back in time: "If you remember, I brought a witness on the stand that testified he had known him ten years. Immediately the defense was up—'no, no, we object.' I have been perfectly willing at all times to go into that question."[48]

In a civilian court, that might have been grounds for a mistrial. Mayes was suggesting what excluded witnesses would have said. This was not a civilian court, which was why the order of the summations was reversed. In a civilian criminal trial, the defense usually closes the case, for it is the defendant's liberty at stake and the defendant who enjoys a presumption of innocence. In Ben's case, Mayes had the privilege of going last, knowing there would be no check on how boldly he broke the boundaries, bent the record, or misstated the law.[49]

Point after point, Mayes trivialized Ben's defense, dismissing Sophia's testimony in a sentence: "I never had a sister but I wish I had had one as refined and as well equipped with the graces that make men bless the name of woman as she, and the Court will understand me when I leave her testimony in the beauty of its devotion and the sacredness of its sacrifice."[50]

Mayes told the jury to reject the idea "that if this man would do this to one man that he would do it to any man that he came in contact with." Like Hudson, Mayes based his argument on men's attitudes toward women, opining that a "homo-sexualist, a man whose sexual desires are reversed . . . has the same desires toward men that normal men have towards women," and that "men do not try to have sexual intercourse with every woman that they meet." He went on: "The loves and desires and sacrifices and jealousies and everything else that pertain to homo-sexuality center on man and they make advances towards people who appeal to them and not to every one."[51]

Mayes was smart to make the comparison explicitly. Asking the jurors to think like the heterosexual men they were, and generalize from that, was an easier sell than asking them to think like reasonable homosexuals. Hudson had failed to do the latter, and now it was too late to argue that if Ben was a "homo-sexualist," then Worcester, Frick, and their "clique" would be the least likely men to "appeal to him," the least likely men to whom he would risk unmasking himself.

Finally, Mayes dismissed the idea that people jumped to conclusions about Ben for incorrect reasons. "I do not see why a man could not be a pervert and still be fond of flowers."[52]

Mayes spoke confidently right up to the end. He told the jurors that the evidence supported findings of guilty, that they were the judges of the witnesses' credibility, and that the specifications and witnesses all supported one another. "I have performed my duty as I saw it, and I think with absolute fairness to the accused. Surely, I have followed the dictates of my own conscience. Now, Gentlemen of the Court, your duties comprise the remainder of this trial."[53]

Kirby asked if Ben had anything further to say, and Hudson said no.

The sun had set long ago. The jurors would eat their dinner, and then, after reconvening at 8:15 p.m., they would begin to discuss Ben's fate. How long a night it would be no one knew.

# CHAPTER THIRTY-SEVEN

# *Deliberations*

CLARENCE DARROW SAID THE criminal justice system was no system at all, but a "method of arraying a defendant in court . . . tried by judges who almost invariably believe in the prisoner's guilt, defended as is usually the case by incompetent lawyers . . . scarcely more liable to lead to correct results than the ancient forms."[1]

As Ben waited for the jury's verdict in the dark quiet of a Plum Island night, he may have harbored thoughts along the same lines. Family money had enabled him to hire a private lawyer, and there was no doubt that Hudson had put in long hours, but Ben had good reason for wondering whether he had been properly defended against all that had been brought to bear against him.

For months, ever since the December meeting with Haan and Sarratt, Ben had anticipated a trial that would reveal a plot against him. Yet, in the end, his own lawyer had all but thrown up his hands. "This conspiracy or whatever it is" came across like a surrender. Katie Ewing's pithy words—"spite work"—sounded far stronger, but Hudson had not even mentioned her testimony.

Should Ben have hired a more hardscrabble attorney? What if Kenly had been allowed to serve as his counsel? Would the closing argument have been more compelling?

Undoubtedly, such questions entered Ben's mind even as he tried to stay optimistic, recalling the ample testimony in his favor. No one knew his behavior at home better than Sophia. As Hudson had pointed out, there were no carpets on the floors, and "if any one walks in these houses . . . you can hear them."[2] Sophia had testified well, even if Mayes dismissed her knowledge in a sentence, reducing her to a biased woman whose words warranted no weight.

Wholly apart from the quality of lawyering inside the courtroom, much had broken against Ben outside the courtroom, beyond his control and well beyond the turbulent waters of Plum Gut: Colonel Davis not telling him of the allegations, Mills not interviewing him, denial of his leave, confusion over his resignation, Mayes's use of his alibis to redraft the charges, and Garrison's prejudicial public statement and order to hasten the trial. On the other hand, the jurors' questions indicated considerable skepticism about the accusers' accounts.

Either way, it appeared that what was going to determine Ben's future had little to do with his day-to-day conduct and the vigilance with which he had carried out the instructions to bring discipline to Fort Terry. Davis "appreciated the spirit which had been developed there under him," according to the sworn answers Davis submitted in lieu of live testimony, but Ben had to wonder why the turnaround at the post was not more of a focal point. Why wasn't there more testimony isolating Worcester and his band, showing that a link among the "scoundrels" was resistance to the order Ben was instilling? Ben could have made those points himself if he had been better coached. But if a fix was in from Washington, did the trial and testimony really matter, or had it all been for show, the grudges of the men at Fort Terry of lesser importance than the bigger grudge held by Leonard Wood against Louis?

During the two-week recess, while the jurors waited for possible deployment to Mexico, they had had something else to think about: Wood's imminent arrival in New York as their boss, bringing with him the same authority to upend their lives as he had Barry's. The timing was uncanny.

It is not known whether Wood spoke with any jurors during the recess to underscore his expectations. That was not the sort of conversation a careful person would commit to writing. Certainly Kirby, as jury president, needed to correspond with the War Department to discuss when the proceedings would resume. With Barry gone, and Evans only two weeks into his interim assignment running the Eastern Department, Kirby may well have communicated directly with Wood. Or Wood may have picked up the phone to call Kirby and ask how things were going. At the very least, Kirby had to know about the history of Wood and Louis Koehler if people at Fort Terry were speaking of it to reporters, which means Kirby likely knew about the claim that Wood had punished the jurors who voted to acquit Louis by separating them from the service.

Ben could not be sure about meddling from Washington, but he surely knew what Louis had endured. Now, Ben was in his own hell. He would never again be so naïve as to give an inspector truthful information only to have it used against him. Still, he remained hopeful that the jury would see Worcester's and Frick's "spite work" for what it was and acquit him.

It was a little before 11:00 p.m. when Kirby sent word that the jury had reached a verdict.

"[C]AN ALL THESE MEN be wrong, and these other men right?"[3] So had Hudson framed the case's fundamental dilemma, the dutiful Ben known by many versus the out-of-control Ben testified to by the accusers.

The jurors debated that question for two and a half hours, though there were really multiple questions, for the jurors did not have to vote the same way on all charges. They would do so if they accepted the fabrication claim as a total defense, but not if they rejected it or concluded it did not extend to all accusers.

Back in the courtroom, Ben tried to read the jurors' expressions and body language. He had entertained several of the jury members in his home. His sister had helped prepare their meals. Could they really have voted to end his military career?

All too soon it became clear that Kirby had no intention of revealing the jury's verdict. He said only that a decision had been reached. For now, the jurors were going to their beds.

Nearby, in the house occupied by the former post commander, Sophia could do little but tell her brother to have faith.

Ben had left LeMars seeking the fullest life he could imagine, richer in honor, novelty, and satisfaction than all the money his siblings engaged in business might earn. He knew he was fortunate that his younger sister had come along for the recent part of the ride. On the most uncertain night of his life, at least he was not alone. Still, as he undressed, carefully hanging his uniform as he had every evening of his adult life, he had to wonder whether he would soon instead be hanging civilian clothes or prison garb. A conviction on any one of the charges would be enough to kick Ben out of the Army with a dishonorable discharge and send him to prison.

The next morning, Ben walked to the makeshift courtroom for the last time, but still he would not leave the building with knowledge of the jury's decision. Only James Mayes, who had written so confidently in his prizewinning essay about "real soldiers," would have that privilege.

# CHAPTER THIRTY-EIGHT

# *Speculation*

A T NINE O'CLOCK ON Friday morning, Kirby officially opened the
court's last session and promptly asked all to leave except the jurors. Ben walked back to his house an unsatisfied man.

On the table in front of Kirby sat a typed, four-page verdict sheet prepared by Mayes. The pages listed all thirty-three charges. Kirby signed
the form and asked Mayes to enter the room. Mayes reviewed the form
and signed his name. By ten o'clock, it was all over. Kirby told the weary
jurors they were free to leave Plum Island. Some would never return.

There were bags to pack and a steamer to board—but first "all the
court officers filed down to Major Koehler's residence, and after chat-
ting with him a few minutes shook hands with him," reported the
*Times*. Their goodbye was so "hearty" that Ben put aside his earlier
trepidation and felt elated, sure of his acquittal. The scene prompted
"jubilation on the part of Major Koehler's adherents."[1]

Of all the men who had spent weeks together inside the small library, only Ben would remain on Plum Island, still wearing a uniform
but stripped of all duties—walking, eating, and sleeping in a kind of
purgatory—yet he was reported to be in "happy spirits," awaiting news
of his vindication. Everyone else left for an awkward ride across the
Sound, the jurors and Mayes knowing the verdict, Hawthorne and
Hudson in the dark.

According to Saturday's *Tribune*, Mayes seemed "pleased at the outcome."[2] As Mayes actually knew the verdict, his mood was perhaps more telling than Ben's, but the press had made mistakes throughout the trial. Articles had cited the closing of the officers' club as the reason for anger toward Ben, for example, but that event played little part in the testimony.

Over the weekend, other papers declined to speculate, reporting only that a verdict had been reached and would be kept secret pending review by Garrison and Wilson. Two weeks passed, cherry blossoms bloomed in Washington, and finally reporters had more than handshakes and demeanor on which to base a prediction.

"KOEHLER VERDICT IN; GUILTY, IS THE GUESS," read a headline in the *Sun* on April 12. The "guess" was that of a reporter who learned of the trial record's arrival at the War Department. As the reporter theorized, "Had there been a verdict of acquittal, announcement would have been made by this time at the headquarters of the Department of the East and it would not have been necessary for the case to be sent to Washington for review."[3]

That was not necessarily true, as someone else named Koehler well knew. Louis's acquittal had not been announced by Taft and Roosevelt until several months after the jury vote. Taft's conclusion in Louis's case, that the president could not convert an acquittal into a conviction, remained the law. To that extent, the *Sun* reporter drew a reasonable inference. Wilson had four options: accept the verdict and sentence, change conviction to acquittal on the ground of insufficient evidence, reduce the recommended penalty, or nullify the trial.

Other papers ran the same story as the *Sun*, but in a matter of days, Garrison ended the need for any more guesses.

"Guilty" *was* the verdict, Garrison confirmed. At least six officers on the jury had sided with the men above and below Ben who wanted him gone, and they imposed the sentence he most feared: expulsion from the Army, dishonorably, though without a prison term.

But guilty of what? Garrison used the same words as Mills: "immoral conduct." Garrison said the findings and sentence were still subject to review by Crowder, the chief of staff, and himself before they went to the president.[4]

It was unusual for a statement to be issued about a verdict that was not yet final, but this was an unusual case, and Leonard Wood wanted to move on. Five days after Garrison's statement, Wood vacated the office of chief of staff. He had stayed in Washington just long enough to see the curtain close on all the marionettes whose strings he had pulled.


IN LEMARS, WHERE BEN's youngest brother and elder sister still lived, the local paper reported on the fate of its former resident, whose pioneer parents lay buried in a hallowed spot in the middle of town. The paper observed that the trial "was one of the most sensational military proceedings ever held in the east. Because of the prominence of Major Koehler, as well as the serious nature of the charges, the case excited interest."[5]

The *LeMars Semi-Weekly Sentinel* also reprinted a curious dispatch from Hastings, Nebraska. The article pointed out that Ben had spent considerable time in Blue Hill where, it was stated, "he was noted for manliness as a boy and his friends there are convinced he is the victim of a conspiracy."[6]

"Manliness as a boy?" What exactly did that mean, and how would a boy have shown it? By using guns, riding well, and playing sports (though perhaps not cricket)? By breaking chicken's necks, instead of raising them for eggs? By flirting with girls, not seeming to avoid them? The paper did not explain, but the excerpt spoke volumes about the era's fixation on manliness, starting with a boy's training and socialization. Ironically, Ben had the kind of upbringing that the Boy Scouts manual lamented the passing of, given how "the hardships and privations of pioneer life . . . did so much to develop sterling manhood."[7] By the time of Ben's court-martial, the pioneer life was a memory being recreated in fiction, along with the rise of the cowboy as male hero, and exhortations for men to get outside—all fantasy stand-ins for the real things Ben had lived, but which did him little good on the East Coast in 1914.[8]

It seems that the case of Major Benjamin Martin Koehler had become a referendum on his manliness after all. As if it wasn't enough that nearly every aspect of Ben's Army life had been raked over for signs of "perversion," now his childhood was being brought into it.

Fortunately for Ben, a few people wanted to focus on the specific charges of which he had been convicted. One was Charles Sloan, the congressman who had intervened with Garrison in January. Sloan, an attorney, took umbrage at the way the government had treated a "Nebraska boy." He obtained a copy of the transcript and the more he read, the more he saw gross injustice. He intervened once again, asking Garrison to slow down the train that was speeding away with Ben's future. As far as Sloan was concerned, Ben Koehler may have been convicted, but he was not "dead morally" yet.

# PART FOUR

# Smear

MAYES AND THE ACCUSERS did not win a clean sweep by any means. As Sloan soon discovered, there was quite a bit of nuance embedded in Garrison's statement of "guilty." The jurors had rejected several claims.

Most significantly, the jury acquitted Ben of trying to kiss Austin Frick upstairs in the bathroom and grabbing his testicles while they danced.

The jurors found Ben not guilty of hugging Sergeant Edison Kirkman and fondling Kirkman's penis in Ben's bedroom and home office.

Ben was declared not guilty of touching Isaac Spears while urinating in a Greenport restroom, and of reaching up from the back of the buckboard, fondling Walter Ensley's private parts, and exposing himself as the electric lights magically turned on to illuminate the incident.

The jurors also rejected Harvey Kernan's claim. They acquitted Ben of stroking Kernan's back in the hospital tent after comparing his penis to a flashlight.

Final score: six wins for Ben, eleven for Mayes in the first set of charges, and ten wins for Mayes in the second set due to the absence of King's claim in the assault counts.

Did this result make any sense?

On the surface, the vote reflected a rejection of a conspiracy premised on every accuser's having lied. Notably, the jurors threw out the claims of the three accusers whom Hudson came closest to calling liars: Frick, Kirkman, and Ensley, the latter of whom the jury president all but called a liar himself. It seemed the jurors had placed stock in Sophia's words after all, for her testimony was at its strongest against Frick and Kirkman. She had said Frick did not go upstairs during dinner and that there was no "little shutter" on Ben's home office door. For the jurors to decide that a woman knew best about what happened in her home was not asking them to stretch their attitudes—not like asking them to credit Katie Ewing for knowing that the conversation she overheard involving Byers and Moody reflected "spite work."

Spears and Kernan had testified to two of the milder acts—touching of the hip and back. As to them, perhaps the jurors accepted Hudson's theory of misinterpretation, especially since Spears admitted to having drunk at least eight beers, rendering his memory suspect. Regarding Kernan, some jurors had slept in the camp tents and knew whether there were electric lights, making a flashlight unnecessary, as Ben said. In that case, the jurors were calling Kernan a liar, not simply a man who had overreacted to a pat on the back. He was the one who vacillated between saying he "knew absolutely nothing based on facts" and saying Ben stroked him.

The jury had no obligation to explain its split verdict, but a ruling that five men were not telling the truth when they said Ben molested them begged the question of why those five men claimed Ben had done so—to Mills, to Mayes, and at the trial. Advance planning was the most plausible explanation for lying by multiple accusers. It strained credulity that they had fabricated elaborate stories of penis and testicle grabbing independently, especially when Frick and Kirkman were friends as well as Worcester's most trusted subordinates.

Frick had been heard on more than one occasion vowing to "get" Ben, and the jury apparently concluded that that is what he was trying to do. The man whose testimony Crowder had singled out as strong, the man who cajoled others into testifying, the earliest proponent of trying to trigger an investigation into Ben's sexuality, was not believed. In his summation, Hudson had let Worcester off the hook but portrayed Frick as the instigator, and the jury apparently agreed. Kirkman was Worcester's first sergeant, whose story Worcester admitted to having discussed in advance of Mills's investigation. Ensley had all but been told to incriminate Ben by his boss, Barrett. Spears served in Worcester's company and was friendly with Putney. Kernan was being challenged about the beer permit. He testified that he went to see Mills only because Worcester told him to do so. For the jury to have concluded that these men were not telling the truth was tantamount to finding that a plot existed and that Worcester was in the thick of it.

Moreover, without the rejected claims, the resulting timeline created an anomaly. The actions of which Ben was convicted left a gap from August 1912 to July 1913. The full set of accusations created the impression of a regular pattern, but now there was the odd picture of a man who restrained himself for eleven months and became sexually assertive again in July 1913, the very month that Davis said better evidence was required.

Deliberating for only two and a half hours, eager to get to bed Thursday night and home on Friday, the jurors may not have focused on the logical defects in their findings. In the end, the jury vote suggests a compromise more than a rational statement about the evidence.

Throughout the trial, at least one member of the jury spoke as if decidedly in Ben's camp. Others were said to be unconvinced or undecided. If Kirby was determined to return a conviction, which seems likely given his curtness toward the end, other jurors may have cut a deal, insisting that the claims told by obviously biased and unreliable accusers be rejected.

But had not all of the jurors been described as giving Ben "hearty" handshakes before their departure? If so, that suggested all the more that they had voted to convict for pragmatic reasons, such as their own futures under Leonard Wood, not because they believed the charges.

There was also the matter of Hudson's closing statement. He had made it relatively easy for the jurors to go along with several of the accusers. Worcester was "immature," not venal. The "clean-cut" Charles Byers "genuinely believed" he was touched. Moody was "not in the same camp" as the others, despite Ewing having heard him talk about an "oath." Had Hudson delivered a cogent portrayal of the plot, persuasively labeling all its members liars, had he conceded nothing and demanded acquittal as a moral imperative, maybe that would have challenged the jury to take on Wood—and Kirby—just as the Louis Koehler jurors had done.

Hudson came nowhere close to meeting that bar. The jurors saved their own skins at the expense of Ben's.

In addition to the jurors' concerns over their careers, there was the large, prejudicial shadow cast by Garrison's threat of multiple court-martials if the verdict went in Ben's favor. According to the *New York Tribune*, "Colonel Kirby denied that a remark of Secretary Garrison that the case must end with a conviction or other court martials would be ordered influenced the court."[1] But if a reporter saw that possibility, it was not trivial. Did Kirby want to sentence one man to dismissal, or numerous fellow officers to future trips to Plum Island to serve as jurors in additional court-martials?

The *Tribune* reporter, though astute, did not accurately quote Garrison's statements. Garrison had not said that a conviction on *any* charge would save all the complainants from court-martials, but rather that "each and every one" found to have lied would be court-martialed. Would Frick and the other four whose charges were rejected face court-martials for perjury? That remained to be seen. The jury had made the need for additional court-martials less burdensome by returning guilty verdicts on nearly two-thirds of the counts. That may well have been the intention—return enough guilty verdicts that Ben looked "weak or insane," as Hudson had put it during an argument, and the Army not so bad.

The jurors realized that the testimony deviated from the specifications. Kirby had used a pen to edit the typed specifications to conform to the testimony. In the case of Moody, Kirby wrote that Ben was "Guilty, except the words 'legs and breasts,' substituting therefor the words 'leg and breast.'" Similar changes were made in other charges:

"grasping" became "touching and pressing" in Wilson's case, "rubbing" was deleted from Elvin Byers's count, obscene talk was excised from the Wilson and Fairey counts. Dates were changed. It took time to find the correct pages in the transcript to make the changes. That is apparently how the jury spent much of Thursday night, consistent with the outcome being predetermined, requiring little discussion.

The verdict was mixed and logically suspect, but reporters were not told that Ben had been acquitted of twelve of the thirty-three counts, including those lodged by one of the two men the press had described as Ben's "principal accusers," one of the two men who were commissioned officers at the time of the alleged offenses.[2]

Holding back the details and making it appear that Ben was guilty as charged had the desired effect of forestalling any questions about court-martials for the five men whose claims were rejected, and it nipped in the bud any questions reporters might have had as to how the jury could find a "principal accuser" and four other men untruthful without that pointing to a broader conspiracy to lie involving the whole group.

The War Department's presentation of the verdict further damaged Ben's reputation and shamed him throughout the country. Papers reported that two officers had been the main witnesses against Ben without noting that the claims by one of those officers had been rejected.

An extreme example appeared on April 19. Ben had spent more of his Army life in New York State than anywhere, so it was not surprising that on the Sunday following announcement of the verdict, the *New York Tribune* devoted half a page to Ben's career and downfall, pointing out his Astor service, rapid rise in rank, "brilliance" as a soldier, and anticipated advancement.[3] Those facts marked the heights from which Ben had fallen, but the article contained damaging inaccuracies as to the reasons for the fall.

The article stated that military men had come from all over the world to testify *against* Ben, when the opposite was true. The witnesses against him were clustered in and around Plum Island, while men from far away came to testify *for* Ben, and more had wanted to come.

The paper wrote that Ben's punishment could have been life in prison, when the maximum term was one year for third-degree assault, which, even if multiplied by the number of convictions, added up to eleven years at most. The jury had needed "only thirty minutes" to reach its verdict, the paper stated, when the record showed the jury deliberated from 8:15 until 10:55 p.m.

The *Tribune* hinted at who might be the source of the misinformation: Mayes. It was noted in the story that he was a former newspaperman, which would have given him a certain veneer of reliability with other journalists in the absence of contrary evidence.

Representative Sloan, however, had access to the transcript and jury form. He enlisted senators and other members of Congress with law backgrounds to review the testimony related to the eleven men whose charges had been sustained. Sloan approached the task this way to minimize any actual or perceived bias due to his friendship with the Koehlers, as well as to hasten the review.[4]

While Sloan had persuaded Garrison to postpone Wilson's final ruling, that did not buy unlimited time, as Army officials well showed with their next action. They could not send Ben to jail, nor discharge him without Wilson's approval, but they could uproot and isolate him.

Once again, Wood proved to be a master manipulator. He had a subordinate, the chief of the Coast Artillery division, write a memo to him recommending Ben's transfer. The reasons given were specious.

The first ground cited for transferring Ben was that "the nature of the charges upon which he was tried are well known at the post, and many of the officers and enlisted men of Fort Terry were material witnesses against him."[5] That was incorrect. Only two commissioned officers at Fort Terry were material witnesses against Ben, and Frick's claims had been rejected. Two privates remained at Fort Terry whose claims had been sustained—Barrett and Fairey—and two noncommissioned officers—Campbell and Elvin Byers. The others either no longer worked at Fort Terry, such as Ward and King, or never had, such as Charles Byers and Moody, who were stationed on Fishers Island. Out of seven hundred men, five was not "many."

The memo went on to state that because of the "above facts," "the relationships now existing between Major Koehler and all of the other officers of the fort is [*sic*] strained. Major Koehler goes about the fort freely. The situation is very embarrassing."

Embarrassing for whom? Nearly all the other officers at Fort Terry had testified for Ben, not against him. That was the source of the embarrassment, not the reverse.

The memo concluded, "It is known that Major Koehler has a following among the enlisted men and his presence, therefore, is injurious as far as discipline is concerned."

Wood had written in December of the need to show enlisted men that the Army could be fair by subjecting an officer to a court-martial. Here he was approving the opposite argument, that because of his good relationship with enlisted men, Ben posed a threat to discipline.

Making Ben Koehler leave his home, friends, garden, and the only stability he knew was one of Wood's last acts before departing Washington. The memo was dated April 18, and Wood approved it right away. On April 21, Ben received orders to leave Plum Island and head "without delay to Fort Wadsworth, N.Y."[6] With those words, the Nebraska boy born in Illinois and raised in Iowa set off for yet another island: Staten Island.

Some say that islands' physical isolation feels protective, giving rise to a special feeling among an island's inhabitants, a freedom from rules and convention, even from time itself. Some say that being surrounded by water creates a sense of community and endless possibility.

None of those appealing factors pertained to Ben Koehler as he headed on April 27 to New York City's least populated borough. Staten Island was a city island with a bulkhead, and from Fort Wadsworth, situated on the coast, Ben did not much like the view. Across the harbor lay Governors Island, the place where Worcester had begun Ben's nightmare. It was not voluntarily that Ben gave up the wildness of Plum Gut for the more domesticated Narrows, which divided New York Bay into two halves.

The two halves of the Koehler household also found themselves divided. Sophia, having given the Army two and a half years of free labor, no longer provided value as the post commander's social hostess. She accompanied her brother one last time on the steamer to New London and the train to Grand Central Terminal. After that, she was on her own, free to purchase a one-way ticket to Iowa.

In April, war in Mexico became a reality. The United States sent troops, and Ben wanted to be among them. If Wilson upheld the verdict, Ben would try to reenlist as a private, his friends told the press. It was another parallel to the Dreyfus case, Ben's "loyalty to the service" being proclaimed. Ben himself would say nothing of substance, not on the record.

"I expect word from Washington in a day or two regarding my court-martial," he was quoted in the *Washington Times* at the end of April. "Until then, I must be silent."[7]

In May, Sloan submitted a lengthy "Review of Evidence and Brief" to Crowder and Garrison as well as the "Opinions of Senators and Representatives" who had reviewed the transcript. Sloan's memo summarized the testimony concerning each sustained charge in two columns, the government's "Support" on the left, the "Opposition" on the right.

Of course, Sloan and his colleagues had not sat at Fort Terry and observed the witnesses. They had not seen the "clean-cut" appearance of Charles Byers, nor the earnestness of Philip Worcester as he spoke of wanting to make the Army "clean." Juries are considered good evaluators of witness credibility because they can assess body language, directness of manner, and other indices of truth telling, yet studies have shown that under certain circumstances the brain may put undue weight on body language and tone of voice over content.

Based on content, Sloan and the other lawyers argued that a miscarriage of justice had occurred. "[A]bsolutely insufficient to sustain any of the specifications offered," wrote Sloan of the prosecution's evidence.[8]

Montana Senator Thomas J. Walsh, who would later be President Franklin Roosevelt's choice for attorney general, pointed out Campbell's use of the phrase "I believe" in several answers about Ben's touching his arm.[9] Walsh wrote, "It seems scarcely credible that if the acts charged ever did take place, and they had the significance attached to them in the charge, the witness would find his recollection of the occurrence so feeble that he would be required to qualify what he had to say about the matter with the expression 'I believe.'" Campbell's testimony "would not support the charge in any court exercising civil jurisdiction and ought not to be deemed sufficient for conviction in any tribunal."[10]

Other reviewers expressed similar opinions. "Very much surprised," wrote Senator George Norris, a former judge and prosecutor, calling Ben's conviction on the Davis charges a "grave injustice" as "all the established circumstances" disproved Davis's testimony. "Ridiculous" wrote the congressman who reviewed the Campbell charges. Representative Moses Kinkaid of Nebraska, also a former judge, said Jones, Lones, and others had "squarely contradicted" Elvin Byers's testimony and that "hearsay and suspicion," not "proper evidence," produced the conviction. Daniel Anthony Jr. wrote of Fairey's unsubstantiated testimony and motive to lie—Ben's failure to promote him—and agreed that the jury's vote to convict could have resulted only from a "general atmosphere of guilt and suspicion which the prosecutor's office of the Government endeavored to build up around the accused."[11]

In conclusion, Sloan asked that the convictions be set aside because the evidence of his character was "so strong and convincing" and the nature of the charges was "so at variance with the modesty, decency and manliness of the accused as testified to by his superior officers as well as his subordinates," not to mention "the suspicious circumstances and the general relation of the parties making the accusations."[12]

Garrison did not meet with Sloan and Gilbert Hitchcock to discuss the memo nor arrange for them to confer with Wilson, as Sloan said Garrison had promised.[13] Nor, apparently, did Garrison raise any concerns with Wilson, for on June 20, Wilson told Garrison he did not see "any basis" for changing the verdict or sentence. The governor of Missouri had urged Wilson to let Ben remain in the Army at reduced standing or resign.[14] Wilson did not do that. On June 23, he confirmed the sentence of dismissal.[15] The adjutant general added his signature, Ben was summoned, and a telegram from Washington conveying the decision was read to him.[16]

Whether anyone actually reviewed Sloan's submission cannot be known. It and the eleven-hundred–page transcript may well have been stamped and filed without a page being turned.

There is no doubt about what happened next to Ben Koehler. Twenty-one years to the month after he had entered West Point, he removed his uniform for the last time and took a ferry across the Narrows back to civilian life. At least he was spared a public shaming ceremony of the sort Dreyfus endured, with officers ripping off his insignia and breaking his sword.

The shaming took place in the press.


"KOEHLER OUT OF ARMY," wrote *The New York Times*. The article repeated the falsehood that "evidence damaging to the accused" had come from all over the world—"from Hawaii and the Philippines, as well as the Pacific Coast" and embellished it with additional falsity: "The testimony piled up until it was stacked in sheets of typewritten foolscap a foot high. Only half an hour was required by the jury to reach a verdict."[17]

The *Times* did note that Ben's "career as an officer has been brilliant." Perhaps someone had checked the *Times* archives and seen his photo in the West Point Class of 1897, back when he was described as one of the best and the brightest, an "embryo general."

Now the *Times* concluded its article with a simpler description: "Major Koehler is a bachelor, 42 years of age."

# CHAPTER FORTY

# *Hawarden*

"WE HAVE FIVE HORSES, two cows, twenty hogs and fifty-three chickens so you see we are some farmers." Such was Ben's new life, as described by Sophia, his housemate once again.

Sophia tended to write to Roy Dimmick when she felt optimistic. Finally, thirty-four weeks after Ben's ouster, she did. In March 1915, the two siblings embarked on a new joint venture as Iowa farmers—far, far away from oceans, beach plums, and military bases. The two-story house they now shared stood far removed from almost everything.

"Came just a week ago," Sophia reported to Roy. "We are still in a mess waiting for the painters to do the walls and woodwork and I think it will be Easter before we are settled."[1]

The eastern bank of the Big Sioux River provided the nearest coast, about a mile from the 240 acres of farmland Ben and Sophia owned thanks to Rudolph, who had acquired the farm in a foreclosure sale and sold it to his siblings. The property lay three miles outside the small city of Hawarden, in Buncombe Township, about fifteen miles of rolling fields northwest of LeMars.

Twenty years earlier, Sophia complained of Rudolph's failure to mail one of her first letters to Roy, then her adolescent crush, but whatever negligence the youngest Koehler brother had displayed as a teen lay buried under years of success in real estate.[2] Of the Koehler siblings' many enterprises, Rudolph's chosen profession proved the most useful to Ben and Sophia in their time of need. They had lived at first with Louis and Maude, who were now back in Leavenworth, but Ben wanted his own place where he could hang his civilian clothes on a permanent basis.

Rudolph came to the rescue by finding property in a community with its own quirky association to Great Britain, Hawarden being the name of a Welsh castle belonging to the nineteenth-century British statesman William Gladstone. The farm's isolation appealed to Ben, if not to his more social sister. Inside the house, Sophia installed features more typical of a city residence, including a stained-glass window and ample shelves for books. Outside, a short walk from the back door, stood a barn, chicken house, and machine shed. The human footprint was small and condensed compared to the vastness of the land, made larger for the Koehlers when Sophia insisted on purchasing eighty adjacent acres that came up for sale.

The Big Sioux River separated northwestern Iowa from South Dakota and flowed into the Missouri River. Unlike the churning waters of Plum Gut, the Sioux moved in one direction, just as Ben was trying to do, set on forgetting the past and reinventing himself.

Ben had spoken at his LeMars graduation of historical turning points. His own turning point was in progress. He had not been a civilian since working at Henry's bank, but Plum Island had taught him one thing: He loved the land and stewarding the life it made possible. If he could supervise an island of 840 acres, he figured he could run a farm of 320.

As Ben's focus narrowed, much was happening in the larger world. Most foreboding, Germany declared war against Russia a month after Ben's dismissal. Deprived of military channels of communication, Ben relied on newspapers for information. Unpleasantly, Leonard Wood's name appeared in much that Ben read; for Wood was fast becoming one of the most outspoken advocates for a bigger and better-trained military in anticipation of U.S. involvement. Roosevelt heartily endorsed Wood's position, but Wood reported to a different commander-in-chief in 1914. Wilson disagreed with the preparedness movement and did not much care for Wood's stridency on the topic.

Wilson used his January 1915 State of the Union address to express pacifist views. Telling Congress and the public that the events in Europe constituted "a war with which we have nothing to do, whose cause cannot touch us," Wilson urged that "friendship and disinterested service" ought to be the attitude of the United States, not "fearful preparation for trouble."[3]

It was a popular position. Senators and representatives applauded, but Wood, Roosevelt, and their allies continued to maintain that the United States was woefully unprepared for a modern war.[4] Wilson did not appreciate being undermined by the highest-ranking officer in the Army, especially when Wood ramped up his words to denounce "fake humanitarians" as "unconscious slayers of their people" if they sent citizens into battle without proper training—words that sounded a great deal like those Mayes had used in his 1910 essay.[5]

After those remarks, Wilson told Garrison to reprimand Wood and ordered Army officers to cease making public statements about "the military situation in the United States or abroad."[6] That did not stop Wood from helping to form the American Legion, a preparedness organization joined immediately by Roosevelt and his four sons. Again, Wilson pushed back, ordering the Legion off Governors Island, where Wood had provided office space.[7]

In May 1915, the British ocean liner *Lusitania* sank off the coast of Ireland, killing nearly 1,200 civilian passengers. Unlike the *Maine*, the cause was clear—a torpedo fired by a German submarine. Wilson still resisted entering the war, and Roosevelt criticized him for weakness.[8] Roosevelt's position gained in popularity, the country inched closer to involvement, and Crowder applied himself to shaping a draft (which would "especially target[ ] unmarried men without gainful employment").[9] The buildup would change all domestic Army installations, but Ben's court-martial had given Fort Terry a head start.

Despite Garrison's grand statements about the reprehensibility of men who would bring false charges, there had been no courts-martial of Frick, Kirkman, Ensley, Kernan, or Spears, nor would there ever be. Instead, the Army found less public and time-consuming ways to clean house and keep the scandal from developing an afterlife.

The day after Ben left Plum Island, the Army named a complete outsider as his replacement: Major James A. Shipton, a man who had spent 1913 in Buenos Aires as military attaché.[10] Shipton was a reset button in a uniform. No underling at Fort Terry could accuse him of favoring one side over the other, and if someone did raise the case, Shipton could silence him with a simple "Before my time." In 1915, Shipton wrote of Worcester: "an excellent officer in every way, energetic and efficient and entirely trustworthy."[11] Worcester apparently got along with his new boss, a married man, much better than his old one.

Other members of the "clique" had little chance to get to know the new commander. Those who joined Worcester and Frick out of revenge for perceived wrongs by Ben, or to teach a suspected homosexual a harsh lesson, had succeeded in engineering Ben's ouster. But any accusers who believed their "spite work" could simply prune Fort Terry of its commander, lopping off the tree's crown and leaving the trunk standing with its branches intact, found that they were badly mistaken. The Army sawed and scattered the branches, a common way for an organization to end a scandal: squelch the stories and oral histories that would perpetuate it by separating the people most likely to talk about it.

Lieutenant Smith, Ben's friend, had been transferred the same December day Wood ordered Barry to the Philippines. Ellis was sent to Fort Slocum before the trial ended. A couple of weeks later, Robinson found himself reassigned to the Quartermaster Corps in Washington, D.C. A few months after that, the Army dispatched Frick to Portsmouth, New Hampshire. Plank-walking had indeed occurred—by people on both sides of the case.

Only Worcester's life played out as he wanted. In August 1915, he moved back to the Hudson Valley with his wife to join the West Point Chemistry Department.[12] Few would ever know how close Worcester came to having a plagiarism accusation derail his teaching career.

In Washington, Sloan took his outrage to the House floor, using a debate in January 1915 about a military appropriations bill as an opportunity to praise Ben and castigate the process that resulted in his conviction. Ben's arrest had come like "a thunderbolt from a clear sky," Sloan told his colleagues. "The moment he was ordered to trial he was damned."[13]

Sloan characterized Mayes as determined to carry out "the wish of Washington," in service of which mission the prosecutor misstated the law, violated the rules of evidence, and created such an aura of suspicion that he obtained convictions based on weak, uncorroborated testimony from discredited witnesses.

In particular, Sloan said, it was simply not a true statement of the law that uncorroborated testimony by one witness was sufficient for conviction given the presumption of innocence and Ben's steadfast denials, not to mention the witnesses who substantiated Ben's accounts and undermined the credibility of the accusers. This point would continue to be debated to the present day in sexual abuse cases. He said/she said (or he said/they said) remains challenging from an evidentiary standpoint, but the seeming stalemate is often illusory, capable of being broken by careful consideration of motives—a key factor in Ben's case.

In his oration on the House floor, Sloan did not shy away from quoting Katie Ewing about the "oath" she had overhead Moody discuss with Byers. Unlike Hudson, Sloan repeated her words verbatim, as did the Senate attorney whom Sloan had asked to review the Elvin Byers charge.

Nor was Sloan afraid to castigate the executive branch and Army for not following through on Garrison's vow to try any accusers determined to have lied. The prosecution's evidence was, in Sloan's words, "so grossly inadequate and flagrantly false that the failure to try the accusing witnesses for their perjury and other forms of mendacity is sufficient warrant for Major Koehler's complaint and to apprise him of the brand of injustice he received."

Sloan noted that for Ben, a guilty verdict on any charge meant far more than "disgrace, degradation, and loss of means of livelihood." It meant "punishment for life," for that was how an "Army officer of rank" regarded dishonorable discharge. With such all-important stakes, Sloan argued, the highest standards of fairness should have been applied. The opposite occurred, he said—and he did not even know about the fake Searcy letter.

Sloan reached the heights of his criticism when he turned to the alleged groping of Charles Byers with Moses nearby. In Sloan's words, conviction on that count showed "how helpless, however innocent, the accused was before that body of men, who seemed to lust for his downfall and the destruction of his prospects and honor rather than find and preserve justice."

The lawyer who reviewed Ben's conviction on that charge termed it "irreconcilable with a rational mind" and opined that a guilty verdict based on Byers's testimony, given the presence of Moses, would "reverse all rules of law and shock the civilized sense of justice"—and yet a conviction had occurred. If the evidence put forward was sufficient, Sloan argued, "then the fundamental basis for personal security has been destroyed; the wisdom of centuries set aside without a precedent, authority, or reason."

Sloan ended with expressions of hope that the court-martial system would be overhauled to protect others from "the cruel and unjust sacrifice" Ben had made and that "[t]he time may come when this House will be the forum to rectify this manifest wrong."

The *Congressional Record* reprinted Sloan's statement, and newspapers reported it with headlines such as "Major Koehler Scandal Is Revived in House."[14] If Ben read Sloan's clearly argued and heartfelt remarks, he may well have wished that Sloan, not Samuel Hudson, had been present on Plum Island to give the closing argument in his behalf.

A copy of Sloan's speech made its way into Ben's file at the adjutant general's office. Apparently, top officials were still watching Ben, hide as he might in pastoral Hawarden.


EVICTION FROM PLUM ISLAND could change the beneficiary of Ben's stewardship, but it did not change his nature. Where before Ben had inspected water pumps and gun batteries, in Hawarden he turned his attention to hatching chickens in the new incubators he and Sophia had purchased, "one a 140 egg one, the other 50 . . . so you see we are busy and aren't going to have scrub chickens," she wrote to Roy.[15] Sophia sounded proud, determined to put the pieces of her and Ben's lives back together. She also sounded glad to be away from New York City. If Roy headed to New York in May, Sophia hoped he would "stop off and see a model Iowa farm," but she was "only afraid it will make New York seem more distasteful than ever."

While he counted his chickens, Ben continued to count the days until his innocence would be declared. He had not given up, nor had his family and friends. A group of them, led by Daniel Anthony Jr., hired a private detective who traveled to New London and was reported to be "more than satisfied" with material he gathered in an effort to reopen the case.[16]

At least one accuser had recanted. As reported in May 1915 in the *Chicago Daily Tribune*, "One man who testified against Koehler at the court martial has since signed an affidavit to the effect that he had seen the accused man only once, and that on that occasion he had to have Koehler pointed out to him. He knew nothing, he admitted, of his private life."[17]

The recanting witness was likely Davis or Charles Byers. Both had testified to having no prior knowledge of Ben. It seemed others might also recant, for the detective was reported to be "looking for three former privates who have since left the army and come to Chicago."

The *Tribune* article was the first post-conviction story that repeated Ben's view of the case, "that Koehler's strict attitude toward the officers under him incurred . . . enmity . . . and that the case against him was a 'frameup.'" According to the article, Ben "does not want reinstatement in the army, seeking only to have his name cleared." He had apparently changed his mind since vowing to enlist.

While the detective pursued leads, Ben passed his time quietly. A lone shade tree stood on the hill behind the white house and red barn on 420th Street just west of Cherry. Sitting on a bench under the tree, Ben could survey his new domain without obstruction. There were gently sloping fields as far as the eye could see, dotted here and there with shrubs or clumps of trees. To the west, the ground dipped, and through that opening Ben could see across the Big Sioux River into South Dakota, though the land knew no borders and the South Dakota acres looked the same as the Iowa acres, golden brown until they met the horizon. There were few signs of humans, just a couple of farmhouses in the distance. From so far away they looked like white dashes, mere punctuation marks on the primary story of the land.

Ben liked his new territory. It did not have a view of an ocean or estuary, nor was it as large as Plum Island, but it was his. He held title to these fields, along with a person he trusted like no other. For seventeen years he had been the Army's tenant. The government could oust him at any time, and it had done so. No one broke his sword, no one ripped the oak-leaf major's insignia off his uniform, no one spat at him, but it was the biggest disgrace and loss of his life.

Seated on the shaded bench, Ben had plenty of time to think—about his graduation motto, "duty before position," about a decision he had made in 1909 to turn down the post of military attaché in Berlin, and about all the other ways in which his life might have turned out differently.[18]

Never again would Ben set foot on an island. The literal detachment islands represented from the mainland, and the emotional detachment from his roots in the Midwest, were over for him, and he would never again fall asleep to the sounds of the Atlantic or create a rise in a crowd by hitting a target in the Pacific.

The waves in his new life would be formed of grain and corn. Those waves were quiet and predictable, unlike the swells of oceans that answered only to the wind.

# *Federal Action*

B EN KOEHLER WAS NEVER a standard-bearer for gay men or men rumored to be gay, and he did not become one after his conviction.

Neither Ben, nor his attorney, nor his supporters framed his trial as a challenge to homophobia. An organization dedicated to gay rights would not emerge until 1924, and its existence would be short-lived.[1] Whatever respect Ben's relationship to Maude Anthony gave him for the protest tactics of the women's suffrage movement, his own training in mass action came from a different source: the military. After Ben's dismissal, as women gained the right to vote in additional states and protested in Washington demanding federal voting rights, the lesson Ben's former bosses extracted from his case was that more strictness was needed, not less, to keep the Army "clean" of homosexuals.

In 1916, General Crowder appealed to Congress for a new clause in the Articles of War prohibiting "assault with the intent to commit any felony" instead of the existing "assault and battery with an intent to commit rape" in "time of war." The proposed change sharpened the articles' applicability to same-sex activity by changing "rape" to "any felony," which included sodomy under state laws. If a groper's intent was anal or oral sex, the grope could be punished under the new clause.[2] Though homosexuality was not mentioned when Crowder testified before congressional subcommittees about the revised wording, a design to penalize sexual behavior is suggested by the fact that Crowder also proposed a separate clause prohibiting "assault with intent to do bodily harm," leaving "any felony" to encompass illegal sex acts that did not involve "bodily harm."[3]

Congress and Wilson went along with the proposed changes in August 1916. "Assault with intent to commit any felony" became part of a new Article 93 entitled "Various Crimes."[4]

Clearer articulation of prohibited conduct might have improved fairness, except that Congress retained the broadly worded article used to prosecute Louis, Ben, and many others—interference with "good order and discipline"—and the similarly broad "conduct unbecoming" clause, both of which owed their genesis to a military code issued by the Earl of Essex in 1642.[5] As long as military superiors had those articles, they could continue to engage in "selective enforcement against servicemen whose conduct offends current military mores."[6] That included speech—not just private talk about "fat boys" and sex, but public speech about matters of social concern. For example, in 1925, a popular colonel and advocate of greater use of air power was discharged for criticizing the military after several fatal plane crashes.[7]

Military defendants who challenged the "good order" and "conduct unbecoming" articles as unconstitutionally vague and overbroad have never succeeded, but the argument gained some traction in a Vietnam War case involving an Army doctor discharged for saying that black soldiers "are sacrificed and discriminated against in Viet Nam by being given all the hazardous duty" and making other antiwar statements.[8] The doctor challenged his expulsion and won the support of two Supreme Court justices, William O. Douglas and Potter Stewart, who agreed that the articles violated due process by failing to give clear notice to officers of what conduct was prohibited and fostering arbitrary, subjective decision-making by higher-ups, inspectors, and juries. Douglas and Stewart also found the articles overbroad, allowing prosecution for speech protected by the First Amendment. The Court's majority disagreed, holding that "The fundamental necessity for obedience, and the consequent necessity for imposition of discipline, may render permissible within the military that which would be constitutionally impermissible outside it."[9]

Dissenting from the lower court's decision that upheld the articles, Judge David Bazelon had observed that a vague grant of authority to the military was problematic because "it leaves the definition, and therefore the creation, of crimes to the discretion of minor executive or military officials."[10] That was true in Ben's case, allowing his conviction to contribute to decades of further discrimination against men perceived to be homosexual. The unreviewed and unchecked moral sensibilities and malice of a few men underlay Ben's prosecution, not any policy deliberated and announced by Congress or a clearly expressed administrative rule backed by findings of fact, as would be required later in the twentieth century for agency actions of all types.

Trial attorney Daniel Kornstein, who was drafted after a year at Yale Law School into the judge advocate general's office during the Vietnam War, notes that "the vagueness doctrine does more than guarantee notice. By compelling government to make an explicit choice, it eliminates or greatly reduces the area for arbitrary or discriminatory enforcement."[11]

That, too, applied to Ben's case. The Army never made clear what it was about his supposed conduct and words that crossed a line. The problem could not have been one man touching another, for the desirable homosocial intimacy of which Kenly spoke allowed a man to put his arm around another in friendship. If the issue was touching with a "suggestion," as Worcester and Mayes put it, what kind of suggestion was impermissible, how serious and recurring did it need to be, and how was that internal mindset to be proved? Given that "conduct unbecoming" is an offense "solely because of the opinions of other people,"[12] was it enough that the person touched *believed* the other man was gay? Was talk of sexual intercourse always grounds for dismissal—or only when spoken by an allegedly gay man?

Guidelines for military recruiters written in 1917 and distributed in 1918 provided specific advice on how to detect "inverts" and "perverts" and keep them out of the service.[13] In 1919, the same year Congress voted to grant women the right to vote, the nation's legislators took an explicit step to regulate homosexual behavior, making "sodomy" a violation of the Articles of War.[14] Whereas the element of "assault"—unwanted touching—had been the criminal nugget in Ben's supposed actions, the addition of "sodomy" in 1920 expressly banned consensual sex between men.[15] Investigators seeking to enforce "moral zones" around bases had discovered "that it was not only women and girls who pandered to the sexual needs of sailors and soldiers."[16] Reminiscent of what state and municipal investigators had written two decades earlier, federal agents now warned of "fairies" in Philadelphia, perverts in New York City, and female impersonators on Long Island.[17]

Such actions, large and small, were part of a years' long process whereby those inclined to participate in same-sex activity—once perceived as a local morality matter curbed, if at all, through municipal decency laws and state penal codes—were increasingly seen as a problem to be dealt with at the federal level, by bureaucrats whose numbers and power were growing. At the same time, medical, social, and legal interest in homosexuality was, according to Margot Canaday, "exploding."[18]

In 1919, the assistant secretary of the navy—Franklin Delano Roosevelt—was so concerned with "vice and depravity" in the services that he authorized a sting operation in which undercover agents propositioned sailors stationed in Newport, Rhode Island, suspected of being part of a homosexual group linked to a local minister.[19] Yet Americans were not all in with the idea that same-gender sex deserved to be rooted out at all costs. When word spread of the government's entrapment techniques, a congressional investigation ensued and an outcry prompted the military to drop the charges.[20]

Legal historians distinguish between centuries-old, religious-based edicts "designed to suppress all forms of non-procreative and non-marital sexual conduct" and "discrimination against a class of people on the basis of their homosexual status," which "developed only in the twentieth century . . . peak[ing] from the 1930s to the 1960s."[21] Ben's case presaged the turn toward homosexual status discrimination, just as the suspicions about single men in post-gold rush San Francisco would reappear in 1930s determinations that unmarried men were unworthy of federal benefits.[22]

After World War II, with the addition of an administrative policing apparatus, the armed services officially moved beyond punishing homosexual "acts" to targeting men perceived as being gay.[23] Then, Worcester's stated goal of making the army "clean" became documented policy, with a means beyond the court-martial or forced resignations to carry it out.

Ben Koehler's case lies at the beginning of that arc, a pre–World War I trial of a senior officer for alleged homoerotic acts that received sustained, national press coverage and the personal involvement of the secretary of war and Army chief of staff. Sixteen men banded together to oust a man they did not want to work for by purporting to "out" him at a time in the United States when challenges to the supremacy of white men from women, immigrants, and a changing economy helped turn an Army base "clique" into early policers of gender conformity.

The very existence of such a detailed record of federal action against a suspected "homo-sexualist" in 1913–14 owes itself to an unusual set of circumstances. Had Ben not been determined to prove his innocence and had Wood not been determined to make Ben suffer, there might never have been a trial. Ben's misfortune is historians' gain, for the transcript provides a unique look at how senior military officers approached a pre–World War I claim that a member of their own elite group was homosexual.

Even more than a century after the trial, the evidence of a plot is overwhelming, including:

- The far-fetched, bold nature of the allegations, at a time when educated, middle-class gay men were doing their utmost to conceal their sexual preference
- The accusers' numerous alterations of dates and descriptions
- Malice of the accusers toward Ben, their friendship with one another, and their failure to mention the claims to anyone

until Frick and Worcester asked if they had anything to report—mostly after Worcester's dispute with Shanley and
Ben's threat to report him for plagiarism

- The rebuttals of the accusers' claims by other witnesses
- The overheard conversation about an "oath" and needing to
  "stick tight"
- Zerphy's corroborated testimony that he was denied a furlough, pass, and promotion for not incriminating Ben, cou-
  pled with Sophia's letter that enlisted men faced the
  guardhouse if they testified for Ben—a fear two privates displayed by leaving the Army the day they testified
- The fake Searcy letter sent when the accusers' testimony was
  declared weak
- The jury's finding that five accusers were not telling the
  truth, including Frick, who had done the most to spread rumors and solicit incriminating stories
- Admission by a sixth accuser, whose claim the jury upheld,
  that he had fabricated his story

Added to the plot from below was Wood's malice from above. Wood
significantly influenced Crowder and Garrison. The indifference
shown to the many factors pointing to Ben's innocence reflects the
extent to which the Army and War Department allowed the case to
turn not on what Ben actually did but on the believability of his depiction as a homosexual. *Could he have done it?* was a far easier question
to answer than *Did he do it?*

In the present day, Chelsea Manning said she enlisted when confused about her gender identity, hoping the Army would "man her
up."[24] Whether Ben relied on the imposed discipline of the Army to
stifle homosexual urges cannot be known. His boyhood interest in a
military career, nurtured by Louis's example, provides an independent reason for his entering the Army. It is also likely that Ben's moralistic parents, and his exposure to radical reformers such as Daniel
Read Anthony and Susan B. Anthony, introduced him to the idea that
self-control over sexual desire was a virtue.[25] Possibly Ben used that

explanation to rationalize to himself his apparent lack of sexual activity with women.

In the end, it is impossible to know whether Ben had homosexual "tendencies," to use Hudson's word, and impossible to know exactly what happened between Ben and any of the accusers. However, all factors point to a set of lies that resulted in the "punishment for life" of an officer long on the kind of loyalty, attention to duty, and fairness the Army claimed to want.

Philip Worcester tossed a lit match into a mixture of male angst, malice, and ill-informed stereotypes. The result was a conflagration still smoldering today.

# A Home at the Prince

SOPHIA MARGARET KOEHLER MARRIED Oscar LeRoy Dimmick on April 2, 1918. It was a small wedding in LeMars. The bride wore blue. If Maude had married "late" at age 31, Sophia's age of 41 made her a very old bride by the standards of the day. Susan B. Anthony would have approved.

After pronouncing Roy and Sophia man and wife, the pastor turned to the youngest guest and christened Wilhelmine Margaret Koehler, daughter of Rudolph and his wife, Minnie. Ben and Margaret Gund served as sponsors.[1]

For three years, Sophia, Rudolph, and other family members had been the mainstay of Ben's social life. Lizzie lived in the Koehler family home on Court Street, where pink roses filled the living and dining rooms for the wedding, and where the siblings had gathered for holiday meals since Ben and Sophia's return to Iowa.

There were no earnest lieutenants, no loyal quartermaster, filling Ben's evenings at the farm. For the most part, when people stopped in, they were Sophia's friends, up from LeMars for a meal or perhaps a swim in the river and an overnight stay. Sophia's outgoing nature also resulted in a few dinner invitations for her and Ben to homes in Hawarden.

At least with respect to Sophia's devotion to Ben, James Mayes had been correct, but as the months passed, it became increasingly wearing for her to live on an isolated farm as companion to a man still nursing a large wound—and still accustomed to being a commander. If she thought entertaining officers on Plum Island was hard work, Sophia found that life on a farm left her exhausted many nights. Eight months after moving in, Ben engaged "two men, one to dig a cave and dig sewer and the other to build a tower for our tank that is to hold the water," as Sophia wrote to Roy. The workers were not her cup of tea: "Of course they stay with us," she wrote, "and I have the extreme pleasure of cooking for the beasts—wish you could see Bill—He is the worst old thing you can imagine—uses abominable tobacco—the only redeeming feature about him is that he doesn't chew nor use snuff. He talks all the time. . . . We have a dreadful time evenings trying to read or do anything except listen to him."[2]

There was a second, smaller house on the property that Ben intended to relocate and rent out, but only after enlarging the cellar of the main house. By the time the workers left, Sophia lamented, "I will be able to run a child's restaurant—You should see them eat cakes in the morning—Bill especially."

Roy had sent another book, but Sophia lacked time to read: "It's bedtime for me for I am weary and I have bread to mix and buckwheat cakes to get ready for morning before I can go to bed so good night— Happy Dreams."

A year later, Sophia sounded more positive. Ben's garden was "wonderful," yielding "turnips, lettuce, radishes, cucumbers and squash by the wheel barrow . . . and we load up everyone that comes from town."[3] Three calves had been born and given British-inspired names: Sir Peter, Sir John Thomas, and Mary Margaret.

The hard work continued: "The dishes are washed for the third time and last, thank Heaven, for today. But tomorrow it will be the same thing over again. If only we didn't have to eat—wouldn't it be joy! Perhaps not to you men who do nothing towards the eats—but eat." That was the most political statement Sophia had ever written to Roy.

Sophia's remedy for male demands on her time was not to march for the National Woman's Suffrage Party but to embrace something

more traditional. After the third growing season came and went, Sophia decided to release herself from further daily duties as Ben's helpmate—for Roy was ready to offer her a different sort of life.

He had always been ready.

At the time of their wedding, Sophia and Roy had been writing to
each other for twenty-three years, beginning with Sophia's letter
mailed in June 1895 complaining of spring rains, telling of dances
and polo matches, flirtatiously inviting Roy to LeMars, and expressing
joy that Ben would soon be home from West Point. To Sophia, the
courtship may have seemed like a meander, the lively teenager with
grand if vague aspirations living singly for many years before marrying a man she had liked in high school.[4] For Roy, the union reflected
years of focus and hope. He had saved every one of her letters, whereas
Sophia did not begin to save Roy's until they became engaged.

"Dear Girl," he wrote from a Rochester hotel in November 1917, as
though going back in time to when he first met Sophia, during her
girlhood visits to Blue Hill.

"I am a lonesome old thing tonight dear," he continued. "Just between you and I, Sunday's [sic] away from home (even though my
home be only a room at the Prince) are not as easy or enjoyable as
they once were."[5]

That room at the Prince George Hotel on 28th Street in Manhattan
would soon be Sophia's home, for Roy planned to "hop off one train
pick up a wife & take another train out of town," as he joked in a letter
written from Detroit a week before the wedding.[6]

It was another one of the O. Henry-like plot twists in Roy and Sophia's history that Roy had arranged to relocate to New York just as
Sophia and Ben were heading west. Consequently, Sophia was marrying a true "Nebraska boy" who now lived in a city she found
"distasteful."

The couple may have spent their engagement apart, but Roy's new
status as fiancé allowed him to begin pouring out his heart. "You
might say why dont [sic] you get acquainted make more friends," he
wrote. "Really my dear most people dont interest me very much unless
I have to do business with them—then I want to know all about them

I can—on the other hand dont suppose I am interesting to other people unless they have business with me."[7]

Roy had always been a loner, and now he asked for Sophia's help. "My good father was different he enjoyed making friends & had 50 where I dont have one—so you must show me how to make & hold friends for your sake," he wrote.

The honesty in Roy's letters is striking. Certainly, Sophia deserved at least that. Her marriage to Roy calls to mind the conclusion of Willa Cather's 1913 novel *O Pioneers!* when, on a Nebraska farm just south of where Roy grew up, Alexandra says to Carl, "I think when friends marry, they are safe."[8]

Considering what an institution charged with keeping people safe had done to Ben, Sophia could hardly be faulted for looking to an old friend for security and companionship. The man who visited a lonely former neighbor in Tacoma, who sent books, nuts, and candy, who traveled across the country time and again hoping to see her presented a good bet to be loyal.

Henry David Thoreau, a famous bachelor, also had a younger sister named Sophia. The name derives from the Greek word for "wise." Like Sophia Koehler, Sophia Thoreau served as a helpmate to her brother, drafting letters for him, illustrating his articles, and reading to him—including on the night before he died.[9] She never left the Concord, Massachusetts, home she shared with him, but on April 2, 1918, Sophia Koehler withdrew the lifeline she had provided to Ben for six and a half years. After a wedding repast in Lizzie's dining room on a Tuesday afternoon, she boarded an evening train to Buffalo with her new husband. From there they would head to New York City and their one-room "home" at the Prince where, at the very least, Sophia would have no kitchen and no obligation to prepare "eats" for anyone.[10]

IT HAD NOT BEEN an altogether easy transition from "brilliant soldier" to farmer for Ben. Seven months before his sister's wedding, he suffered an accident. While helping workers construct Sioux County's first pit silo on his land, Ben slipped and his left hand became caught in the bucket that was hoisting dirt. As the local paper told the story, "he was drawn clear to the top before the hoisting apparatus could be stopped and then had to be lowered to the bottom again in order to loosen his hand. The hand was pretty badly mashed, but no bones were broken, and no other injuries resulted. It was certainly a narrow escape."[11]

A mashed hand was a milder injury than might have occurred had Ben rejoined the Army, which Representative Sloan tried to effectuate by introducing a bill in 1916 to reinstate Ben at his former rank and grade.[12] Sloan had said in 1915 that he hoped the House would rectify the "manifest wrong" done to Ben, and this was his effort to make that happen.

Except that the new secretary of war, Newton Baker, saw no wrong. Asked for comments, Baker wrote that Ben had been tried on "charges alleging specific acts indicating sexual perversion and the approaches of a sexual pervert . . . [T]he sentence was approved by the Secretary of War, Mr. Garrison, and the President of the United States, only after the most careful personal consideration . . ."[13]

"I cannot recommend the passage of the bill for his reinstatement," Baker concluded, prompting Sloan to take to the floor of the House once again, praising Ben's war record, his reforms at Fort Terry, his "looking after the welfare, social and otherwise, of his men," and his curbing of "lewdness and lechery" by others at the post.

"But . . . these men who were being disciplined, with not sufficient activity on their hands to keep them out of mischief, organized a cabal against him," Sloan continued, calling Frick "a lecherous liar" and Worcester "the other leading conspirator." Sloan said Garrison's instruction to Mayes before the investigation that finding for Ben would require court-martialing all the accusers "condemned [Ben] then and there": "Edmund Burke once said that you could not indict a whole people. Neither could you court-martial a whole fort."[14]

Sloan's words sounded strong, but they did not change Ben's situation. His former colleagues deployed to domestic readiness camps while he grew turnips and raised chickens.

Baker, a former city solicitor and prosecutor in Cleveland, also heard from an influential resident of his native city, George Gund of the Gund Brewing Company. "Nothing is clearer than that a great wrong was done Major Koehler in this case," wrote Gund, noting that the Koehlers "are our cousins and I know they have the highest ideals and have been considered among the strongest families of Iowa."[15] Gund continued, "I do hope that you can right this wrong. To us who know him the charge cannot be understood. We feel sure that your investigation will prove our contention, that he is deserving of full and complete reinstatement in the army."

Baker replied that he had reviewed the "voluminous" record "with patient care, and regret to say that . . . I am obliged to conclude that the trial was fair and the conviction justified by the evidence."[16]

Baker wrote that "there seems no possible way to account for so much concurrence" among the sixteen accusing witnesses. "It would have required intricate, elaborate and long continued preparation to work up a conspiracy with so many details, and clearly nobody had a sufficient motive to undertake so serious and fearful a thing."

One wonders how effective a prosecutor Baker could have been with such a marked propensity to underestimate human malice. His letter ignored the jury's rejection of the stories of five accusers, which posited a good way to account for "so much concurrence": lying.

And yet, Baker cited his prosecutorial experience as the reason why he could help the mystified Gund understand his cousin's perversion; for Baker believed his work had made him "familiar with these strange manifestations of sexual repression and inversion." He stated: "Apparently men of the highest culture and of the most refined instincts are sometimes the victims of these impulses, and those who know these men are wholly unable to believe them capable of such conduct."

Baker told Ben's cousin that "these cases are more properly referred to doctors and medical specialists than to punishing tribunals."


IN JULY 1916, WILSON took the unusual step of promoting more than one thousand Army officers. "Never before in the history of this country has a President been able to reward at one stroke so many officers of the land arm of the United States service," wrote *The New York Times*.[17]

Louis Koehler advanced to colonel, as did William Kenly, William Haan, Delamere Skerrett, James Shipton (Ben's replacement at Fort Terry), and Charles Hagadorn (the man sensitive to Russian weather). Richard Ellis rose to major and Edward Putney to captain. Even Frick's former roommate, Raycroft Walsh, finally rose to first lieutenant—a rank Frick had already attained at Fort Monroe, where he worked as a Coast Artillery instructor.[18]

Were he still in the Army, Ben would almost certainly have advanced to lieutenant colonel, if he had not already been promoted.

In May 1917, a month after the United States formally entered World War I, Ben's supporters made another attempt to reinstate him. Hitchcock, the Senate sponsor, wrote to Baker that "there always has been very grave doubt as to the justice of the [court-martial and discharge] and the credibility of the testimony. In any event, he was an able officer with a fine record and on account of the serious doubt I hope the Department will favorably consider a bill authorizing the President to reinstate him."[19]

Baker was unmoved:

> This case has been brought to my attention on more than one occasion and I have carefully and repeatedly examined it's [*sic*] records and can come to no other conclusion than that the sentence awarded was only appropriate for the offense committed, and will be constrained to make an unfavorable report on any bill presented for the restoring of Major Koehler to the army.[20]

What all this meant for Ben, sadly, was that, despite the recanting of an accuser, neither the Chicago detective hired by Daniel Anthony Jr. nor Representative Sloan and Senator Hitchcock had succeeded in helping Ben clear his name.[21]

Of all the men involved in Ben's court-martial, Andy Moses would rise the furthest in rank. Though the Army did not trust him to say what he saw from a distance of a few feet, it elevated Moses all the way to Major General. His long career would not end until his retirement in 1938. He had, indeed, been an "embryo general" back in 1897.

Philip Worcester also did well. Two weeks after Sophia's wedding, with the temporary rank of colonel, Worcester sailed to France by way of England as Ordnance Officer of the 82nd Division. He would go on to receive a Distinguished Service Medal for his administration of ordnance supplies with "untiring energy and loyal devotion to duty" during two offensives.[22]

Austin Frick would eventually attain the rank of major, a long way from being court-martialed for perjury.[23]

If Ben could not fight for his country, he derived some satisfaction in seeing that Leonard Wood's dream was also crushed. Wood did not secure the appointment he coveted as commander of the American Expeditionary Force in Europe. That position went to General John Pershing. "Not only was Wood passed over for command of the AEF," writes Wood scholar Jack Lane, "but he was excluded from any active participation in the war in Europe . . . [F]or an officer who had served long years in anticipation of just such a command as was available in Europe, the period of American intervention was a time of frustration and despair."[24]

Wilson also dealt Theodore Roosevelt a blow, denying his proposal to lead a volunteer unit to Europe the same day Wilson signed the nation's first Selective Service Act and announced that he was sending soldiers to France under Pershing.[25] Though Roosevelt possessed "fine vigor and enthusiasm," he was not, Wilson said, a military expert whose involvement was "calculated to contribute to the immediate success of the war."[26]

Nor did Louis Koehler play the role in World War I he might have liked. A bad knee kept him in the United States. Maude's health was uneven, and the couple never had children, Susan B. Anthony having hinted at an unsuccessful pregnancy early in the marriage.[27] Seeking a warmer climate, Louis and Maude moved to Los Angeles, where they built a house that still stands, and Louis spent the war years training soldiers—soldiers who began World War I under an Army chief of staff whom Louis once accused of negligence toward soldiers' welfare. Despite earlier opposition to his qualifications by Representative Daniel Anthony Jr., Hugh Scott had attained the most senior post in the Army a few months after Ben's dismissal.[28] A Philippine newspaper once opined that Louis's complaints about Scott and Leonard Wood would lead to changes in the "autocracy of rank in the army."[29] It had not exactly worked out that way.


IN 1918, THE ARMY deployed the Fort Terry units to Europe and placed the fort on "caretaker" status. In Iowa, Fort Terry's former commander also felt his status change. Ben felt isolation in a wholly new way. Not being part of World War I was a loss of honor, action, and ambition, but not having a partner with whom to watch the thistle and fleabane bloom was a loss registered in the senses and more acutely experienced. Sophia's departure left Ben newly alone. There was no one to greet him in the morning, no one to read with him in the evening, no one to share the day's disappointments and accomplishments.

In contrast, life was full of fresh possibilities for the new Mrs. Roy Dimmick. New York proved to be her home for only for a short while. Moving around was Roy's specialty, and he managed to extricate himself and his wife from their room at the Prince George within a matter of months. They headed west, past Iowa and Nebraska to the other coast, all the way to Portland, where women had been allowed to vote since 1912.

There, in January 1920, at the age of 43, Sophia gave birth to a son, whom she and Roy named Louis. To have married at 41 was unconventional. To bear a child at 43 was highly unusual—but Sophia carried it off. She came from strong stock, and now Sophia showed what physical strength, determination, and indifference to the negative opinions of others could mean for a woman of her day—or any era. Sophia had spent years caring for her mother and for Ben. Now she would raise her own offspring, though she and Roy proved to be strict parents from Louis's point of view.

Ben became a regular visitor to Portland. He also saw a good deal of Rudolph and their nephew Ben, a son of Barthold, whom Representative Sloan appointed to the Naval Academy in Annapolis—almost as though creating a new military man named Ben Koehler could expunge the injustice done to the first one.[30] If nothing else, this action rewarded Navy football fans, for a touchdown scored by the young Ben Koehler gave them a victory in the 1920 Army–Navy game.[31]

After World War I, military justice became a major issue in Washington. Senators and representatives, saying they had remained mum out of respect to soldiers in action, now publicly castigated Wood, Crowder, and others for a system that, in their view, imposed excessive sentences for trivial offenses and favored discipline over justice.[32]

Sloan had left Congress in March 1919, deciding not to seek a fifth term, or he might have brought up Ben's case once more as an example of military injustice that predated World War I. In early 1918, when another member of Congress pressed for reinstatement of a captain said to have been wrongly convicted, Sloan agreed that "a number of injustices are done some of the best men of America right now." In what was likely a reference to Ben, Sloan went on, "I have one in mind, because the Secretary of War would not do—" but he was cut off by another representative.[33] Apparently, Sloan's colleagues knew what he was going to say.

A star of the congressional hearings in 1919 was Brigadier General Samuel T. Ansell, the acting judge advocate general, "who ruined his military career when he vigorously attacked the harsh system of military justice that existed during and after World War I."[34] Describing a recent court-martial as "one of the unfairest and most illegal of trials," Ansell sparked a discussion among senators on the Committee of Military Affairs that seemed to reprise Ben's case. One senator spoke of how court-martial jurors were not "free agents" when casting their votes if "presided over, we will say, by a superior officer and dominated by a judge advocate determined to convict."[35]

"I can see how it is easy to create an atmosphere of intimidation, particularly where the finding is not in accord with what the controlling influence requires," continued the senator.

One month after Ansell's appearance before the committee, the "controlling influence" in Ben's case, Leonard Wood, lashed out at Ansell and demoted him. It became Wood, Baker, and Crowder on one side, Ansell on the other, splashed across the front pages for weeks. In the end, Congress enacted reforms, such as requiring that all court-martial defendants be provided with counsel. No soldier should have to defend himself, as Louis Koehler had been left to do in Jolo. In Ben's court-martial, a colonel had decided the questions of law, framed on behalf of the Army by a nonlawyer without regard to the rules of evidence. Those practices also met their end. Henceforth, special law officers would rule on legal questions, and the rules of evidence approved for use in civilian courts would be followed. Power dynamics remained intact, however, as did the vaguely written penal articles. Fifty years later, the U.S. Supreme Court would still characterize the court-martial as "not yet an independent instrument of justice but . . . to a significant degree, a specialized part of the overall mechanism by which military discipline is preserved."[36]

Wood had plenty of critics in Congress, but he remained popular with "the upper classes of the big cities and . . . eager young patriots in the colleges" as a result of his preparedness speeches.[37] In 1920, Ben watched from Iowa as Wood sought the ultimate seat of power: the presidency. Roosevelt had died in 1919, and many of his supporters turned to Wood, the angry man's candidate, according to journalist Walter Lippmann, who wrote that Wood appealed to those for whom the war had not gone on "long enough to consume their energy," and whose "hatreds and violence which were jammed up without issue in action against the enemy, turned against all kinds of imaginary enemies—the enemy within, the enemy to the South, the enemy at Moscow, the Negro, the immigrant, the labor union—against anything that might be treated as a plausible object for unexpected feeling."[38]

By that description, Wood had not changed since stalking Geronimo. In 1886, he considered himself the "right sort" of white man to subjugate Native Americans, and now he was running a presidential campaign appealing to others who considered themselves the "right sort." He did not succeed. Although Wood entered the Republican primary with the largest number of committed delegates, more than five hundred delegates were uncommitted, and on the ninth vote the deadlock was broken in favor of Warren Harding, a less controversial candidate.[39] Harding won the general election and gave Wood a taste of his own medicine, sending Wood to the Philippines.

In Iowa, Ben also became involved in government—at a far more modest scale. Having led the Fort Terry hop committee, Ben joined the entertainment committee of Buncombe Township's farm bureau association, sometimes preparing lunches for its members after meetings at his house.[40] He served as a local judge for elections and represented his town at statewide meetings, including as a "road delegate."[41] Improving the streets around Hawarden, with a population of approximately 2,500 in 1920, ranked as small potatoes by Washington standards, but Ben had always shown more concern—and aptitude—for taking care of the environment in which he found himself than expanding his sphere of influence.

Ben did retain one vestige of his time in New York City, and it set him apart: Though he lived in a solid Republican county, he belonged to the Democratic party. When Ben visited Portland one fall, the Hawarden paper reported the resulting lack of a single Democratic vote being cast in his voting precinct on primary day.[42] However, to the surprise of local observers, Ben ran as a Republican in 1928 and won election as a town trustee.[43]

Even with Sophia gone, Ben was not entirely alone. Tenants who helped him manage the farm lived in the second house, about three-quarters of a mile away, but that house burned to the ground in 1921 only two years after Ben had rebuilt it following a fire "of a mysterious origin."

"It would seem that Mr. Koehler is having more than his share of misfortune," the *Hawarden Independent* wrote, noting that Ben had immediately "started hauling lumber . . . for a new dwelling and construction work in this will be pushed with the utmost speed."[44]

By 1921, having lost his military career, reputation, and government-provided home, Ben was accustomed to having "more than his share of misfortune." If Ben suspected arson, perhaps even by a local vigilante aware of his dishonorable discharge from the Army, nothing was ever said of that in the local papers, which wrote of Ben and his property, public service, health, and accidents as if he were any local resident—albeit a Democrat.

Other losses affected Ben around this time. Brother George died in 1918, then Christian in 1921, both in Blue Hill. Ben served as a pallbearer. In 1924, Louis died.[45] The Army gave him an officer's funeral at Arlington National Cemetery, as it had Edgar. Rudolph traveled to Washington for the event—but Ben did not. Apparently, he could not bear seeing all those men in uniform still in the world from which he'd been expelled. He stayed away from the pomp and eulogies for his favorite brother, the person he had tried to emulate, but whose vindication by the Army's disciplinary system had proven to be a tour de force Ben could not repeat.

In 1926, Ben attended the funerals of the two brothers who had intervened in his case, Henry in Missouri and Barthold in Nebraska.

In 1927, Wood returned to Boston to undergo surgery for a brain tumor and died on the operating table. It was a humble death for the doctor-turned-general-turned-presidential aspirant. Like Edgar, who had been deprived of speech by a bullet, Wood could utter no final words.

The Army would not commemorate Wood's legacy in a lasting way until the 1940s, when a basic training post in Missouri became Fort Leonard Wood. Today, the sprawling fort trains thousands of military personnel and civilians each year, with a focus on chemical, biological, radiological, and nuclear capabilities. Ironically, the fort lies only a few miles to the west of the Mark Twain National Forest. Foes in life, the imperialist and the critic are officially immortalized by the U.S. government in large blocks of real estate in central Missouri, positioned like two big eyes, each one watching the other.

Ben's older sister, Lizzie, died in LeMars in 1933, and by that point, Ben had been out of the Army for nearly as long as he had been in it. The "Ben Koehler farm" was now a landmark in Hawarden. He had a quiet life, revolving around land, family, and civic duty, yet it suited

Ben. He had plenty of time to read and to command his small corner of the world without interference.

At the end of 1933, Philip Worcester made his exit from the military and from life itself. Death, the ultimate sentence, imposed itself on Worcester early, at the age of 54. He died at Walter Reed General Hospital from pneumonia complicated by meningitis. Posthumously, the Army promoted him from lieutenant colonel to colonel, the rank he had held in World War I. Worcester received an Arlington funeral. He also received obituaries in *The New York Times* and the West Point annual report, neither of which mentioned his role in the Ben Koehler case.[46]

In 1940, Ben paid a long visit to Portland, the last good time with Sophia and her husband. Sophia had developed an interest in mysticism after taking philosophy courses, and her faith was soon tested, for Roy would die in 1941 and Sophia would be diagnosed with breast cancer. She moved to California to be near old friends from LeMars. They cared for her during a painful and prolonged demise. She died on December 8, 1943, and was buried in Claremont.[47]

It turned out that selling tobacco products had been lucrative. Roy was paid in stock by the American Tobacco Company and he and Sophia were frugal, so Louis Dimmick inherited considerable assets at the age of 23 upon his mother's death. He married a classmate from Pomona College and the couple lived modestly, so that the stock was quite valuable by the time he and his wife, Dorcas, decided to use it. They invested in land in California and did well. Louis also used a significant amount of the stock for philanthropic purposes. Louis's two daughters both graduated from Pomona and then took different paths on different coasts, as though living out two sides of the Koehler legacy. Kathleen became a drama teacher at Bennington College, marrying a playwright and settling in New York City. Mary, the older sister, emulated her great-uncle's comfort with detail in an accounting career and then, like him, found herself drawn to the land. She and her husband started a vineyard in California's Anderson Valley.

Louis rarely spoke to his daughters about Sophia, Roy, or his Uncle Ben. It had been a rather lonely childhood for him, the only child of parents who were much older than the parents of his peers. Sophia had outgrown her desire to "bowl and have a good time," but Louis understood the quiet devotion and drama that underlay his parents' union. Just as Roy had saved all of Sophia's letters, so did Louis, along with the post-engagement letters written by Roy. Louis's daughter Mary found them in a shoebox in her father's office after he died in 2001.[48]

AFTER SOPHIA'S DEATH, BEN's health began failing while another world war proceeded without him, full of reminders of the military life he once lived. The Pacific campaign was led by Douglas MacArthur, son of the general under whom Ben had fought in the complicated archipelago of the Philippines, where he lost a brother and risked his own life carrying out orders to weaken the native people who opposed American domination.

On Plum Island's East Point, where Ben had once cantered, inspecting soldiers and fortifications, the United States built three additional batteries from which a new crop of soldiers waited for signs of enemy torpedo boats. In nearby waters, American submarines practiced torpedo shots, and Air Force pilots honed the accuracy of their bomb drops by aiming at Fort Tyler, no longer habitable due to rising seas around Gardiner's Island Point. In decades to come, as the idea of armed ships sailing into Long Island Sound came to seem more fanciful than threatening, Fort Tyler's remains would attract leisure craft, especially those equipped with fishing rods, for upwelling caused by the confluence of rough and still waters brought many fish to the surface.[49] Terns would colonize the sandy shoals nearby, and long after V-day the darkened cement walls jutting out of the sea would be known by a new name: the Ruins.

JUDGED ON THE BASIS of longevity, Ben's short body had served him well, better than Worcester's tall one by decades. Having survived both loved ones and foes, Ben left the farm in 1944 at the age of 73 and moved into a boxy rental house Rudolph found for him in LeMars on the other side of town from the wealthier enclave in which Ben had spent his adolescence.

Ben knew few people in LeMars, which was a different place from when he was young. Ice cream was the rage, due to the success of a local family named Wells, whose company advertised its Blue Bunny brand with cards that included an illustration entitled "Problem Solvers" that showed a Native American, standing amidst slayed members of his tribe, surrendering to two white men.[50] Louis had fought in the Indian Wars back in the 1880s, and Ben knew that Louis would never have used Native American deaths to sell ice cream.

Ben mostly stayed at home, feeling his age, and on Christmas morning 1946, Rudolph arrived at the house to find Ben dead. He had suffered a cerebral hemorrhage attributed to cardiovascular disease. Just like Sophia, Ben came into the world in January and left it in December, though Ben's tombstone at the LeMars Memorial Cemetery is surely unique in bearing the dates of both New Year's Day and Christmas. Like so much about Ben Koehler, even his tombstone presents him in a false light, chiseling in stone an association between a man whose essence was hard work and two of the year's most celebrated days off.

Ben's remains and his tombstone would have been placed many miles east in Arlington National Cemetery but for some "scoundrels" whose interests differed from his at a brief moment in time on a small New York island. Ben's obituary in the Hawarden paper made no mention of the scandal from long ago, noting only that Ben had graduated West Point and "served in the United States army" until he bought "a farm northeast of Hawarden and lived here until 1944."[51]

One can see the Koehler family plot from the sidewalk, near monuments inscribed with British names, but no one named Koehler lives in LeMars today, and the alumni record for the LeMars High School class of 1889 makes no mention of Benjamin Koehler ever having served in the military. He is described as "retired farmer." On his death certificate, his "usual occupation, industry or business" is given as "Farming own farm."[52]

Sophia and Ben had once agreed that whoever survived the other would receive the whole interest in the farm. On his last trip to Portland, Ben brought a deed giving his share to Sophia but she refused to accept it, and she wound up predeceasing Ben, leaving instructions that her interest should pass to her nieces and nephews in Nebraska.

After Ben's death, her son Louis tried to carry out "Mother's wishes as I understand them," as he wrote to Rudolph, the last of the eleven Koehler siblings still living.[53] In response, Rudolph sent an old photo of Louis and his Uncle Ben along with a letter describing the whereabouts and success of various relatives, including the younger Ben Koehler, whom Rudolph described as "the greatest football player ever at [Annapolis]." All three of Barthold's sons "have done very well and have gathered quite a lot of property." Anthony's son "made a lot of money," and Rudolph reported that his daughter, Wilhelmine, was married, "well cared for," and living in Sioux City.

Obviously capable of bestowing praise, Rudolph offered none for Ben, writing only this: "Looked after Ben for 34 years most of the time and he was some charge."[54]

Dependent on Rudolph for information, Louis found it difficult to ascertain the true status and value of the land, which Rudolph had rented to tenant farmers after Ben moved to LeMars. The situation was complicated by a purported transfer of the farm by Ben to Rudolph when Ben was sick. Louis obtained the help of a Portland lawyer, Paulus Newell, a close friend of his parents.[55] Eventually, Louis and the lawyer succeeded in transferring Sophia's half of the farm in equal thirds to the three people she had specified.

Rudolph rented out the remaining half of the farm until his death in 1958. His estate sold the property to a family of Dutch heritage, who built a house near the one Ben had shared with Sophia. The newer house is where Steve, grandson of the purchasers, lives today, farming Ben's former land and additional acres he owns in South Dakota. His mother Kay lives nearby.

Cats prowl outside the old Koehler house. A fallen tree lies near the barn, which could use some repairs and a coat of paint. It remains very quiet on 420th Street, and the pit silo where Ben injured his hand still stands. A shade tree grows on the hill behind the house, where the stone bench under its thick branches looks like it will last for a long time.

When the new owners took possession, they found old books and pamphlets in the attic of the barn. There were math books, history books, and works on geography, but by far the greatest number concerned military strategy.

Someone told them a colonel once lived in the house.

The books wound up in Kay's cellar, until water damage coated them with mildew and she threw them away. She always presumed that the colonel had fought in the Civil War, until a stranger from New York stopped by one autumn morning. The two women had coffee and spoke of Ben Koehler, the real man, not the one the concocted from spite, bias, and ignorance.

Truth, like all the laws of nature, has a way of surviving.

# Epilogue

THREE YEARS AFTER BEN Koehler's death, the Army regimented discrimination: Class I "aggressive" gay men were subject to general court-martial. Class II active but nonaggressive homosexuals could avoid court-martial by accepting a dishonorable discharge. Class III was the most pernicious. It gave the Army the power to oust a man through general or honorable discharge simply for professing or exhibiting homosexual "tendencies"—the same word Samuel Hudson had used in his closing argument in 1914.[1]

In this way, the government assumed broad authority to say what made a "real man," for unacceptable "tendencies" ranged from physical traits (such as lack of body hair) to emotional ones (any apparent form of weakness, maybe even a penchant for flowers). Decisions were subjective and made without higher review. Meanwhile, in England, fifty-five years after Oscar Wilde's undoing, a brilliant mathematician and codebreaker, Alan Turing, was convicted of homosexuality in 1952. He underwent chemical castration and committed suicide two years later.[2]

Ben Koehler had entered the Army to protect his country from external threats. In the end, for him, domestic attitudes about masculinity and sexuality proved the bigger threat.

"It's bad for the military to kick good people out." That is Sue Fulton's number-one reason for inclusiveness in the armed services.[3] Fulton graduated West Point in 1980 in the first coed class, served in Germany, came out as a lesbian in 1993, and began chairing the U.S. Military Academy Board of Visitors in 2015, the first woman and openly LGBTQ veteran to do so. Her message is simple: "If you're willing to serve your country and you're qualified, other factors don't matter."[4]

It took a while for other leaders to reach the same conclusion.

In 1993, President Bill Clinton altered the rules, beginning the era of Don't Ask, Don't Tell. Ben may have been the first allegedly gay commander to be publicly vilified by the modern federal state, but the pain of many more people inspired Clinton's change, including a woman who became an activist after her son was bludgeoned to death by other soldiers who thought he was gay.[5] In 2010, Congress repealed Don't Ask, Don't Tell at the urging of President Barack Obama, who said it was "time to recognize that sacrifice, valor and integrity are no more defined by sexual orientation than they are by race or gender, religion or creed."[6]

In 2016, the military announced that transgender individuals would be allowed to serve in 2018, and Eric Fanning became secretary of the Army, the first openly gay person to head a branch of the U.S. military.[7]

Even the Boy Scouts changed its policies and its name. The organization founded to dilute the influence of women on boys announced in 2017 that it would begin accepting transgender boys.[8] Then it invited girls and changed its name to "Scouts" before admitting, in 2020, to hundreds of sexual abuse cases.

Such reforms hardly ended LGBTQ discrimination in the military or in society. Although a majority of Americans support LGBTQ rights, President Donald Trump has appointed federal judges "with explicit, unabashed hostility to gay and transgender rights."[9] He also barred trans individuals from military service effective April 2019, despite a finding by the RAND National Defense Research Institute that service by trans individuals in foreign militaries had "no significant effect on cohesion, operational effectiveness, or readiness."[10]

While violence and suicides involving members of the LGBTQ community have increased, sexual harassers and their enablers have started to face serious consequences. In 2016 came the removal of a university president (Ken Starr, Baylor University) for neglecting claims about sexual abuse by other men, and the resignation of a news executive following reports of his own abuses (the late Roger Ailes, Fox News). Then the dam of denial broke in late 2017 under the weight of the #MeToo series of allegations, and the resignation, firing, or suspension of powerful men in Hollywood, New York, or somewhere in between became a regular occurrence.[11] Along with the increased publicity given to women's—and men's—allegations of sexual predation came the defensive claim by some, notably Harvey Weinstein, that they were being falsely accused.

The word "falsity" is a big blanket in this context, covering both instances when the accused admits to physical contact with the claimant but says the contact was consensual, and situations when the accused denies any contact at all—as Ben Koehler did.[12]

As Secretary of War Garrison said in 1913, intentionally false accusations are "reprehensible," but anyone influenced by the myth that women are less trustworthy than men in matters of sexuality must reckon with the coordinated, premeditated "spite work" by sixteen men on Plum Island over a century ago.[13] Nothing alleged by a #MeToo accused against his female accuser(s) comes close to such mendacity.[14]

Today, when cases of male-female sexual misconduct are reported, whether one's instinct is to believe the alleged victim or wrongdoer often depends on whether one sympathizes with patriarchal norms. Yet personal and sociocultural attitudes about gender and sexuality are a poor way for cases to be decided. In an ideal world, each and every person would be treated as an individual, free from stereotypes and preconceptions. In an American courtroom, even a military tribunal, the Constitution requires it.[15]

Since the groundbreaking work of Catharine MacKinnon, it has been recognized that sexual assault and sexual harassment may be more about power than sex, and that for sexual abusers "it is precisely the power imbalance that's erotic."[16] Tarana Burke, founder of

#MeToo, calls "power and privilege" the "building blocks of sexual violence."[17] Priests have power over altar boys, just as studio heads have power over actresses, which brings one back to the real issue underlying the Koehler case: the definition of manhood. What if the definition was not linked to power—or to the "warrior" role?[18]

In *Angry White Men*, Michael Kimmel writes compassionately of American men who "are feeling cheated, unhappy, and unfulfilled," men who "bought the promise of self-made masculinity" only to experience its "foundation . . . all but eroded."[19]

Kimmel's tone turns critical, however, when he writes of the reaction by some: "The game has changed, but instead of questioning the rules, they want to eliminate the other players . . . they fall back upon those same traditional notions of manhood—physical strength, self-control, power—that defined their fathers' and their grandfathers' eras, as if the solution to their problem were simply 'more' masculinity."

Kimmel argues that rather than allowing men to pass on to their children "the same tired and impossible ideals of manliness and the same sense of entitlement," we must recognize the problem "and act both to defuse and to diffuse the anger."

Kimmel wrote his words before the election of Donald Trump, who conducts himself as though he believes that "more masculinity" is just what the nation needs.

Trump's rationale to ban trans individuals from the armed services was the same disproven one used against African-Americans, women, and gays—that they could not do the job and would pose a distraction.[20] The Trump administration has also reversed civil rights policies and rules intended to reduce discrimination against members of the growing LGBTQ community in such essential areas as access to health care.[21] As Jennifer Finney Boylan, a trans woman, wrote in 2019, "There are times—especially since 2016—when all of our progress feels very much at risk. There are times when it feels as if Stonewall were still going on and the battle that began that night can still be lost."[22]

Irrational fear of sexual predation underlies some of the antipathy directed at trans people. A trans high school girl lamented that those who sought to ban her from the women's room had created a "fictional being": a boy masquerading in female trappings who secretly wanted to molest girls and gawk at their nude bodies.[23]

The major said to have fondled penises at Fort Terry was also a fictional being created by the fears and self-interest of others. The tragic irony was that the real Ben Koehler presented the sort of egalitarian officer that Army higher-ups said they wanted, but the definition of "desirable men" needed to change for that to happen. For Wood to complain about a surfeit of autocratic officers was like a trainer teaching a dog to kill and then expressing surprise that the dog did not lay down with lambs.

As Frank Bruni wrote in an essay, neither British nor Mexican men surveyed in a recent study "described a [male] gender construct as musky, musty and unyielding as the one that Americans detailed"—a "Man Box, constricted by a concept of manhood that includes aggression, hypersexuality, and utter self-sufficiency."[24]

If the aggressive, muscular definition of manhood ascended as recently as the late 1800s and early 1900s, it can be retired and replaced—as many men have already done with it. Today's men are "less likely to marry and have children, and when they do, they spend a lot more time with those kids than their dads could've imagined. They spend more time cooking and cleaning, and worry about work-life balance and spiritual fulfillment."[25] In the political sphere, 2019–20 saw the first serious presidential bid by an openly gay man, Pete Buttigieg, who once thought his sexual identity was the "one thing that might have meant that it would be better not to have any aspirations related to politics," but who came to believe it "could be the very thing that anchors the moral and emotional purpose of this entire campaign."[26]

In the study cited by Bruni, 75 percent of 1,300 men between 18 and 30 said "they're supposed to act strong even when scared or nervous," and 63 percent said "they're exhorted to seize sex whenever available." While those figures are high and troubling, many men did not agree with the statements.

Bruni observed that the Man Box has consequences not only for other people and the country but also for those inside it, for the study found that "men who registered narrow, clichéd instructions about manhood were more likely to act out in self-destructive ways, such as substance abuse, and in outwardly destructive ones, such as online bullying."

Perhaps it is not only justice to others that comes from trying to judge each person as an individual but also justice to the self.[27]

The Man Box was being constructed in 1913 and 1914 when Worcester and his "clique" decided they did not want to keep saluting Benjamin Koehler, and today, the target from inside the Man Box has expanded. While harassment and violence are still directed at individuals, anger is also directed at the institutions and laws that protect individual rights.[28] Yet would anyone want to be tried by a court as ruled by stereotypes and manipulation, and lacking in protections for the individual, as the tribunal that convicted Ben Koehler?[29]

Gross injustice ended Ben and Sophia's usefulness to the Army, and changes in methods of war ended the perceived usefulness of Fort Terry to the nation. The United States had bought Plum Island to defend against a foreign foe that never showed up. After World War II, the government decided to use the island to fight another unseen enemy: germs. Fort Terry closed and the Plum Island Animal Disease Center came into being, operated by the Departments of Agriculture and Homeland Security (since 2001) with a focus on preventing hoof and mouth disease from entering the country's meat supplies.[30] Take a ferry across Long Island Sound and you can see the lab buildings from the starboard deck shortly after departing Orient Point. (While you are at it, imagine scared soldiers rowing a boat the same distance to avoid testifying.)

On the east side of the island, the buildings Ben Koehler worked so hard to improve sit decaying, as the federal government contemplates what to do with Plum Island, where more than 220 species of birds have been counted and twenty-five natural communities identified.[31] A coalition of more than 105 organizations seeks to preserve at least 80 percent of the island and open parts for limited public access when the lab moves to Kansas (scheduled for 2023). Others have golf greens and profits in mind, but the coalition contends that the values of history, nature, and public trust ought to prevail.

If the island, or a large part of it, becomes a preserve, visitors could see and smell the sea as their forebears did, imagine the place when Native Americans came to grow corn, chart the stages of the country, perhaps crawl into a tent on the old parade ground and hear waves breaking as soldiers once did. They could learn about Long Island Sound forts and the changing nature of war. They could be introduced to Ben Koehler and learn of the bumpy road toward inclusiveness in the armed services.

Of course, there would have to be refugia off-limits to people—for seals and endangered piping plovers, roseate terns, and other species that rely on the island, much of which has been relatively undisturbed by humans for decades. These creatures need their space away from us. Granting that space, and telling people why, would be consistent with the Ben Koehler story, encouraging respect for what is different—like a bachelor in an era committed to marriage or women who decide not to marry and procreate.[32]

History buffs think the remains of Fort Terry deserve restoration. So does Ben Koehler's reputation. In 1915, Representative Sloan proclaimed to his colleagues, "Justice may not forever sleep. The time may come when this House will be the forum to rectify this manifest wrong." That time has come. Ben Koehler should be pardoned out of respect for his service and suffering, and all the men and women who have ever been vilified, victimized, or dehumanized on account of seeming different.

# ACKNOWLEDGMENTS

Fascination with a place led to this book. Thanks to Nancy Kelley, director of The Nature Conservancy's Long Island Chapter, for assigning me over a decade ago to advocate for Plum Island's protection due to its important role in a magnificent coastal system.

In 2016, my then-colleague Randy Parsons handed me a copy of *A World Unto Itself: The Remarkable History of Plum Island*. Reading the excellent chapter by historian Amy Kasuga Folk about the Koehler court-martial, I was astonished that such a significant, virtually unknown trial had taken place in eastern Long Island. I am grateful to Amy for supporting my effort to add a lawyer's perspective to her work. Amy cared about Ben Koehler's tragic fate in the same way that I did, as a writer trying to get beyond the facts and inhabit the inner world of a man who left scant record of his emotions.

Many thanks to editors David Lamb and Cathy Suter, and other readers who provided valuable feedback: Ruth Ann Bramson, John Lacy Clark, Jennifer Clarke, Chris Elias, Marcy Friedman, Scott Fain, Bruce Horwith, Dan Kornstein, Ann Northrop, and John Turner. Thanks to Gordon Bliss, Chris Zeeman, and Bolling Smith of the Coast Defense Study Group for providing information about Fort Terry. Special thanks to Mary Dimmick Elke, Sophia's granddaughter and Ben's grand-niece, for providing letters, photographs, and recollections. I am grateful to Greg Jacob, an ex-Marine and former advocate for the Service Women's Action Network, who is a tenacious colleague in the effort to preserve Plum Island, as are my friends at Save the Sound, Chris Cryder, Louise Harrison, and Leah Schmalz.

Wayne and June Marty generously led me around LeMars, Iowa. I'll never forget coffee with Kay O. in Hawarden after finding her son in one of his fields across the Iowa border in South Dakota.

My gratitude to Liz Parker, Monica Banks, Philip Schultz, and Mary Landergan for their efforts to see the book published, and to Lucy Cutler, Paul D'Andrea, Stuart Lowrie, Monica Wagner, Peter Strauss, Jeremy Kessler, Logan Schendel, Sally Behr Schendel, and Peter and Suzanne Clifton Walsh for their encouragement and advice. Thanks to Emily Herrick and Michael Denslow for all the dinners and dog walks while I wrote an early draft, and appreciation to my wonderful publisher, Pauline Neuwirth (introduced to me by Priscilla Garston), editor Colin Bertram, and the capable staff of Neuwirth & Associates.

This book would not have been possible without the help of librarians and researchers across the country, who ably steward the records of our past.

Anciently formed Plum Island may have launched the book, but concerns with social justice kept me going. For his example, and all that he taught me the year I was fortunate to clerk for him, I pay tribute to the late Hon. Harold H. Greene, a refugee from Nazi Germany who advanced the fight to end racism as a key drafter of the Voting Rights Act. He made the dignity of every individual central to many acts and decisions as head of the District of Columbia's court system and a federal district court judge. By demonstrating that a public servant could embody the highest ideals, he gave this ex-reporter an enduring foundation for hope.

Last but hardly least, deepest gratitude to my son, Justin Melville DePay, for his creativity, open-mindedness, patience, and love.

# NOTES

## CHAPTER ONE – CROSS-DRESSING FOR HALLOWEEN

1. Transcript, "Trial by General Court Martial at Fort Terry, New York, of Major Benjamin M. Koehler," Record Group 153: Records of the Judge Advocate General's Office (Army), Entry 15: Court-Martial Case Files (July 1894–1917), Box #4637, Court-Martial Case File #84967, date-stamped May 21, 1914, National Archives (hereafter "Koehler Transcript"), 63, 69, 71–72.
2. Worcester said he was wearing bathing trunks. Koehler Transcript, 59.
3. Ibid.
4. Matthew D. Schlesinger, Alissa L. Feldmann, Stephen M. Young, "Biodiversity and Ecological Potential of Plum Island, New York," New York Natural Heritage Program (2012), 4.
5. Koehler Transcript, 763–64.
6. Ibid., 750. The Worcester home was next to the Koehler home, according to a press account. "Koehler's Counsel Charge Conspiracy," *(N.Y.) Sun*, March 5, 1914.
7. Koehler Transcript, 62, 71.
8. Ibid., 725, 727.
9. Ibid., 751.
10. Ibid., 723-24.
11. Ibid., 75.
12. Ibid., 726.
13. Mazhar had been brought to the United States from Egypt in 1893 to perform at the fair. Her "danse du ventre" was "a particularly powerful draw . . . Rumors spread of half-clad women jiggling away, when in fact the dance was elegant, stylized, and rather chaste." Erik Larson, *The Devil in the White City: Murder, Magic, and Madness at the Fair that Changed America* (New York: Vintage Books, 2004), 207-08. Mazhar married a Greek coffeehouse proprietor, moved to Rochester, and protested her depiction in the film *The Great Ziegfeld*, saying her dancing was "neither vulgar nor shocking," nor was she ever "nearly nude." "Little Egypt, Dance Queen of 1893 World's Fair, Dies," *Rochester Democrat and Chronicle*, April 6, 1937. Worcester said he had danced the hoochie-coochie "very many times," but in the "presence of ladies, I did it modestly." Koehler Transcript, 73.
14. Koehler Transcript, 753.
15. Ibid.
16. Ibid., 55, 58.

## CHAPTER TWO – PERVERSION

1. Remarks of Charles Henry Sloan, *Congressional Record*, 63rd Congress, Vol. 52, pt. 2, Jan. 21, 1915, 2188.
2. "Summary of Efficiency Reports," for Koehler, Benjamin M., 1913, entry by Col. John V. White, Coast Artillery Corps, commanding North Atlantic Coast Artillery District, Record Group 94: Records of the Adjutant General's Office, Entry 25: Adjutant General's Office Document Files/AGO Doc. Files (1890–1917), Box #430, Major Benjamin Koehler, AGO Doc. File #58077, National Archives (hereafter "Koehler AGO File").
3. Hugh Ryan, *When Brooklyn Was Queer* (New York: St. Martin's Press, 2019), 24.
4. Michael S. Kimmel, *Manhood in America: A Cultural History*, 4th ed. (New York: Oxford University Press, 2017), 85–86.
5. George Chauncey, *Gay New York: Gender, Urban Culture, and the Making of the Gay Male World 1890–1940* (New York: Basic Books, 1994), 103. "Queer people were coming into focus" after 1910, writes Hugh Ryan. They were being noticed, studied, categorized, and punished. In 1914, a New York City gynecologist "attempted to disentangle what we would call being transgender (which he . . . referred to as transvestitism) from being gay" in an article published in the *New York Medical Journal*, in which he opined that homosexuality was a "morbid sex state" arising from "the crude powerful sensation of sex," whereas transvestitism, defined as a man's desire to wear women's clothing, was an aesthetic preference "found mostly in individuals possessing the so called artistic temperament." According to Ryan, another early commentator who "separate[d] homosexuality from being transgender—sort of" was Dr. Alfred W. Herzog, publisher of the *Medico-Legal Journal*, who in 1918 published a three-volume series about a trans woman, Jennie June, called *Autobiography of an Androgyne*. Ryan states that the first volume was "completed around 1899, but it took her nearly twenty years to find a willing publisher." Herzog wrote an introduction arguing "for a complicated legal approach to queerness, which basically was to allow trans women such as Jennie June to live freely, because it was their nature, but to work to prevent or punish all other forms of queerness." Ryan, *When Brooklyn Was Queer*, 69, 80–83, 88. Concepts and language to express gender identity and sexual orientation continue to expand and evolve.
6. Excerpt of testimony by Joel S. Harris, "Report of the Special Committee of the Assembly appointed to investigate the Public Offices and Departments of the City of New York and of the counties therein," Vol. 2 (Albany: James B. Lyon, 1900), 1429. The committee was a "special legislative body . . . composed of upstate politicians, mostly Republicans" who sought to embarrass New York City's Democratic leaders by portraying the city as a haven for vice and corruption. Jonathan Ned Katz, *Gay American History: Lesbians & Gay Men in the U.S.A.* (New York: Meridian, 1992, originally published by T. Y. Crowell, 1976), 46–47.
7. The author of the report, an inspector named Marcus Braun, "reported on the existence of 'a lively and frequent intercourse between the American and European male prostitutes, as well as among the Pederasts of the two hemispheres.'" Margot Canaday, *The Straight State: Sexuality and Citizenship in Twentieth-Century America* (Princeton, NJ: Princeton University Press, 2009), 19. Braun relied heavily on the story of a German count and military officer who had supposedly paid his male lover turned extortionist to emigrate to the United States.
8. Canaday, *The Straight State*, 22–23. According to Canaday, "relatively few aliens were so policed." Her review of archival records found thirty-one cases in which

foreigners appealed a finding that they should be "excluded or deported for perversion in the first quarter of the twentieth century." While that number omits people who did not appeal, or whose records were lost, it reflects the limited extent of gender policing that the Bureau of Immigration practiced in the early 1900s. The Bureau had a small staff and was only "beginning to have . . . a vague sense of what it was looking for."

9. Canaday, *The Straight State*, 20, quoting comments on Braun's report by Daniel Keefe, commissioner-general of the Bureau of Immigration. The Bureau, created in 1895, succeeded the Office of the Superintendent of Immigration formed by the Immigration Act of 1891. Ibid., 20 n.3, citing G. T. Kurian, ed., *A Historical Guide to the U.S. Government* (New York: Oxford University Press, 1998), 305–8.

10. Canaday, *The Straight State*, 20.

11. Ibid., 21.

12. Ibid., 25 (italics in original). The "public charge" clause would gain attention in late 2019 when the Trump administration began to use it as a basis for denying green cards to immigrants. "'Shoot Them in the Legs,' Trump suggested: Inside His Border War," *New York Times*, Oct. 1, 2019.

13. Canaday, *The Straight State*, 25, 31. Sometimes these traits were ascribed to particular nationalities or races, especially Europeans and Asians. In women, "mannishness" drew suspicion of nonnormative sexual proclivities. Ibid., 30–33. As Ryan notes, the early twentieth century eugenics movement, which held that "social problems were rooted in deviant bodies and inheritable traits," was "trotted out to prove that . . . queer people were a biological dead end that threatened to contaminate good (white) Americans." "Coarse" facial features were among the "surprisingly large number of body parts [that] could communicate unwholesome or downright psychopathic personality traits." The inability to whistle was another indication. *When Brooklyn Was Queer*, 76–77 (describing views held by Dr. Robert Wilson Shufeldt, who wrote about trans woman Loop-the-Loop in 1917, calling her a "passive pederast").

14. "Screening at the border 'was among the very first examples of psychological expertise being deployed by the federal government in an important area of public policy,'" Canaday, *The Straight State*, 21, quoting Ellen Herman, *The Romance of American Psychology: Political Culture in the Age of Experts* (Berkeley: University of California Press, 1996).

15. Canaday, *The Straight State*, 62, quoting Army Special Regulations No. 65, Physical Examination of Recruits, written in 1917 and distributed to draft boards and medical advisory boards in March 1918.

16. Koehler Transcript, 379 (testimony of John Cashman).

17. Koehler Transcript, 1101, 1173. Scholars believe the word "homosexual" originated in a German pamphlet in 1868 and was first used in the United States in 1892. Jonathan Ned Katz, "The Invention of Heterosexuality," *Socialist Review* 20 (January-March 1990), 7–34. Sexual norms changed significantly in the late 1800s/early 1900s, as did medical, political, and social interest in the topic of sexuality. The word "sexy" was coined in 1892, following the appearance of "sexful" in 1890. "Hot Property," *New York Times Magazine*, Jan. 14, 2018, 11. See also George Chauncey et al., "The Historians' Case Against Gay Discrimination," *amicus curiae* brief submitted in *Lawrence v. Texas*, 2002: "[T]he very concept of homosexuality as a discrete psychological condition and source of personal identity was not available until the late 1800s," 2. The word "homosexual" first appeared in the *New York Times* in November 1914. Ryan, *When Brooklyn Was Queer*, 92.

18. Sodomy laws were not enacted as anti-homosexual measures, according to the *amicus* brief referenced in the preceding note filed in the Supreme Court case that invalidated sodomy laws in Texas and thirteen other states in 2003: "In colonial America, regulation of non-procreative sexual practices—regulation that carried harsh penalties but was rarely enforced—stemmed from Christian religious teachings and reflected the need for procreative sex to increase the population. Colonial sexual regulation included such non-procreative acts as masturbation, and sodomy laws applied equally to male-male, male-female, and human-animal sexual activity. 'Sodomy' was not the equivalent of 'homosexual conduct.' It was understood as a particular, discrete, act, not as an indication of a person's sexuality or sexual orientation" (p. 2). Before World War I, there were few prosecutions under state sodomy laws involving consenting adults, and in the nineteenth century, prosecutions under state morals codes were aimed primarily at "predatory men assaulting children, women, and animals" or "people of color and foreign-born individuals, all 'alien' to middle-class WASP America." William N. Eskridge, Jr., *Gaylaw: Challenging the Apartheid of the Closet* (Cambridge, MA: Harvard University Press, 1999, paperback ed., 2002), 19, 159.

19. Article 61 stated that "Any officer who is convicted of conduct unbecoming an officer and a gentleman shall be dismissed from the service." Article 62 stated that "All crimes not capital, and all disorders and neglects, which officers and soldiers may be guilty of, to the prejudice of good order and military discipline, though not mentioned in the foregoing Articles of War, are to be taken cognizance of by a . . . court-martial according to the nature and degree of the offense, and punished at the discretion of such court." *Comparison of Proposed New Articles of War with the Present Articles of War and Other Related Statutes,* (Washington, DC: Government Printing Office, 1912), https://www.loc.gov/rr/frd/Military_Law/pdf/A-W_book.pdf. The articles became sections 133 and 134, respectively, in the Uniform Code of Military Justice adopted in 1951. *Parker v. Levy,* 417 U.S. 733 (1974), 745–46.

20. Daniel J. Kornstein, "Taps for the Real Catch-22," 81 *Yale Law Journal* 1518, 1521, 1524 (1972).

21. Koehler Transcript, 104.

22. Letter from Sophia Koehler to Roy Dimmick, Jan. 22, 1914.

23. Koehler Transcript, 767.

24. Ibid., 116, 142 (testimony of Austin Frick).

25. Kimmel, *Manhood in America,* 4th ed., ix.

26. Stacey M. Robertson, "'Aunt Nancy Men': Parker Pillsbury, Masculinity, and Women's Rights Activism in the Nineteenth-Century United States," *American Studies* 37 (Fall 1996).

27. Kimmel, *Manhood in America: A Cultural History,* 1st ed. (New York: Free Press, 1996), 8.

28. Wrote Whitman of one amputee whom he comforted, "He has suffered a great deal, and still suffers—has eyes as bright as a hawk, but face pale—our affection is quite an affair, quite romantic—sometimes when I lean over to say I am going, he puts his arm round my neck, draws my face down, &C." *Prose Works 1892,* ed. Floyd Stovall (New York: New York University Press, 1963-1964), 1: 32–33, 43, quoted in Jerome Loving, "Caresser of Life: Walt Whitman and the Civil War," *Walt Whitman Quarterly Review* 15 (Fall 1997), 68. https://doi.org/10.13008/2153-3695.1521.

29. This is not to suggest that men suspected of homosexuality had a free pass in America until the late 1800s, or that Whitman's poetry did not raise eyebrows.

As Eskridge points out in *Gaylaw*, 19, "Eminent Bostonians tried to dissuade Walt Whitman from publishing the homoerotic *Calamus* poems as part of the 1860 edition of *Leaves of Grass*, but there was no effort at legal censorship of his 'love of comrades' until 1882."

30. E. Anthony Rotundo, *American Manhood: Transformations in Masculinity from the Revolution to the Modern Era* (New York: Basic Books, 1993), 84; John Ibson, *Picturing Men: A Century of Male Relationships in Everyday American Photography* (Chicago: University of Chicago Press, 2006).

31. "The two were ardently close friends as well as bedmates for more than three years." Rotundo, *American Manhood*, 88. Whether or not Lincoln was gay or bisexual is a matter of debate.

32. Ibid., 85.

33. While people "after the Civil War increasingly noticed gender and sexual non-conformities," arrests for oral or anal sex did not significantly increase until the 1910–21 period. Eskridge, *Gaylaw*, 8, 20, 25. Tolerance of gender fluidity waned elsewhere as well. During Japan's Edo period, which ended in 1868, young men known as *wakashu* were socially approved to have sex with men or women. The practice ended in the second half of the nineteenth century, partly due to western influences. "When Japan Had a Third Gender," *New York Times*, March 11, 2017.

34. Rotundo, *American Manhood*, 6.

35. See *Parker v. Levy*, 417 U.S. 743 (1974), 774 (Stewart, J., dissenting).

36. Chauncey, *Gay New York*, 115–16.

37. Sophia to Roy, Jan. 22, 1914.

### CHAPTER THREE – EMBRYO GENERALS

1. Sophia to Roy, June 11, 1895.

2. "Class of '97, West Point," *New York Times*, June 27, 1897.

3. Ibid.

4. John Pettegrew, *Brutes in Suits: Male Sensibility in America, 1890-1920* (Baltimore: Johns Hopkins University Press, 2007), 198, 200–01.

5. Pettegrew, *Brutes in Suits*, 210. Roosevelt said in 1897 at the Naval War College: "All the great masterful races have been fighting races, and the minute that a race loses the hard fighting virtues, then, no matter what else it may retain, no matter how skilled in commerce and finance, in science or art, it has lost its right to stand as the equal of the best." H. W. Brands, *TR: The Last Romantic* (New York: Basic Books, 1997), 317. In the same speech, he said, "[I]n the last resort we can only secure peace by being ready and willing to fight for it . . . [A] rich nation which is slothful, timid, or unwieldy is an easy prey for any people which still retains those most valuable of all qualities, the soldierly virtues." See also Kristin L. Hoganson, *Fighting for American Manhood: How Gender Politics Provoked the Spanish-American and Philippine-American Wars* (New Haven, CT: Yale University Press, 1998), 35 (publicly expressed concerns that "organized women and their moralistic allies were undermining the manly basis of politics, if not manhood itself"), 62 (male "fraternalism and honor" versus "obsessive pursuit of profit"), 96 ("late-nineteenth-century revival of the Civil War-era belief that military endeavors and manliness were linked").

6. Letter from Alexander Frederick Richmann to Newton Baker, Aug. 1, 1916, Koehler AGO File.

7. Numerous documents in Ben's Army file give his birth year as 1872, as do newspaper accounts. His gravestone, however, states 1871. As Ben was the likely

source of his age in the Army documents, and Rudolph the likely source of the date on the gravestone, the year 1872 is considered more credible.

8. Though Grant's feelings for Galena were ambivalent, its citizens' regard for him was anything but. Local businessmen bought Grant and his family a house in hopes of ensuring at least regular visits by the famous man. Ron Chernow, *Grant* (New York: Penguin Press, 2017), 559.

9. Ibid., 118.

10. "LeMars, Sixth Annual Review of Its Progress by the Sentinel," *LeMars Sentinel*, Jan. 4, 1877, 2.

11. "An Interview with Clyde Kluckhohn," *New York Times*, March 27, 1949.

12. Ibid.

13. It was a "popular advice manual," according to Kimmel, *Manhood in America*, 1st ed., 140.

14. As another Brit put it, "in America there is baseball instead of society." Virginia Woolf, "American Fiction," *Saturday Review of Literature*, Aug. 1, 1925, 1–2.

15. Peter Pagnamenta, *Prairie Fever: British Aristocrats in the American West, 1830–1890* (New York: W. W. Norton, 2013), 198, quoting a letter from Close.

16. Ibid., 197-200, quoting Close's pamphlet distributed in England, "Farming in Northwest Iowa."

17. Ibid., 206.

18. Alumni records of LeMars High School, reviewed at Plymouth County Historical Society, LeMars, Iowa.

19. "[S]issy, pussy-foot, and other gender-based terms of derision became increasingly prominent in late-nineteenth-century American culture, as men began to define themselves in opposition to all that was 'soft' and womanlike.'" Chauncey, *Gay New York*, 114–15, citing John Higham, "The Reorientation of American Culture in the 1890s," in *Writing American History: Essays on Modern Scholarship* (Bloomington: Indiana University Press, 1970). Chauncey notes that in the 1910s and 1920s, "queer culture encouraged . . . an interest in the arts, décor, fashion, and manners that were often regarded by outsiders as effete, if not downright effeminate." Moreover, "pronounced Anglophilia" became "a significant tendency in portions of middle-class gay male culture" to deflect suspicion and present an image starkly different from flamboyant fairies. *Gay New York*, 105–6.

20. Koehler Transcript, 1102.

21. LeMars High School Program, "Graduating and Entering Exercises of the Classes of '88 and '91," May 25, 1888.

22. Willa Cather, *My Antonia* (Boston: Houghton Mifflin, 1918), 7.

23. This district no longer exists since Iowa's 4th and 5th congressional districts were eliminated and merged with the 3rd, https://en.wikipedia.org/wiki/Iowa%27s_5th_congressional_district.

24. Chernow, *Grant*, 19.

25. As Andrew Solomon writes in *Far From the Tree* (New York: Scribner, 2012), 4, "Anomalous bodies are usually more frightening to people who witness them than to people who have them."

26. Sophia to Roy, June 11, 1895.

27. For a discussion of the history of this association, and how the perception of it came to undermine a New Deal social welfare program for transient single men, see Canaday, *The Straight State*, 91–117. Use of "gay" to refer to a homosexual may owe its etymology to the hobo association, as the phrase "gay cat," as far back as 1893, was slang for a young transient who annoyed older wanderers by getting "gay" or "fresh." *Online Etymology Dictionary*, https://www

.etymonline.com/word/gay; Cara, "More Than Words: Gay Pt. 2—Gay Cats," *Autostraddle*, Feb. 10, 2014, https://www.autostraddle.com/more-than-words -gay-pt-2-gay-cats-222847/.

28. "Koehler's Counsel Charge Conspiracy," *(N.Y.) Sun*, March 5, 1914.

29. "Class of '97, West Point," *New York Times*, June 27, 1897. The reference to "survival of the fittest" was typical in the late 1800s, when Darwinian thought greatly influenced American discourse, including the view that "Americans needed to become tougher in order to compete" in international affairs. Hoganson, *Fighting for American Manhood*, 12.

30. Koehler AGO File.

31. *Army and Navy Register*, Aug. 5, 1906, 3–4 (ineligibility of married students initially prescribed by regulation in 1878, then mandated by law in 1892).

32. Henry Koehler to Hon. George D. Meiklejohn, June 5, 1897, Koehler AGO File.

33. John S. Hoover to Sen. John M. Thurston, June 23, 1897, Koehler AGO File.

34. Thurston to the Assistant Secretary of War, June 23, 1897, Koehler AGO File.

35. Oath of office signed by Benjamin Martin Koehler, July 19, 1897, in LeMars, IA, Koehler AGO File.

36. Richard Ellmann, *Oscar Wilde* (New York: Vintage Books, 1988), 477.

37. In Wilde's case, a marquess sought to end a relationship between Wilde and the marquess's son. Wilde's notoriety in the United States is unclear. Citing Thomas Beer, *The Mauve Decade*, (1926), 129, Ellmann writes that in the United States, "at least nine hundred sermons were preached against [Wilde] between 1895 and 1900. *Oscar Wilde*, 548. However, Katz "found few American references to Wilde's trouble." *Gay American History*, 577 n.60.

38. Ellmann, *Oscar Wilde*, 476.

## CHAPTER FOUR – ISLANDS

1. In late May 1898, the *Times* described the "important arrest" on a steamer off Key West, Florida, of a Spaniard "supposed to have obtained information concerning New York Harbor and its defenses, with charts of the harbor, which he is attempting to get to the Spanish authorities." "Spy Caught at Key West: Alleged that He Was Carrying Information About New York City's Defenses to the Spanish," *New York Times*, May 25, 1898. The next day, the *Times* updated its New York-centric story when the charts turned out to pertain to the entire Atlantic coast. "Spanish Spy an Officer," *New York Times*, May 26, 1898.

2. As the *Times* wrote, "The general discussion of the possibility of war with Spain has caused considerable uneasiness among many of the seashore residents, especially those who have Summer cottages to let, as it has had a tendency to put somewhat of a damper on the leasing of them for the coming season." "One Effect of War Talk: Renting of Cottages on the New Jersey Coast Put Back— Some of Those Already Taken," *New York Times*, March 14, 1898.

3. The Endicott Report, commissioned at the behest of Congress, had warned in 1886 that the country's coastal defenses were weak and outdated and recommended massive investment in twenty-seven ports. Ruth Ann Bramson, Geoffrey K. Fleming, and Amy Kasuga Folk, *A World Unto Itself: The Remarkable History of Plum Island, New York* (Southhold, NY: Southold Historical Society, 2014), 136.

4. "New York Cedes Plum Island: To be Used by the United States as a Site for Fortifications," *New York Times*, Sept. 15, 1897. The first purchase consisted of 193 acres. Bramson et al., *A World Unto Itself*, 137.

5. Hoganson, *Fighting for American Manhood*, 51. Cuban rebels had a public relations office in New York and "received priceless support from the American yellow press, which played the plight of suffering Cuba for all it was worth . . . " Brands, *TR*, 311.
6. Hoganson, *Fighting for American Manhood*, 54, 61.
7. Ibid., 10.
8. Jack C. Lane, *Armed Progressive: General Leonard Wood* (Lincoln: University of Nebraska Press, 1978, paperback ed., 2009), 25; James Bradley, *The Imperial Cruise* (New York: Back Bay Books, 2009), 70–71.
9. Hoganson, *Fighting for American Manhood*, 46–54.
10. Ibid., 47, quoting Rep. John S. Williams, May 20, 1897. Williams was lamenting what historians refer to as a shift from "producer manhood" to "consumer manhood," resulting from a variety of economic and social forces including changes in the means of production, from independent small businesses to factories, and the rise of mass marketing by brand-building companies.
11. Ibid., 45. In the 1800s, that system was called "chivalry," whereas today it is "misogyny" in the lexicon of philosopher Kate Manne, who posits that "misogyny, though often personal in tone, is most productively understood as a *political* phenomenon," i.e., "the system that operates within a patriarchal social order to police and enforce women's subordination to uphold male dominance." Whereas sexism provides the ideology or purported justification for treating women as inferior to men, misogyny "should be understood primarily as the 'law enforcement' branch of a patriarchal order" operating in nasty, belittling, shaming ways. Manne, *Down Girl: The Logic of Misogyny* (New York: Oxford University Press, 2018, paperback ed., 2019), 33, 79.
12. Hoganson, *Fighting for American Manhood*, 83, 153.
13. "There are even wisps of evidence that [Roosevelt] was a devotee of recapitulation theory: a belief, propounded by a professor of pedagogy and psychology, G. Stanley Hall . . . that 'overcivilization was endangering American manhood.' According to Hall, American boys were becoming effeminate and needed to return to primitivism instead of wallowing in Victorian-era 'ideologies of self-restrained manliness.'" Brinkley, *The Wilderness Warrior*, 349.
14. Kimmel, *Manhood in America*, 1st ed., 121, referring to Rabbi Solomon Schindler and noting that "[p]ercentages of women teachers were even higher in major cities." On average, women occupied three-quarters of the school teaching jobs in 1900, four-fifths in 1910.
15. Kimmel, *Manhood in America*, 4th ed., 94. As Virginia Woolf put it, "The Suffrage campaign was no doubt to blame [for men becoming 'stridently sex-conscious']. It must have roused in men an extraordinary desire for self-assertion." *A Room of One's Own* (London: Harcourt Brace Jovanovich, 1929, Harvest/HBJ Book ed.), 103.
16. Kimmel, *Manhood in America*, 4th ed., 105.
17. Chauncey, *Gay New York*, 47.
18. A cartoon in the *New York Journal* "depicted McKinley in a bonnet and apron futilely trying to sweep back a stormy sea convey[ing] the . . . conviction that if the president countered the will of American men, he would become as politically potent as a feebleminded old woman." Hoganson, *Fighting for American Manhood*, 103–4.
19. Brinkley, *The Wilderness Warrior*, 312; Hoganson, *Fighting for American Manhood*, 95.
20. Theodore Roosevelt, *The Rough Riders* (Charles Scribner's Sons, 1899, republished by Corner House Publishers, Williamstown, MA, 1971), 3. See also Lane,

*Armed Progressive*, 26, quoting from a letter Roosevelt wrote to his daughter Alice, June 18, 1897, found in Elting E. Morison, ed., *The Letters of Theodore Roosevelt*, I:628 (Cambridge, MA: Harvard University Press, 1954) (describing Wood's stories as "harassing beyond belief").

21. Roosevelt, *The Rough Riders*, 1, 3–5.
22. Ibid.
23. "By 1890, one in six of the labour force was a woman; by 1900, nearly one in five." Andrew Sinclair, *The Emancipation of the American Woman* (New York: Harper Colophon Books, 1965), 172.
24. Eleanor Flexner, *Century of Struggle: The Woman's Rights Movement in the United States* (New York: Atheneum, 1973, originally published by Harvard University Press, 1959), 224–225. The suffrage amendment passed except in San Francisco, Oakland, and Alameda, where the liquor vote prevailed. A "change of 13,400 votes would have put California in the suffrage column in 1896."
25. Hoganson, *Fighting for American Manhood*, 30.
26. For a discussion of early women's suffrage in western states, see Sinclair, *The Emancipation of the American Woman*, 204–19.
27. Sophia graduated from the University of Nebraska, Lincoln, in February 1902 with an A.B. Alumni Directory, University of Nebraska, Graduates 1869–1912 (Lincoln, NE: Lincoln Publishing Co., 1912), 91. "Personal," *LeMars Semi-Weekly Post*, Feb. 21, 1902. Only two percent of people aged 18–24 went to college in 1899–1900. Of that small number 36 percent were women. *120 Years of American Education: A Statistical Portrait* (National Center for Education Statistics, 1993), 67. Some men regarded a woman's interest in higher education as a sign of lesbianism. Ryan, *When Brooklyn Was Queer*, 68.
28. "What a tempestuous life he has had," Susan B. Anthony wrote of Daniel years later when he was ill, "and his death seems to be equally so—It is to [*sic*] bad we have to suffer so to get out of this world." Susan B. Anthony to Maud Anthony Koehler (Rochester: Nov. 7, 1904) (courtesy Central Library of Rochester and Monroe County—Susan B. Anthony Letters Collection). Anthony spelled her niece's name her own way—Maud—even though her niece used Maude.
29. Susan B. Anthony to Jessie Anthony (Rochester: Oct. 29, 1904), 2 (Library of Congress, Susan B. Anthony Papers).
30. Susan B. Anthony to Maud Anthony Koehler (Rochester: May 29, 1897) (underscoring in original) (courtesy Central Library of Rochester and Monroe County—Susan B. Anthony Letters Collection). Even to a close relative, Anthony signed her full name: "Well with lots & lots of love—I am as ever Your affectionate aunt - Susan B. Anthony."
31. Ibid. (underscoring in original). Anthony's three-story brick home at 17 Madison Street, Rochester, NY, is now the National Susan B. Anthony Museum and House, surrounded by the Susan B. Anthony Historic Preservation District.
32. Denigration of men who supported women's rights went back to the Seneca Falls Convention, when Frederick Douglass and other male supporters were called "Aunt Nancy Men," "manmilliners" and "Miss-Nancys." Kimmel, *Manhood in America*, 4th ed., 60–61; Robertson, "'Aunt Nancy Men.'" As Robertson writes, when Parker Pillsbury, Susan B. Anthony, and Elizabeth Cady Stanton began publishing a women's rights newspaper called *The Revolution* in 1868, "the popular press attacked the radicals' sexual identity in an effort to reinforce the traditional gender roles which the women's rights movement openly challenged." Robertson, "'Aunt Nancy Men,'" 33. "Such a debate illustrates a theme we encounter again and again throughout American history," writes Kimmel. "Support for feminism or civil rights has been seen as an indication

that a man is less than manly—as if support for inequality somehow made one *more* of a man." *Manhood in America*, 4th ed., 61.

33. Whereas mid-1800s suffragists—mostly white, privileged women—had stressed their similarity to men consistent with the "natural right" basis for equality, in the late 1800s, "new arguments for suffrage evolved, emphasizing the ways in which women differed from men." Those differences included "the reforms that women voters could effect." Aileen S. Kraditor, *The Ideas of the Woman Suffrage Movement 1890-1920* (Garden City, NY: Anchor Books, 1971, originally published by Columbia University Press, 1965), 38–39.

34. LeMars High School Program, "Graduating and Entering Exercises of the Classes of '88 and '91," May 25, 1888.

35. The *Maine* was one of the Navy's best midsize battleships. Spain had agreed to the ship's arrival in Havana with the goal of easing tensions with the United States. Brands, *TR*, 250.

36. *The World*, Feb. 17, 1898.

37. *New York Journal*, Feb. 17, 1898.

38. Carl Schurz, quoted in Kimmel, *Manhood in America*, 1st ed., 112.

39. Pettegrew, *Brutes in Suits*, 200–21.

40. "Increase of the Artillery," *San Francisco Call*, March 8, 1898.

41. "B.M. Koehler, Succinct Account of Services," Koehler AGO File, signed oath of office and letter accepting commission as 2nd lieutenant for artillery, Ft. McHenry, April 8, 1898, Koehler AGO File.

42. After a Republican called a Democrat "a liar" and the Democrat "hurled" a book in response, spectators "screamed" as members "ran . . . and crowded up the adjoining aisles, clinching, tugging, hauling at each other like madmen. It was like free fight in the street." "Blows Averted in the House," *New York Times*, April 14, 1898.

43. Historian Richard J. Barnet points to the Spanish-American War as an example of "popular support for decisions taken by a handful of government officials [being] swiftly and skillfully engineered." Barnet, *Roots of War: The Men and Institutions Behind U.S. Foreign Policy* (Baltimore: Penguin Books, 1971), 243.

### CHAPTER FIVE – MOCK BATTLE, REAL DEATH

1. "Astor Battery Nearly Filled," *New York Times*, May 31, 1898; Justin Kaplan, *When the Astors Owned New York* (New York: Penguin Books, 2016, originally published by Viking, 2006), 134.

2. "Astor Battery Nearly Filled," *New York Times*, May 31, 1898.

3. Untitled dispatch with Washington dateline, *New York Times*, May 31, 1898.

4. Roosevelt, *The Rough Riders*, 1. Roosevelt first inquired about a commission in the New York State militia but "there were no vacancies." Ibid., 6. In early May, after McKinley authorized three new federal regiments of volunteers and the secretary of war requested "frontiersmen possessing special qualifications as horsemen and marksmen," Roosevelt "leaped at the opportunity" and resigned as assistant secretary to join. Roosevelt and Leonard Wood received authorization to form the First United States Volunteer Cavalry, with Wood in command and Roosevelt a lieutenant colonel. Roosevelt declined to take the lead due to his lack of military experience. Brinkley, *The Wilderness Warrior*, 312–13.

5. "The Astor Battery Home," *New York Times*, Jan. 23, 1899.

6. Ibid.

7. Reports by Commanding Officers, filed with Efficiency Record of Koehler, Benjamin M., Koehler AGO File.

8. Efficiency Record of Koehler, Benjamin M., Koehler AGO File.

9. "[T]he characteristics of the damage are consistent with a large internal explosion" likely caused by a fire in a coal bunker, wrote a Navy admiral after an analysis by ship and weapons experts. "There is no evidence that a mine destroyed the Maine." H. G. Rickover, "How the Battleship Maine Was Destroyed," 1976, excerpts available at http://people.usm.maine.edu/rklotz/rickover.htm.

10. Hoganson, *Fighting for American Manhood*, 141.

11. "The Astor Battery Home," *New York Times*, Jan. 23, 1899.

12. Handwritten note to "Maj. Johnston," presumably John Alexander Johnston as the initials "J.A.J." follow the "Yes." Koehler AGO file.

13. Special Orders, No. 14, Headquarters of the Army, Adjutant General's Office, Jan. 18, 1899, Koehler AGO file.

14. In December 1898, Koehler asked to remain in the Philippines with Light Battery D although his official assignment, Light Battery F, meant he should return to New York. "Koehler did not return with the Astory battery!" wrote a headquarters officer in January 1899, suggesting that early in his career, Koehler showed more concern with field demands than protocol. The Army went along, revoking its order and assigning him to Battery D. Koehler AGO file, Document #191401.

15. Risen, "The Rough Riders' Guide to World Domination," *New York Times*, June 2, 2019, Week in Review.

16. Hoganson, *Fighting for American Manhood*, 134–35.

17. Ibid., 165.

18. Ibid., 141.

19. Ibid. See generally Chapter 7, "The National Manhood Metaphor and the Fight over the Fathers in the Philippine Debate," 156–79.

20. Ibid., 179.

21. Ibid., 139.

22. "Has been engaged in all expeditions which I have commanded," wrote Lawton. AGO Doc. #282942, Koehler AGO File.

23. Hawthorne to Adjutant General, First Division, Eighth Army Corps, June 23, 1899, Koehler AGO file.

24. Koehler Transcript, 742.

25. B. M. Koehler to Adjutant General, Aug. 12, 1899, Koehler AGO file.

### CHAPTER SIX – THREE SONS AT RISK

1. Richmann to Baker, Aug. 1, 1916.

2. "Died," *[LeMars] Evening Sentinel*, Sept. 5, 1885.

3. Ibid.

4. "Pioneer Woman Dead," *LeMars Semi-Weekly Sentinel*, June 23, 1911.

5. Elizabeth Koehler Struble to Roy Dimmick, Jan. 21, 1913.

6. See, e.g., "Gordon Gund," Greater Cleveland Sports Hall of Fame, http://www.clevelandsportshall.com/gund-gordon/; "The Museum of Modern Art Elects New Officers/Agnes Gund Named Chairman," Museum of Modern Art press release, Nov. 10, 1993, https://www.moma.org/momaorg/shared pdfs/docs/press_archives/7201/releases/MOMA_1993_0108_66.pdf; "Agnes Gund, Arts Patron and President Emerita, Museum of Modern Art: Grooming the Next Generation of Arts Leaders," *Philanthropy News Digest*, Oct. 28, 2008, https://philanthropynewsdigest.org/newsmakers/agnes-gund-arts-patron -and-president-emerita-museum-of-modern-art-grooming-the-next-generation -of-arts-leaders.

7. "Meets His Death," *LeMars Semi-Weekly Sentinel*, March 8, 1900.

8. Letter from Wendell L. Simpson to commanding officer, 9th U.S. Infantry (Fort Trumbull, CT: Nov. 18, 1898), National Archives. Record Group 94: Records of the Adjutant General's Office, Entry 25: Adjutant General's Office Document Files/AGO Doc. Files (1890–1917), File of Edgar Koehler ("Edgar Koehler File").

9. Ibid.

10. Ezra P. Ewers, 1st Division brigade commander, wrote that Edgar "remained mounted thus making the services rendered most frought and effective." Ewers to Secretary of War (San Luis, Cuba: Feb. 12, 1899), Adelbert Ames, brigadier general of the Volunteer Army, wrote, "I most urgently recommend Lieutenant Edgar F. Koehler . . . to be made a Captain and Asst. Quartermaster, U.S. Army." Ames to Secretary of War, (Camp Wikoff, NY: Aug. 18, 1898). "Lieutenant Koehler's action on this occasion, as being the only officer that ascended San Juan Hill mounted, not only exposed him to the fire of the enemy as a particular object, but by being mounted enabled him to move with rapidity to points where he was ordered, to assist in the direction of the troops charging the enemy on the hill," wrote Colonel William Powell, commander of Edgar's regiment, in his recommendation that Edgar "be awarded a Gold Medal for conspicuous gallantry and fearless intrepidity" that "distinguished him above others." Powell to Army Adjutant General, Washington, DC (Madison Barracks, NY: Nov. 23, 1898), Edgar Koehler File.

11. Colonel Charles Wikoff was the brigade commander killed early in the battle.

12. Roosevelt, *The Rough Riders*, 134.

13. Lane, *Armed Progressive*, 282 n.39, quoting Margaret Leech, *In the Days of McKinley* (New York, 1959), 250–51.

14. Roosevelt was awarded a Medal of Honor posthumously in 2001.

15. Nellie Powell Koehler to McKinley, Aug. 23, 1899, Edgar Koehler File.

16. Lawton was the highest-ranking officer to die in the Spanish-American and Philippine wars. His promotion to brigadier general took effect the day of his death.

17. Letter from John M. Sigworth, Capt. 9th Infantry, to Adjutant General, Washington, DC (Tarlac, the Philippines: March 4, 1900), Edgar Koehler File ("Sigworth Letter"). See also "Officer Killed in Ambush," *New York Times*, March 7, 1900; "Meets His Death," *LeMars Semi-Weekly Sentinel*, March 8, 1900.

18. Sigworth Letter. Sigworth ordered his men to kill the twenty-seven detained Filipinos. The Americans also burned the barracks they discovered in the forest and lit fire to the entire barrio after permitting residents to remove their belongings. In answer to questions from Washington, Major General Elwell Otis wrote that while "Action of this character is not encouraged . . . [t]he treachery practiced by the guerrilla bands and the consequent barbarities suffered by some of our troops merit an occasional severe retaliatory punishment." Elwell S. Otis, Major Gen., US Volunteers, 2nd endorsement to Sigworth Letter, March 8, 1900, Edgar Koehler File. See also "Meets His Death," *LeMars Semi-Weekly Sentinel*, March 8, 1900.

19. Telegram from Margaret Koehler to Secretary of War (LeMars, IA: March 6, 1900, 11:30 a.m.). A handwritten note on the Army's copy states: "Telegram was sent her before this was received." Edgar Koehler File.

20. "Meets His Death," *LeMars Semi-Weekly Sentinel*, March 8, 1900.

21. Mark Twain, *New York Herald*, Oct. 15, 1900.

22. Twain castigated the United States for having played "the European game,"

which was "to send out an army—ostensibly to help the native patriots put the finishing touch upon their long and plucky struggle for independence, but really to take their land away from them and keep it." Mark Twain, "To the Person Sitting in Darkness," *North American Review*, Feb. 1901, 169, 171, https://archive.org/details/jstor-25105120.

## CHAPTER SEVEN – SINGLE IN SAN FRANCISCO

1. Edith Huntington Makes Formal Debut at Brilliant Ball Given in Her Honor," *San Francisco Call*, Jan. 25, 1902.
2. "Brilliant Wedding," *Los Angeles Herald*, Dec. 16, 1902.
3. Alice Roosevelt Longworth, *Crowded Hours* (New York: Charles Scribner's Sons, 1933), 72, as quoted in Bradley, *The Imperial Cruise*, 20.
4. Bradley, *The Imperial Cruise*, Chapter 3; Howard Jones, *Crucible of Power: A History of American Foreign Relations to 1913* (Lanham, MD: Rowman & Littlefield, 2009), 165.
5. Clare Sears, *Arresting Dress: Cross-Dressing, Law, and Fascination in Nineteenth-Century San Francisco* (Durham, NC: Duke University Press, 2015), 29.
6. Ibid., 32–33, reproducing cartoon from *San Francisco Examiner*, Inaugural Ball Supplement, Jan. 29, 1895.
7. Ibid., 32.
8. The law stated: "If any person shall appear in a public place in a state of nudity, or in a dress not belonging to his or her sex, or in an indecent or lewd dress, or shall make any indecent exposure of his or her person, or be guilty of any lewd or indecent act or behavior, or shall exhibit or perform any indecent, immoral or lewd play, or other representation, he should be guilty of a misdemeanor." San Francisco Board of Supervisors, Revised Orders of the City and County of San Francisco, quoted in Sears, *Arresting Dress*, 42.
9. Ibid., 38.
10. Eskridge, *Gaylaw*, Appendix A2, 338–41. Sears states that San Francisco adopted the law in 1863; Eskridge says 1866. Either way, San Francisco was the first western city to ban cross-dressing by well over a decade, based on Eskridge's table of municipal ordinances, which shows Oakland as the next western city to do so, in 1879.
11. Sears, *Arresting Dress*, 57.
12. Hoganson, *Fighting for American Manhood*, 154.
13. Nan Alamilla Boyd, *Wide Open Town: A History of Queer San Francisco to 1965* (Berkeley: University of California Press, 2005), 27.
14. Ibid., 26.
15. Ibid.
16. "Soldiers and Veterans Ready," *San Francisco Chronicle*, May 31, 1902.
17. "Smashes Target into Splinters," *San Francisco Call*, Jan. 9, 1903.
18. Ibid.
19. "Provost Guard Stopped a Riot," *San Francisco Chronicle*, March 28, 1902.
20. Boyd, *Wide Open Town*, 28
21. Sears, *Arresting Dress*, 111–12.
22. Ibid., 115–16.
23. Chauncey, *Gay New York*, 36–37. Chauncey notes that slumming was a popular activity "among middle-class men (and even among some women), in part as a way to witness working-class 'depravity' and to confirm their sense of superiority." For a fuller discussion of slumming and how it was mostly wealthy white tourists and residents who were shepherded through poor and

working-class neighborhoods, see Chad Heap, *Slumming: Sexual and Racial Encounters in American Nightlife, 1885-1940* (Chicago: University of Chicago Press, 2010).

24. Chauncey, *Gay New York*, 44–45. He writes that "At a time when New York was a notoriously 'wide-open' city, 'degenerate resorts' and 'fairy back room saloons' were a highly visible feature of the city's sexual underworld, spotlighted by the press and frequented by out-of-town businessmen and uptown slummers alike . . . One investigator reported seeing some seventy-five fairies at a single saloon in 1901."

25. By 1900, twenty-eight cities forbade cross-dressing. By World War I, the total was more than forty—but not New York, where state law "made it a crime to wear a mask or costume *only* while attempting to commit another crime." Ryan, *When Brooklyn Was Queer*, 86. See also Sears, *Arresting Dress*, 4; Eskridge, *Gaylaw*, 27. Nonetheless, police did sometimes make arrests for cross-dressing in New York in the 1910s, such as the arrest of Elizabeth Trondle wearing a "natty blue serge suit and trousers" in a Brooklyn saloon in 1913. The judge told the arresting officer, "It is no crime for a woman to dress in any attire she desires unless to commit a crime." Ryan, *When Brooklyn Was Queer*, 84–86. On his night in jail, Trondle drafted a letter to President Wilson asking for a "permit" to "appear as a man and do man's work," which Trondle shared with the judge the next day. The letter was published in newspapers around the country "taking Trondle from local news to nationwide infamy overnight."

26. Sears, *Arresting Dress*, 92.

27. Ibid.

28. Presidio Treatment Record No. 6221 (Feb. 26–March 14, 1901, "Bronchitis, acute"), Presidio Treatment Record No. 13419 (Nov. 9–15, 1901, "Fever malarial intermittent tertian"), Presidio Treatment Record No. 15159 (April 29, 1902, "fistula in ano," transferred for operation to Army General Hospital), Presidio Treatment Record No. 11348 (April 29–May 9, 1902, "fistula in ano"), Koehler AGO File.

29. "Personal," *LeMars Semi-Weekly Post*, April 1, 1902; "Personal," *LeMars Semi-Weekly Sentinel*, Oct. 21, 1902.

30. "Society," *San Francisco Chronicle*, April 22, 1903. Among his other activities in San Francisco, Ben served on a court-martial jury and served as an usher in an Army wedding. "Army Orders," *San Francisco Chronicle*, July 24, 1902; "Exchange Vows in Christ Church," *San Francisco Chronicle*, June 10, 1903.

31. Koehler Transcript, 314, 320.

32. Ibid., 812, 1055.

33. Sophia to Lucile Dimmick, July 7, 1911 (underscoring in original).

### CHAPTER EIGHT – PLUM ISLAND

1. Bramson et al., *A World Unto Itself*, 11.

2. Ibid., 9–11.

3. Jason Epstein and Elizabeth Barlow, *East Hampton–A History & Guide* (New York: Random House, 1985, originally published by Medway Press, 1975), 16; *Between Ocean and Empire: An Illustrated History of Long Island*, ed. Robert B. MacKay, Geoffrey L. Rossano, and Carol A. Traynor (Northridge, CA: Windsor Publications, 1985), 20–21.

4. *Between Ocean and Empire*, 21. However, the Montauketts began paying tributes to the British after the defeat of the Pequots. Epstein and Barlow, *East Hampton*, 16.

5. Epstein and Barlow, *East Hampton*, 15. It is also said that Wyandanch gave the island to Gardiner in appreciation for Gardiner's rescue of Wyandanch's daughter after she was taken prisoner by a rival tribe. The island remains in the Gardiner family, the oldest continuous land grant in the United States. Cora Simons, "A Guide to Local Place Names," *The Gazette* (Amagansett, NY), 1993–94, 6. The Town of East Hampton holds a conservation easement limiting development on the island. "An American Eden: Gardiners Island in the Age of the Goelets," *Avenue on the Beach*, Aug. 2013, 93.

6. John A. Strong, "The Plum Island Deed Game: A Case Study in the Dispossession of Indian Land on Long Island," *Journal of the Suffolk County Historical Society*, Vol. 31, Dec. 2017, 3, 5–6. Strong notes scholars' conclusions that "Indians considered these transactions to be ceremonial, sealing an alliance with the English that might serve as a basis for trade and military support in the future [citations omitted]. The land was a reciprocal gift given by the Indians for the use of the English." Native Americans did not realize that for the British, "use" meant exclusivity.

7. Bramson et al., *A World Unto Itself*, 20. According to Strong, a Corchaug had previously purported to sell Plum Island to Governor Theophilus Eaton of New Haven but stood silent in 1659 when Wyandanch told local officials that the land was his to sell. The British had declared Wyandanch the "grand" or "chief" sachem in eastern Long Island largely to settle such intertribal disputes over land grants. Strong, "The Plum Island Deed Game," 9–10, 12.

8. Bramson et al., *A World Unto Itself*, 20, 22.

9. Ibid., 34–35.

10. Ibid., 60.

11. Ibid., 87–99.

12. Ibid., 70–73.

13. Pastors refused to wed the couple. "Refused Astor's $10,000; Pastor Offered This to Wed Him, Says Bishop Hamilton," *New York Times*, Sept. 23, 1911; "Pastor is Congratulated: Clergyman Who Refused to Marry Astor Gets Approving Messages," *New York Times*, Sept. 8, 1911. The Astors sought to evade the disapproval by traveling to Europe and down the Nile on a houseboat. Madeleine Talmage Force Astor would survive the *Titanic*'s sinking in 1912—her pregnancy was the reason for the couple returning home—but for Astor the escape to Europe proved to be a one-way trip. "The Tragedy of the Titanic—A Complete Story," *New York Times*, Special Section, April 28, 1912; "Astor Lives and Astor Wives, Part II," *New York Social Diary*, July 27, 2006, http://www.newyork socialdiary.com/social-history/2006/astor-lives-and-astor-wives-part-ii; Kaplan, *When the Astors Owned New York*, 159.

### CHAPTER NINE – GRUDGES TAKE HOLD

1. Koehler Transcript, 394.

2. Robert J. Hefner, Historic Resources Survey, Plum Island, New York, Vol. 5, Appendix B ("Resources Associated with Fort Terry/Post Buildings"), prepared for U.S. Dept. of Agriculture, 1998; War Department, O.Q.M.G. reports for Fort Terry (provided by Gordon Bliss, Coast Defense Study Group).

3. See, e.g., Michael C. Carroll, *Lab 257: The Disturbing Story of the Government's Secret Germ Laboratory* (New York: HarperCollins, 2005); "Plum Island Animal Disease Research Center," Dept. of Homeland Security website, https://www.dhs.gov/science-and-technology/plum-island-animal-disease-center.

4. Tom Migdalsk, "Plum Gut," *The Fisherman*, Dec. 2, 2018, https://www.the

-fisherman.com/index.cfm?fuseaction=feature.display&feature_ID=1029& ParentCat=8.

5. Sophia to Roy, Jan. 20, 1912 (dated 1911 by Sophia but 1912 postmark).
6. Sophia to Roy, March 27, 1908.
7. Sophia to Roy, Jan. 20, 1912.
8. Koehler Transcript, 548.
9. Ibid., 545–46, 799.
10. Ibid., 549.
11. Ibid., 802.
12. Ibid.
13. Ibid.
14. Ibid., 800.
15. Ibid., 273–74.
16. Ibid., 386–88.
17. Ben said he was told that "Sergeant Barrett thought I had it in for him." Ibid., 801.

### CHAPTER TEN – A CHILL IN THE AIR

1. Sophia to Roy, Sept. 30, 1912.
2. Ibid.
3. Koehler Transcript, 767.
4. Sophia to Roy, Sept. 30, 1912.
5. Koehler Transcript, 985, 1047.
6. Ibid., 1050, 1053.
7. Sophia to Roy, Sept. 30, 1912.
8. Sophia to Roy, Oct. 30, 1912.
9. Ibid.
10. Koehler Transcript, 418, 425.
11. Ibid., 119, 512.
12. Ibid., 530.
13. Ibid, 528.
14. Ibid., 527.

### CHAPTER ELEVEN – LIVING WITH A MAN

1. Koehler Transcript, 1083.
2. Ibid., 1086.
3. Ibid., 1085–86.
4. Ibid.
5. William Menninger, *Psychiatry in a Troubled World* (New York: Macmillan, 1948), 224. Concerns "that military life created the conditions for perversion to thrive" began to be expressed in the early 1900s. Canaday, *The Straight State*, 70.
6. The same point has been made about close relationships between nineteenth-century women. See, e.g., Ryan, *When Brooklyn Was Queer*, 33, discussing artist Mary Hallock Foote and Helena de Kay Gilder and quoting historian Carroll Smith-Rosenberg that "The essential question is not whether these women had genital contact and can therefore be defined as homosexual or heterosexual. The twentieth-century tendency to view human love and sexuality within a dichotomized universe of deviance and normality, genitality and platonic love, is alien to the emotions and attitudes of the nineteenth

century . . . " Carroll Smith-Rosenberg, *Disorderly Conduct: Visions of Gender in Victorian America* (New York: Knopf, 1985), 58–59.

7. Smith-Rosenberg, *Disorderly Conduct*, 36.

8. Kimmel, *Manhood in America*, 1st ed., 172.

9. Chauncey, *Gay New York*, 113.

10. Ibid., 115.

11. Kimmel, *Manhood in America*, 1st ed., 104. Chauncey, writing in 1994, used the phrase "masculinity crisis" to characterize the 1890–1920 period, whereas a more recent view is that the socially constructed concept of masculinity in America has always been unstable and contested, with more intense displays of such angst occurring in certain eras. See, e.g., Kimmel, *Manhood in America*, 4th ed., 1–8.

12. Kimmel, *Manhood in America*, 1st ed., 168.

13. Ibid., 169.

14. Quoted in Kimmel, *Manhood in America*, 1st ed., 170, citing Betty Keller, *Black Wolf: The Life of Ernest Thompson Seton* (New York: HarperCollins, 1985), 189. "[S]eemingly endless details" support the claim that the British man whose ideas inspired the Boy Scouts' founding, Lord Robert Baden-Powell, was gay. Gip Plaster, "Was the Founder of the Scouting Movement Gay?" The Gayscribe Archive, https://gayscribe.com/author/gayscribe/, discussing Tim Jeal, *Baden-Powell: Founder of the Boy Scouts* (New Haven, CT: Yale University Press, 2007, originally published as *The Boy-Man: The Life of Lord Baden-Powell, 1990*).

15. Koehler Transcript, 1087.

16. Ibid.

17. Ibid. Cf. Andrew Solomon, writing that before he came out as gay he adopted "an affected Victorian prudery, aimed not at masking but at obliterating desire." *Far From the Tree*, 10.

18. Koehler Transcript, 1088.

19. The strong influences exerted by social Darwinism, eugenics, and sexology can be seen, in the words of Smith-Rosenberg, "all as parts of a metaphoric discourse in which the physical body symbolized the social body, and physical and sexual disorder stood for social discord and danger." All forms of sexuality other than heterosexuality "became organically 'unnatural,' atavistic, degenerate— symbols of social disorder." *Disorderly Conduct*, 40.

20. Chauncey, *Gay New York*, 115–16.

21. Catherine S. Manegold, "Playing it Straight: The Odd Place of Homosexuality in the Military," *New York Times*, April 18, 1993, Week in Review.

22. Koehler Transcript, 1099. Ben's attorney implied that the observation was made by Master Gunner King at Grand Central Terminal in the spring of 1912, when Ben "came to the train with his friend, Colonel Kenly."

23. Koehler Transcript, 130–31.

24. Ibid., 421.

25. Ibid., 768.

26. Ibid.

27. https://sanjuanpuertorico.com/casa-blanca-museum-old-viejo-san-juan/. Ponce de León died before the house was completed and never lived there, but his family and descendants did for 250 years.

28. Louis received the assignment in July 1912. War Department Special Orders, No. 175, July 26, 1912.

29. Even so, there was concern about Wood's confirmation of the posting, for Louis's brother-in-law, Daniel Anthony Jr., in early July 1912 spoke to President Taft, who "assured [him] my order would be out so I could sail on August 3rd

boat," according to Louis. Koehler to Col. H. P. McCain, Adjutant General, July 27, 1912, Record Group 94, National Archives File #1938524-A. Louis did not receive the order until July 29. Telegram from Adjutant General to Koehler, July 29, 1912. National Archives File #1938524.

30. Sophia to Roy, April 27, 1913.


### CHAPTER TWELVE – LADIES "WEARIN' PANTALOONS"

1. Thomas P. Walsh, *Tin Pan Alley and the Philippines: American Songs of War and Love, 1898–1946* (Lanham, MD: Scarecrow Press, 2013), 152–53.

2. Hoganson, *Fighting for American Manhood*, 134-35. Hoganson observes that while "the martial spirit" was considered manly in American men, Filipinos were described as savages fighting from animalistic instincts. "Rather than being rational in battle, they were frenzied. Rather than being honorable, they were cruel, revengeful, and merciless." The descriptions of Filipinos as savage "had antecedents in negative depictions of Native-American men [and] also paralleled the images of African-American men as bestial rapists that white supremacists were working so hard to disseminate in this period."

3. Ibid., 137.

4. Susan B. Anthony died of pneumonia a few months later, in March 1906. She had felt unsteady for some time but took walks and campaigned for women's suffrage nonetheless. See, e.g., Letter from Susan B. Anthony to Maud Koehler, Dec. 14, 1904, Library of Congress (marked "Anthony Family Collection") ("I took a walk last night and the girl, Carrie, lent me her arm. I do dread going out awfully, but am going to try to pluck up courage every day to start out for a walk.")

5. Adrian Chen, "The Tough Guy," *The New Yorker*, Nov. 21, 2016, 68.

6. The southern Philippines remains an area of unrest. The predominantly Muslim city of Marawi, on the island of Mindanao, was devastated in 2017 in fighting between Islamic State loyalists and Filipino forces from the north, backed by U.S. air strikes. "Filipinos Find Their Home City in Tatters," *New York Times*, April 11, 2018. In January 2019, twenty died in a bombing in Jolo. "Cathedral Bombing Shows Global Reach of the Islamic State," *New York Times*, Jan. 29, 2019. In 2019, the United States advised against travel to the Sulu Archipelago, https://travel.state.gov/content/travel/en/traveladvisories/traveladvisories/philippines-travel-advisory.html.

7. On July 4, 1902, Roosevelt declared peace and granted amnesty to Filipinos "in all parts of the archipelago except in the country inhabited by the Moro tribes, to which this proclamation does not apply." Proclamation 483—Granting Pardon and Amnesty to Participants in Insurrection in the Philippines, http://www.presidency.ucsb.edu/ws/index.php?pid=69569.

8. "600 Moros Slain in Jolo Battle," *Chicago Tribune*, March 10, 1906.

9. Among Wood's friends were Senator Henry Cabot Lodge and Secretary of War Elihu Root. Those ties helped Wood secure a nomination to brigadier general in 1901, elevating him over 509 other officers in a move that "smacked of rank favoritism" and prompted numerous editorials in opposition. Nonetheless, Congress went along. Lane, *Armed Progressive*, 115, 120–27.

10. Ibid., 124.

11. Ibid.

12. James R. Arnold, *The Moro War: How America Battled a Muslim Insurgency in the Philippine Jungle, 1902–1913* (New York: Bloomsbury Press, 2011), 177.

13. Lane, *Armed Progressive*, 125.

14. Taft to Wood, Dec. 10, 1903; Wood to Taft, Dec. 16, 1903, as quoted in Lane, *Armed Progressive*, 126.

15. John S. D. Eisenhower, *Teddy Roosevelt and Leonard Wood: Partners in Command* (Columbia: University of Missouri, 2014), 15.

16. Roosevelt, *The Rough Riders*, 4.

17. Jack C. Lane, ed., *Chasing Geronimo, The Journal of Leonard Wood, May-September 1886* (Lincoln: University of Nebraska Press, 2009), 13.

18. Arnold, *The Moro War*, 78.

19. Wood Journal Entry May 4, 1886, reprinted in Lane, *Chasing Geronimo*, 26.

20. Ibid., Wood Journal Entries May 11 ("Went out after deer in order to get something for a change. Did not get any. Indians picked up a couple"); May 12 ("Indians picked up a couple of deer"); July 31 ("Saw many deer but got none"); May 13 ("[T]he main trail led southwest and presented signs which the Indians say indicate that the squaws and the great portion of the bucks are with this party"); July 8 ("Our Indians did some wonderful trailing, keeping the trail for miles when it seemed to be all washed out"); Aug. 6 ("[T]he Indians made a fire with dry sticks, the first time I have ever seen it done").

21. Ibid., Wood Journal Entries Aug. 29, Aug. 30.

22. Ibid., Wood Journal Entry Sept. 7.

23. Ibid., Wood Journal Entries June 26, 131 n.3. Wrote Lawton, "I really do not feel any sympathy when I hear that the Indians have killed a half a dozen or more of the [Mexicans]. I think the Indians better than the Mexicans." Letter of Henry Lawton to Mame, June 30, 1886, Lane, *Chasing Geronimo*, 49.

24. Ibid., 136–37 n.17.

25. Lane, *Armed Progressive*, 64-65.

26. Ibid., 65. Lane contends that a newspaper editor was actually the source of the information.

27. Pettegrew, *Brutes in Suits*, 235.

28. Hoganson, *Fighting for American Manhood*, 131. Wrote Roosevelt about black infantrymen in Cuba, "No troops could have behaved better [than] the colored soldiers had behaved so far; but they are, of course, peculiarly dependent upon their white officers. Occasionally they produce non-commissioned officers who can take the initiative and accept responsibility precisely like the best class of whites; but this cannot be expected normally, nor is it fair to expect it." *The Rough Riders*, 143. This comment and others by Roosevelt drew denunciation from the black press. Pettegrew, *Brutes in Suits*, 240.

29. Hoganson, *Fighting for American Manhood* , 128–29.

30. Ibid., 130.

31. Flexner, *Century of Struggle*, 248. Washington State broke the "doldrums" in 1910.

32. Wood Journal Entry May 29, 1886, reprinted in Lane, *Chasing Geronimo*.

33. Ibid., Wood Journal Entries July 12, July 13, July 16 ("Was so sick and dizzy that I kept falling down while on foot . . . Was taken very sick, not expected to live. Delirious all night, with a high fever").

34. Lane, *Armed Progressive*, 14; Arnold, *The Moro War*, 79 ("commendable conduct, but hardly worth the Congressional Medal of Honor"). Wood's receipt of the medal would still be controversial thirty years later in 1916. "Army Bill Joker Aims to Rob Wood of Honor Medal," *New York Times*, May 20, 1916.

35. Lane, *Armed Progressive*, 14–15. Lane, *Chasing Geronimo*, 8–9, describing Miles as "an exceedingly ambitious officer." Miles, like Wood, lacked a West Point degree, and he benefited from relationships with powerful people, having married the niece of General William Sherman and Senator John Sherman. See

also Arnold, *The Moro War*, 79 (in the Geronimo campaign, Wood revealed "a deep understanding of how to play army politics").

36. Roosevelt, *The Rough Riders*, 5.
37. Arnold, *The Moro War*, 81.
38. Roosevelt, *The Rough Riders*, 4.
39. "Koehler to Face Trial for Intemperate Phrase," *Washington Post*, Aug. 6, 1906.
40. Taft to Roosevelt, March 22, 1907, part of War Department General Orders, No. 65, March 26, 1907. ("1907 General Orders, No. 65"). Record Group 94: Records of the Adjutant General's Office, Entry 25: Adjutant General's Office Document Files/AGO Doc. Files (1890-1917), File #4473-ACP-85, Lewis M. Koehler ("Lewis Koehler File").
41. Secretary of War Elihu Root, Taft's predecessor, was the primary advocate of "put[ting] the War Department on an economical, businesslike basis with a single, clear chain of command. His key word was 'efficiency.'" Joseph W. A. Whitehorne, *The Inspectors General of the United States Army 1903–1939* (Washington, DC: Office of the Inspector General and Center of Military History, U.S. Army, 1998), 11.
42. Louis received a Silver Star for his conduct in Papaya, Luzon, in June 1900. Cullums Register, Vol. VII, 225.
43. Letter from Brigadier General Jesse M. Lee to Lewis Koehler, Greencastle, Indiana, Nov. 13, 1901, ("Lewis Koehler File").
44. L. M. Koehler to Taft, March 23, 1906, part of ("1907 General Orders, No. 65").
45. "Army Probe Imminent," *Washington Post*, Dec. 10, 1908.
46. "Army Officers Stand By Capt. Louis Koehler," *Leavenworth Weekly Times*, Dec. 20, 1906.
47. "Koehler to Face Trial for Intemperate Phrase," *Washington Post*, Aug. 6, 1906; 1907 General Orders, No. 65.
48. Kornstein, "Taps for the Real Catch-22," 1524. The U.S. Supreme Court would later invalidate as unconstitutional a civilian law penalizing "annoying" conduct. *Coates v. Cincinnati*, 402 U.S. 611 (1971).
49. Even if being "difficult to please" was a social no-no, it was a stretch to say that attitude caused "reasonably direct and palpable" harm to the Army, a construction given to Article 62 in a nineteenth-century treatise cited approvingly by the Supreme Court as reducing the clause's vagueness. See Kornstein, "Taps for the Real Catch-22," 1522–23 n.37; *Parker v. Levy*, 417 U.S. 733, 754–55 (1974) (majority) and 773 (Stewart, J., dissenting).
50. Taft to Roosevelt, March 22, 1907, General Orders, No. 65.
51. "Bud" means "mountain" in the Tausug language.
52. Arnold, *The Moro Battle*, 148-68.
53. Jack McCallum, *Leonard Wood: Rough Rider, Surgeon, Architect of American Imperialism* (New York: New York University Press, 2006), 228.
54. Robert Fulton, "Uncle Sam, the Moros, and the Moro Campaigns, Timeline of the 1st Battle of Bud Dajo—1906."
55. See, e.g., Report of J. W. Hayward, Midshipman, U.S. Navy, Commanding U.S.S. *Pampanga*, Jolo, Philippines, March 9, 1906 (ship arrived at 4:00 a.m. March 7, unloaded two Colt Automatic guns and nine men at 7:00 a.m., and reported to Wood "upon his arrival") ("Hayward Report").
56. Fulton, "Uncle Sam, the Moros, and the Moro Campaigns." See also Hayward Report ("In ten minutes all the Moros in the trenches were killed"); Lane, *Armed Progressive*, 134.
57. Lane, *Armed Progressive*, 134 (fifty-two wounded); "Duterte Reminds US of Bud

Dajo Massacre," *Sun Star Philippines*, April 21, 2016 (seventy wounded). Officers under Wood wanted to search for survivors but Wood ordered them to leave. That evening, he dined at the officers' club with another officer "who had aggressively manufactured evidence to provide a rationale for the campaign." Arnold, *The Moro War*, 169–70.

58. "Women and Children Killed In Moro Battle," *New York Times*, March 11, 1906.
59. Ibid.
60. Telegram from Taft to Wood, March 12, 1906, included in U.S. Senate Document No. 289, 59th Congress; "Attack by United States Troops on Mount Dajo," Letter from the Secretary of War transmitting Complete Copies of All Communications that have been received in or sent from the War Department Pertaining to the Recent Attack by troops of the United States on Mount Dajo, March 26, 1906 ("Mount Dajo Report").
61. Cables from Wood to Taft, March 12, 1906, March 19, 1906, contained in Mount Dajo Report.
62. Hoganson, *Fighting for American Manhood*, 182–90.
63. Samuel Clemens, "Comments on the Moro Massacre," March 12, 1906, originally published in *Mark Twain's Autobiography*, ed. Albert Bigelow Paine (New York: Harper and Brothers, 1924); reprinted in *Mark Twain's Weapons of Satire: Anti-imperialist Writings on the Philippine-American War*, ed. Jim Zwick (New York: Syracuse University Press, 1992), 170–73, https://www.historyisaweapon.com /defcon1/clemensmoromassacre.html.
64. Colonel Joseph W. Duncan, 6th Infantry, "Report of Engagement with Moro Enemy in Bud Dajo, Island of Jolo, March 5th, 6th, 7th, 8th, 1906," March 10, 1906, referencing Major Omar Bundy.
65. Ibid., 46.
66. "Philippine's Duterte Keeps Lashing Out at United States—Over Atrocities a Century Ago," *Washington Post*, July 24, 2017; "Duterte Reminds US of Bud Dajo Massacre," *Sun Star Philippines*, April 21, 2016, http://www.sunstar.com .ph/article/96464/. The *Washington Post* quoted Duterte as saying, with reference to criticism of his extrajudicial killings of suspected drug sellers and users, "You're investigating me and the internal affairs of my country? I'm investigating you, and I will investigate you, and I will expose it to the world what you did to the Filipinos, especially to the Moro Filipinos."
67. AGO Records of Philip Worcester, Document 530055; RG 94, Entry 25, AGO Document File, 1890-1917, Stack 8W3, 13/29/4, Box 3702, 164; Obituary, Sixty-Fifth Annual Report of the Association of Graduates of the United States Military Academy at West Point, June 11, 1934, 224, http://digital-library .usma.edu/cdm/ref/collection/aogreunion/id/21016.
68. Koehler Transcript, 104, 106.

### CHAPTER THIRTEEN – THE PRESIDENT DISAPPROVES

1. L. M. Koehler to Taft, March 23, 1906, 1907 General Orders, No. 65.
2. "Army Officers Stand By Capt. Louis Koehler," *Leavenworth Weekly Times*, Dec. 20, 1906.
3. "Wood Gets Prize Post," *Washington Post*, April 2, 1907.
4. Edgar C. Ellis to Taft, Aug. 7, 1906, Lewis Koehler File.
5. In a move the *Leavenworth Weekly Times* termed "unprecedented," Wood detained senior officers in the Philippines until the prosecutor found a jury he considered unbiased. *Leavenworth Weekly Times*, Dec. 20, 1906.
6. Ibid.

7. 1907 General Orders, No. 65.
8. Taft to Roosevelt, March 22, 1907, reprinted in 1907 General Orders, No. 65.
9. Roosevelt Statement, March 22, 1907, included in 1907 General Orders, No. 65. Ainsworth immediately cabled Wood, saying, "Proceedings findings and acquittal court-martial case Lewis M. Koehler disapproved by the President. Action published in orders." Ainsworth to Wood, March 23, 1907, No. 3177. Lewis Koehler File. While Louis and his family spelled his name "Louis," the Army wrote it as "Lewis."
10. See, e.g., "President Saves Wood," *New York Times*, March 23, 1907; "Court-Martial Is Overruled," *Los Angeles Times*, March 23, 1907; "Captain Koehler's Case Disposed Of," *Boston Evening Transcript*, March 23, 1907. Numerous other papers ran the story. The case was considered so significant that Major William F. Flynn's official West Point biography notes that he was "selected as Senior Counsel in the Koehler trial and successfully defended Captain L. M. Koehler, 4th Cavalry, before a presidential court martial." Biographical Register of the Officers and Graduates of the U. S. Military Academy at West Point, N.Y., Vol. 5.
11. Richmann to Baker, Aug. 1, 1916. After his acquittal was made public, Louis did not let the matter drop, requesting an investigation into why he was held in arrest for months despite a vote of acquittal. The Army's senior lawyer found no wrongdoing. Lewis Koehler File.
12. "Wood Gets Prize Post," *Washington Post*, April 2, 1907.
13. "A reviewing authority may mitigate a sentence, but it can not change a finding of acquittal to one of conviction," Taft wrote to Roosevelt. 1907 General Orders, No. 65.
14. "Evidence in Wood Case: Major Runcie Tells of Magazine Article Attacking General Brooke: Written at Wood's Request," *Arizona Daily Star*, Nov. 28, 1903; "Root Called in Wood Case," *New York Times*, Dec. 16, 1903, reporting on Runcie's testimony that the article about Brooke "was prepared practically at [Wood's] suggestion and dictation," and other testimony "that Gen. Wood was untruthful in many matters affecting public affairs."

## CHAPTER FOURTEEN – HATCHED ON PLUM ISLAND

1. Sophia to Roy, April 27, 1913. She told Roy of a sight in Puerto Rico she thought would interest him: "a lovely trip over the mountains [where] I saw the American Tobacco Co's tobacco growing—most of it all under white net—making the valleys and mountains look as though covered with snow."
2. Ibid.
3. "I guess it was 50 feet wide, possibly 75, from 100 feet to 150 feet in length," Ben said of the garden's dimensions. Koehler Transcript, 785.
4. Ibid., 784.
5. Ibid., 421–22 (testimony of Sidney Jordan).
6. Ibid. 195 (testimony of Edison Kirkman).
7. Ibid., 428–29 (testimony of Sidney Jordan).
8. Ibid., 809.
9. Ibid., 453 (testimony of John Fuller).
10. Ibid., 273.
11. Sophia to Roy, April 27, 1913.
12. Chauncey, *Gay New York*, 117.
13. Koehler Transcript, 139.
14. Ben noticed a female dog in front of Brown's quarters in violation of a post rule. Brown, the same man who had been scolded for not sleeping in his camp

bunk, was ordered to remove the dog on the next boat. Brown also brought pigs to Fort Terry despite being told that they were prohibited. Those, too, Ben ordered removed. Koehler Transcript, 988–89, 1048–49.
15. Koehler Transcript, 797.
16. Ibid., 1057.
17. Ibid., 153.
18. Ibid., 897 (interrogatory answers of Col. Richmond Davis).
19. Ibid., 899.
20. Ibid., 896.
21. Ibid., 418.
22. Ibid., 154.
23. Ibid., 1057.
24. Ibid., 831.
25. Ibid., 153.
26. Ibid., 1056.
27. Ibid., 474, 502 (testimony of Andrew Moses).
28. Ibid., 744.

### CHAPTER FIFTEEN – A HURRIED INVESTIGATION

1. Koehler Transcript, 744.
2. U.S. Constitution, Art. 1, Sec. 8.
3. Koehler Transcript, 744.
4. Ibid.
5. Ibid., 756–57.
6. Stephen C. Mills, "Does the Enlisted Soldier Need 'Regeneration'?" *Journal of the Military Service Institution of the United States*, Vol. 38, Jan.–Feb. 1906, 314, 324.
7. Charles W. Larned, "A Reply to Colonel Mills," *Journal of the Military Service Institution of the United States*, Vol. 38, Jan.–Feb. 1906, 326a.
8. When questioned, Koehler replied, "I examined this man and found him to be exceptionally intelligent. He spoke and read French and German; he wrote English perfectly and understood what he read. His recommendations were excellent. His reading was not good because his pronunciation was poor." Report of B. M. Koehler re Frederick Kurzman, Dec. 21, 1910, AGO Doc. #1729776.
9. Letter from Samuel Silverman to the Adjutant General, Feb. 20, 1911, Record Group 94: Records of the Adjutant General's Office, Entry 25: Adjutant General's Office Document Files/AGO Doc. Files (1890-1917), Box #4959, Private Samuel Silverman, Company H, 11th U.S. Infantry, AGO Doc. File #1265503 ("Silverman File").
10. Endorsement signed by B. M. Koehler, Dec. 7, 1910, Silverman File, Doc. #1724115.
11. "[H]ad Silverman lost or destroyed his discharge he could have been enlisted," wrote Ben. Endorsement signed by B. M. Koehler, Dec. 15, 1910, Silverman File, Doc. #1727241.
12. Letter by Major S. Wadhaus to the Adjutant, Ft. Slocum, Dec. 7, 1910, Silverman File.
13. Endorsement signed by B. M. Koehler, Dec. 7, 1910, Silverman File, Doc. #1724115.
14. "Everything I did in this case was done with knowledge and approval of the Chief Recruiting Officer New York City," wrote Ben. Silverman File, Doc. #1727241.
15. Ainsworth endorsement, Dec. 29, 1910, Silverman File, Doc. #1721426.

16. Kenly to Koehler, Sept. 11, 1911, Koehler AGO File.
17. Lane, *Armed Progressive*, 160–67.
18. If handwriting is any gauge of self-confidence, the flourishes Ben used when signing his name had increased in size and ornateness since his early oaths of office. By 1910, the distance between the left side of his wide 'B' and the top of the curved stroke that began his middle initial 'M' spanned more than an inch.
19. There had been reports of homosexual activity and rapes of women by soldiers in the Philippines, and much contact with prostitutes. Whether the Philippine War was debasing American men instead of inculcating manly virtues became a matter of public debate. See, e.g., Hoganson, *Fighting for American Manhood*, 142.

### CHAPTER SIXTEEN – LONG WALK FROM QUARTERMASTER DOCK

1. Trust for Governors Island website, https://govisland.com/history.
2. While on Governors Island, Wood concealed near paralysis of his left side. The condition was corrected by removal of a tumor pressing on his motor cortex, an operation Wood submitted to after Taft announced his promotion to chief of staff. Lane, *Armed Progressive*, 146–47. The next Eastern Department commander did not live on Governors Island. Barry assumed the position in August 1912 and moved into the commander's quarters.
3. Koehler Transcript, 745.
4. Ibid., 835.
5. Ibid., 745.
6. "Artist Files Lawsuit Claiming Extortion," *New York Times*, Nov. 17, 2018.
7. Sherwood Anderson, "Hands," in *Winesburg, Ohio* (New York: Compass Books, 1958), 32.
8. Lillian Hellman, *The Children's Hour* (1934). The play was based on an incident that took place in Scotland in the early 1800s, the subject of a 1930s book. "Drumsheugh: Lesbian Sex Row Rocked Society," *The Scotsman*, Feb. 25, 2009.
9. Katz, *Gay American History*, 29, describing the case of Edward McCosker, who arrested a man for disorderly conduct. The arrested man claimed he was defending himself against sexual advances by McCosker. McCosker denied the allegation, but after testimony, an administrative board found against him and he lost his job.
10. William C. Robinson, *Elementary Law* (Boston: Little, Brown and Company, 1910), 632, citing Clark and Marshall. The threatened man paid the money but went to the authorities, and the individual who had made the threat was charged with robbery—a crime that requires not only taking property but also putting the victim in fear. Fear of prosecution for sodomy was considered sufficient.
11. The Army's incorporation by reference of state sodomy laws is analogous to the Bureau of Immigration's practice of looking at state convictions of foreigners under state and local moral turpitude laws.
12. Havelock Ellis, *Studies in the Psychology of Sex*, Vol. 1. *Sexual Inversion* (London: University Press, 1897), Chapter 2.
13. Ryan, *When Brooklyn Was Queer*, 83.
14. Canaday, *The Straight State*, 58.
15. See, e.g., David K. Johnson, *The Lavender Scare: The Cold War Persecution of Gays and Lesbians in the Federal Government* (Chicago: University of Chicago Press, 2004), about firings of thousands of alleged homosexuals from their federal government jobs during the McCarthy era, as well as the 2017 documentary of the same name, https://www.thelavenderscare.com/.

16. "Obama Ends 'Don't Ask, Don't Tell' Policy," *New York Times*, July 22, 2011.
17. Koehler Transcript, 745, 833, 834.
18. Ibid., 831, 833.

## CHAPTER SEVENTEEN – A MARCH, THEN A BRAWL

1. Koehler Transcript, 467, 471 (testimony of Katie Ewing).
2. "Army Sensation in Trial of Koehler," (*N.Y.) Sun*, Feb. 23, 1914. According to the article, the fight in the club broke out after one officer accused another of sleeping with his wife.
3. Koehler Transcript, 368 (testimony of Edward Shanley).
4. Ibid., 361, 367.
5. Ibid., 96.
6. Ibid., 762. "I told him that was no way to conduct an organization," said Ben.
7. Ibid., 96.
8. Ibid., 85.
9. Ibid., 362. "[H]e told lies down there against me," said Private George Krouchonoskie.
10. Ibid., 85.
11. Ibid., 368.
12. Ibid., 752.
13. Ibid., 757.
14. Ibid., 89–90.
15. Both men were young when their fathers died. According to the Worcester family genealogy, Philip Henry Worcester was born in Norfolk, Virginia, in June 1879, and his father, Henry Parker Worcester, died in October 1882. Worcester was the oldest male of four children. After her husband's death, Worcester's mother, Justina Rea Worcester, returned to her native Portland, Maine, where Worcester grew up, http://www.worcesterfamily.com/ninth.htm#1701.
16. Rotundo, *American Manhood*, 6.
17. Frick was commissioned in 1910 after his graduation from Pennsylvania State College with a degree in chemistry. Penn State Alumni Quarterly, Vol. III, July 1913, 218.
18. Koehler Transcript, 771.
19. Ibid., 72.
20. Ibid.
21. Ibid., 384, 386.
22. Magnus Hirschfeld, *Homosexuality in Men and Women* (1914), as quoted in Katz, *Gay History*, 77.
23. Chauncey, *Gay New York*, 37–40, 66–67, 355. For a discussion of how the Brooklyn Navy Yard provided jobs and other "conditions that allowed early queer lives to flourish," see Ryan, *When Brooklyn Was Queer*, 17–24.
24. Obituary, Philip Henry Worcester, *Sixty-Fifth Annual Report of the Association of Graduates of the United States Military Academy at West Point*, June 11, 1934, 224–25 ("Worcester West Point Obituary"); AGO Doc. #1485198.
25. Special Orders, No. 158, Aug. 22, 1910. Robert C. Richardson Jr., *West Point: An Intimate Picture of the National Academy and of the Life of the Cadet* (New York: Knickerbocker Press/G.P. Putnam's Sons, 1917), 348–49. https://www.gutenberg.org/files/57316/57316-h/57316-h.htm
26. Special Orders, No. 129, June 20, 1913.
27. Koehler Transcript, 762–63.

28. Ibid., 763, 817, 823.
29. 1911 Efficiency Report of Philip H. Worcester signed by Maj. Gen. Thomas H. Barry. In August 1912, thousands of men including Worcester participated in the Connecticut Maneuver Campaign, a large simulation of an invasion. As chief ordnance officer of a division, Worcester spent "considerable time at Governors Island at the close of the maneuvers attempting to settle all reports and returns." He received permission to return to Governors Island in the fall of 1912 to complete the work. Memo from Worcester to Superintendent, United States Military Academy, Sept. 24, 1912, Record Group 94: Records of the Adjutant General's Office, Entry 25: Adjutant General's Office Document Files/AGO Doc. Files (1890-1917), Box #3701, AGO Doc. File 530055 ("Worcester AGO File"), Doc. #1957046.
30. Koehler Transcript, 763.

### CHAPTER EIGHTEEN – ORDERS

1. "Army Sensation in Trial of Koehler," (*N.Y.*) *Sun*, Feb. 23, 1914.
2. "Garrison Shifts a Dozen Generals," *New York Times*, Dec. 19, 1913. Wood left in place two candidates for his position, William Wotherspoon and Hugh Scott.
3. Special Orders, No. 296, Dec. 19, 1913, issued by Leonard Wood on behalf of the secretary of war.
4. Daniel Anthony Jr. referred to Wood as having made the decision to court-martial Ben, though the revocation of the leave appears to have been communicated by someone at the Eastern Department. Koehler Transcript, 746; Anthony to Garrison, March 12, 1914, Lewis Koehler File.
5. Two days after the announcement, the *New York Times* published a letter asserting that Barry had more foreign service than most generals, and more than twice as much as Wotherspoon, who was not reassigned. "General's Foreign Service, Secretary Garrison's Statement Not Borne Out by the Records," Letter to the Editor signed by "A Line Officer," *New York Times*, Dec. 21, 1913. Most likely, the letter was written by a Barry ally, given that the author was able to obtain service information about a dozen generals so quickly.
6. Koehler Transcript, 826.
7. Richmann to Baker, Aug. 1, 1916.
8. Anthony to Garrison, March 12, 1914.
9. Ibid. (underscoring in original).
10. Memo of C. C. Hodges to Chief of Staff, March 11, 1914. Lewis Koehler File.
11. Special Orders, No. 303, Dec. 29, 1913, signed by Wood. "Louis had a four-year detail at Porto Rico" according to the 1916 Richmann letter to Baker. The assignment began in August 1912. Special Orders, No. 175, July 26, 1912. Record Group 94: Records of the Adjutant General's Office, Entry 25: Adjutant General's Office Document Files/AGO Doc. Files (1890-1917), File #3965-ACP-88, Doc. #1938524.
12. Koehler Transcript, 833.

### CHAPTER NINETEEN – ALL HAIL WASHINGTON

1. Wilson has been described as an "unapologetic racist." Editorial, "The Real Meaning of 'Send Her Back,'" *New York Times*, July 19, 2019. He "fill[ed] his administration with segregationists," according to columnist Brent Staples, "extend[ing] Jim Crow into Washington's offices, cafeterias, and lavatories" and firing large numbers black civil servants, according to historian Kevin

Boyle. Brent Staples, "When White Supremacists Ruled the Capital," *New York Times*, Sept. 29, 2017; Kevin Boyle, *Arc of Justice: A Saga of Race, Civil Rights, and Murder in the Jazz Age* (New York: Picador/Holt and Co., 2004), 88. On another rights issue, women's suffrage, Wilson's initial attitude was "lukewarm at best," though he later changed his position. "Woodrow Wilson and the Women's Suffrage Movement: A Reflection," The Wilson Center, June 4, 2013, https://www.wilsoncenter.org/article/woodrow-wilson-and-the-womens -suffrage-movement-reflection. While a professor at Princeton, Wilson complained of immigration by "multitudes of men of the lowest class from the south of Italy." Adam Hochschild, "Obstruction of Injustice," *The New Yorker*, Nov. 11, 2019, 28, 30. Perhaps the reputation of southern Italian men as relatively accepting of homosexual relations was a factor underlying Wilson's disparagement. See Chauncey, *Gay New York*, 72–83 (discussing the association, both real and perceived, among Italian male immigrants, the emergence of a "bachelor subculture," and homosexuality in the 1890–1920 period).

2. Wood to James A. Reed, Dec. 27, 1913, Koehler AGO File.

3. Ibid.

4. Wood to Adjutant General, Dec. 27, 1913, Koehler AGO File.

5. Wood to Garrison, Dec. 27, 1913, addressed to The Marlborough-Blenheim, Atlantic City. Lindley M. Garrison Papers, Seeley G. Mudd Manuscript Library, Princeton University, Box 5, FF12, Code MC060 ("Garrison Papers").

6. Wood to Garrison, Dec. 27, 1913, Garrison Papers.

7. Lindley M. Garrison, "What the War Department Has Done," *Harper's Weekly*, March 7, 1914, 9, 10.

8. Koehler Transcript, 353 (testimony of George Krouchonoskie).

9. Ibid., 756–57.

10. Ibid., 1052.

11. Ibid., 526.

12. Garrison, "What the War Department Has Done," 10.

13. Memo for Chief of Staff by Enoch Crowder, Dec. 27, 1913, Koehler AGO File.

14. Crowder to Maj. Albert Payne Duval, Sept. 25, 1925, Enoch H. Crowder Papers, State Historical Society of Missouri ("Crowder Papers").

15. "Travelog of Linn, Grundy, Macon, Sullivan, Morgan and Hickory Counties," *St. Louis Daily Globe-Democrat*, Sept. 20, 1925.

16. Later, when Crowder served as ambassador to Cuba in Havana, he and an aide would request that "a married man be sent here" to serve as embassy secretary "to have available a woman who would be in a position to relieve [Crowder] of a great many of the social details which he now has to look after himself." Letter from Richard B. Southgate to Frederic R. Dolbeare, Jan. 21, 1926, Crowder Papers.

17. Koehler Transcript, 1058–59.

18. Lieutenant Gorham identified Frick as Ben's only "enemy" at the post. Koehler Transcript, 1141. Lieutenant Humphreys said Frick complained about the assignments Ben gave him: "He wanted to go to town and complained sometimes of different things, different duties, complained a good many times about tug duty, which was not very hard." Ibid., 541. Humphreys also said that Frick had a "reputation for telling falsehoods" and "repeating gossip" to the extent that "if you repeat something at all that you have heard, somebody will laugh and say 'Frick must have told you that' if it was something that sounded rather funny." Ibid., 532.

19. Chauncey, *Gay New York*, 122–23, 102, 110–11. Some of the doctors beginning to write about male-male sex during this period distinguished between "'inverts' (who, as feminine in character, were naturally attracted to men)

and 'perverts' (who, as conventionally masculine men, perverted their normal sexual drive when they responded to the advances of someone who appeared anatomically to be another man . . .)." There was a strong class element to attitudes and practices regarding male-male sex both outside and inside the gay world. "Fairies" tended to be working-class men, and working-class men were generally more accepting than middle-class men of men who had sex with other men. In contrast, middle-class gay men, "queers" in the parlance of the day, "typically displayed their homosexuality only in more private settings or by using signals." They tended to disparage "faggots" and "fairies" for their "effeminacy and flagrancy." At the same time, queers benefited from the fairies' flagrancy, for "the flamboyant stereotype diverted attention from other, more guarded men, and made it relatively easy for them to pass as straight."

20. There was one other handwritten change in the final letter. In the original typed version, Wood had called the evidence against Ben "abundant." In the final version, Wood—presumably after receiving Crowder's memo—crossed out "abundant" and substituted "sufficient," so that the sentence read "I believe the evidence is sufficient."

21. Not until a book was published in 1970—*The Brownsville Raid* by John D. Weaver (New York: Norton)—did the Army find the discharged men innocent. After a new review, President Richard Nixon issued pardons to all.

22. The Constitutional League of the United States, based in New York City, represented the soldiers. Typical of the evidence introduced to show that the investigation violated due process was an affidavit from a black soldier that "General Garlington would not allow this affiant to explain anything relative to conditions . . . the location of his comrades, or the material facts relative to the night in question." Affidavit of Luther Thornton, Nov. 23, 1908, as found in "Affair at Brownsville, Texas," 60th Congress, 1st Session, Senate Documents, 1908, printed in United States Congressional Serial Set, Government Printing Office (1908).

23. Bolling W. Smith, "The Court-Martial of Maj. Benjamin M. Koehler, C.A.C., Fort Terry, NY," *Coast Defense Journal*, Feb. 2005, 81, 83.

24. In his memo to Wood, Crowder had pointed out that "under the New York Penal Code (the law applicable at Fort Terry)" the "acts charged against Major Koehler" would constitute misdemeanor "minor assaults (third degree), punishable with the maximum punishment of one year's imprisonment; of $500.00 fine; or of both such fine and imprisonment." Memo for Chief of Staff, Dec. 27, 1913, Garrison Papers.

25. Henry Koehler to J. P. Tumulty, Dec. 30, 1913, Koehler AGO File.

26. George C. Scott to Garrison, Jan. 6, 1914, Koehler AGO File.

27. Henry Breckinridge to George C. Scott, Jan. 7, 1914, Koehler AGO File.

28. W. P. Borland to Garrison, Jan. 10, 1914, Koehler AGO File.

29. W. O. Bradley to Breckinridge, Jan. 8, 1914, Koehler AGO File.

30. Bryan was a strong Wilson supporter until he resigned in protest of Wilson's war policies in 1916.

31. Hoganson, *Fighting for American Manhood*, 97.

32. Telegram from W. J. Bryan to Garrison, Jan. 6, 1914, Koehler AGO File.

33. Crowder to Garrison, Jan. 12, 1914, Garrison Papers.

34. Garrison to Crowder, Jan. 12, 1914, Koehler AGO File.

35. Gilbert M. Hitchcock to Garrison, Jan. 15, 1914, Garrison Papers.

36. Garrison to Hitchcock and Sloan, Jan. 15, 1914, Koehler AGO File.

37. Telegram from Barry to the Adjutant General, quoting telegram from B. M. Koehler to Barry, Jan. 15, 1914, Koehler AGO File.

38. Sophia to Roy, undated, on stationery of the Beverwyck, where Sophia said she would be staying in a note sent to Roy dated Dec. 27, 1913.
39. Sophia to Roy, Jan. 22, 1914.

### CHAPTER TWENTY – THE MEANING OF "START"

1. "Major Hagadorn Before Army Court," *New York Times*, Dec. 26, 1913; "Hagadorn Guilty Is Court Verdict," *Brooklyn Daily Eagle*, Dec. 26, 1913.
2. Garrison to Wood, Jan. 15, 1914, Garrison Papers.
3. Endorsement by George Andrews to Commanding General, Eastern Dept., Jan. 13, 1914, Koehler AGO File.

### CHAPTER TWENTY-ONE – UNTHINKABLE

1. "Plans Cadet Corps to Strengthen Army," *New York Times*, March 6, 1910. The essay won the 1909 Gold Medal of the Military Service Institution and appeared in the March-April 1910 issue of the Institution's journal. See note 5 below.
2. Ibid.
3. Hoganson, *Fighting for American Manhood*, 175, quoting Roosevelt's speech "The Strenuous Life," delivered April 10, 1899, https://voicesofdemocracy .umd.edu/roosevelt-strenuous-life-1899-speech-text/.
4. 1913 review by Lieutenant Colonel Richmond P. Davis, Summary of Efficiency Reports, Benjamin M. Koehler, Koehler AGO File. Davis's 1912 review reads similarly, as does the 1911 review by Colonel William C. Rafferty.
5. James J. Mayes, "What Military Training and Education Should Be Required in Educational Institutions of All Grades, and What Legal Exactions of Military Service on the Part of the Government is Wise and Compatible with our Institutions?," *Journal of the Military Service Institution*, Vol. XLVI, No. CLXIV, March-April 2010.
6. Wood to Adjutant General, Feb. 7, 1914, Koehler AGO File.

### CHAPTER TWENTY-TWO – CONFUSION

1. Telegram from Garrison to Barry, Feb. 9, 1914, Garrison Papers.
2. Telegram from Barry to Garrison, Feb. 10, 1914, 2:12 a.m., Garrison Papers.
3. Telegram from Barry to Garrison, Feb. 10, 1914, 3:52 p.m., Garrison Papers.
4. Telegram from Garrison to Barry, Feb. 10, 1914, Koehler AGO File.
5. Koehler Transcript, 748.
6. See, e.g., "Brooklyn Diocese Creates Program to Compensate Sex Abuse Victims," *New York Times*, June 23, 2017. The Brooklyn Diocese knew of at least 280 abuse victims, some with claims dating back to the 1930s, involving at least fifty-four priests in Brooklyn and Queens.
7. See, e.g., "Baylor's Pride Turns to Shame in Rape Scandal," *New York Times*, March 10, 2017.
8. See, e.g., Gary Noling, "Restoring My Daughter's Honor," *New York Times*, Aug. 9, 2016 ("From 2009 to 2015, 25 percent of service members who left the military after reporting a sexual assault were discharged because of some kind of misconduct. About a third of those discharges were related to alcohol or drug use, which is frequently linked to PTSD"). The author's daughter, a Marine, reported being raped by a senior Marine. "Her peers and her supervisor isolated and abused her," she developed a drinking problem, was discharged, and died of acute alcohol poisoning. Between 2017 and 2019, the number of unreport-

ed sexual assaults at the top three military academies increased by almost 50 percent, according to a Pentagon study, despite efforts to encourage women to report incidents. "More Assaults Unreported on Campuses of Academies," *New York Times*, Feb. 1, 2019. In the services, a study found that under one-third of attacks were reported in 2014, and 62 percent of women who reported sexual assault "said they had faced retaliation for doing so." "Trump Faulted for His Notions About Assaults," *New York Times*, Sept. 9, 2016. From 2016 to 2018, sexual assaults against women in the military rose by 50 percent over the prior two-year period. "Pentagon Survey Finds Increase in Sexual Assaults Reported by Women," *New York Times*, May 2, 2019. This is despite the repeal of the Don't Ask, Don't Tell policy, which had the pernicious effect of allowing men whose overtures were rebuffed to accuse women of being lesbians and begin proceedings to have them dismissed on that ground. Christin M. Damiano, "Lesbian Baiting in the Military: Institutionalized Sexual Harassment Under 'Don't Ask, Don't Tell, Don't Pursue,'" *American University Journal of Gender, Social Policy & the Law* Vol. 7, no. 3 (1999), 499–522.

9. While the professed lack of impact may be seen as undercutting the men's claims, the manliness ethos might have constrained the accusers from admitting physical or emotional injury. This norm endures in the reluctance of some male soldiers and police officers to acknowledge symptoms of trauma and seek help out of concern that it will make them seem weak. See, e.g., "As Suicides Rise, Police Leaders Battle Mental Health Stigma," *New York Times*, June 28, 2019 ("[F]or many officers, emotional vulnerability is incompatible with their desire to be seen as heroes, according to researchers who study police stress").

10. Garrison to Crowder, Jan. 12, 1914, Garrison Papers (emphasis added).

11. Quoted in Lane, *Armed Progressive*, 209. Writes Lane, "Wood was a self-righteous man whose beliefs hardened into moral principles. He tended to pursue those beliefs with the certitude usually reserved to evangelistic crusaders."

12. In particular, Crowder wanted the Army to find out "whether any or all of the witnesses had a grievance or an animus against the accused that could be utilized by counsel in an attack upon their credibility." Crowder to Garrison, Jan. 12, 1914, Garrison Papers.

13. Endorsement by George Andrews to Commanding General, Eastern Dept., Jan. 13, 1914, Koehler AGO File.

14. Koehler Transcript, 749.

15. Ben had received excellent reviews but once, in 1903, a superior identified a potential weakness. In answer to the question "Is he . . . resourceful?" the commander of the Presidio had written "Somewhat." The question about resourcefulness was eliminated from later versions of the evaluation form, but the commander's answer highlighted a fundamental aspect of Ben's character that did not vanish along with the question: Ben was earnest; he was dutiful; he was capable. He could be overly confident at times, and as events had shown and would continue to show, he could also be self-destructively naive.

### CHAPTER TWENTY-THREE – AN OLD NEMESIS RETURNS

1. "Army Sensation in Trial of Koehler," *(N.Y.) Sun*, Feb. 23, 1914.

2. A dispatch reprinted in Ben's hometown paper stated that "the particulars were such that they could not be handled by a newspaper." "Trial By Court Martial," *LeMars Semi-Weekly Sentinel*, Feb. 24, 1914.

3. That Wood was solely in control of information dispensed by the War Department to the media about "even the most trivial" matters was the claim of an unnamed member of Congress whose letter highly critical of Wood was printed

in the *Army and Navy Register* on February 28, 1914. "An Army Press Agency," Letter to the Editor, *Army and Navy Register*, Vol. 55, no. 1754, 1.

4. "Army Board to Try Major B. M. Koehler," *New York Times*, Feb. 23, 1914.

5. In 1907, while serving as the fire commander during a drill at Fort Monroe, watching officers and enlisted men fire into Chesapeake Bay, Ben saw several things he did not like. There were visitors on the floating command post, presenting a distraction in Ben's view. Also, men from the same company as the shooters were measuring the accuracy and length of the shots. That struck Ben as a conflict of interest, unfair to other companies. Ben recommended against both practices in his written report, which Skerrett, the artillery officer for the Department of the East, read as an impertinent act of criticism of the colonel in charge of the exercises. Skerrett made a note of his displeasure with Ben, the first written criticism placed in Ben's file. Koehler Transcript, 8. Shortly afterwards, Kenly tapped Ben for a new assignment, removing him from Skerrett's sphere of influence.

6. "Army Board to Try Major B. M. Koehler," *New York Times*, Feb. 23, 1914

7. "Retirement of Colonel Hawthorne," *Army and Navy Register*, Nov. 5, 1914.

8. "Army Sensation in Trial of Koehler," *(N.Y.) Sun*, Feb. 12, 1914.

9. Koehler Transcript, 8.

10. Ibid., 9.

11. Ibid., 28.

12. "Army Board to Try Major B. M. Koehler," *New York Times*, Feb. 23, 1914.

13. The sets differed in number because King's claim involved words only, not touching, and did not fall within the state assault statute on which the second set of charges was based. Two counts in each set pertained to Austin Frick, one for the bathroom claim, one for the dance claim.

14. "On February 27, 1914, shortly after midday, we started down the River of Doubt into the unknown," Theodore Roosevelt, *Through the Brazilian Wilderness* (1914) (republished by The Lakeside Press, 2016), 221.

### CHAPTER TWENTY-FOUR — "ANY SUCH TENDENCIES"

1. For a discussion of such cases extending back to 1827, see *Parker v. Levy*, 417 U.S. 743 (1974).

2. The *Times* reporter had apparently spoken to supporters of Ben while staked out on Water Street in New London. In an article headlined "Say Koehler Asked to be Put on Trial," the correspondent wrote that "it was said that he demanded a full investigation of the charges against him, contending that he was innocent of the gross accusations, and intended to see the whole affair through to the finish." *New York Times*, Feb. 26, 1914. In contrast, there was no denial contained in the two-paragraph article that appeared directly below the Koehler piece, reporting that the Navy planned to court-martial a lieutenant commander found in a Newport News hotel room with another man "the morning after a valentine party." The charges were "maltreating an inhabitant" and "scandalous conduct." In that case, unlike Ben's, there was corroborating evidence of contact as the men were found together.

3. "Secret Trial for Koehler," *New York Times*, Feb. 25, 1914; "Say Koehler Asked to be Put on Trial," *New York Times*, Feb. 26, 1914.

4. The procedures have since changed. Opening statements now occur in court-martials.

5. Koehler Transcript, 54. Unless otherwise noted, this chapter's references to the court-martial proceedings are based on Koehler Transcript, 54–106.

6. The same attitude—an affront to a heterosexual man's dignity—formed the

basis for the "gay panic defense," first used in a court in 1868 (in Massachusetts) and still extant in some states. As broadened during the twentieth century, the defense allowed an "unwanted, nonviolent homosexual advance [to
be] an adequate provocation for heat-of-passion killing," reducing a murder
charge to manslaughter. Pettegrew, *Brutes in Suits*, 308.

7. Later in his testimony Worcester was asked, "By the way, when Major Koehler
grasped you the way you described did he hurt you?" "No, sir," he answered.
8. Chauncey, *Gay New York*, 4, 6–7, 107.
9. Carol Flora Brooks, "The Early History of the Anti-Contraceptive Laws in Massachusetts and Connecticut," *American Quarterly*, Vol. 18, no. 1 (Spring 1966), 3,
6-8. The Massachusetts bill was entitled "An Act Concerning Offences against
Chastity, Morality and Decency." Boston, Hudson's city, had been a center of
crusading by the New England Society for the Suppression of Vice.

### CHAPTER TWENTY-FIVE – A CLEVER WITNESS

1. Koehler Transcript, 103–4. Unless otherwise noted, this chapter's references to
the court-martial proceedings are based on Koehler Transcript, 81–111.
2. Kimmel, *Manhood in America*, 1st ed., 123.
3. Memo of H. L. Hawthorne to James J. Mayes re "Request to be furnished with
the military record of Maj. Benjamin M. Koehler C.A.C., Feb. 26, 1914." As
noted in the fourth endorsement on the request, the records were not sent
from Washington until March 10, 1914. Koehler AGO File.

### CHAPTER TWENTY-SIX – UNGRATEFUL GUEST

1. Unless otherwise noted, this chapter's references to the court-martial proceedings are based on Koehler Transcript, 111–42.
2. Koehler Transcript, 772 (testimony of Ben Koehler).
3. Koehler Transcript, 1057 (testimony of Ben Koehler).
4. Sophia to Roy, April 27, 1913.

### CHAPTER TWENTY-SEVEN – AN AMERICAN DREYFUS?

1. "Liken Him to Dreyfus," *Washington Post*, March 1, 1914.
2. Adam Gopnik, "Trial of the Century," *The New Yorker*, Sept. 28, 2009, 72.
3. Ibid.
4. Ibid.
5. "Liken Him to Dreyfus," *Washington Post*, March 1, 1914.
6. Kimmel, *Manhood in America*, 1st ed., 100.
7. "Major Koehler's Friends Strive to Keep Trial Secret," *St. Louis Post-Dispatch*,
March 1, 1914.
8. "Say Koehler Asked to Be Put on Trial," *New York Times*, Feb. 26, 2014.
9. Gopnik, "Trial of the Century," 74–75; Benjamin F. Martin, "The Dreyfus Affair
and the Corruption of the French Legal System," in *The Dreyfus Affair: Art,
Truth, and Justice*, ed. Norman L. Kleeblatt (Berkeley: University of California
Press, 1987), 37.
10. Telegram from Garrison to Barry, Feb. 26, 1914, Garrison Papers.
11. Telegram from Barry to Garrison, Feb. 26, 1914, Koehler AGO File.
12. Kirby to Barry, quoted in telegram from Haan to Adjutant General, Feb. 26,
1914, Koehler AGO File.
13. "We do it in the interest of decency," Kirby was quoted as saying. "The interests

of justice, our country, the service and the accused demand that the court be closed. I do not think that the citizens of the United States want matters put before them that are not in the interest of moral decency . . . You should not pry into matters that do not concern the public. The newspapers have their rights, but the army also has its rights. These matters are sacred . . ." "Koehler is Defended," *LeMars Semi-Weekly Sentinel,* March 10, 1914.

14. "Enmity Blamed for Koehler Charges," *Washington Times,* March 1, 1914.
15. Telegram from Haan to Adjutant General, Feb. 26, 1914, Koehler AGO File.
16. Telegram from Garrison to Haan, Feb. 27, 1914, Koehler AGO File.
17. According to the *Washington Post,* one juror dissented and wanted the trial open. "Liken Him to Dreyfus," *Washington Post,* March 1, 1914.
18. "Koehler Trial Not Thrown Open," *New York Times,* March 1, 1914.
19. "Liken Him to Dreyfus," *Washington Post,* March 1, 1914.
20. "Major Koehler's Friends Strive to Keep Trial Secret," *St. Louis Post-Dispatch,* March 1, 1914.
21. Richmann to Baker, Aug. 1, 1916, 3. Koehler AGO File. The claim is plausible because at least five members of the jury were retired or reassigned within a few years after the verdict: Lieutenant Colonel Charles Varnum was retired for disability in October 1907, https://en.wikipedia.org/wiki/Charles _Varnum; jury president Brigadier General Winfield Edgerly was retired for disability in 1909, https://en.wikipedia.org/wiki/Winfield_Scott_Edgerly; Major Andrew Rowan was retired in 1909, https://en.wikipedia.org/wiki/Andrew _Summers_Rowan; Colonel Walter S. Scott was directed to report to an Army retiring board in 1911, *Army and Navy Register,* May 13, 1911, 20; and Colonel Joseph Duncan, who had led the Battle of Bud Dajo, was assigned to the general staff in August 1907—though four years later, shortly before his death, he became brigadier general, *Army and Navy Register,* June 1, 1912, 20. In contrast, other members of the Louis Koehler jury stayed in the Army for many years. While it is unknown who among the jurors voted for acquittal, the five people retired or reassigned may well have done so. It appears from a Wood telegram dated November 2, 1906, that four jurors may have been absent or removed due to challenges, leaving a jury of nine people. Accordingly, a vote of five would have been sufficient to acquit. Lewis Koehler File.
22. "Gen. Wood to Come Here," *New York Times,* Dec. 20, 1913. The change would take place April 1, 1914, according to the announcement, made the day after Wood ordered Ben's court-martial and Louis's reposting.
23. "Wood to Replace Gen. Grant Here," *New York Times,* April 1, 1907.
24. Richmann to Baker, Aug. 1, 1916, 3–4.

## CHAPTER TWENTY-EIGHT – IRREGULARITIES

1. "Enmity Blamed for Koehler Charges," *Washington Times,* March 1, 1914.
2. The referenced parts of Ward's testimony are found in Koehler Transcript, 147–63.
3. Hudson suggested that Ward had lied about his marital status on his enlistment papers, but Ward declined to say whether he had been married at the time on the grounds that the answer might incriminate him.
4. Wilson's testimony is found in Koehler Transcript, 166–75.
5. Koehler Transcript, 776.
6. Ibid., 373–74 (testimony of William Proctor).
7. "Enmity Blamed for Koehler Charges," *Washington Times,* March 1, 1914.
8. "To Try Koehler in Public," *New York Times,* Feb. 27, 1914.

9. The New London Association of Congregational Ministers condemned the Sunday session. "Koehler Case Now Tangle of Inquiries," *(N.Y. Sun)*, March 4, 1914.

## CHAPTER TWENTY-NINE – A FAKE LETTER MAKES THE ROUNDS

1. Opinion of Judge-Advocate General, p. 485, 2 D-9, referenced in Koehler Transcript, 237.
2. Koehler Transcript, 147. "Here" in Ward's sentence referred to the brick building that housed the gymnasium and school as well as the library where the court-martial was taking place. "Koehler's Counsel Charge Conspiracy," *(N.Y.) Sun*, March 5, 1914.
3. Koehler Transcript, 773–74.
4. Ibid., 168–69.
5. Ibid., 750.
6. Letter dated Feb. 28, 1914, addressed to "the Honorable Secretary of War," with "A. J. Searcy" typed as the sender's name, AGO Document #2133497, Koehler AGO File.
7. Soldier's Application for Pension, No. 14739, signed by A. J. Searcy, June 30, 1909, notarized by Brazos County (TX) Judge A.G. Boards based on representations of two witnesses who had served with Searcy. Texas State Library and Archives Commission.
8. Memo from Crowder to Garrison, March 3, 1914, Koehler AGO File, bearing March 3, 1914 date stamp from the "Secretarys Office."
9. Martin, "The Dreyfus Affair and the Corruption of the French Legal System," 40.
10. Letter from E. A. Bolmes, Texas Commissioner of Pensions, to the Adjutant General, War Department, Washington, DC, attached to Searcy's Soldier's Application for Pension. While the letter is undated, the timing of summer 1909 is proved by the June 1909 date of the application, the Aug. 21, 1909, date on the adjutant general's response, and the "approved" date stamp of Aug. 31, 1909 on the application.
11. Letter from Ainsworth to the Commissioner of Pensions, State of Texas, Aug. 21, 1909, obtained from the Texas State Library and Archives Commission, bearing AGO document #1557356.
12. While one hopes that the most senior general in the Army was not a forger, Wood had been accused of planting untruths about more senior Army men than Koehler, such as General Brooke. The last sentence of the Searcy letter echoed a point made by Wood in his memo to Garrison: "I sincerely pray to God that in justice to the poor, unfortunate, enlisted men you will see that this vile scoundrel is given his just deserts." If, as Garrison would write in *Harper's Weekly* in "What the War Department Has Done," March 7, 1914, he was deeply concerned over relations between officers and enlisted men, who would know that better than Wood? On the other hand, his concern may have been well enough known that a shrewd junior officer would think to mention it.
13. Koehler Transcript, 180, 181, 191.
14. Ibid., 1006.
15. Ibid., 1007.
16. Ibid., 1013.
17. Davis told Mills the incident took place during battle practice in 1913, but Ben had pointed out to Mayes that Lieutenant Colonel Jordan supervised the Battle Station in 1913 while Ben served in another location. Koehler Transcript, 1045.

18. Ibid., 781.
19. Ibid., 184.

### CHAPTER THIRTY – A LITTLE SHUTTER AND A GREEN SHADE

1. Charles Johnson Post, "The Honor of the Army," *Harper's Weekly*, Feb. 28, 1914, 12.
2. "Is Our Army System Sound?" *Harper's Weekly*, Feb. 28, 1914, 1.
3. "Libel of the Army," *Army and Navy Register*, Feb. 28, 1914, Vol. 15, no. 1754, 267.
4. Kirkman's testimony is found in Koehler Transcript, 192–212.
5. "Testify Against Koehler," *New York Times*, March 4, 1914.
6. "Damaging Case Against Koehler," *New York Tribune*, March 2, 1914; "Dramatic Scenes at Koehler Trial," *New York Times*, March 2, 1914.
7. Byers's testimony is found in Koehler Transcript, 212–21.
8. Spears's testimony is found in Koehler Transcript, 221–33.
9. Koehler Transcript, 788.
10. Moody's testimony is found in Koehler Transcript, 233–51.
11. Marcus Aurelius, *Meditations*, Book IV, No. 49 (Gateway Edition, Henry Regnery Co., 1956, 43). Aurelius also equated sexual desire with feminine traits, writing that "he who offends through desire, being overpowered by pleasure, seems to be in a manner more intemperate and more womanish in his offences." Book II, No. 10.
12. "Koehler Witnesses Escape in Rowboat," *New York Times*, March 3, 1914.

### CHAPTER THIRTY-ONE – SO MUCH TALK ABOUT FAT BOYS

1. "Koehler Witnesses Escape in Rowboat," *New York Times*, March 3, 1914.
2. "Risk Lives to Flee from Koehler Trial," *(N.Y.) Sun*, March 3, 1914.
3. "Koehler Witnesses Escape in Rowboat," *New York Times*, March 3, 1914.
4. "Storm Damage Breaks Record for Last Quarter of Century," *(N.Y.) Sun*, March 3, 1914.
5. Koehler Transcript, 253.
6. Ibid., 269.
7. Barrett's testimony is found in Koehler Transcript, 269–87.
8. Chauncey, *Gay New York*, 114 ("What the historian Elliot Gorn has called a 'cult of muscularity' took root in turn-of-the-century middle-class culture").
9. Kimmel, *Manhood in America*, 1st ed., 127.
10. "Meets His Death," *LeMars Semi-Weekly Sentinel*, March 8, 1900.
11. "Koehler's Counsel Charge Conspiracy," *(N.Y.) Sun*, March 5, 1914.
12. Ensley's testimony is found in Koehler Transcript, 287–313.
13. Koehler Transcript, 789.
14. Campbell's testimony is found in Koehler Transcript, 313–20.
15. Koehler Transcript, 811. Mayes apparently arranged for the court reporter to alter Fairey's first description of Ben's alleged wrongdoing. Where the transcript first read "and he pinched me on the leg," the words "and he goosed me" were added. Mayes signed his initials approving the addition.
16. Koehler Transcript, 335.
17. Ibid., 336, 346. Ben said he declined to give a positive endorsement, but King minimized the issue on the stand.
18. The specifications gave the date as "on or about May 23, 1912." However, the record of King's furlough showed that it ended in April. Mayes applied

his usual fix: King changed the date to April 12 while testifying. Koehler Transcript, 1104.

19. Koehler Transcript, 336–37.

20. Ibid., 341–42, 814–15.

21. Ibid., 346–47.

22. More than a century later, the testimony of multiple victims would be considered so prejudicial that it would be significantly limited in the high-profile sex abuse trials of entertainer Bill Cosby. Numerous women told prosecutors that Cosby had abused them, but the statute of limitations precluded Cosby's prosecution for all but one incident. In the first trial, the judge allowed one other victim to testify. The jury failed to reach a verdict. The judge allowed five other victims to testify in the second trial, and Cosby was convicted. "Jury Finds Cosby Guilty in a Sexual Assault Case Seen as a Turning Point," *New York Times*, April 27, 2018. By no means is this comparison meant as criticism of the ruling in the second trial, nor is it possible to know with certainty that the testimony of additional victims was the deciding factor leading to the different result. Courts are not laboratories where "all else being equal" conclusions can be drawn—hence, lawyers' desire to control as much as they can.

23. "Koehler Case Now Tangle of Inquiries," *(N.Y.) Sun*, March 4, 1914.

24. For example, the *Sun* wrote incorrectly that Charles Byers had testified about "advances" by Ben "for nearly eight years back," the first incident occurring at the Presidio "on the night before the San Francisco earthquake and fire in the spring of 1906"—well after Ben had left San Francisco for the east coast. The same article described Jordan as a witness against Ben when the opposite was true. "Risk Lives to Flee from Koehler Trial," *(N.Y.) Sun*, March 3, 1914. Both the *Sun* and *New York Tribune* wrote that Ben faced a ninety-nine-year prison term when the maximum was sixteen years, and wrongly reported that an incriminating photo had been entered into evidence. "Damaging Case Against Koehler," *New York Tribune*, March 2, 1914; "Maj. Koehler Faces Long Prison Term," *(N.Y.) Sun*, March 2, 1914. The *Tribune* purported to describe Ben's testimony given March 6 when he did not take the stand until March 9 and said few of the things attributed to him in the article. "Koehler On Stand Denies Charges," *New York Tribune*, March 7, 1914.

25. "Evans in Command of Eastern Department," *Courier-Journal* (Louisville, KY), March 1, 1914.

26. Telegram from Wood to Commanding General, Eastern Dept., requesting "such action taken as may be necessary to extend representatives of the press the usual facilities and courtesies in the way of transportation and being allowed to land at Fort Terry," quoted in Memo from Eastern Department Commander to Adjutant General, March 3, 1914, #3024 DJA.

### CHAPTER THIRTY-TWO – PSYCHOLOGY MAKES AN APPEARANCE

1. "Koehler's Counsel Charge Conspiracy," *(N.Y.) Sun*, March 5, 1914.

2. "Koehler Defense Begun," *New York Times*, March 5, 1914; "Koehler's Counsel Charge Conspiracy," *(N.Y.) Sun*, March 5, 1914.

3. "Two Women Testify in Koehler's Defence," *(N.Y.) Sun*, March 6, 1914.

4. "Major Benjamin M. Koehler Who Is on Trial at Fort Terry," *Leavenworth Post*, March 16, 1914.

5. "Two Women Testify in Koehler's Defence," *(N.Y.) Sun*, March 6, 1914.

6. Koehler Transcript, 371–73.

7. Ibid., 354.

8. The argument between Mayes and Hudson is in Koehler Transcript, 354–60.
9. Ibid., 378–82.

## CHAPTER THIRTY-THREE – FEMALE ADVOCATES

1. "Do you remember all the people who came there that day?" Mayes asked, referring to Jones's most recent birthday. "I didn't have any; I am too old," she replied. Koehler Transcript, 437. Later, a juror asked, "What dessert was it you put back in the ice box?" Jones answered, "I think we had that day rice pudding or custard, I am not sure which." Ibid., 444–45.
2. Ibid., 414–16.
3. Ibid., 384–88, 393–94, 400.
4. Ibid., 388 (Smith), 445–56 (Fuller).
5. Ibid., 418–19.
6. State laws restricting jury service to men, approved in dictum by the U.S. Supreme Court in 1879, *Strauder v. West Virginia*, 100 U.S. 303, were not ruled unconstitutional until 1975 in *Taylor v. Louisiana*, 419 U.S. 522.
7. Ewing's testimony is found in Koehler Transcript, 457–72.
8. The press conformed to the perception of women as oddities in the courtroom with headlines such as "Women at Koehler Trial" in the *New York Times*, March 6, 1914.
9. Shanley's testimony is found in Koehler Transcript, 362–69.
10. Ibid., 352.
11. Ibid., 563. Zerphy's testimony is found in Koehler Transcript, 561–70.
12. "Maj. Koehler Faces Long Prison Term," *(N.Y.) Sun*, March 2, 1914.
13. Moses's testimony is found in Koehler Transcript, 473–503.
14. "Witnesses Give the Accused Good Name," *Salt Lake Tribune*, March 8, 1914.
15. "Koehler Case Now Tangle of Inquiries," *(N.Y.) Sun*, March 4, 1914.
16. "Women at Koehler Trial," *New York Times*, March 6, 1914.
17. "Koehler Case Now Tangle of Inquiries," *(N.Y.) Sun*, March 4, 1914.

## CHAPTER THIRTY-FOUR – DETAILS, DETAILS

1. Some press accounts described Sophia's appearance, which was generally not done when the witnesses were male. "She is a slender little woman of quiet manner and much personal charm," wrote the *Sun*, "a slender woman of prepossessing appearance, her hair slightly tinged with gray," according to the *Times*. "Koehler Court Said to be Evenly Divided," *(N.Y.) Sun*, March 9, 1914; "Koehler's Sister Called," *New York Times*, March 10, 1914.
2. Koehler Transcript, 730. Sophia's testimony is found at 723–40.
3. "Makes A Good Witness," *LeMars Semi-Weekly Sentinel*, March 24, 1914, reprinting "A Dispatch from New London, Conn., to the New York Herald of Last Week."
4. Ibid.
5. Hawthorne's testimony is found in Koehler Transcript, 741–44.

## CHAPTER THIRTY-FIVE – THE ACCUSED SPEAKS

1. Koehler Transcript, 753. "Suck up your stomach," was a common command addressed to new cadets during inspections at West Point. Richardson, *West Point*, 124.
2. Koehler Transcript, 826.

3. Ibid., 766.
4. Ibid., 779–80.
5. "Did you ever direct Private Davis to telephone to Battery Steele for ranges to points in the Sound from Battery Steele?" Hudson asked Ben, who replied, "Never had occasion to, because we had no base line . . . We had no plotting board and no base line; it is a vertical instrument." Koehler Transcript, 781.
6. Ibid., 808.
7. Ibid., 796.
8. Ibid., 793, 798.
9. Ibid., 798.
10. Ibid., 810.
11. Ibid., 829.
12. Roosevelt, *Rough Riders*, 236.
13. Koehler Transcript, 832.
14. Ibid., 830.
15. Ibid.
16. Chauncey, *Gay New York*, 115.
17. Koehler Transcript, 835.
18. Ibid., 829.
19. Ibid., 828–29.
20. "A command is speech brigaded with action," wrote Justice William O. Douglas in his dissent to a majority opinion upholding the constitutionality of the successors to the articles under which Ben was prosecuted. *Parker v. Levy*, 417 U.S. 743 (1974), 768 (Douglas, J., dissenting).
21. Rotundo, *American Manhood*, 278. As Kimmel notes, "The increased fears of feminization eroded the casual coexistence between homosexual and heterosexual men that had characterized urban life in the 1870s and 1880s." *Manhood in America*, 1st ed., 122.
22. "Koehler is Defended," *LeMars Semi-Weekly Sentinel*, March 10, 1914.
23. "Major Koehler Victim of Feud, Says Sister," *(N.Y.) Sun*, March 10, 1914.
24. "Koehler Plans Appeal Direct to President," *(N.Y.) Sun*, March 12, 1914.
25. "I Alone to Blame," *Washington Post*, March 11, 1914.
26. "Makes A Good Witness," *LeMars Semi-Weekly Sentinel*, March 24, 1914, reprinting "A Dispatch from New London, Conn., to the New York Herald of Last Week."
27. "I Alone to Blame," *Washington Post*, March 11, 1914.
28. Ibid.; "Makes A Good Witness," *LeMars Semi-Weekly Sentinel*, March 24, 1914.
29. "Hurries Trial of Koehler," *Washington Post*, March 12, 1914.
30. D. R. Anthony Jr. to Garrison, March 14, 1914, Garrison Papers.
31. "Interference with Army Trial," *Army and Navy Register*, Vol. 55, no. 1756, March 14, 1914, 330.
32. Ibid.
33. "Hurries Trial of Koehler," *Washington Post*, March 12, 1914 ("[T]he War Department today telegraphed instructions ordering the hurrying along of the trial").
34. "Koehler's Sister Called," *New York Times*, March 10, 1914.
35. Koehler Transcript, 931–32.
36. Brown's testimony is found in Koehler Transcript, 972–1001.
37. King and Brown were friends, "together all the time," Brown said. Theirs were the two tent bunks Ben found empty during camp. Brown likely blamed Ben for the departure of his friend, as King had felt it necessary to leave to get the promotion Ben did not endorse. Brown admitted that during a visit by King to

Fort Terry in February, Brown and King spoke about the timing of King's furlough and Ben's trip to New York City. After that, King received the telegram telling him to see Mayes on Governors Island. Koehler Transcript, 345.

38. O'Brien's testimony and the resulting lawyers' argument are found in Koehler Transcript, 1018–38.

39. Record Group 94: Records of the Adjutant General's Office, Entry 25: Adjutant General's Office Document Files/AGO Doc. Files (1890–1917), AGO Document File for William J. O'Brien.

40. "Koehler Court Said to be Evenly Divided," *(N.Y.) Sun*, March 9, 1914.

41. Koehler Transcript, 862.

42. Ibid., 1043–44.

43. Ibid., 853–54.

44. Ibid., 854–57.

45. Ibid., 1059–60.

46. Ibid., 1058–59.

47. Ibid., 1061.

48. Canaday, *The Straight State*, 53.

49. "Koehler On Stand Denies Charges," *New York Tribune*, March 7, 1914.

50. Koehler Transcript, 951.

51. Ibid., 1058.

52. Ibid., 1054–55.

53. Koehler Transcript, 1055. Ben recalled that Campbell came to his house "once last summer and asked me to go fishing with him," an invitation Ben declined. Perhaps it was Campbell's intention to set up a story by creating a situation when he and Ben would be alone.

54. Koehler Transcript, 1056–57.

55. Ibid., 1068.

56. Ibid., 1079.

57. "Mexican Crisis May Save Major Koehler From Court Martial," *Democrat and Chronicle* (Rochester, NY), March 13, 1914.

58. "Koehler Trial Suspended," *New York Times*, March 13, 1914.

### CHAPTER THIRTY-SIX – MANLINESS

1. "Makes Final Plea for Major Koehler Today," *New York Tribune*, March 26, 1914.

2. Koehler Transcript, 1087–88.

3. "Kohler [*sic*] Court Martial Behind Closed Doors," *Allentown Democrat* (Allentown, PA), March 27, 1914.

4. See, e.g., Boyle, *Arc of Justice*, 292–96, 331–34, chronicling Darrow's successful defense in the 1920s of a black doctor in Detroit charged with murder for defending his house against a rock-hurling white mob. The first trial ended in a mistrial, the second in acquittal.

5. Hudson said he "would not try this case in an open court for any compensation that a man could give me." Koehler Transcript, 1161.

6. Ibid., 1102, 1163.

7. Ibid., 1153.

8. Ibid., 1144, 1145.

9. Ibid., 1137.

10. Ibid., 1147.

11. Ibid., 1140.

12. Ibid., 1139.

13. Ibid., 1127.

14. Ibid., 1098.
15. Ibid., 1099–100. "Does the Astor Battery suggest anything to you?" asked Hudson. "Is there anything that might have been thought by these soldiers of the Astor Battery that would not be said of any other Battery?"
16. Koehler Transcript, 1101, 1104.
17. Cf. Manne, *Down Girl*, 117–18, discussing how patriarchal norms may lead a man to feel entitled to prevent a woman "from competing with him for, or otherwise robbing him of, certain masculine-coded prizes" and how such thinking can intersect with other norms "to produce distinctively anti-LGBTQ forms of misogyny."
18. Koehler Transcript, 1128, 1136.
19. Ibid., 1153.
20. Ibid., 1104. The same defense theory has been articulated in the contemporary case of the actor Cuba Gooding, who was accused by several women of groping them. Gooding's lawyer called the accusations a "distorted overreaction" to innocent acts. "Third Person Accuses Actor Of Sex Abuse At City Bars," *New York Times*, Nov. 1, 2019.
21. Ibid., 1107–8.
22. Ibid., 1102.
23. Ibid., 1114, 1141.
24. Ibid., 1118, 1119.
25. Ibid., 1124.
26. Ibid., 1132.
27. Ibid., 1135.
28. Ibid., 1131–32. Hudson also took issue with Elvin Byers's testimony that Ben "exhibited indications of passion" when Byers described "a surgical operation on a man." Said Hudson: "Now I don't understand it, but if a surgical operation on a man's private parts described minutely will make another man feel passionate, that it [*sic*] is beyond me. It seems to me that would have the direct opposite effect." Koehler Transcript, 1120.
29. Ibid., 1134.
30. Ibid., 1157–58.
31. Ibid., 1100–01. The nine were Worcester, Frick, Kirkman, Byers, Spears, Barrett, Ensley, Campbell, and Fairey. In addition, Ward "was a Sergeant in the Post Exchange under Captain Ellis."
32. Hudson may have thought it unwise to rely heavily on a woman's words, especially on behalf of a client challenging the perception of him as unmanly. Mayes had asked whether Ewing was "a particular friend" of Ben's, to which he answered no, but the question implied both a woman's bias and something odd about a man having a female friend. Koehler Transcript, 1054.
33. Ibid., 1147.
34. Ibid., 1106.
35. Ibid., 1119.
36. Ibid., 1114.
37. Manne, *Down Girl*, 185-96. Manne posits that credibility deficits come into play "in situations of conflict, for example, 'he said'/'she said' scenarios . . ." She notes that "Another locus of concern is the punishment and policing of men who flout the norms of masculinity," 192–93. Blending these two ideas, it can be seen that Ben, accused of being unmanly, was all too easily placed in a suspect testimonial position similar to that of a woman testifying against a man. Manne cites the work of Gaile Pohlhaus Jr. for the premise that a testimonial bias can go well "beyond failing to glean who is trustworthy, and hence what

really transpired" and become "a *refusal* to acknowledge what is revealed by the evidence" (emphasis in original), 190. A lawyer who served in Congress would make a related point when he wrote that "some charges are of such a nature that the charge itself, in the feeling of resentment and disgust which it encites, frequently takes the place of proof, whereas the exact reverse should be the case." Memo of William Borland to Enoch Crowder, May 1914; "U.S. vs. Major Benjamin M. Koehler, Review of Evidence and Brief by Hon. Chas. H. Sloan, Opinions of Senators and Representatives," Record Group 153, AGO Doc. #2166541, National Archives, date stamped May 21, 1914.

38. Koehler Transcript, 1146.
39. Ibid., 1146.
40. Ibid.
41. Ibid., 1162.
42. Ibid., 1102.
43. Ibid., 1163.
44. Ibid.
45. Ibid., 1166.
46. Ibid., 1167.
47. Ibid., 1166–67.
48. Ibid., 1168–69.
49. Ibid., 1169. Mayes asserted, for example, that "[A] crime of this character is so secret that it is presumed there will be no other witnesses. Therefore, it has been specifically held that offenses of this nature may be established by the testimony of one witness uncorroborated."
50. Ibid., 1171.
51. Ibid., 1173.
52. Ibid., 1174.
53. Ibid.

## CHAPTER THIRTY-SEVEN – DELIBERATIONS

1. "Makes Final Plea for Major Koehler Today," *New York Tribune*, March 26, 1914.
2. Koehler Transcript, 1087–88.
3. "Kohler [*sic*] Court Martial Behind Closed Doors," *Allentown Democrat* (Allentown, PA), March 27, 1914.

## CHAPTER THIRTY-EIGHT – SPECULATION

1. "Victory for Koehler?" *New York Times*, March 29, 1914.
2. "Koehler Case Ends, Finding is Secret," *New York Tribune*, March 28, 1914.
3. "Koehler Verdict In; Guilty, is the Guess," *(N.Y.) Sun*, April 12, 1914.
4. "Major Koehler Guilty," *(N.Y.) Sun*, April 15, 1914.
5. "Finding is Announced," *LeMars Semi-Weekly Sentinel*, April 17, 1914.
6. Ibid.
7. Kimmel, *Manhood in America*, 4th ed., 145, quoting the Boy Scout manual *Scouting* by Daniel Beard (1914).
8. See generally Kimmel, *Manhood in America*, 4th ed., 122–34.

## CHAPTER THIRTY-NINE – SMEAR

1. "Koehler Case Ends, Finding is Secret," *New York Tribune*, March 28, 1914.
2. "Koehler Case Now Tangle of Inquiries," *(N.Y.) Sun*, March 4, 1914.

3. "Major Koehler's Fall—A Case That Stirred Army and Nation," *New York Tribune*, April 19, 1914.
4. Remarks of Charles Henry Sloan, *Congressional Record*, 63rd Congress, Vol. 52, pt. 2, Jan. 21, 1915, 2191.
5. Memo from E. M. Weaver to Wood, April 18, 1914, Koehler AGO File.
6. Memo from E. M. Weaver to adjutant general, April 21, 1914, Koehler AGO File.
7. "Major Koehler Ready to Enlist as Private," *Washington Times*, April 30, 1914.
8. Hon. Chas. H. Sloan, "U.S. vs. Major Benjamin M. Koehler, Review of Evidence and Brief," Record Group 153, AGO Doc. #2166541, National Archives, date stamped May 21, 1914 ("Sloan Memo").
9. Walsh died en route to Washington in 1933 to accept the attorney general appointment, https://www.senate.gov/artandhistory/history/common /generic/Featured_Bio_Walsh.htm.
10. Letter from T. J. Walsh to Sloan, May 26, 1914, with handwritten note affixed stating "Left with me by Mr. Sloan—May 27, 1914. L.M.G. [Lindsey M. Garrison]," Garrison Papers.
11. The quotations are taken from excerpts of the reviewers' opinions printed in the *Congressional Record*, 63rd Congress, Jan. 21, 1915, 2188–94.
12. Sloan Memo.
13. Richmann to Baker, Aug. 1, 1916.
14. Elliott W. Major to Wilson, April 21, 1914. Major, the state's former attorney general, described Henry Koehler as "a most estimable gentleman and friend" and wished to save Ben and his family from "humiliation."
15. General Orders, No. 48, War Department, June 25, 1914. The order listed the "guilty" and "not guilty" counts, but it is not known whether the order was made public. No press accounts reported the acquittals.
16. Telegram of R. K. Evans to adjutant general, June 26, 1914, Koehler AGO File.
17. "Koehler Out of Army," *New York Times*, June 28, 1914.

### CHAPTER FORTY – HAWARDEN

1. Sophia to Roy, March 10, 1915.
2. Sophia to Roy, June 12, 1895 ("I wrote to you before I left [to visit relatives in Marcus, IA] but I find that my brother hasn't mailed it so I thought I had better writer another").
3. Woodrow Wilson, Second Annual Message to Congress, Dec. 8, 1914, http:// www.presidency.ucsb.edu/ws/index.php?pid=29555.
4. Lane, *Armed Progressive*, 187.
5. Ibid., 188.
6. Ibid., 190.
7. Ibid., 191.
8. "Nation in Danger, Roosevelt Cries," *New York Times*, March 30, 1916. Roosevelt and Wood had fervent supporters. See, e.g., "How Weak We Are Shown by Gen. Wood," *New York Times*, May 25, 1916 ("General Wood was the last speaker. The whole assembly [1,000 members of the Merchants' Association] arose and cheered . . .").
9. Canaday, *The Straight State*, 60, referencing the work of Gerald Shenk.
10. "Army Officers Abroad," *Army and Navy Register*, Sept. 21, 1912, 335.
11. 1915 Efficiency Report of Philip Worcester, Worcester AGO File.
12. Ibid.
13. Charles Henry Sloan, *Congressional Record*, 63rd Congress, Jan. 21, 1915, 2188.
14. "Major Koehler Scandal Is Revived in House," *Washington Herald*, Jan. 22, 1915.

See also "Sloan Defends Major Koehler," *Lincoln Star*, Jan. 22, 1915; "Denounces Court-Martial," *Omaha Daily Bee*, Jan. 22, 1915.

15. Sophia to Roy, March 15, 1915.
16. "Glynn in Koehler Case," *St. Joseph (MO) News-Press/Gazette*, May 15, 1915.
17. "Army Man Tries to Clear Name," *Chicago Daily Tribune*, May 15, 1915.
18. "Captain B. M. Koehler to Berlin?," *The Coffeyville Daily Journal*, April 7, 1909.

## CHAPTER FORTY-ONE – FEDERAL ACTION

1. The organization was the Society for Human Rights in Chicago, which published a newsletter entitled "Friendship and Freedom." Membership was small and the group disbanded in 1925 after a series of arrests. "#7 [of 20 Chicago innovators]: First gay rights group in the US (1924)," *Chicago Tribune*, Nov. 19, 2013. Some members were involved in later gay rights organizations, including the Mattachine Society, founded in Los Angeles in 1950, which, in association with Frank Kameny and others, played a significant role in the gay rights movement of the 1960s. See, e.g., the documentary *The Lavender Scare*, produced by Josh Howard (2017), https://www.thelavenderscare.com/.
2. The accuser who came the closest to alleging that was Kirkman, with his story about Ben suggesting they sleep together and get "something doing before morning," but the jury rejected his claim.
3. Crowder and members of Congress may have been reluctant to discuss the issue openly to avoid the appearance that homosexuality was a problem in the domestic armed services, lest it affect image and recruitment. This was in contrast to acknowledging a problem in the Philippines, where male-male encounters could be blamed on sex-crazed, degenerate Filipinos, just as some officials blamed the more permissive French for corrupting American soldiers in World War I.
4. "Wilson Completes Defense Program," *New York Times*, Aug. 30, 1916. The language is set forth in Senate bill 3191, 64th Congress, 1st Session, printed in "Revision of the Articles of War," Calendar No. 122, Senate Report 130, Feb. 9, 1916, enacted as 39 Stat. 650, U.S. Comp. Stat. (1916) Section 2308a. The revised article had been proposed but not enacted in 1912 and 1914. It read in full: "Any person subject to military law who commits manslaughter, mayhem, arson, burglary, robbery, larceny, embezzlement, perjury, assault with intent to commit any felony, or assault with intent to do bodily harm, shall be punished as a court-martial may direct." See generally "Comparison of Proposed New Articles of War with the Present Articles of War and Other Related Statutes," Military Legal Resources, Library of Congress, 4, https://www.loc.gov/rr/frd/Military_Law/pdf/A-W_book.pdf.
5. *Parker v. Levy*, 417 U.S. 743 (1974). In the 1916 version, the two articles were renumbered 95 (dismissal for conduct "unbecoming an officer and a gentleman") and 96 (making "disorders and neglects to the prejudice of good order and discipline" subject to court-martial along with other crimes "not mentioned in these articles").
6. Kornstein, "Taps for the Real Catch-22," 1525.
7. Billy Mitchell's comments included the statement that "These incidents are the direct result of the incompetency, criminal negligence and almost treasonable administration of the national defense by the Navy and War Departments." "The Billy Mitchell Court-Martial," *Air & Space Smithsonian*, https://www.airspacemag.com/history-of-flight/the-billy-mitchell-court-martial-136828592/9.

8. *Parker v. Levy*, 417 U.S. 743 (1974), 76Plu.

9. Id., 758.

10. *Levy v. Corcoran*, 389 F.2d 929 (D.C. Cir. 1967).

11. Kornstein, "Taps for the Real Catch-22," 1539.

12. Ibid. Kornstein writes that the crux of the offense "is that when people learn of the conduct, they think less of the actor and perhaps of the institution with which he is associated."

13. "Examiners were advised to watch for male recruits who 'present the general body conformation of the opposite sex, with sloping narrow shoulders, broad hips, excessive pectoral and pubic adipose deposits, with lack of masculine [hair] and muscular markings.'" Special Regulations no. 65, Physical Examination of Recruits, decimal 342.15, box 795, central decimal files 1917–1925, Records of the Adjutant General, RG 407, as quoted in Canaday, *The Straight State*, 62.

14. The revision of Article 93 added sodomy, housebreaking, and forgery as military crimes, and added a second type of assault with intent to commit bodily harm—"with a dangerous weapon, instrument, or other thing."

15. "The Manuals for Court-Martial from 1917 defined sodomy as anal penetration of either a man or a woman by a man; oral sex did not constitute sodomy. After the 1920 revision, however, the Manuals for Court Martial redefined sodomy to include oral and anal penetration between two men or between a man and a woman," Rhonda Evans, "U.S Military Policies Concerning Homosexuals: Development, Implementation and Outcomes," prepared For the Center for the Study of Sexual Minorities in the Military, Univ. of California at Santa Barbara, 8 n.4.

16. Canaday, *The Straight State*, 60–61. The "moral zones" were created by the Draft Act and enforced by Newton Baker, who had dismissed all appeals in Koehler's behalf. Baker established the Commission on Training Camp Activities whose anti-prostitution investigators soon discovered male-male coupling. CTCA investigators received help from anti-vice groups such as New York's Committee of Fourteen.

17. Ibid.

18. Ibid., 2–7.

19. Ibid., 71–75.

20. "Lay Navy Scandal to F.D. Roosevelt; Senate Naval Sub-Committee Accuses Him and Daniels in Newport Inquiry. Details Are Unprintable, Minority Report Asserts Charges of Immorally Employing Men Do Officials Injustice," *New York Times*, July 20, 1921.

21. "The Historians' Case Against Gay Discrimination," *amicus curiae* brief, Lawrence v. Texas, 2002. Canaday makes the point that the acts of exclusion, discharge, and shaming—in the military, immigration decisions, and later in determining eligibility for welfare benefits—actually helped create the homosexual identity as a political and legal concept. *The Straight State*, 4.

22. Canaday, *The Straight State*, 90–134.

23. Ibid., 86.

24. Matthew Shaer, "The Long, Lonely Road of Chelsea Manning," *New York Times Magazine*, June 12, 2017. Manning transitioned to female while serving time in an Army prison for providing diplomatic cables and other sensitive government information to WikiLeaks.

25. See, e.g., Robertson, "'Aunt Nancy Men.'" Robertson writes that "radical reformers led the way in advocating rigid self-control in relation to the body. This concern with bodily self-control motivated [Parker] Pillsbury to support only reasonably regulated sexual relations as an element of true manhood. Abstinence was acceptable—and much preferred to lasciviousness." She notes that

Pillsbury wrote his wife "that she should assure her bachelor brother, Charles Sargent, 'to hold his head and maintain his right to sleep alone as long as he pleases. A true man's history can be written in other characters *than baby hieroglyphics*,'" n. 62 (emphasis in original). See also Chauncey, *Gay New York*, 119 ("Several generations of middle-class men had considered sexual self-control to be crucial to their image as middle-class gentlemen").

## CHAPTER FORTY-TWO – A HOME AT THE PRINCE

1. "A Pretty Home Wedding," *LeMars Semi-Weekly Sentinel*, April 5, 1918.
2. Sophia to Roy, Nov. 11, 1915.
3. Sophia to Roy, Sept. 13, 1916.
4. Sophia had lived through years of what Chauncey calls "a heterosexual counterrevolution"—the stigmatization of unmarried women in the early twentieth century. Whereas "as many as 50 percent of the graduates of some women's colleges in the late nineteenth century never married," choosing to pursue careers and social reform, acceptance of this choice waned as demonstrations of heterosexuality, through socialization with and marriage to a woman, increasingly became the expectation for men. In the 1920s, the "age of first marriage dropped [for women], the percentage of women who married increased, and many women left autonomous women's organizations to join the dominant (and male-dominated) political and professional organizations of their day." This trend "undermined the middle-class women's culture that had sustained a generation of challenges to the male-dominated professions and social order." *Gay New York*, 118.
5. Roy to Sophia, Nov. 25, 1917.
6. Roy to Sophia, March 24, 1918.
7. Roy to Sophia, Nov. 25, 1917.
8. Willa Cather, *O Pioneers!* (Boston: Houghton Mifflin, 1913; New York: Vintage Classics ed., 1992), 159.
9. Kevin Dann, *Expect Great Things: The Life and Search of Henry David Thoreau* (New York: Penguin Random House, 2017) 304, 341–42.
10. The Prince George, at Fifth Avenue and 28th Street, went on to be New York City's largest welfare hotel and homeless shelter, possibly the largest in the nation. In 1996, a nonprofit converted it into a residence for lower-income working single adults and the formerly homeless. "A New Chapter for the Building Once Called 'Hell's Embassy in Manhattan,'" *New York Times*, Aug. 15, 2016.
11. "Had Narrow Escape," *Hawarden Independent*, Sept. 20, 1917.
12. H.R. 14998, 64th Congress, 1st Session, introduced April 24,1916. A companion bill in the Senate, S. 6669, was introduced by Senator Hitchcock on July 19, 1916. Neither bill passed.
13. Baker to Chairman, Committee on Military Affairs, House of Representatives, May 19, 1916, Koehler AGO File.
14. *Congressional Record*, Vol. 53, 64th Congress, 1st Session, June 21, 1916, 9737–38.
15. George Gund to Baker, Aug. 4, 1916, Koehler AGO File.
16. Baker to Gund, Koehler AGO File.
17. "Wilson Moves Up 1,000 Army Officers," *New York Times*, July 16, 1916.
18. In May 1917, Frick would be reassigned to coast defenses in Savannah, Georgia. "Coast Artillery Courses of Instruction are Closed," *Official Bulletin*, Committee on Public Information, Washington, DC, May 28, 1917, 7 (a war-related committee formed by order of President Wilson).
19. Hitchcock to Baker, May 26, 1917, Koehler AGO File.

20. Baker to Hitchcock, 1917 (undated, referring "to your letter of May 26th"), Koehler AGO File.

21. Another letter came from LeMars banker E. A. Dalton, a member of one of Le-Mars's British families, who wrote: "His sister and my wife are intimate friends and as a consequence, I see the Major frequently." He, too, claimed to "have read the evidence gathered during the trial and have talked with attorneys and from what I have learned I do not see how he could ever have been found guilty." Dalton to Baker, June 7, 1917, Koehler AGO File.

22. Worcester West Point Obituary.

23. "Coast Artillery Corps," *Army and Navy Register*, Oct. 30, 1920, 452.

24. Lane, *Armed Progressive*, 203.

25. "President Calls Nation to Arms; Draft Bill Signed; Registration on June 5, Regulars Under Pershing to go to France," *New York Times*, May 19, 1917.

26. "Will Not Send Roosevelt," *New York Times*, May 19, 1917.

27. "[H]ow tickled the lieutenant will be," wrote Anthony, "—when to his Maud is added a second one for him to love & cherish—well if all this is for nothing—let it all go that may—and whichever may—Aunt Susan's best love & sympathy always go with her niece Maud." Letter of Susan B. Anthony to "Darling Niece Maud," May 24, 1897, Susan B. Anthony Collection, Library of Congress.

28. Wood admitted in 1906 that he had unsuccessfully urged Scott's promotion to brigadier general six times in four years. "Officers Stand By Koehler," *LeMars Semi-Weekly Sentinel*, Dec. 21, 1906. In 1908, when it was rumored that Roosevelt might announce Scott's advancement, Daniel Anthony Jr. vowed to prevent Senate confirmation, saying Scott had "no military record or service that justified his promotion" above others. "Army Probe Imminent," *Washington Post*, Dec. 10, 1908. Scott did not become brigadier general until 1913.

29. "Army Officers Stand By Capt. Louis Koehler," *Leavenworth Weekly Times*, Dec. 20, 1906, quoting commentary by the *Manila American*.

30. "Hawarden and Vicinity," *Hawarden Independent*, Sept. 9, 1920.

31. http://armynavygame.com/sports/2016/10/4/army-navy-through-the-years.aspx?path=football. "[A] short Army punt set up the lone score of the day, a 7-yard pass from Vic Noyes to Bennie Koehler. It marked Navy's first offensive touchdown against Army in 10 games (a span of 13 years)."

32. "Bill to Reform Courts-Martial," *New York Times*, May 19, 1919, quoting Sen. George Chamberlain as saying, "the primary principle of the present bill is to establish military justice and regulate it by law rather than by mere military command"; "Courts-Martial Plan Rapped By Generals Wood and Scott/Control of Discipline Urged," *Cincinnati Enquirer*, April 17, 1919. For particularly strident criticism of Crowder and the court-martial system—"It works not justice but tyranny, oppression, and the destruction of the souls and spirits of human beings"—see Extension of Remarks of Dan V. Stephens, *Congressional Record*, March 10, 1919, 5384–86. Stephens, like Sloan, represented Nebraska and wrote a section of the brief criticizing the Koehler verdict.

33. *Congressional Record*, Vol. 56, 65th Congress, 2nd Session, Feb. 4, 1918, 1678.

34. Daniel H. Benson, "Military Justice in the Consumer Perspective," 13 *Arizona Law Review* 595, 596 (1971).

35. Senator Charles Thomas, quoted in *Trials by Courts-Martial*, U.S. Senate Report, Committee of Military Affairs, Feb. 15, 1919, 128.

36. *O'Callahan v. Parker*, 395 U.S. 258, 265 (1969).

37. Lane, *Armed Progressive*, 248.

38. Walter Lippmann, "Leonard Wood," *New Republic* (March 17, 1920), 22, in Lane, *Armed Progressive*, 248–49.

39. Lane, *Armed Progressive*, 247.

40. "Planning for Joint Meeting," *Hawarden Independent*, Feb. 17, 1921.
41. "Map Out Year's Road Program," *Hawarden Independent*, Feb. 11, 1932.
42. "At the primary last week not a single democratic vote was cast in that precinct. For quite a few years Ben Koehler cast the only democratic ballot in primaries there and was thus unable to maintain any great degree of secrecy as to the candidates whom he supported. But Mr. Koehler is visiting in Portland, Ore., at present and did not vote in the recent primary." "Strongest G.O.P. Precinct," *Hawarden Independent*, June 13, 1940.
43. "Smoke Rings," *Hawarden Independent*, Nov. 1, 1928 "[I]imagine my amazement when I chanced to look at a sample ballot for Buncombe township and discovered that Ben Koehler is running for township trustee on the republican ticket."
44. "Fire Destroys Tenant House," *Hawarden Independent*, Nov. 24, 1921.
45. "Death Ends Long Military Career," *LeMars Globe Post*, July 17, 1924.
46. "Lt. Col. P. H. Worcester: Coast Artillery Corps Officer, 54, Won Citations for Gallantry," *New York Times*, Dec. 5, 1922; Worcester West Point Obituary.
47. "Sister of Local Man Died Dec. 8," *Hawarden Independent*, Dec. 16, 1943.
48. Author interview with Mary Dimmick Elke, July 25, 2016.
49. "Fort Tyler: Historic Fortress Bombed into Ruins," *Dan's Papers*, June 6, 2013, http://www.danspapers.com/2013/06/fort-tyler-the-historic-fortress-in-east-hampton-bombed-into-ruins/.
50. Advertisement on display at the Plymouth County Historical Society, Oct. 2016.
51. "Ben Koehler Dies Christmas Morning at Home in LeMars," *Hawarden Independent*, Jan. 2, 1947.
52. Alumni record viewed at Plymouth County Historical Society.
53. Louis Dimmick to Rudolph Koehler, April 10, 1947.
54. Rudolph Koehler to Louis Dimmick, Feb. 8, 1947.
55. Paulus E. Newell to Louis Dimmick, Feb. 6, Feb. 7, March 27, 1947.

### EPILOGUE

1. "Homosexuals in the Military," 37 Fordham L. Rev. 465 (1969), 468–69.
2. Turing's story is told in the 2014 film *The Imitation Game*, which won an Academy Award for best adapted screenplay. British laws against same-gender sex remain in effect in many countries, even though Britain repealed its own law in 1967. "Kenya's High Court Upholds Colonial-Era Ban on Gay Sex," *New York Times*, May 25, 2019. "[O]ver 70 countries still criminalize consensual same-sex acts, and in 11 of them, punishments include the death penalty." Moises Kaufman, "A Dangerous Euphoria," *New York Times*, June 23, 2019, "Years of Pride" Section.
3. "Sue Fulton Thinks Equal Rights Make the Military Stronger," interview with Ana Marie Cox, *New York Times Magazine*, Jan. 15, 2017, 58.
4. "Brenda 'Sue' Fulton, Openly Gay Veteran, Named to West Point Advisory Board," *Huffington Post*, July 6, 2011, updated Sept. 5, 2011.
5. "Patricia Kutteles, Driven by Tragedy to End 'Don't Ask, Don't Tell,' Dies at 67," *New York Times*, Nov. 23, 2016. According to Damiano, "Lesbian Baiting in the Military," the regulation "actually worsened the plight of gay and lesbian service members in many circumstances" and hurt all military women by allowing male superiors to accuse them of being lesbian and open investigations if they declined an advance or reported sexual harassment/sexual abuse.
6. Office of the Press Secretary, the White House, "Remarks by the President and Vice President at Signing of the Don't Ask, Don't Tell Repeal Act of

2010," https://obamawhitehouse.archives.gov/the-press-office/2010/12/22
/remarks-president-and-vice-president-signing-dont-ask-dont-tell-repeal-a.
Some 17,000 service members were discharged under the Don't Ask, Don't
Tell policy. "Obama Signs Away 'Don't Ask, Don't Tell,'" *New York Times*, Dec.
22, 2010.

7. After an eight-month confirmation process, Fanning served as Secretary of the
Army for only eight months, from May 18, 2016 until January 20, 2017, the date
of Donald Trump's inauguration. In 2018, he became president of the Aero-
space Industries Association. "Former US Army Secretary to Replace Melcher as
AIA Boss," *Defense News*, Sept. 18, 2017.

8. "In Historic Shift, Boy Scouts Will Accept Girls," *New York Times*, Oct. 12, 2017.

9. Frank Bruni, "The Gay Truth About Trump," *New York Times*, June 23, 2019.
Bruni reports that "in poll after poll, most Americans say that transgender people should be able to serve in the military, with 70 percent of them indicating
support in one survey."

10. "Assessing the Implications of Allowing Transgender Personnel to Serve
Openly," RAND Corporation, 2016, 60, https://www.rand.org/pubs/research
_reports/RR1530.html. "Transgender Military Service," Human Rights Cam-
paign, https://www.hrc.org/resources/transgender-military-service. Lawsuits
concerning the policy reversal may yet lead to a different result.

11. "How #MeToo Realigned the Corridors of Power," *New York Times*, Oct. 24, 2018.

12. When the issue concerns consent, a woman accused of predation may also
claim "falsity," such as the professor who claimed her graduate student willing-
ly accepted her sexual overtures. "A Female Professor, Her Male Student and
the Limits of #MeToo," *New York Times*, Aug. 14, 2018.

13. An extreme assertion to the contrary was that of Eugene Quay, who wrote in
1961 that women were prone to lie about sexual assault in order to obtain
a legal abortion. "Justifiable Abortion—Medical and Legal Foundations," 49
*Georgetown Law Journal* 395 (1961).

14. There is a recent case of a man claiming that a number of men lied about his
alleged gropings. See, e.g., "Many Accusations, Few Apologies," *New York Times*,
March 4, 2018, Styles, describing allegations against photographer Mario Tes-
tino. Unlike in the Koehler case, the men making the claims did not work
together or know each other. There have also been recent reports of men
claiming abuse by a former coach or doctor, but in such cases the issue can
be not whether contact occurred but the appropriateness of the contact. See,
e.g., "For Wrestlers, #MeToo Stirs Buried Beast," *New York Times*, Aug. 3, 2018.
Indeed, one former wrestler said he told himself for years, "He's a doctor, I'm
sure he's got a reason to be doing it." Cf. "Yoga is Finally Facing Consent and
Unwanted Touch," *New York Times*, Nov. 8, 2019.

15. Male-generated doubt about women's veracity has resulted in decades of un-
derreported sexual abuse. As one woman wrote, "It's no wonder that the federal Bureau of Justice Statistics reported that from 2006 to 2010, 65 percent of
sexual assaults went unreported. What's the point, if you won't be believed?"
Amber Tamblyn, "I Am Done With Not Being Believed," *New York Times*, Week
in Review, Sept. 16, 2017. See also "I Can Finally Tell My Weinstein Story," *New
York Times*, Oct. 6, 2019, Week in Review, describing laughter when abuse was
reported because "[w]ho would ever believe us over the most powerful man in
Hollywood?" followed by pressure, including sleep deprivation, to sign a non-
disclosure agreement; Chanel Miller, *Know My Name* (New York: Viking, 2019),
288. ("The real question we need to be asking is not, *Why didn't she report*, the
question is, *Why would you?*").

16. Moises Velasquez-Manoff, "Real Men Get Rejected, Too," *New York Times*, Sunday Review, Feb. 24, 2018. See Catharine A. MacKinnon, *Sexual Harassment of Working Women* (New Haven, CT: Yale University Press, 1979).
17. Tarana Burke, TED Talk, Nov. 30, 2018, https://blog.ted.com/watch-tarana-burkes-ted-talk-me-too-is-a-movement-not-a-moment/.
18. Philosopher Tom Digby asserts that the warrior concept of manhood is at the root of stunted emotions in men and male discrimination against both women and men. "Male Trouble: Are Men Victims of Sexism?" *Social Theory and Practice*, 2003, https://www.academia.edu/10460232/Male_Trouble_Are_Men_Victims_of_Sexism.
19. Michael Kimmel, *Angry White Men: American Masculinity at the End of an Era* (New York: Nation Books, 2013), 15.
20. "Our military must be focused on decisive and overwhelming victory and cannot be burdened with the disruption that transgender in the military would entail," Trump wrote in a series of posts on Twitter.
21. See, e.g., "Trump Plan Could Curb Transgender People's Access to Health Services," *New York Times*, April 22, 2018. According to a 2018 Gallup poll 4.5 percent of Americans identified as lesbian, gay, bisexual or transgender in 2017, up from 3.5 percent in 2012. https://news.gallup.com/poll/234863/estimate-lgbt-population-rises.aspx
22. Jennifer Finney Boylan, "In the End, Love," *New York Times*, June 23, 2019, "Years of Pride" Section.
23. "Transgender Student Won a Battle. Now It's War," *New York Times*, April 3, 2017.
24. Frank Bruni, "Manhood in the Age of Trump," *New York Times*, April 2, 2017, Week in Review.
25. Richard Dormen, "The Diverse Men of 2020," *New York Times*, March 17, 2019, Week in Review.
26. "'The Daily' and Mayor Pete Buttigieg," *New York Times*, Nov. 23, 2019.
27. See, e.g., "Trump's Justice Department Redefines Whose Civil Rights to Protect," *New York Times*, Sept. 4, 2018, writing of the U.S. Department of Justice, "the focus has shifted to people of faith, police officers and local government officials who maintain they have been trampled by the federal government."
28. Ibid.
29. The use of sexual stereotypes persists to such an extent that an openly gay Afghan teenager seeking to escape persecution at home was denied asylum by Austria on the ground that "Neither your walk, nor your behavior nor your clothing give [*sic*] the slightest indication that you could be gay." "Gay Afghan Boy Denied Asylum in Austria, Rights Group Says," *New York Times*, Aug. 17, 2018, quoting the decision.
30. In *Lab 257*, Michael Carroll alleges that immediately after World War II, the Army employed ex-Nazi scientists to experiment with agents of biological warfare on Plum Island, including the possible use of ticks as vectors.
31. Schlesinger et al., "Biodiversity and Ecological Potential of Plum Island, New York ("Few publicly owned islands are as poorly known, misunderstood, and shrouded in mystery as Plum Island, New York"). The statement well synthesizes lessons of the Koehler case: secrecy enables injustice, and misunderstanding enables discrimination.
32. Discriminatory attitudes a woman may encounter today for not marrying or having children are the subject of Glynnis MacNicol's book, *No One Tells You This: A Memoir* (New York: Simon & Schuster, 2018).

# INDEX